FRONT OFFICE SERVICES

FRONT OFFICE SERVICES

Editor
Desmond Waller

DPH

DISCOVERY PUBLISHING HOUSE
INDIA

Published by:

DISCOVERY PUBLISHING HOUSE
4383/4B, Ansari Road, Darya Ganj
New Delhi-110 002 (India)
Phone : +91-11-23279245; 23253475; 43596065
+91 9811179893 / +91 9871656464
E-mail : discoverybooksindia@gmail.com
orderdphbooks@gmail.com
namitwasan9@gmail.com
web : www.discoverypublishinggroup.com

First Published: **2024**

ISBN: 978-81-19365-27-2

Front Office Services

Printed at:
Infinity Imaging Systems
Delhi

PREFACE

The hospitality industry is constantly evolving to enhance the guest experience and improve the level of service provided by hotels. The hotel front desk is a crucial component of the Front Office operations as it creates the guest's first impression. Therefore, hotels have adopted new practices to enhance the performance and service offered, with each guest being treated with utmost consideration to make them feel special.

In today's competitive market, hotels are distinguishing themselves by adopting innovative practices to attract more guests. Traditionally, the front office has been seen as a check-in and check-out point for guests, a source of infinite information, and a problem-solving center. However, the front office personnel's role and management's expectations have created a "gap," leading to a breakdown in communication and service delivery.

Effective management credit policies are essential in certain circumstances, but the awkwardness of many situations could have been avoided by allowing front office agents to assume some responsibility. By using their judgment and seeking management assistance only when they feel uncomfortable, a friendly and compatible first impression could have been achieved.

Hotels are always seeking new ways to enhance the customer experience and thrive as a company. The hotel front desk plays a vital role in Front Office operations and is responsible for making the guest feel welcome and valued. With so much competition in the industry, hotels must implement new and creative ways to attract more customers. The front office staff of a hotel must possess a diverse range of skills, including the ability to use various technologies like printers, fax machines, and phones.

This book "Front Office Services" is designed to educate and train individuals who aspire to become leaders in the hotel industry. It provides a detailed understanding of front office systems and procedures that are essential for the smooth functioning of a hotel's front desk operations. This book is a valuable resource for those who want to learn about the various tasks involved in front office management and how to perform them efficiently.

The editor has collected reliable and scientifically proven information from various credible sources to provide readers with the latest and most accurate information available. The book is a compilation of contributions from various experts in the field, and the editor expresses gratitude to these contributors for sharing their knowledge and expertise.

Editor

CONTENTS

CHAPTER 1

Service Customer Loyalty: An Evaluation Based on Loyalty Factors

Neringa Vilkaite-Vaitone and Ilona Skackauskiene

Management Department, Vilnius Gediminas Technical University, Sauletekio av. 11, LT-10223 Vilnius, Lithuania

ABSTRACT

This study sheds light on customer loyalty based on three groups of factors (customer, service provider, and environment). Noting the diversity of the effects of customer loyalty factors, this research investigates the impact of every factor upon customer loyalty. This paper provides an innovative insight into how a variety of customer loyalty factors might be combined into a single measure of customer loyalty. Finally, this study examines phases of customer loyalty and identifies the factors that prevent a peak of customer loyalty. The factors determining customer loyalty explain why customers move across different loyalty phases over time. The results of the empirical testing confirmed the practical applicability of the suggested approach for evaluating customer loyalty based on these factors. An innovative approach to the evaluation of customer loyalty is essential for marketers because it will help them to evaluate loyalty in cases where data about customer behavior are not collected. The findings of the research contribute to a better understanding of which factors are a viable basis for increasing customer loyalty, specifically in the catering and beauty markets, and offer guidance to marketing managers on how to shift customers to more desirable loyalty phases.

Keywords: *loyalty; service; service industries; consumption; customer*

INTRODUCTION

Companies are experiencing difficulties in attracting and maintaining customers as a result of service markets becoming increasingly competitive. Therefore, the need to motivate customer loyalty is getting stronger. In this environment, loyalty becomes an important marketing tool that is not only to be aimed at the customer, but is also a significant indicator of the success of a business [1,2]. Strengthening the focus on the customer places a spotlight on the service providers' profits and the potential development of the sources of income in the future. Therefore, customer loyalty is prioritized as the main aim of an organization and its marketing. It is the biggest asset of any organization and a requirement for the foundation of any organization. The majority of managers understand the importance of the loyalty of their customers and therefore pay attention to increasing the loyalty of existing customers, attracting new loyal customers, and choosing a strategy of customer loyalty management. This is extremely important in mature markets, where expansion to new loyal customers is not possible.

Customer loyalty evaluation is an important condition for the development of customer loyalty. A range of customer loyalty evaluation instruments has been developed by marketing scholars over the last few decades [3,4,5,6,7,8,9,10,11,12, 13,14,15,16]. Instruments for the evaluation of customer loyalty can be classified as behavioral, attitudinal, and multidimensional [4,5,6,7,8]. Previous research in the field of customer loyalty evaluation has shown that behavioral data are the superior choice on which to base the evaluation of customer loyalty [6,8]; however, in some cases, the required data (value of purchases, frequency of purchases, etc.) might be unavailable or even not collected by a company. An alternative technique in such cases would be questionnaire research, which usually concentrates on the evaluation of factors determining customer loyalty [4,5]. Even though there is no doubt that an understanding of customer loyalty factors is essential for businesses to survive in an extremely competitive environment, a comprehensive set of customer loyalty factors and their evaluation and synthesis into one particular numerical value representing the level of customer loyalty has not yet been fully demonstrated. A numerical value of this type would be an innovative and expedient choice for the measurement of customer loyalty when the behavioral data essential for the measurement are not available.

The goal of the present research is to contribute to customer loyalty research in the service industry. We do so by proposing a comprehensive set of customer loyalty factors and empirically testing the applicability of the set in cases where behavioral data that are essential for the evaluation of customer loyalty are unavailable. That is, we develop a set of factors and, in a detailed manner, explain every factor's impact on customer loyalty. We test our alternative for the evaluation of customer loyalty in the context of the service industry using data obtained from a catering company and a beauty studio in Lithuania. To summarize, the study is aimed at answering the following research questions:

1. What factors have the potential to reflect customer loyalty in cases when behavioral data are unavailable?
2. What impact does each factor have on customer loyalty and how might these impacts be merged into one loyalty measure?
3. Does the proposed approach reveal customer loyalty in service companies? If so, what are the implications for managers and scholars interested in building loyalty?

The confirmation of the possibility of evaluating customer loyalty based on factors would confirm the aptitude of the chosen factors for this purpose and provide managers with more specific, expedient, and clear guidance in the options of how to evaluate customer loyalty in cases when behavioral data are unavailable. Even though our findings are based on data from a catering company and a beauty studio, we discuss how our research can benefit all service establishments in developing customer loyalty.

The remainder of the article is structured as follows. The next section presents the theoretical background of factors determining customer loyalty. The Materials and Methods section describes the sequence of the research and the data used. The Results section presents the results of our empirical research on customer loyalty in a catering company and at a beauty studio. The Discussion section reviews the theoretical and practical implications of the results. The last section provides conclusions and suggests directions for future research.

THEORETICAL BACKGROUND

Factors Determining Customer Loyalty

Customer loyalty is not a new concept. It has been explored since the 1930s [9]. Since then, many definitions have been suggested. In reference to previous research in the field of customer loyalty, authors have suggested defining this concept as a customer's positive attitude in regards to the service (and its attributes), i.e., an attitude that enhances customer preference in the form of the purchase of certain types of services from a certain provider [17].

Customer loyalty is determined by many factors. Identifying the determinants of loyalty is an initial step in the evaluation of customer loyalty. Over the last four decades, research on customer loyalty factors has been a prolific field. Marketing scholars [9,11,13,14,15,16,18,19,20] have developed and validated more than one hundred different factors determining customer loyalty. Classifications of factors determining customer loyalty show that researchers' opinions on collections of factors vary. The number of factors that determines customer loyalty also varies a lot—researchers indicate between 3 and 30. Notably, authors who analyzed how only one determining factor had an impact on customer loyalty were deliberately not included in this analysis (as an acknowledgement that there are many factors determining customer loyalty) because in these studies, there was only one factor mentioned and the rest remained unknown. The factors determining customer loyalty are very wide-ranging, but they have certain specifications that allow them to be divided into categories. However, in scientific sources, there is no agreement on these categories. In most classifications, factors were not grouped at all; nonetheless, there were attempts to allocate factors to: Customer [16], psychological state [19], emotional state [21], service provider [22,23], communications [24], situation [25], marketing mix [26,27], and environment [18].

There is no doubt that the existence of a service is necessary for the occurrence of customer loyalty. This service is provided by the organization that is forming the loyalty. Due to the inseparability between the service itself and the service provider, a group of factors is integrated into the list of service provider factors. External factors may influence both the participants of the process of loyalty creation, i.e., the customer and the service provider. The marketing mix is the result of the organization's functional marketing; therefore, it is not defined as a factor equal to customer, service, service provider, and communications. Psychological and emotional factors form a part of customer factors, but the situational factors of customer loyalty are not included in the classification because the situational factor category is linked with other group factors. Thus, all of the factors determining customer loyalty are divided into three categories by the authors of this article: The customer, the service provider, and the environment characteristics (Figure 1). To determine customer loyalty, it is appropriate to choose those factors that are not accidentally mentioned in other classifications and those that do not overlap with each other.

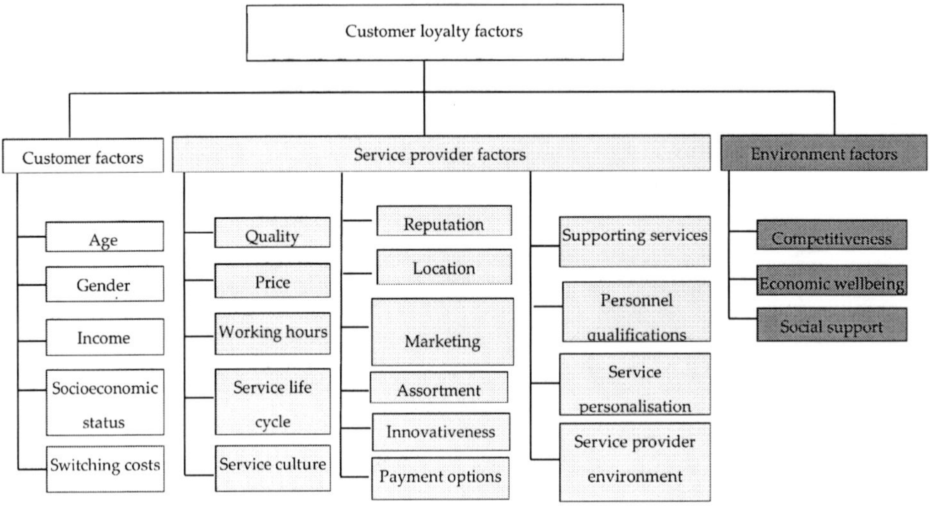

Figure 1. *A set of factors determining customer loyalty.*

All of the factors that are included in the named categories must be evaluated based on the following principles:

- Scales (names, ranks, and relationship scales) are applied for the evaluation of every factor;
- the effect of each factor on loyalty is evaluated within individual grades; ranks are arranged in ascending order;
- the effect on loyalty is expressed by an index. The meanings of the index may be included in the interval [−1;1]; however, characteristics of every factor may adopt different minimum values, depending on their impact on loyalty;
- evaluation of the factors is determined by the standard, average value, maximum value, and the requirements to meet the factor; therefore, some factor evaluations are inseparable from the market.

Customer Factors

The group of customer factors includes age, gender, income, socioeconomic status, and switching costs. Each of these factors has a certain impact on customer loyalty. As was confirmed by S. Homjitr, Sato [10] and Srivastava [12], loyalty is not the same during different stages of a customer's life. More mature customers show a higher level of loyalty than those who are younger. According to Anderson and Sharp [28], the younger the customer is, the easier it is for a competitor to attract them. More senior customers are less interested in changing service providers, mainly due to the social benefits they may receive, exceptional customer service, and the strong relationship based on trust that has been created. Belas et al. [29] stated that older customers believe that the organization's offer is the best. Older customers are more satisfied with their service; their perceptive value is greater. In particular, loyalty increases when a person's social network narrows down (children leave parental homes, individual retires, etc.). Quite often, it is not a very easy task to fill that social gap. As a result, keeping in touch with service providers becomes an opportunity to fill that social gap. As a customer of the same service provider (e.g., hairdresser, medical center, sports facility, etc.), they are recognizable and, therefore, the customer feels closeness. For senior citizens, such connections are a lot more important than for the younger generation [30]. Older customers tend to be more critical towards change and tend not to have a strong desire to try new things, which leads to a direct and positive correlation between age and loyalty. Taking into consideration all of the factors mentioned above, it can be said that loyalty grows stronger as the age of a customer increases. However, this statement cannot be applied to all services, as some services are never or seldom used by a younger age group (e.g., prosthetic dentistry, kinesiatrics, etc.), or vice versa—a large proportion of the customers of a service is made up of younger people (e.g., night clubs, the education sector, etc.). It is therefore very likely that exceptions in certain services may exist—customer loyalty may become weaker with age, or it may not have such tendencies and is simply different in individual age groups (Table 1). Therefore, the data presented in Table 1 show that stronger customer loyalty among young customers is evident in the transport and security, professional, scientific, and technical fields, as well as in educational services. Information and communication activities cover both younger and older customers. The impact on loyalty by age group on the remaining service groups is direct—loyalty increases as age increases. Since the effect of customer loyalty based on age group varies depending on the type of activity of the service provider, the impact of loyalty must be based on a scale, where the effect on loyalty increases when the age of the customer goes up, or vice versa. If the aim is to evaluate the loyalty of the customers of a service that are not the youngest among the age groups of customers (or vice versa—not the oldest), then, it is suggested that customers' ages be regrouped.

According to Homjitr, Sato [10], Tweneboah-Koduah, Farley [25], and Belas et al. [29], customer behavior is one of the fields where significant differences appear between men and women. Interpersonal communication between women

Table 1. *The impact on customer loyalty in different age groups by type of service.*

Services	Authors	Impact
Passenger transport, car servicing	Parahoo et al. [31], Jiang, Zhang [32], Bekk et al. [33]	Younger customers are more loyal
Graphic design	Loureiro, Holger [34]	
Computer games, IT solutions, instant messaging	Kim, Kim [35]	
Physical education	Dragan [36]	
Catering	Anderson, Sharp [28]	Older customers are more loyal
Supply of internet connection, mobile phone networks	Anderson, Sharp [28], Cambra-Fierro et al. [37]	
Insurance, credit cards, banking	Anderson, Sharp [28], Belas et al. [29], Tweneboah-Koduah, Farley [25]	
Car rental, tourism	Anderson, Sharp [28], Patterson [30]	
Health care, dentistry	Anderson, Sharp [28], Patterson [30]	
Gambling	Prentice [38]	
Hairdresser/barber	Patterson [30]	

is much stronger than it is between men. Women's shopping behavior is heavily affected by interpersonal relationships. In comparison to men, women are more involved in shopping. Women also experience higher satisfaction in the shopping process. They trust the information they receive while shopping more than men do. Moreover, women go shopping more often and seek better deals more actively than men. Shopping for women is a part of their social identity; they identify the elements of acquiring a tangible product [39]. Their propensity to recommend the services of the organization to their peers is significantly stronger [29]. Customers can be held as a key concept in communications marketing, the main communications marketing goal, or the result of communications marketing. Therefore, women are valued as being superior in maintaining connections and showing stronger customer loyalty to organizations. The weaker loyalty of men is highlighted by Tweneboah-Koduah, Farley [25], and Kamath et al. [40]. The results of this research allow the quantification of the impact of gender on the formation of customer loyalty.

The income of the customer is claimed to be an important factor in customer behavior, and it is included in the segmentation of market decisions. Customer income analysis shows that individuals with lower incomes tend to have stronger loyalties [41,42]. Customers with lower incomes prefer a certain service provider in the majority of cases, as these customers are limited by service choices that are affordable to them. In contrast, customers on higher incomes have the opportunity to constantly change their preferences within a wide range of services [42]. Customers with higher incomes tend to have received higher levels of education. As a result, the quality of communication and information exchange between service providers and higher-earning customers can be more intense, which results in weaker loyalty. In addition, customers with higher incomes have fewer consumption restrictions. To evaluate customer income, the calculation of relative income as a ratio of a customer's monthly income and the highest income in terms of customers of service organizations is suggested. Due to the lower consumption restrictions and the more intensive changes in service providers, a higher relative customer income has a smaller impact on loyalty compared to lower relative customer income, which is seen to have a stronger impact on customer loyalty.

Two types of socioeconomic status are distinguished in the scientific literature: Material status and educational status [43]. Educational status is more important than material status. In addition to that, to evaluate the material status aspect, the income factor has to be taken into consideration. Therefore, the socioeconomic status of service customers is only based on the education factor. There is no doubt in the scientific literature on the relationship between education and customer loyalty; it is agreed that the education factor is significant: Lower educational achievement leads to customer loyalty [25]. Customers with higher education achievements tend to acquire services from more than one provider. This is the case because customers with higher education levels tend to gain more information, process it better, and base their decisions on that information, whereas lower education has the opposite effect; the need for such a solution does not occur. In addition to that, higher education almost always guarantees higher income; as a result, customers with a higher income seem to switch service providers more frequently.

Switching costs are the actual or perceived costs that are incurred in the process of switching from one service provider to another [44]. These costs include search costs, shut-down and set-up costs, integration costs, accrued benefit loss, risk of non-performance and opportunistic behavior, and relationship building costs [45]. It is relatively easy to calculate the costs of search and accrued benefit loss, but it is very difficult to calculate integration, shut-down, and set-up costs; therefore, calculations may be very inaccurate. It must be noted that actual and relative costs in changing service providers may be very different. Because customers can perceive the same costs very differently, it is preferred to calculate the actual costs of changing service providers. It is suggested that these calculations include the shut-down and set-up costs, integration costs, and costs of accrued benefit loss. For the evaluation of customer loyalty, it is suggested that relative costs are calculated as a ratio of the switching costs for a particular customer and maximum switching costs in terms of the same service provider. Service providers' ability to create service provider switching costs undoubtedly builds customer loyalty [46]. When the relative switching costs are high, the customer tends not to change service providers. Therefore, relatively larger switching costs make a greater impact on loyalty, whereas the non-existence of switching costs is associated with negative impacts on customer loyalty.

Service Provider Factors

Service provider factors include factors related to the service (e.g., price, product assortment, innovativeness, quality, supporting services, service personalization, service life cycle) and the convenience of its provision (location, working hours). Some factors reveal attractiveness (reputation, marketing, service provider environment attractiveness), while others define other characteristics of the service provider (personnel qualifications, payment options) (Figure 1).

Price is viewed as an important factor, especially for middle-income earners and/or in commodity-based sectors [13,47]. Customers tend to compare the price of the service provider of a particular type of service with prices of other providers offering the same service. If the price offered by a particular provider is less than other service providers' prices, it is more likely that the customer will become loyal to that particular provider. However, if the price for the service is a lot larger, the purchase will likely remain a one-off.

Innovation includes the steps by which one organization is quicker to achieve transformation than other organizations. Consequently, the innovativeness of the service is when an unprecedented service is achieved before other organizations. Services may be classified according to their innovativeness in very different ways. According to one of the earliest classifications, the novelty of the service may be classified as follows: (1) Changes in the techno-economic paradigm (significant changes of technology systems affecting the economy); (2) changes in the technology system (changes that have a large-scale impact on various industries); (3) radical innovations (small and localized changes); (4) incremental innovations (small-scale or continuous improvement of a service) [48]. According to Lemy et al. [49], in pursuit of customer loyalty, the service provider must create innovations. Therefore, innovative services strengthen customer loyalty. Since minor changes to the service are considered necessary for any organization that is providing a service, such changes are seen to have little effect on loyalty.

Assortment is defined as all of the products that the organization sells. With reference to Bhatnagar et al. [9], assortment has a significant influence on the customer when choosing one organization over another; the wider the range of products, the more appealing the organization is to the customer. When choosing larger assortment providers, customers know that the likelihood of getting their required service is a lot higher than choosing a provider with a smaller variety of services. Therefore, variety is claimed to be an essential characteristic of assortment. To evaluate service assortment, it is suggested that the number of all of the available types of different options in the organization is calculated and compared to the maximum assortment in organizations providing that particular type of service. The higher the value of the indicator, the higher the probability that the service offered will match the needs of customers. Therefore, a higher value of the indicator is seen as more acceptable as customers are offered a larger range of services.

Supporting services do not contribute towards the main service, but they create additional value to the customer and highlight what an organization offers compared to its competitors. According to Small et al. [50], supporting services complement the main service. To calculate the value of supporting services, it is suggested that the number of services offered in an organization is calculated and compared to the highest number of supporting services in any of the organizations providing that particular type of service. Supporting services, regardless of whether they are provided directly or online, provide extra benefits for the customer. Therefore, providing these services will encourage the formation of a positive opinion about the organization. Supporting services also guarantee additional sales, which increase the values of purchases. As a result, larger relative values of supporting services will have a greater impact on customer loyalty, while a low value is linked to a neutral or a very weak impact on loyalty.

Customers may choose to pick certain providers' services based on their quality [13,14,20]. Berezny and Konecny [51] state that customers judge service quality based on the number of complaints received. In an attempt to evaluate the quality of service, it is suggested that the customer complaints about the quality of the service of particular organizations received by national institutions are assessed. Normally, these national institutions provide yearly data reports on customer complaints based on different types of services. Therefore, based on this information, the average number of complaints to providers of particular types of services can be determined. By comparing complaints about the service provider with the market average, the relative quality of the services provided by the organization is determined. The better quality of a particular service provider compared to other providers of the same type of service will have a stronger impact on customer loyalty.

When services are not personalized, all customers are offered the same; when their differences and profitability are not taken into consideration, then the added value is very restricted [52]. Personalized service is when any action is taken to adapt the service for a particular customer. Personalization is not a one-dimensional category, but a combination of the following attributes: Process, communications, assortment, price, and location [53]. As service customization increases customer loyalty [54], a growing level of customization has a bigger impact on customer loyalty. The non-personalization of the service is claimed to have no effect on loyalty. The highest level of service personalization, taking into consideration all five features, has a very large influence on customer loyalty.

A positive reputation of a service provider is an intangible asset that guarantees competitive advantages to the service provider. It is proposed that the evaluation of reputation is based on the number of complaints. The total number of complaints does not reflect the real status of the reputation of the organization; therefore, Morgan and Rego [55] suggest calculating the proportion of the complaining customers against all of the customers of the service provider. Researchers [55] found that the average value of this indicator is 20%. A lower value of this indicator shows a better reputation of the service provider, which leads to a stronger impact on loyalty.

The length of a typical working week is from 35 to 40 hours. Therefore, a working week of 35–40 hours is considered to be normal, and its effect on loyalty is considered to be average. Working hours of less than 35 per week or working hours that are planned and known to the customer are considered to be restricted. Very restricted working hours are when access to the service is very limited for the customer and arranged beforehand (Table 2). On the one hand, it is more difficult to acquire the required service when working hours are very restricted, but, on the other hand, this working time is usual in some activities (insurance, night clubs, etc.), and it is therefore considered to have a neutral effect on loyalty. The length of working hours is one of the most important factors for service customers when choosing a specific service provider [56]. As it is more convenient for the customer to use the service at the time that is more acceptable to them, a service provider

Table 2. *Types of service providers with reference to working hours.*

Number of Working Hours Per Week	Type	Impact on Loyalty
Limited to the customer and arranged beforehand	Very restricted	0.00
Less than 35	Restricted	0.25
35–40	Average	0.50
41–104	Adapted	0.75
105–168	Unlimited	1.00

with unlimited working hours is valued more. This working time increases the likelihood of multiple purchases, as the customer has an opportunity to receive the service at the time that is most convenient to them.

A convenient location increases demand and service usage opportunities. Tripathi [57] suggests measuring the distance between a customer's home or place of work to evaluate the convenience of the location. An acceptable distance from the customer's home or place of work may vary greatly depending on the type of service. For example, the acceptable distance from a customer's home or working place varies from 4.83 km in the case of spatial service brokerage [58] to 10.78 km in the case of catering [59]. Knowing the acceptable distance between a service organization and a customer's home or place of work is important, and it is recommended that the proportion of customers that live or work 7.80 km away from the service organization is calculated. If data are available on both the customer's place of living as well as their place of work, then an average of these two distances is used. The convenience of the location is based not only on the distance, but also on sufficient availability of car parking spaces (a 1000 m^2 service area requires at least five car parking spaces), the convenience of the horizontal and vertical arrangement of the building, and the level of crime in the area [60]. The location of the organization that meets all of the criteria named above is considered to be excellent, and the one meeting none of the criteria: Dissatisfactory. The former evaluation of location will have either a neutral or a very insignificant effect on customer loyalty.

Personnel qualification involves the professional experience and education of a service provider's personnel [61]. Without a doubt, both features affect customer loyalty, as through work experience, professional experience, and acquired qualifications, a member of a staff learns about customers, who they are, and why they choose the services of the organization. This knowledge is reflected in actions that develop customer loyalty [62]. It is claimed that longer professional experience has a stronger impact on the loyalty of customers. Higher education is also claimed as a condition for stronger customer loyalty, based on the difficulty of gaining access to higher levels of education [63]. To evaluate general staff qualification levels and their impact on customer loyalty, the average of both professional and educational qualifications needs to be calculated.

Customer loyalty also depends on the marketing budget [64]. It is suggested that, to evaluate the impact of marketing budget, the share of the marketing budget in sales should be calculated first [65] and then compared to the relative budget values of other providers of that particular type of service. Higher marketing budgets strengthen customer loyalty [64]; this type of budget shows that more money is spent on attracting customers, and when more are attracted, the likelihood of loyalty is higher. A separate evaluation of marketing budget does not show whether the assets were used effectively; therefore, it is suggested that the valuation of marketing content is supplemented with further assessment. According to Empen et al. [66], the largest share of marketing budgets goes to sales promotion. Therefore, it is useful to calculate the share of expenses for sales promotions in the total marketing budget. The larger the portion of sales promotion expenses in the marketing budget, the stronger the influence on loyalty. Guided by the values of marketing budget and content, the average impact on loyalty can be calculated.

The product life cycle is a period divided into certain stages: It starts with the introduction of the services into the market and ends with their elimination. The traditional model of a product life cycle consists of four phases: Introduction, growth, maturity, and decline [67]. During the introduction stage, the service is new and known very little by customers; it is often ordered only for trial purposes. At this stage, the service is only used by innovative customers. Following the evaluation of the service, these customers spread information about the service, and, therefore, the customer circle expands. It is only natural that at the stage of introduction, the service cannot make a big impact on customer loyalty; however, its impact is bigger than at the stage of extinction. The growth phase of the service is linked to an exceptionally strong relationship between the customer and service provider and, during this stage, the provider adjusts the offer according to the customers' needs regarding price, distribution, and innovation. Due to the growing recognition of the service, it is believed that loyalty for it grows as well. During the maturity stage, sales scales stabilize. At the beginning of the phase, the number of customers stays the same, but later, the number starts to go down due to the appearance of new service providers that offer the same solution service–as a result, sales decrease, which leads to a decline in the effect on loyalty. During the decline phase, the number of sales constantly decline; the service is at risk of extinction and, therefore, it is believed that the effect on loyalty is neutral.

According to Padma and Wagenseil [68], customer service culture is a system of shared meanings guiding employees in what they should do. Christopher [69] established the following cultural aspects of customer service: The quality of the order placement, timely delivery, order accuracy, and precise billing and returns. To evaluate the culture of customer service, it is suggested that the secret shopper method be used, although it would only consist of the first element of valuation, due to the other elements requiring a deal. The customer service culture of ordering is characterized by the following qualities: The greeting provided by customer service staff, the use of a uniform by members of customer service staff, the advice provided by customer service staff, the capability of customer service staff to provide information about the service, and the ability of staff to determine waiting times (or specify waiting times). A high-quality customer service culture encourages members of staff to focus on the customer, and this is the first step towards the development of an organization that is focused on customer needs, which undoubtedly leads to customer loyalty. This means that a service organization that fulfils more of the attributes of customer service culture claims higher customer loyalty.

Researchers [70,71] established the following ways of paying for services: Cash, card, bank transaction, payment deferral, cheque. The ways that customers prefer to pay for the service can vary and depend on personal customer traits and features of the forms of payment [70]. This means that a service organization that accepts a variety of payment methods claims higher customer loyalty.

The service delivery environment is associated with physical attributes. An attractive service environment would be new, with wide transitions, a creative layout, bright colors, and new and modern equipment. A less attractive environment would be considered to be one with narrower transitions, a darker interior, and older and poorly maintained equipment (some requiring replacement) [66]. Scientists have identified the following physical elements of the service environment: Cleanliness and tidiness, temperature, interior, and ventilation [72,73]. Significant features of these elements have been evaluated in the service environment (Table 3).

Table 3. *Elements and features of the service delivery environment.*

Elements	Author(s)	Features
Cleanliness and tidiness	Bashar et al. [73]	The organization has a cleaning plan, the cleaning plan is being actioned, and the overall cleanliness of the premises is appropriate
Temperature	Bashar et al. [73]	During the cold season, the temperature is 18–22 °C; during the warm season, the temperature is 18–28 °C
Interior	Richardson [72], Bashar et al. [73]	The plan of the interior is customer-friendly; the interior design has unconventional features; dominant colors in the premises are attractive to the customers (warm colors—red, yellow, orange); lighting is sufficient
Ventilation	Richardson [72], Bashar et al. [73]	The facility has a ventilation/recuperation system; premises have fragrance appliances; artificial scents are used

If the service delivery environment of the organization fulfils the elements (see Table 3), the element expression will have a strong impact on customer loyalty, as an attractive environment increases the likelihood of a larger purchase value [73]. Customer loyalty based on all of the elements of the service provider environment is determined by the number of satisfactory attributes.

Environmental Factors

The last group of factors is that of environmental factors (Figure 1). This encompasses competitiveness, economic wellbeing, and social support.

It is very common to measure organizational competitiveness by profitability, productivity, market share, and other factors [74,75]. To establish customer loyalty, one of the above indicators is purposed to assess competition: Market share. Market share is calculated as a ratio of sales of a particular type of service from a particular provider and the total sales of that particular type of service. The greater the proportion of the organization's market share, the stronger the loyalty of customers is.

The economic situation in a country can be evaluated within the scope of gross domestic product (CDP) per capita [76]. It is suggested that a comparison of the value of this indicator within the area to the GDP per capita in the country can show the economic situation of a service provider. Given that the growth of GDP is linked to the weakening of customer loyalty due to fewer restrictions on consumerism, the growth of GDP is linked to weaker effects on loyalty.

Customer loyalty also depends on the level of social security in the country [77]. Social support is evaluated as a ratio between the average social support received by customers of a particular service provider and the average income of customers of a particular service provider. Higher values of social support are associated with a higher tendency towards risk and trying different services [78]. Therefore, it is claimed that higher values of average social support will weaken customer loyalty.

Estimation of Customer Loyalty Phase

Customer factors, service provider factors, and environmental factors compose a set of factors determining customer loyalty (Figure 1). All factors can have minimum values individually selected for each factor, depending on their effect on loyalty. Scales, impact intervals, and the courses of impact on loyalty for the evaluation of these factors are outlined in Table 4.

To evaluate customer loyalty based on the evaluation of loyalty factors, it is important not only to have data on the service provider that is being researched, but also trusted data from other organizations that provide the same services.

Customer loyalty evaluation based on loyalty factors allows the evaluation of customer loyalty using the previously developed evaluation indicator system. This type of customer loyalty evaluation allows customer loyalty to be split into levels (Figure 2).

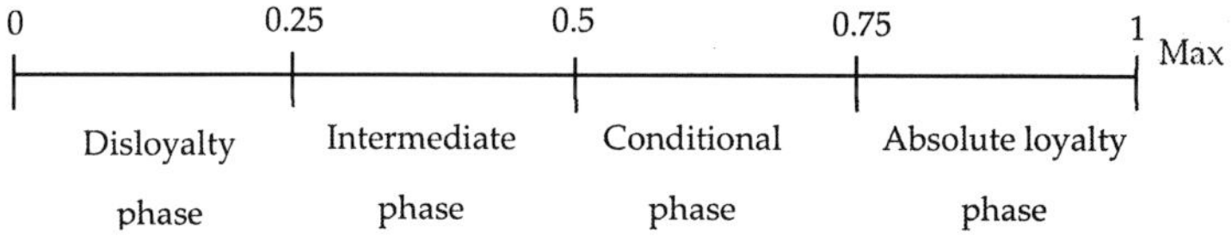

Figure 2. *Service customer loyalty evaluation scale and its linguistic interpretation.*

Service customer loyalty is divided into four phases: Disloyalty, intermediate loyalty, conditional loyalty, and absolute loyalty. The motivation for the usage of an ordinal scale for the evaluation of customer loyalty is that loyalty is a latent variable that is difficult or even impossible to evaluate directly. The choice of an ordinal scale was also determined by the dominance of the use of these scales in social sciences [79]. The content of disloyal and absolutely loyal customer statuses is clearly described in scientific and professional literature [80,81]. More uncertainty is caused by the intermediate state of loyalty. The customer in an intermediate state is undecided, they are selecting, deliberating, and, at any point, may change their status, but not necessarily toward greater loyalty. The conditional loyalty phase is reached when the loyalty evaluation is above average, but the service customers are not absolutely loyal yet. Absolute loyalty is when a customer does not have any intention of searching for alternative providers of a particular type of service.

Table 4. *Scales, impact intervals, and courses of impact on loyalty.*

Factors	Scales	Impact Interval	Impact on Loyalty
Age	Ratio	0.20–1.00	Every age group has the potential for loyalty. The impact of age on loyalty depends on the type of service. Younger customers are more loyal to providers of passenger transport, car servicing, graphic design, computer games, IT solutions, instant messaging, and physical education services, while older customers demonstrate stronger loyalty for providers of catering, internet, mobile phone networks, insurance, credit cards, banking, car rental, tourism, health care, dentistry, gambling, and hairdresser/barber services.
Gender	Nominal	0.40–0.60	Women, due to their strong aptitude for interpersonal relationships, have stronger customer loyalty potential than men.
Income	Ratio	0.20–1.00	Lower-income customer loyalty is stronger because of the lack of available choices.
Socioeconomic status	Ordinal	0.20–1.00	The loyalty of customers with lower education levels is stronger. Customers with higher education levels tend to gain more information, process it better, and base their decisions on that information.
Switching costs	Ratio	0.00–1.00	Non-existent or relatively low switching costs have a negative impact on customer loyalty. Larger costs are associated with a stronger impact on loyalty.
Assortment	Ratio	0.20–1.00	Higher relative assortment (selection) of products makes a stronger impact on loyalty.
Innovativeness	Ordinal	0.00–1.00	Customer loyalty is built on an organization's ability to innovate services. The more innovative a service is, the higher the impact on loyalty it has.
Supporting services	Ratio	0.00–1.00	The higher the relative value of services, the higher the impact on loyalty.
Service personalization	Ordinal	0.00–1.00	Service personalization has an impact on loyalty. The highest level of service personalization has the highest impact on loyalty.
Service life cycle	Ordinal	0.00–1.00	The strongest loyalty to the service is shown during the growth stage, while the weakest loyalty is seen during the decline stage.
Price	Ordinal	0.00–1.00	When the price is lower than other service providers', the likelihood of loyalty increases; therefore, lower prices are associated with higher impacts on loyalty.
Quality	Ordinal	0.00–1.00	Superior quality to other market players makes an extremely strong impact on customer loyalty.
Working hours	Ordinal	0.00–1.00	An organization that has unlimited working hours is evaluated as the best in terms of loyalty.
Location	Ordinal	0.00–1.00	The location of the organization that is within a reasonable distance and with an acceptable number of car parking spaces, is on the ground level, and has a relatively low level of criminal activity criteria is valued as having the most impact on loyalty.
Marketing	Ratio	0.10–1.00	Larger budgets for marketing and a greater sales promotion share in the marketing budget mean stronger impacts on loyalty.
Attractiveness of service delivery environment	Ordinal	0.00–1.00	A more attractive service delivery environment has a stronger impact on customer loyalty.
Reputation	Ratio	0.00–1.00	A better reputation of the service provider has a stronger impact on loyalty.
Service culture	Ordinal	(–0.25)–1.00	A service organization that fits in with more cultural attributes of the service customer attracts higher customer loyalty.
Payment options	Ordinal	0.00–1.00	A service organization that offers a wider variety of payment options claims higher customer loyalty.
Personnel qualifications	Ratio	(–0.10)–1.00	Higher qualifications of employees are considered to be a stronger condition of customer loyalty.
Competitiveness	Ratio	0.00–1.00	Higher relative market shares of the organization are associated with a stronger impact on loyalty.
Economic wellbeing	Ratio	0.00–1.00	GDP growth is associated with a stronger effect on loyalty.
Social support	Ratio	0.00–1.00	A higher relative value of social support has a weaker impact on loyalty.

Estimations of customer loyalty phases show whether the measures put in place to instigate customer loyalty were selected well and whether their implementation was effective. The value of service customer loyalty farthest from the maximum unit shows that the service provider is not fully utilizing its potential of loyalty.

MATERIALS AND METHODS

The application of the suggested set of factors to a catering company and a beauty studio was conducted to evaluate customer loyalty. Both companies are small business units operating in an average-size city in Lithuania (Table 5).

Table 5. *Characteristics of the researched companies.*

Characteristics	Catering Company	Beauty Studio
Location	Siauliai, Lithuania	Siauliai, Lithuania
Date of establishment	23 February 2012	7 June 2010
Number of employees (December, 2019)	9	4
Income, EUR (2019)	25,213	40,118

The management of both companies provided specific data from the companies' loyalty program databases and financial reports. The following documents were also requested: Rules for participation in the loyalty program, cleaning plans, temperature logs, room plans, service delivery standards, results from secret shopper researches, CVs of employees, etc. (Table 6). Additional efforts to collect data from customers were not initiated due to the specific approach to the evaluation of customer loyalty: The set of factors used intends to evaluate customer loyalty in cases when behavioral data are unavailable. This approach provides the possibility of evaluating the loyalty of a whole customer base of the company, not of a particular customer.

The collected data let the authors identify the demographic characteristics of the customers of both service providers. The typical customer of the catering company was a female who is 21–40 years old and has a higher education level. In the case of the beauty studio, the typical customer was female as well; however, the age group of 41–60 years was found to be dominant (29.19% of the whole customer base). Customers with a higher education comprised a considerable share of the customer base of the beauty studio.

Methods of content analysis and document analysis were chosen for the analysis of the collected data. Every data source was carefully checked in order to find the required data for the evaluation of every factor. When the analysis of the provided data sources was finished, it was noticed that there were still some informational gaps. To fill them, the management was contacted once again.

Values for factors were determined based on the factor valuation scale, loyalty impact range, and the loyalty effect direction set out in Table 4. Assigning quantifying values to factors makes it possible to calculate the loyalty value, to find out average values of different loyalty groups [16,18,22,23], and to determine

Table 6. *Data sources.*

Factors	Data Source	Specification of Data
Age, gender, income, socioeconomic status, location	Database of the customer loyalty program	Customers' dates of birth, distribution of customers according to gender, income, social status, and living place, number of customers who had complaints during the last year, number of participants of the customer loyalty program, number of customers during the last year, the value of customers' social support
Switching costs	Rules of the customer loyalty program	Service provider's switching costs
Assortment, supporting services, price	The price list of services	Number of services provided, prices
Innovativeness, service life cycle, quality, working hours, attractiveness of service delivery environment, reputation, payment options	Interviews with top management	Innovativeness of services, possibilities to provide services in electronic environments, possibilities to provide services in other physical locations, phase of the service life cycle, number of complaints related to the quality of services, number of working hours, specification of a ventilation system, specification of aromatization system, number of payment options
Attractiveness of service delivery environment	Cleaning plan	(Non-)existence of a cleaning plan, the degree of compliance with a cleaning plan
Attractiveness of service delivery environment	Temperature monitoring system	Temperature monitoring data
Marketing	Financial accounts	Marketing budget, promotion budget, income
	Scheme of the building	The layout of the interior
	Interviews with personnel	The number of foreign languages known, possibilities to adapt services
Location, attractiveness of service delivery environment	Photos of interior	Interior design, dominant colors, lighting solutions
Service personalization	Service standard	Possibilities of customer participation in service provision, possibilities to devote extra time for a customer, possibilities to advise customers, possibilities for personal communication with customers, possibilities to congratulate customers on their birthdays, possibilities to adapt services, possibilities to adjust the price
Location	City scheme	Number of parking spaces
Service culture	Results of a secret shopper research	The greeting provided by customer service staff, the use of a uniform by members of customer service staff, the advice provided by customer service staff, the capability of customer service staff to provide information about the service, the ability of staff to determine waiting times (or specify waiting times)
Personnel qualifications	CVs of employees	Professional experience, education
Competitiveness, economic wellbeing, social support	Statistics Office	GDP per capita, the income of organizations providing a particular service, size of social support

the loyalty status: Disloyalty, intermediate, conditional, or absolute loyalty [80,81]. We reassured the management of both companies that the results would be used solely for research purposes.

RESULTS

Customer loyalty to the catering company and the beauty studio services was determined by the evaluation of the impact of customer, service provider, and environmental factors. The results showed that the impacts of factors on loyalty vary widely, from −1 to 1 (Table 7).

Both service providers fell into the category of services where older customers seem to be more loyal (Table 1). Due to the dominance of younger customers in both companies, the impact of age upon customer loyalty was weaker (0.48 and

Table 7. *The impacts of factors on loyalty.*

Group of Factors	Factors	The Impact on Loyalty	
		Catering Company	Beauty Studio
Customer	Age	0.48	0.47
	Gender	0.52	0.58
	Income	0.32	0.74
	Socioeconomic status	0.28	0.34
	Switching costs	−1.00	−1.00
Service provider	Assortment	0.60	0.20
	Innovativeness	0.25	0.00
	Supporting services	0.25	0.00
	Service personalization	0.80	1.00
	Service life cycle	0.25	0.50
	Price	0.75	1.00
	Quality	1.00	1.00
	Location	0.50	0.75
	Working hours	0.75	0.75
	Marketing	0.33	0.58
	Attractiveness of service provider environment	0.75	1.00
	Reputation	1.00	1.00
	Service culture	1.00	0.75
	Payment options	0.75	0.00
	Personnel qualifications	0.59	0.62
Environment	Competition	0.00	1.00
	Economic welfare	0.75	1.00
	Social support	0.25	0.50

0.47, respectively). Based on theoretical assumptions and identified scales, impact intervals, and the course of impact on loyalty (Table 4), numeric values of loyalty were attributed to the remaining factors that belong to the customer, service provider, or environmental groups.

Regarding the catering company, among the individual factors, the strongest positive impacts on customer loyalty were quality, reputation, and service culture, whereas the strongest negative effects were made by switching costs (more specifically, the absence of them). The effect of all factors on loyalty was not very strong (0.49). This value of loyalty indicates that the loyalty of customers of the catering company was at the intermediate stage. Factors that belong to the service provider group had the strongest effect on loyalty (0.64) (Figure 3); in terms of these factors, customer loyalty to the catering company is at the conditional stage. The effects of environmental and customer factors on loyalty were significantly weaker (0.33 and 0.12, respectively). Therefore, based on environmental factors, customer loyalty is at the intermediate stage, while the factors of the customer group indicate disloyalty to the catering company.

In relation to the beauty studio, service personalization, price, quality, the attractiveness of the environment, reputation, competitiveness, and economic prosperity had the strongest positive effects—all of these factors had a strong impact on loyalty (0.64). When assessing the groups of factors, it can be seen that the environmental factors had the strongest impact on loyalty (0.83). In terms of these factors, the loyalty of the beauty studio customers was at the phase of

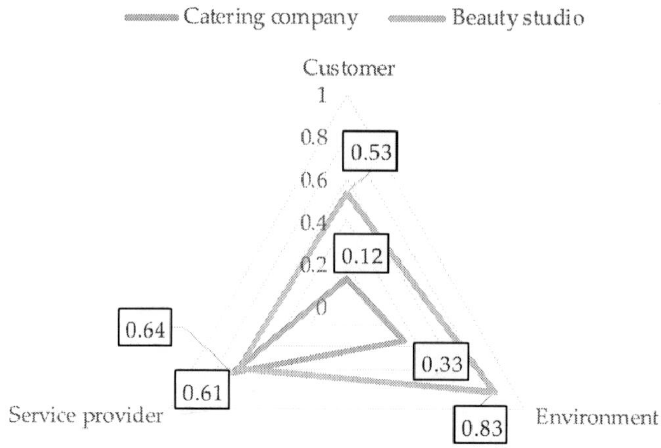

Figure 3. *Average values of factors on loyalty by group.*

absolute loyalty. The impacts of the service provider and customer factors on loyalty seemed to be weaker (0.61 and 0.53, respectively). This means that, in terms of the factors mentioned above, service customer loyalty was at the stage of conditional loyalty.

Determining loyalty by measuring the impact of factors is a superior method, as it allows the determination of loyalty-restricting factors and, based on that information, the service provider can choose the most effective tools to promote loyalty. All factors were divided into three groups according to the effect on loyalty (Table 8).

Table 8. *The differentiation of the strengths of factors' impacts on loyalty.*

Impact on Loyalty	Strength of Impact	Factors	
		Catering Company	**Beauty Studio**
Negative	Very strong	Switching costs	Switching costs
Neutral	Neutral	Competitiveness	Innovativeness, supporting services, payment options
Positive	Very slight	Innovativeness, supporting services, service life cycle, social support	Assortment
	Slight	Socioeconomic status, income, marketing, age, location	Service life cycle, marketing, personnel qualifications, age, socioeconomic status, social support
	Strong	Gender, personnel qualifications, assortment, price, working hours, attractiveness of service delivery environment, payment options, economic wellbeing	Location, working hours, service culture, gender, income
	Very strong	Service personalization, service quality, reputation, service culture	Service personalization, price, service quality, attractiveness of service delivery environment, reputation, competitiveness, economic wellbeing

The breakdown of customer loyalty factors according to their loyalty trends and strength indicates that the loyalty of the catering service customers was mostly limited by switching costs. Competition was a neutral factor that had neither a positive nor negative effect on customer loyalty. The greatest impacts on customer loyalty were the quality, reputation, and culture of the delivery service. In the beauty studio example, customer loyalty was also mostly limited by switching costs. Innovation, additional services, and payment options were neutral factors that had neither positive nor negative effects on customer loyalty. The greatest impacts on customer loyalty were service personalization, price, quality, the attractiveness of the service delivery environment, reputation, competition, and economic wellbeing. If the beauty studio is aiming for a higher rating of customer loyalty, then all of the other factors should be altered. It should be noted that increasing the value of customer loyalty by 5% determined an increase in net profit of from 25% to 85% [82].

To summarize the evaluation of customer loyalty factors, it can be stated that the service customers of the catering company were at the intermediate loyalty stage, while the beauty studio customers' loyalty was at the conditional stage.

DISCUSSION

Customer loyalty evaluation has always been of interest to academics and marketers. However, past research into customer loyalty evaluation in cases where behavioral data are unavailable resulted in the choice of questionnaire research. This study sheds light on an alternative by evaluating customer loyalty based on factors.

This research aimed to contribute to customer loyalty research in service industries. To reach this aim, the authors prepared a set of customer loyalty factors for the evaluation of customer loyalty and tested its applicability to service industries. The suggested set of customer loyalty factors supports the findings of other researchers [16,18,22,23] who suggested the classification of factors based on the main participants in loyalty formation, i.e., the customer, the service provider and the environment.

The findings of this theoretical research contribute to marketing literature in several ways. Firstly, we offer a deeper understanding of the typology of factors that determine customer loyalty. Our study reveals that, taking into consideration customer, service provider, and environmental group factors, the impact of every factor can vary from negative to positive. This finding is supported by the results of empirical testing on both a catering company and a beauty studio. The study was based on objective data obtained from the service companies. Secondly, this study extends prior research on factors determining customer loyalty by systemically developing a framework for the evaluation of customer loyalty based on the evaluation of every particular factor. We used multiple sources of data to empirically examine how customer, service provider, and environmental characteristics influence the phase of customer loyalty. Our findings, summarized in Figure 2, give a better understanding of which types of factors have a considerable impact on customer loyalty. Our findings suggest important differences in loyalty-building mechanisms between the catering company and the beauty studio. Customer age, service provider assortment, innovativeness, supporting services, service culture, and payment options were found to have considerable impacts on the development of customer loyalty in the catering company. In the case of the beauty studio customers, gender, income, socioeconomic status, switching costs, service personalization, service life cycle, price, quality, location, working hours, marketing, attractiveness of the service provider environment, reputation, personnel qualifications, competition, economic welfare, and social support were all responsible for the increasing customer loyalty to the beauty studio.

We have found that customers may be classified into four phases of loyalty: (1) The disloyalty phase, (2) the intermediate phase, (3) the conditional phase, and (4) the absolute loyalty phase. Customers entering the absolute loyalty phase are the most valuable segment, as they devote a considerable share of their expenditure to that particular service provider. These findings are in line with the results of other research [80,81].

The results of the research provide managers with information about the impacts of customer, service provider and environmental factors on customer loyalty across two different service industries. For a beauty studio seeking absolute customer loyalty, it is important to build in switching costs, increase service innovativeness, expand the range of additional services, and improve payment method options. In the case of the catering company, the following factors should be strengthened: Switching costs, competitiveness, innovativeness, supporting services, service life cycle, and social support. Looking from a managerial perspective, these insights call for changes when designing relationship marketing strategies.

CONCLUSIONS

Customer loyalty factors have been gaining considerable attention in the marketing literature. In this study, we draw on a conceptual set of customer loyalty factors applicable to the evaluation of loyalty in the catering and beauty industries. We have investigated the impact of three particular groups of loyalty factors (i.e., customer, service provider, and environmental) upon the formation of customer loyalty. The results support the applicability of the suggested set of customer loyalty factors. The empirical evidence in this paper reveals failures to establish switching costs in both the catering company and the beauty studio, while the factors that have a strong or very strong positive impact upon customer loyalty in the mentioned industries vary considerably. This research highlights that the service provider factors had the strongest effects on loyalty in the case of the catering company, while the loyalty of the customers of the beauty studio was most intensely impacted by environmental factors. We were able to identify that the loyalty of customers of the catering company was at the intermediate stage, and the loyalty of the customers of the beauty studio indicated conditional loyalty. In order to understand the reasons for these differences, research into other service markets is necessary. In addition, further factors, such as green marketing or greenwashing practices, should be explored.

Our research has some limitations. Even though the objective of the research was to contribute to recent literature examining customer loyalty in the service industry, the aim was reached by testing the applicability of the set of customer loyalty factors for the evaluation of customer loyalty in only two industries. We had to limit the number of researched industries due to data accessibility. The inclusion of additional industries in the research would have substantially confirmed the universality of the suggested set of customer loyalty factors. One more limitation is the failure to test the model in the case of e-services. Therefore, it may be interesting to consider customer loyalty and its factors for e-services. Overcoming the mentioned limitations in future studies is expected to be expedient not only to companies providing catering and beauty services, but also to marketers in other areas. We believe that our findings will be interesting for academics and marketers and will provide valuable avenues for future research. For instance, our research on customer loyalty evaluation can be expanded by examining enterprises that represent different channels; for example, online versus offline channels. Furthermore, it would be important to repeat the research in the same catering company and beauty studio after a year or two.

Author Contributions

Conceptualization, I.S. and N.V.-V.; methodology, I.S. and N.V.-V.; formal analysis, I.S. and N.V.-V.; investigation, I.S. and N.V.-V.; resources, I.S. and N.V.-V.; data curation, I.S. and N.V.-V.; writing—original draft preparation, I.S. and N.V.-V.; writing—review and editing, I.S. and N.V.-V.; visualization, N.V.-V.; supervision, I.S. All authors have read and agreed to the published version of the manuscript.

REFERENCES

1. Topcu, B.; Duygun, A. The impacts of customer loyalty on negative word-of-mouth communication and repurchase intention. *J. Mark. Manag.* **2015**, *6*, 16–27.
2. Bergel, M.; Frank, P.; Brock, C. The role of customer engagement facets on the formation of attitude, loyalty and price perception. *J. Serv. Mark.* **2019**, *33*, 890–903.
3. Toufaily, E.; Ricard, L.; Perrien, J. Customer loyalty to a commercial website: Descriptive meta-analysis of the empirical literature and proposal of an integrative model. *J. Bus. Res.* **2013**, *66*, 1436–1447.
4. Kamran-Disfani, O.; Mantrala, M.K.; Izquierdo-Yusta, A.; Martinez-Ruiz, M.P. The impact of retail store format on the satisfaction-loyalty link: An empirical investigation. *J. Bus. Res.* **2017**, *77*, 14–22.
5. Srivastava, M.; Kaul, D. Exploring the link between customer experience-loyalty-consumer spend. *J. Retail. Consum. Serv.* **2016**, *31*, 277–286.
6. Bilgihan, A.; Madanoglu, M.; Ricci, P. Service attributes as drivers of behavioral loyalty in casinos: The mediating effect of attitudinal loyalty. *J. Retail. Consum. Serv.* **2016**, *31*, 14–21.
7. Al-hawari, M.A. How the personality of retail bank customers interferes with the relationship between service quality and loyalty. *Int. J. Bank Mark.* **2015**, *33*, 41–57.
8. Bahri-Ammari, N.; Niekerk, M.V.; Khelil, H.B.; Chtioui, J. The effects of brand attachment on behavioral loyalty in the luxury restaurant sector. *Int. J. Contemp. Hosp. Manag.* **2016**, *28*, 559–585.

9. Bhatnagar, S.B.; Syed, A.A.; Mishra, J.K. Identifying customer loyalty supporting factors in the retail banking context: An empirical examination. *J. Relatsh. Mark.* **2017**, *16*, 197–225.

10. Homjitr, S.; Sato, S.C. Factors affecting brand loyalty of essence of chicken brand towards consumers in Bangkok. *Utcc Int. J. Bus. Econ.* **2017**, *9*, 33–47.

11. Ou, Y.C.; Verhoef, P.C.; Wiesel, T. The effects of customer equity drivers on loyalty across services industries and firms. *J. Acad. Mark. Sci.* **2017**, *45*, 336–356.

12. Srivastava, R.K. How differing demographic factors impact upon customer loyalty towards national or international fast-food chains: A comparative study in emerging markets. *J. Food Prod. Mark.* **2017**, *23*, 901–925.

13. Gomez, M.; Martin-Consuegra, D.; Diaz, E.; Molina, A. Determinants and outcomes of price premium and loyalty: A food case study. *J. Consum. Behav.* **2018**, *17*, 64–74.

14. Ofori, K.S.; Boakye, K.; Narteh, B. Factors influencing consumer loyalty towards 3G mobile data service providers: Evidence from Ghana. *Total Qual. Manag.* **2018**, *29*, 580–598.

15. Auapinyakul, W.; Deebhijarn, S. A structural equation modelling on factors related to the brand loyalty of diners to certified Thai restaurants in the United States. *Asia Pac. Soc. Sci. Rev.* **2019**, *19*, 155–163.

16. Tefera, O.; Migiro, S. The relationship amongst customer satisfaction, loyalty, demographic and tripographic attributes: A case of star rated hotel guests in Ethiopia. *J. Econ. Behav. Stud.* **2019**, *10*, 16–29.

17. Skackauskiene, I.; Vilkaite-Vaitone, N. *Paslaugų Vartotojų Lojalumas*; Technika: Vilnius, Lithuania, 2017.

18. Faisal, S.; Hamid, N.A.A.; Abdullah, N.H. Cultural factors affecting persuasive design of smartphone applications to maintain customer loyalty. *Adv. Sci. Lett.* **2018**, *24*, 4603–4608.

19. Jamaludin, M.; Aziz, A.; Mariapan, M. Millennial travellers decision making influenced through user-generated contents and psychological attributes on destination loyalty to a tropical island. *J. Tour. Hosp. Environ. Manag.* **2018**, *3*, 44–55.

20. Vazifehdust, H.; Jaberi, M. Factors affecting customer loyalty through satisfaction in traditional retail stores: Structural equation modelling approach. *Int. J. Sci. Manag. Dev.* **2018**, *6*, 1–8.

21. Elsäßer, M.; Wirtz, B. Rational and emotional factors of customer satisfaction and brand loyalty in a business-to-business setting. *J. Bus. Ind. Mark.* **2017**, *32*, 138–152.

22. Nyadzayo, M.W.; Khajehzadeh, S. The antecedents of customer loyalty: A moderated mediation model of customer relationship management quality and brand image. *J. Retail. Consum. Serv.* **2016**, *30*, 262–270.

23. Shafei, I.; Tabaa, H. Factors affecting customer loyalty for mobile telecommunication industry. *Euromed J. Bus.* **2016**, *11*, 347–361.

24. Reyes-Menendez, A.; Palos-Sanchez, P.R.; Saura, J.R.; Martin-Velicia, F. Understanding the influence of wireless communications and wi-fi access on customer loyalty: A behavioural model system. *Wirel. Commun. Mob. Comput.* **2018**, *2018*, 1–16.

25. Tweneboah-Koduah, E.Y.; Farley, A.Y.D. Relationship between customer satisfaction and customer loyalty in the retail banking sector of Ghana. *Int. J. Bus. Manag.* **2016**, *11*, 249–262.

26. Wu, Y.; Li, E. Marketing mix, customer value, and customer loyalty in social commerce: A stimulus-organism-response perspective. *Internet Res.* **2018**, *28*, 74–104.

27. Othman, B.A.; Harun, A.; Rashid, W.N.; Nazeer, S.; Kassim, A.W.M.; Kadhim, K.G. The influences of service marketing mix on customer loyalty towards Umrah travel agents: Evidence from Malaysia. *Manag. Sci. Lett.* **2019**, *9*, 865–876.

28. Anderson, K.; Sharp, B. Do growing brands win younger consumers? *Int. J. Mark. Res.* **2010**, *52*, 433–441.

29. Belas, J.; Chocholakova, A.; Gabčova, L. Satisfaction and loyalty of banking customers: A gender approach. *Econ. Sociol.* **2015**, *8*, 176–188.

30. Patterson, P.G. Demographic correlates of loyalty in a service context. *J. Serv. Mark.* **2007**, *21*, 112–121.

31. Parahoo, S.K.; Harvey, H.L.; Radi, G.Y.A. Satisfaction of tourists with public transport: An empirical investigation in Dubai. *J. Travel Tour. Mark.* **2014**, *31*, 1014–1017.

32. Jiang, H.; Zhang, Y. An investigation of service quality, customer satisfaction and loyalty in China's airline market. *J. Air Transp. Manag.* **2016**, *57*, 80–88.

33. Bekk, M.; Sporrle, M.; Landes, M.; Moser, K. Traits grow important with increasing age: Customer age, brand personality and loyalty. *J. Bus. Econ.* **2017**, *87*, 511–531.

34. Loureiro, S.M.C.; Holger, R. Differential effects of atmospheric cues on emotions and loyalty intention with respect to age under online/offline environment. *J. Retail. Consum. Serv.* **2014**, *21*, 211–219.

35. Kim, S.T.; Kim, J.W. A study of consumer loyalty on instant messaging services. *Int. J. Manag. Sci.* **2010**, *16*, 67–80.

36. Dragan, A.A. Segmenting and profiling fitness club customers: A case study. *Rev. Manag. Ing. Econ.* **2013**, *12*, 125–138.

37. Cambra-Fierro, J.; Berbel-Pineda, J.M.; Ruiz-Benitez, R.; Vazquez-Carrasco, R. Managing service recovery processes: The role of customers' age. *J. Bus. Econ. Manag.* **2011**, *12*, 503–528.

38. Prentice, C. Service quality perceptions and customer loyalty in casinos. *Int. J. Contemp. Hosp. Manag.* **2013**, *25*, 49–64.

39. Borges, A.; Babin, B.J.; Spielmann, N. Gender orientation and retail atmosphere: Effects on value perception. *Int. J. Retail Distrib. Manag.* **2013**, *41*, 498–511.

40. Kamath, P.R.; Yogesh, P.P.; Prabhu, K.P. Building customer loyalty in retail banking: A serial-mediation approach. *Int. J. Bank Mark.* **2019**. ahead of print.

41. Tasci, A.D.A. A quest for destination loyalty by profiling loyal travellers. *J. Destin. Mark. Manag.* **2017**, *6*, 207–220.

42. Orhan, S.; Kaplan, Z. Analysis on brand preference and loyalty of physical education and sports teachers. *Univers. J. Educ. Res.* **2018**, *6*, 2471–2477.

43. Ballew, M.T.; Pearson, A.R.; Goldberg, M.H.; Rosenthal, S.A.; Leiserowitz, A. Does socioeconomic status moderate the political divide on climate change? The roles of education, income, and individualism. *Glob. Environ. Chang.* **2020**, *60*, 102024.

44. Li, Y.; Liu, H.; Lim, E.T.K.; Goh, J.M.; Yang, F.; Lee, M.K.O. Customer's reaction to cross-channel integration in omnichannel retailing: The mediating roles of retailer uncertainty, identity attractiveness, and switching costs. *Decis. Support Syst.* **2018**, *109*, 50–60.

45. Xiao, B.; Feng, Y.; Roche, E. Uncertain switching costs and purchase decisions in electronic markets. *Ann. Oper. Res.* **2005**, *135*, 179–196.

46. Koo, B.; Yu, J.; Han, H. The role of loyalty programs in boosting hotel guest loyalty: Impact of switching barriers. *Int. J. Hosp. Manag.* **2020**, *84*, 102328.

47. Singh, P.K.; Pattanayak, J.K. The impact of brand loyalty on consumers' sportswear brand purchase. *IUP J. Brand Manag.* **2014**, *11*, 40–52.

48. Klarin, A. Mapping product and service innovation: A bibliometric analysis and a typology. *Technol. Forecast. Soc. Chang.* **2019**, *149*, 119776.

49. Lemy, D.; Goh, E.; Ferry, J. Moving out of the silo: How service quality innovations can develop customer loyalty in Indonesia's hotels. *J. Vacat. Mark.* **2019**, *25*, 462–479.

50. Small, A.; Russell, S.V.; Paavola, J. Corporate environmental sustainability and ecosystem services: A 21st century solution? In Proceedings of the Academy of Management Annual Meeting, Boston, MA, USA, 9–13 August 2019; Volume 1, pp. 1–5.

51. Berezny, R.; Konecny, V. The impact of the quality of transport services on passenger demand in the suburban bus transport. *Procedia Eng.* **2017**, *192*, 40–45.

52. Torn, I.A.R.; Vaneker, T.H.J. Mass personalization with Industry 4.0 by SMEs: A concept for collaborative networks. *Procedia Manuf.* **2019**, *28*, 135–141.

53. Asif, M.; Krogstie, J. Mobile services personalization evaluation model. *Int. J. UE Serv. Sci. Technol.* **2013**, *6*, 1–12.

54. Wu, C.W. The study of service innovation for digiservice on loyalty. *J. Bus. Res.* **2014**, *67*, 819–824.

55. Morgan, N.A.; Rego, L.L. The value of different customer satisfaction and loyalty metrics in predicting business performance. *Mark. Sci.* **2006**, *25*, 426–439.

56. Flores, M.; Wenzel, T. Shopping hours and price competition with loyal consumers. *BE J. Econ. Anal. Policy* **2015**, *16*, 393–407.

57. Tripathi, S.N. An analysis of customer-pull factors and the process of store loyalty. *Paradigm* **2009**, *9*, 91–103.

58. Ali, R.Y.; Eftelioglu, E.; Shekhar, S.; Athavale, S.; Marsman, E. Supply-demand ratio and on-demand spatial service brokers: A summary of results. In Proceedings of the 9th ACM SIGSPATIAL International Workshop on Computational Transportation Science, San Francisco, CA, USA, 31 October 2016; pp. 7–12.

59. Laska, M.N.; Graham, D.J.; Moe, S.G.; Van Riper, D. Young adult eating and food-purchasing patterns: Food store location and residential proximity. *Am. J. Prev. Med.* **2010**, *39*, 464–467.

60. Waters, S. Choosing a Retail Store Location. 2014. Available online: http://retail.about.com/od/location/a/selecting_site.htm (accessed on 25 January 2020).

61. Benesova, A.; Tupa, J. Requirements for education and qualification of people in industry 4.0. *Procedia Manuf.* **2017**, *11*, 2195–2202.

62. Wang, C.C.; Wang, Y.M.; Chieh, W.H. The moderating role of customer knowledge on the relationship between satisfaction and loyalty. *J. Econ. Bus. Manag.* **2016**, *4*, 292–295.

63. Ulrich, D.; Brockbank, W. *Personalo Vadyba: Vertės Pasiūlymas*; Verslo žinios: Vilnius, Lithuania, 2007.

64. Ziliani, C.; Ieva, M. Loyalty in the omnichannel environment. In *Loyalty Management. From Loyalty Programs to Omnichannel Customer Experiences*; Routledge: New York, NY, USA, 2020.

65. Miller, C.E.; Skudienė, V.; Reardon, J. Managing customer loyalty in the entertainment industry in a transitional economy. *Rev. Manag. Innov. Creat.* **2013**, *6*, 114–129.

66. Empen, J.; Loy, J.P.; Weiss, C. Price promotions and brand loyalty. *Eur. J. Mark.* **2015**, *49*, 736–759.

67. Wu, J.; Chang, C.T.; Teng, J.T.; Lai, K.K. Optimal order quantity and selling price over a product life cycle with deterioration rate linked to expiration date. *Int. J. Prod. Econ.* **2017**, *193*, 343–351.

68. Padma, P.; Wagenseil, U. Retail service excellence: Antecedents and consequences. *Int. J. Retail Distrib. Manag.* **2018**, *46*, 422–441.

69. Christopher, M. *Logistika ir Tiekimo Grandinės Valdymas: Pridėtinės Vertės Tinklų Kūrimas*; Eugrimas: Vilnius, Lithuania, 2007.

70. Shiliashki, M. The untapped potential of digital loyalty programmes. *J. Paym. Strategy Syst.* **2013**, *7*, 106–111.

71. Huynh, K.P.; Nicholls, G.; Shcherbakov, O. Explaining the interplay between merchant acceptance and consumer adoption in two-sided markets for payment methods. *Bank Can. Staff Work. Pap.* **2019**, *32*, 1–31.

72. Richardson, P.; Jain, A.K.; Dick, A. The influence of store aesthetics on evaluation of private label brands. *J. Prod. Brand Manag.* **1996**, *5*, 19–28.

73. Bashar, A.; Ahmad, I.; Wasiq, M. A study on influence of demographic factors on consumer impulse buying behaviour. *J. Manag. Res.* **2013**, *13*, 145–154.

74. Rodriguez-Pose, A.; Hardy, D. Firm competitiveness and regional disparities in Georgia. *Geogr. Rev.* **2016**, *107*, 384–411.

75. Aguiar, G.P.; Silva, J.C.G.L.; Frega, J.R.; Santana, L.F.; Valerius, J. The use of constant market share (CMS) model to assess Brazil nut market competitiveness. *J. Agric. Sci.* **2017**, *9*, 174–180.

76. Churchill, S.W.; Ivanovski, K. Electricity consumption and economic growth across Australian states and territories. *Appl. Econ.* **2020**, *52*, 866–878.

77. Morgeson, F.; Mithas, S.; Keiningham, T.L.; Aksoy, L. An investigation of the cross-national determinants of customer satisfaction. *J. Acad. Mark. Sci.* **2011**, *39*, 198–215.

78. Pont, M.; McQuilken, L. An empirical investigation of customer satisfaction and loyalty across two divergent bank segments. *J. Financ. Serv. Mark.* **2005**, *9*, 344–359.

79. Arvidsson, R. On the use of ordinal scoring scales in social life cycle assessment. *Int. J. Life Cycle Assess.* **2019**, *24*, 604–606.

80. Ngobo, P.V. The trajectory of customer loyalty: An empirical test of Dick and Basu's loyalty framework. *J. Acad. Mark. Sci.* **2017**, *45*, 229–250.

81. Schneider, P.J.; Zielke, S. Searching offline and buying online—An analysis of show rooming forms and segments. *J. Retail. Consum. Serv.* **2020**, *52*, 101919.

82. Aksoy, L.; Keiningham, T.L.; Oliver, R.L. 3 loyalty: Its many sources and variations. *Handb. Serv. Mark. Res.* **2014**, *37*, 37–51.

CHAPTER 2

The Effects of Perceived Value, Website Trust and Hotel Trust on Online Hotel Booking Intention

Seo Yeon Kim[1], Jong Uk Kim[2] and Sang Cheol Park[3]

[1]*Department of ITS Business Planning, SK Holdings, 26, Jong-ro, Jongro-gu, Seoul 03188, Korea*

[2]*School of Business, Sungkyunkwan University, Sungkyunkwan-ro, 25-2, Jongro-gu, Seoul 03063, Korea*

[3]*Department of Business, Daegu University, 201 Daegu-Ro, Gyeongsan-si, Gyeongbuk 38453, Korea*

ABSTRACT

With the rapid development of information technology in hotel booking context, it is no doubt that many hotels consequently enhance the needs of integrating information technologies into their overall business operations. In this study, we developed a research model which consists of perceived value, trust toward a third party online booking site, and trust toward hotels, and tested it by using partial least square techniques. Survey data were collected from 307 individuals who have prior experiences on making a reservation using third-party online booking sites. Based upon our findings, we found that the perceived value, which was affected by both price and quality, was positively related to individuals' intention to book. We also found that both trust toward third-party online booking sites and trust toward hotels, which was influenced by online review, have positive impacts on individuals' intention to book. The implications of these findings for both research and practice are discussed.

Keywords: *intention to book; online hotel booking; perceived value; trust toward a third-party online booking sites; trust toward hotels*

INTRODUCTION

The development of information technology enables most hotels to change their business operations rapidly. Nowadays, it is no doubt that many hotels consequently enhances the needs of integrating information technologies (hereafter, IT) into their overall business operations. A good example of combination of IT and business operations in overall hotel industry would be third-party online hotel booking sites [1]. Prior to the emergence of third-party online hotel booking sites, consumers would have to directly contact a department of hotel reservation by phone. However, the advent of third-party booking sites (e.g., Hotels.com, Booking.com, TripAdvisor, and HotelsCombined) give consumers various benefits before making a reservation. As third-party online booking sites have become sophisticated, they have been transformed into a variety of mobile platforms such as on smart phones (Android, iPhone, Blackberry, etc.) or tablet PC (iPad, etc.). For example, consumers can use mobile devices to book accommodation using mobile apps via a smart phone [2]. The mobile platform has made hotel booking much easier, since the booking is completed on third-party online booking sites itself and users are not redirected to a hotel's website [3]. Thus, a better mobile experience for hotel booking enhances value for the consumers and increases online bookings [4].

In prior work, the perceived value has been considered as a salient factor to predict individuals' purchase behavior; perceived value could play an important role for those who want to make hotel reservations using third-party online booking sites [5,6]. For example, according to Krasna's work [7], the perceived value influences consumers' decision on both hotel choice and booking intention [8], since the value was closely related to price and quality. It is well known that both price and quality could be salient factors for calculating individuals' perceived value before they make final decisions [9]. Consistent with prior work [10], this study has also considered individuals' perceived value as one of the determinants that could affect their intention to book a hotel. This study further attempts to examine how both price and quality could influence individuals' perceived value in our context.

Otherwise, as a consequence of online market development, trust also plays a more important role in the online market than in traditional offline markets, due to the perceived risk and uncertainty present in online transactions [11]. While lack of trust can be the reason consumers avoid purchasing online [12,13], trust is the main concern for many consumers who make a purchase [14]. When a consumer trusts an online website, they are more likely to purchase from the website. Previous studies on online purchase have argued that trust in the online store positively influences the consumers' intentions to purchase from the online store [15,16,17]. While consumers need to rely on the information provided by a third-party online booking site to book, they then need to trust the online booking site with their offering of hotels' information and hotel rates needed for any booking. In this study, we further pay attention to trust toward third-party online booking sites, which should greatly influence intention to book.

In this research area, some research has revealed that the main reason individuals were reluctant to purchase online was related to the lack of trust toward online channels [12,13,14]. The role of trust toward third-party online booking sites could be similar to the findings from previous work (e.g., [12,13,14]). For instance, individuals usually use third-party booking sites when they believe those sites are trustworthy. Once third-party booking sites guarantee their own competences, integrity and reliability toward consumers, consumers could feel that the sites have excellent reputations to offer reliable service and integrity [18,19]. Therefore, we also consider the trust toward third-party online booking sites as one of key factors affecting individuals' intention to book.

In general, consumers are more likely to trust a hotel that makes its services and policies available and informs them about new offerings [20]. Trust toward the hotel could ultimately lead to consumers' booking intention [21]. Therefore, trust toward hotels could be an important factor in predicting individuals' intention to book. In addition, trust toward hotels would be established based on the level of feedback from individuals who had prior experiences staying in those hotels [22,23] Individuals' feedback could be represented as online reviews. Especially, positive online reviews make individuals trust a specific hotel [24]. In this study, we further examine the relationship between online reviews and trust toward hotels.

In summary, this study aims to better understand consumers' intention to book in the third-party online booking site context. In doing so, we seek to answer the following research question:

> *To what extent do perceived value, trust toward the third-party online booking sites, and trust toward hotels help us to predict consumers' intention to book?*

While prior research has examined the impact of trust and value on individuals' intention to book [21,24], we know of no research that has examined the effects of perceived value and two different types of trust (i.e., trust toward third-party websites and hotels) on consumers' intention to book. By addressing the above research question, this study contributes to the current body of knowledge regarding consumer behavior in hotel reservation context. From the standpoint of research implications, this study has presented integrative theoretical views of perceived value and two types of trust in a single research model that may contribute to individuals' intention to book. In practical standpoint, ours could offer some hotels, which connected with the third-party online booking sites, some guidance to establish operational strategies for themselves.

LITERATURE REVIEW AND HYPOTHESES

Price

From the consumer's perspective, price was seen as the amount of money consumers must give up to get a product and service [9]. Several prior studies have long presented that price is regarded as either a monetary sacrifice for obtaining a product or a quality signal of a product [9,25,26]. As a financial sacrifice, price has long been found to have a negative effect on a product's value for money [9,27,28]. Price is one of the major considerations in deciding to purchase as evaluating value. Consumers compare prices offered by online websites with reference prices, and then find the cheapest alternative possible [29]. Prior research found that a lower price for a given quality (i.e., perceived price is reasonable) strongly affects consumer's perceived value [27,30]. If a price is perceived as reasonable, consumers could find high value with financial transaction in their purchase [31]. Under competitive circumstances, reasonable prices help hotels allow consumers to perceive a relative advantage [32]. Price is one of the most important aspects in hotels, and influences accommodation selection decision [33]. According to prior studies, price has been proposed as an effective way to enhance consumers' value [34] and to positively influence perceived value of services [35], as well as hotel booking. Although price is considered as a consumer's perception that their selected hotels' prices represent the best dollar-for-dollar value, consumers do not really expect the hotels to meet the price of an inferior product [36]. Therefore, in the acceptable price range, a given more reasonable price consequently leads to a higher perceived value [15,27]. Therefore, we can present the following hypothesis:

Hypothesis 1. *Reasonable price positively influences perceived value.*

Quality

In general, perceived quality has been used as a measure of how well the service provided by hotels matches consumers' expectations [37]. Previous research has defined perceived quality as the consumer's judgment about a product or a service's overall excellence [9,15]. Quality in hotels was also related to increase consumer's expectations with core service offering of hotels [38] as well as developing a significant relationship between consumers and hotels [39]. Since consumers generally tend to find value by balancing reasonable price and quality [9], quality could be one of key drivers in terms of formulating the perceived value. Sweeney and Soutar [40] have also suggested that quality could be one of the functional sub-factors that contribute to perceived value. In addition, several prior studies have examined the role of quality in individuals' intention to book a hotel [41,42,43]. Specifically, the quality of hotels contains evaluation of room cleanliness, convenience of location, value for money and friendliness of employees [44,45]. Based upon assessing quality of hotels, consumers could perceive their value by figuring out the quality [41,46]. Therefore, this study proposes the following hypothesis:

Hypothesis 2. *Quality positively influences perceived value.*

Perceived Value

The perceived value has been widely defined as the trade-off between price and quality, with a concept of value-for-money [28,40]. It has been regarded as a salient factor that has a great influence on the decision making process of customers, having a significant role in determining customer satisfaction, decision making and purchase behavior [47,48]. For example, Zeithaml [9] has presented the value act as a mediator between quality and purchase in purchase decision. Most studies on perceived value have found a relationship between value and intention to purchase in online [16,25,27]. In online hotel booking context, we also predict that the relationship between individuals' perceived value and intention to book would be positively related. Therefore, we could state the following research hypothesis:

Hypothesis 3. *Perceived value positively influences intention of booking a hotel.*

Trust toward a Third-Party Online Booking Sites

Trust has been defined as "the willingness of a party to be vulnerable to the actions of another party based on the expectation that the other will perform a particular action important to trustor, irrespective of the ability to monitor or control that other party" ([49], p. 712). It is one of the central features of buyer–seller relationships [15], and has long been an important factor in the decision to buy or not to buy a certain product in a certain store [16,50]. In marketing, trust has been considered as a psychological state comprising intention to accept vulnerability based on positive expectation of the consumers' intention [51]. Bijlsma-Frankema and Woolthuis [52] argued that consumers do indeed buy more from a trusted than a distrusted salesperson.

Previous research discussed the challenges which consumers had to face in traditional ways of booking a hotel, such as travel agents, broadcast media, printed advertisement, etc. [53,54]. With the growth of the internet, many online platforms enable online consumers to make more considered decisions with detailed information of the hotels, such as individual comments or experiences about the hotels as well as online reviews from past consumers on hotel booking websites [54]. While they easily obtain information about the hotels, building trust toward websites is a key determinant in their booking intentions.

When consumers trust the online website, they tend to expend less effort searching for information about the website or vendor and less effort when carrying out transactions with the website [25]. While lack of trust can lead to the reason consumers avoid purchase online [12,13], trust is the main concern for many consumers for those who plan to travel [14]. When a consumer trusts an online website, they are more likely to purchase from the website. Previous studies on online purchase have argued that trust in the online store positively influences the consumers' intentions to purchase from the online store [15,16,17]. While consumers need to rely on the information provided by hotel booking website to get information, they also need to trust the website. Online hotel booking websites offer hotels' information and ratings, which are needed for any booking. Chen and Dibb [55] further suggest the importance of the websites which influence consumer's online intention, as the websites provide consumers information to proceed with their online hotel booking decision [15,54,56]. Hence, the following hypothesis is developed.

Hypothesis 4. *Trust toward a third-party online booking sites positively influences intention to book.*

Online Reviews

Most people generally read online reviews before making a reservation. While previous consumers share their hotel experiences in online reviews, a potential consumer receives more detailed information about a target hotel, which gradually increases expectation before making a decision. Online reviews provide easily accessible up-to-date information on hotels, which is more reliable than content posted by service providers themselves [57]. A positive review especially induces a positive change of attitude toward the hotel [24]. Ye et al. [58] have presented that positive online reviews can significantly increase the number of bookings in a hotel. While prior studies [22,23] found that online reviews provide useful references for potential consumers before purchase, consumers increasingly depend on online customer reviews. For example, Elwalda et al. [59] examines that online reviews significantly affect customer intention and trust in e-vendors, particularly for customers who frequently use online reviews before making a purchase. Based upon the above, we can posit the following hypothesis:

Hypothesis 5. *Online reviews positively influence trust toward hotels.*

Trust toward Hotels

While lack of trust toward a hotel might be a major obstacle to book a room [60], consumers normally have a more cautious behavior to book a hotel. Before making a reservation, consumers tried to collect all information for reducing uncertainty regarding inexperienced product or service. To avoid from this uncertainty, hotels need to present a trustworthy image on booking websites by providing detailed information, which should be consistent with the website's promises [9,54]. Previous studies on trust toward hotel domains have suggested that consumers believe there is less risk associated with online purchase when they have greater trust toward hotels [61], and have eventually more positive towards intention to book [62]. While Jarvenpaa et al. [63] found that trust is still a critical challenge even when purchasing from a known online vendor, such as a hotel booking website in hotel contexts, the level of trust toward hotels affects online hotel booking intentions. Therefore, we propose the following hypothesis:

Hypothesis 6. *Trust toward hotels positively influences intention to book.*

Figure 1 illustrates our proposed research model. As noted in Figure 1, perceived value, trust toward third-party online booking sites and trust toward hotels all have a direct influence on customers' intention to book a hotel. We also examine the relationships among price, quality and perceived value as well as test the relationship between online review and trust toward hotels.

DATA COLLECTION

This study performed an online survey as a methodology to test the proposed hypotheses. The online survey instrument consisted of questions from prior studies which have proven their validity and reliability. Empirical data to support the proposed model were collected from Korean-speaking respondents who have online hotel booking experiences.

A pilot test with 30 part-time MBA students at Korean private university was conducted to assure the content validity and reliability of the questions translated from English to Korean because meaning could be affected by the particular context of the actual survey. Through the pilot test, we examined whether the survey

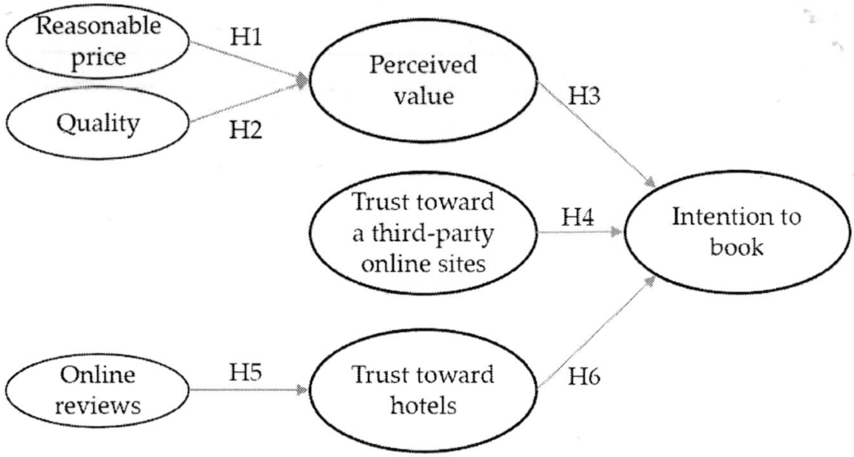

Figure 1. *Research Model.*

questions work correctly, and confirmed the format, readability, and clarity. The final survey contained 24 questions.

The online survey was available between 16 April and 15 May 2016. By voluntarily participating in the study, respondents were notified via mobile or email message that contained participation instruction and a hyperlink to access the online survey.

All questions were anchored on a five-point Likert-type format, and respondents rated from 1 (strongly disagree) to 5 (strongly agree). Table 1 presents our measurement items based on previous studies. Each of four items were borrowed from scales previously used to measure price and quality [31,40]. Four of the perceived value items were adapted from Chiang [31]. The variables of trust in websites in this study use three items to access the compatibility, which were borrowed from Bilgihan et al. [64]. Trust toward hotels were measured by six items developed by Sparks and Browning [21]. Online review was operationalized with three items, as proposed by Zhao et al. [65]. Finally, consumers' intention to book was measured with four items developed by Chiang [31].

A total of 313 respondents participated, and this study finally obtained 307 valid questionnaires after eliminating problematic answers. The collected data consisted of 59.3% male and 40.7% female respondents aged 20–59 years old, with average age of 30 (55.4%). Table 2 shows the demographic profile of respondents. As shown, respondents had had more than one online booking experience, and they reported using Hotels.com (30.6%), HotelsCombined (15.3%), Agoda (14.3%), and booking.com (12.1%), which are the top four online third-party hotel booking sites around the world.

DATA ANALYSIS AND RESULTS

Since all constructs adopted reflective indicators, multiple items were used to measure the constructs for this study. For evaluating the research model, the measurement model was tested by examining the reliability and validity of the measures used to represent each construct [66].

Table 1. *Measurement Scales.*

Factor		Questionnaire	References
Reasonable Price	Price1	Price is reasonably priced for the hotel.	[31,40]
	Price2	Price offers value for money.	
	Price3	Price is a good for the price	
	Price4	Price would be economical.	
Quality	Quality1	The hotel would be excellent.	[64]
	Quality2	The hotel would be of high quality.	
	Quality3	The hotel would be superior.	
	Quality4	The hotel would be favorable.	
Trust toward a third-party online booking sites	Trust-W1	The hotel booking site will always be honest with me.	[64]
	Trust-W2	I believe in the information that this website provides.	
	Trust-W3	This hotel booking website is genuinely concerned about its customers.	
Trust toward hotels	Trust-H1	I believe this hotel would be trustworthy.	[21]
	Trust-H2	I believe this hotel would be reliable.	
	Trust-H3	I believe this hotel would be responsible.	
	Trust-H4	I would have confidence in this hotel.	
	Trust-H5	This seems like a good quality hotel.	
	Trust-H6	If I was to discuss this hotel with others, I would probably say positive things.	
Perceived Value	Value1	The hotel offers good value for the price.	[31]
	Value2	It is worth to book the hotel.	
	Value3	It is a very good bargain to book the hotel at this price shown.	
	Value4	The overall expected value of staying at the hotel is very high.	
Online reviews	Review1	The online reviews are mostly negative (R).	[65]
	Review2	After having read online reviews, I would not book this hotel.	
	Review3	After having read online reviews, I cannot say I like this hotel.	
Intention to book	Intention1	If I am going to book this hotel, I would consider booking this hotel at the price shown.	[31]
	Intention2	The probability that I would book this hotel is very high.	
	Intention3	My willingness to book this hotel is very high.	
	Intention4	I would book the hotel from this booking site.	

Reliability was examined by internal consistency for each block of measures. Thus, Cronbach's alpha, composite reliability, and average variance extracted (AVE) for each construct and cross loadings of all items were examined to show internal consistency and discriminant validity for establishing measurement reliability (Table 3). The Cronbach's alpha coefficients for all constructs are higher than threshold value of 0.7. All of the constructs in our measurement model are higher than Cronbach's alpha of 0.723 composite reliabilities of 0.821 in this measurement model. The average variance extracted (AVE) for all constructs exceeded its threshold value of 0.5, meaning that 50% or more variance of the indicators is accounted for [67]. Thus, all of the constructs in the measurement model exceeded the threshold to be acceptable for all the measures of construct reliability.

Individual item reliability was determined by examining the cross-loading of items. As shown in Table 4, all items resulted in loadings greater than 0.7, i.e., all

Table 2. *Demographic Profiles.*

Items	Category	Frequency	Percept
Gender	Male	182	59.3
	Female	125	40.7
Age	20–29	117	38.1
	30–39	170	55.4
	40–49	17	5.5
	50–59	3	1.0
Area of Employment	Clerical	209	69.4
	Retail	13	4.3
	Professional	23	7.6
	Technical	15	5.0
	Edu. and Public Admin.	13	4.3
	Student	26	8.6
	Homemaker	5	1.7
	Other	3	1.0
Number of online booking experience	1–2	63	20.5
	3–4	95	30.9
	5–6	48	15.6
	7–8	24	7.8
	Over 9	77	25.1
Number of hotel visits	1–2	24	7.8
	3–4	40	13.0
	5–6	43	14.0
	7–8	32	10.4
	Over 9	168	54.7

Table 3. *Results of composite reliability and convergent validity.*

Variables	Cronbach's Alpha	Composite Reliability	AVE
	Total Sample (n = 307)		
Intention to book	0.827	0.886	0.661
Reasonable Price	0.762	0.845	0.581
Quality	0.827	0.883	0.654
Online Review	0.788	0.870	0.691
Trust toward hotels	0.881	0.910	0.629
Trust toward a third-party online booking sites	0.758	0.859	0.670
Perceived Value	0.802	0.871	0.631

constructs indicated adequate internal consistency reliability. The measurement model exhibited significant discriminant validity, while the loading of each item also had a higher loading with its construct than a cross-loading with all the other constructs.

Discriminant validity can be also assessed comparing the variances between all constructs with the average variance from each construct. As shown in Table 5, the square root of a construct's AVE is higher than the correlations between all constructs within the model.

Table 4. *Loadings and cross-loadings of measurement.*

Constructs	Total Sample (n = 307)							
	Items	**Inten**	**Price**	**Qual**	**Review**	**Thotel**	**Tweb**	**Value**
Intention to book	Inten1	0.751	0.320	0.363	0.231	0.372	0.407	0.483
	Inten2	0.891	0.357	0.474	0.164	0.573	0.412	0.548
	Inten3	0.873	0.325	0.507	0.179	0.547	0.502	0.550
	Inten4	0.725	0.292	0.324	0.021	0.318	0.417	0.432
Reasonable price	Price1	0.362	0.838	0.252	−0.008	0.276	0.299	0.454
	Price2	0.351	0.821	0.332	0.183	0.398	0.211	0.444
	Price3	0.321	0.796	0.309	0.070	0.268	0.238	0.427
	Price4	0.085	0.561	0.056	−0.130	0.062	0.020	0.186
Quality	Qual1	0.408	0.283	0.842	0.164	0.503	0.344	0.392
	Qual2	0.396	0.302	0.865	0.209	0.546	0.326	0.350
	Qual3	0.325	0.132	0.739	0.099	0.445	0.200	0.237
	Qual4	0.510	0.327	0.783	0.215	0.493	0.315	0.440
Online Review	Review1	0.130	0.074	0.164	0.779	0.150	0.165	0.210
	Review2	0.150	0.000	0.156	0.794	0.128	0.087	0.076
	Review3	0.184	0.097	0.236	0.914	0.270	0.121	0.232
Trust toward hotels	Thotel1	0.521	0.319	0.546	0.204	0.884	0.338	0.542
	Thotel2	0.494	0.301	0.525	0.163	0.864	0.298	0.530
	Thotel3	0.423	0.309	0.436	0.178	0.807	0.349	0.437
	Thotel4	0.372	0.235	0.442	0.031	0.734	0.267	0.339
	Thotel5	0.344	0.285	0.445	0.155	0.689	0.383	0.379
	Thotel6	0.510	0.265	0.524	0.302	0.762	0.427	0.499
Trust toward a third party online sites	Tweb1	0.399	0.295	0.332	0.137	0.384	0.828	0.370
	Tweb2	0.527	0.135	0.352	0.134	0.397	0.851	0.400
	Tweb3	0.357	0.303	0.215	0.079	0.263	0.775	0.386
Perceived Value	Value1	0.458	0.582	0.349	0.153	0.452	0.364	0.799
	Value2	0.566	0.425	0.400	0.214	0.518	0.365	0.878
	Value3	0.520	0.430	0.329	0.093	0.397	0.388	0.824
	Value4	0.427	0.158	0.387	0.231	0.507	0.397	0.661

Since the evaluation of the measurement model examined the reliability and validity of the measures used to represent each construct, the structural model was tested to evaluate the hypothesized relationships among the constructs in the research model [68]. The structural model of this study was evaluated using partial least squares (PLS) analysis to examine all of the paths simultaneously in this research framework.

Given the sample of 307 used in this study, a strict significance level of 0.05 was used for all statistical tests. As shown in Figure 2, the results of the path analysis indicate that all four paths were significant. The path between reasonable price and perceived value ($\beta = 0.414$, $t = 9.178$); the path between quality and perceived value ($\beta = 0.316$, $t = 7.027$); the path between perceived value and intention to book ($\beta = 0.353$, $t = 6.999$); the path between trust toward a third-party online booking sites and intention to book ($\beta = 0.259$, $t = 5.535$); the path between online review and trust toward hotels($\beta = 0.244$, $t = 4.331$); and the path between trust toward hotels and intention to book ($\beta = 0.252$, $t = 4.495$) were all significant at $p < 0.05$.

Table 5. *Squared pairwise correlations and assessment of discriminant validity.*

		Inten	Price	Qual	Review	Thotel	Tweb	Value
	Inten	**0.813**						
Total	**Price**	0.398	**0.762**					
sample	**Qual**	0.521	0.340	**0.809**				
(n = 307)	**Review**	0.190	0.080	0.232	**0.831**			
	Thotel	0.571	0.361	0.618	0.244	**0.793**		
	Tweb	0.535	0.281	0.378	0.148	0.436	**0.818**	
	Value	0.621	0.521	0.456	0.216	0.585	0.470	**0.794**

Note: Leading diagonal shows the squared root of AVE of each construct; Legend: Inten, intention to book; Price, Reasonable price; Qual, Quality; Thotel, Trust toward hotels; Tweb, Trust toward a third party online sites; Value, Perceived value.

While the R^2 value presents the variances explained, it was examined for meaningful interpretation of path coefficients in this study. The final dependent construct explained 50.2% of intention to book. The intermediate variable was 36.0% of perceived value and 6.0% of trust toward hotels for the total sample of data. Although the R^2 value for trust toward hotels is relatively low for online reviews, the p-value still indicates a significant relationship between online reviews and trust toward hotels. There may be other factors which influence the trust toward hotels and still need to be determined.

DISCUSSIONS AND FUTURE RESEARCH

While investigating the consumer experience in online hotel booking is an emerging area of research, online hotel booking is a useful source of potential consumers for planning a trip to generate their hotel booking intentions. To achieve

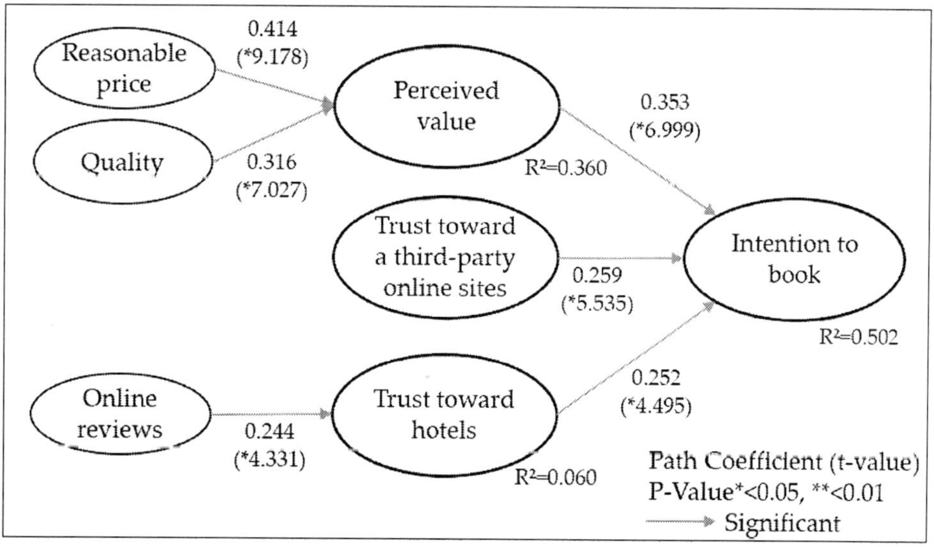

Figure 2. *PLS results for the proposed research model (n = 307).*

this objective, this study proposed a research model that addresses the influential factors to intention to book a hotel on online booking sites. To test the proposed hypotheses, this study performed an online survey as a methodology and collected valid data from 307 respondents. The results via partial least squares (PLS) analysis were based on the analysis of research framework and six research hypotheses were proposed. The research model of this study addresses that perceived value, trust toward third-party online booking sites and trust toward hotels all have a direct influence on customers' intention to book a hotel. In addition to the direct relationships, while both price and quality influences directly the perceived value, online reviews have direct effects on trust toward hotels. Additionally, while the perceived value is significantly derived from reasonable price and quality, the price and quality are important antecedents of value in an online hotel booking context. At the same time, the online review is a relevant antecedent to have trust toward in online hotel booking.

Based on our findings, this study has the following research contributions. First, according to our results, we have found that the perceived value plays the most significant role in online hotel booking context since they may book a hotel online when they perceive benefits of more reasonable price and higher quality of hotel. Compared to results from previous work [9,15,26], this study has also obtained consistent patterns of results in terms of examining the relationships among price, quality and perceived value. Second, we have also found that both trust toward third-party online booking sites and trust toward hotels have significant effects on individuals' intention to book. In this study, we considered two types of trust (i.e., trust related to the third-party websites and trust related to a hotel itself) as major determinants of affecting an individual's intention to book. In online booking a hotel context, two types of trust could play critical roles in predicting individuals' intention. Unless individuals overcome online uncertainty and transactional risk by increasing trust toward two objects (i.e., websites and hotels), they will be reluctant to make a reservation. Based on our findings, which related to online review on trust toward hotels, we further found that the effect of online review on trust toward hotels was significant. The results we obtained were consistent with those reported by Elwalda et al. [59] in examining the relationship between online review and trust toward hotel booking context.

Besides the above research implications, our study also holds several implications for practice. First, the study emphasizes that hoteliers and managers in the hotel industry should focus their efforts on the perceived value of their offering, since value proves to have decisive impact on consumers with benefits of more reasonable price and higher quality of the hotel. The understanding of consumers' perceived value allows the managers to better design their offerings of price and quality corresponding operational strategies around online hotel booking environment. Hence, both hoteliers and managers should keep in mind how perceived value can be fostered by adding the benefits of price and quality consumers emphasize. Second, it also highlights that consumers' intention to book is consistent with trust toward a third-party online booking sites and trust toward hotels. Therefore, both hotels and third-party websites should exert more efforts to encourage customers to build up trust through online hotel booking process. Consequently, it is indeed possible to build up the hotel trust by enhancing and promoting online reviews on websites. The reason behind this may be found in this study that consumers prefer to rely on online reviews to build trust as reducing the online uncertainty associated with intangibility about a hotel. Therefore, hotel companies should be aware that gathering online reviews is an important determinant for gaining customers' trust toward hotels. Thus, the present study's findings have also revealed some important implications for academic researchers, as well as making a relevant practical implication for the hotel industry and online hotel booking websites to improve their business strategies. While value and trust appear to be particularly important determinants of online hotel booking, it is meaningful for hotel related industry to understand the factors that promote consumers' booking intentions.

Despite having both research and practical implications in our study, it is appropriate to point out the limitations associated with our study. First, our data in this study was collected in South Korea. This reflects the intention of South Korean hotel contexts, but not corresponding cross-cultural consumer behavior, while any comparable study and data analysis from different cultures. Hence, future research needs to collect a larger dataset with broader participation of different demographic segments to obtain generalization. Second, due to the parsimonious model in predicting individuals' intention to book, we did not examine how individuals' intention to book on third-party online booking sites may lead to hotels' performance [69]. We believe that additional research is warranted to address these limitations. Third, different types of consumers, hotels and third-party sites might be considered for future research. The respondents of the conducted survey may not be reflective of many different types of "consumers" in this study and broad generalization should not be made. In addition, the information provided by the conducted survey may not be accurate, while most of the consumers were not interested in letting the researcher conduct the survey on premise, which leads to their limited hotel booking experiences. There should be more detailed information on data collection and detailed characteristics of respondents for the future study. Consequently, all hotels and third-party sites are also assumed identical in this study. Hence, different hotels, third-party sites or price may also be effective in intention to book for future study.

Author Contributions

Seo Yeon Kim had developed the proposed research model by reviewing relevant literature, analysed the data, and wrote the paper; Jong Uk Kim and Sang Cheol Park designed the research, analysed the data, contributed to develop both research and practical implications in the paper, and revised the manuscript.

REFERENCES

1. Provider of Hotel Reservation and Distribution Technology Improves Service to Customers by 13%, Reduces Costs 35%. NTT Data, 2012. Available online: https://us.nttdata.com/en/-/media/nttdataamerica/files/resource-library-pdf/provider-of-hotel-reservation--distribution-technology-improves-service-to-customers-by-13-reduces-c.pdf (accessed on 10 October 2017).

2. Benckendorff, P.J.; Sheldon, P.J.; Fesenmaier, D.R. *Tourism Information Technology*; Centre for Agriculture and Bioscience International (CABI): Wallingford, UK, 2014.

3. Team, T. Who Will Benefit from Travelzoo's Hotel Booking Platform and How. 2 May 2014. Available online: https://www.forbes.com/sites/greatspeculations/2014/05/02/who-will-benefit-from-travelzoos-hotel-booking-platform-and-how/#49214c7423ed (accessed on 27 November 2017).

4. Mogelonsky, L. *Hotel Llama: Essays in Hotel Marketing and Management*; AuthorHouse: Bloomington, IN, USA, 2015.

5. Chen, H. The Influence of Perceived Value and Trust on Online Buying Intention. *J. Comput.* **2012**, *7*.

6. Dong, Y.; Ling, L. Hotel Overbooking and Cooperation with Third-Party Websites. *Sustainability* **2015**, *7*, 11696–11712.

7. Krasna, T. The influence of perceived value on customer loyalty in Slovenian hotel industry. *Turizam* **2008**, *12*, 12–15.

8. Chiang, C.; Jang, S.S. The Effects of Perceived Price and Brand Image on Value and Purchase Intention: Leisure traveler's attitudes toward online hotel booking. *J. Hosp. Leis. Mark.* **2007**, *15*, 49–69.

9. Zeithaml, V.A. Consumer Perceptions of Price, Quality, and Value: A Means-End Model and Synthesis of Evidence. *J. Mark.* **1988**, *52*, 2–22.

10. Browning, V.; So, K.; Sparks, B.A. The Influence of Online Reviews on Consumers' Attributions of Service Quality and Control for Service Standards in Hotels. *J. Travel. Tour. Mark.* **2013**, *30*, 23–40.

11. Head, M.; Hassanein, K. Trust in e-Commerce: Evaluating the Impact of Third-Party Seals. *Q. J. Electron. Commer.* **2002**, *3*, 307–325.

12. Turban, E.; King, D.; Lee, J.; Warkentin, M.; Chung, H. *Electronic Commerce: A Managerial Perspective*; Prentice Hall: Upper Saddle River, NJ, USA, 2002.

13. Wu, J.; Chang, Y. Towards understanding members' interactivity, trust, and flow in online travel community. *Ind. Manag. Data Syst.* **2005**, *105*, 937–954.

14. Lewis, I.; Semeijn, J. The Impact of Information Technology on Travel Agents. *Transp. J.* **1998**, *37*, 20–26.

15. Lien, C.; Wen, M.; Huang, L.; Wu, K. Online hotel booking: The effects of brand image, price, trust and value on purchase intentions. *Asia Pac. Manag. Rev.* **2005**, *20*, 210–218.

16. Gefen, D.; Karahanna, E.; Straub, D.W. Trust and TAM in online shopping: An integrated model. *MIS Q.* **2003**, *27*, 51–90.

17. Everard, A.; Galletta, D.F. How Presentation Flaws Affect Perceived Site Quality, Trust, and Intention to Purchase from an Online Store. *J. Manag. Inf. Syst.* **2005**, *22*, 56–95.

18. Ceaparu, I.; Demner, D.; Hung, E.; Zhao, H.; Shneiderman, B. In Web We Trust: Establishing Strategic Trust among Online Customers. 2001. Available online: https://www.cs.umd.edu/users/ben/papers/Ceaparu2002In.pdf (accessed on 30 June 2016).

19. Kim, S.; Kim, D. Antecedents of Corporate Reputation in the Hotel Industry: The Moderating Role of Transparency. *Sustainability* **2017**, *9*, 951.

20. Agag, G.; El-Masry, A.A. Understanding the determinants of hotel booking intentions and moderating role of habit. *Int. J. Hosp. Manag.* **2016**, *54*, 52–67.

21. Sparks, B.A.; Browning, V. The impact of online reviews on hotel booking intentions and perception of trust. *Tour. Manag.* **2011**, *32*, 1310–1323.

22. Chevalier, J.A.; Mayzlin, D. The Effect of Word of Mouth on Sales: Online Book Reviews. *J. Mark. Res.* **2006**, *43*, 345–354.
23. Senecal, S.; Nantel, J. The Influence of Online Product Recommendations on Consumers' Online Choices. *J. Retail.* **2004**, *80*, 159–169.
24. Vermeulen, I.E.; Seegers, D. Tried and tested: The impact of online hotel reviews on consumer consideration. *Tour. Manag.* **2009**, *30*, 123–127.
25. Kim, H.; Xu, Y.; Gupta, S. Which is more important in Internet shopping, perceived price or trust? *Electron. Commer. Res. Appl.* **2012**, *11*, 241–252.
26. Lichtenstein, D.R.; Ridgway, N.M.; Netemeyer, R.G. Price Perceptions and Consumer Shopping Behavior: A Field Study. *J. Mark. Res.* **1993**, *30*, 234–245.
27. Dodds, W.B.; Monroe, K.B.; Grewal, D. Effects of Price, Brand, and Store Information on Buyers' Product Evaluations. *J. Mark. Res.* **1991**, *28*, 307–319.
28. Monroe, K.B. *Pricing: Making Profitable Decisions*, 2nd ed.; McGraw-Hill: New York, NY, USA, 1990.
29. Kim, H.; Gupta, S. A comparison of purchase decision calculus between potential and repeat customers of an online store. *Decis. Support Syst.* **2009**, *47*, 477–487.
30. Yoon, S.; Oh, S.; Song, S.; Kim, K.K.; Kim, Y. Higher quality or lower price? How value-increasing promotions affect retailer reputation via perceived value. *J. Bus. Res.* **2014**, *67*, 2088–2096.
31. Chiang, C. The Effects of Perceived Price and Brand Image on Value and Purchase Intention: Leisure Travelers' Attitudes toward Online Hotel Booking. *J. Hosp. Leis. Mark.* **2007**, *15*, 49–69.
32. Bojanic, D.C. Consumer Perceptions of Price, Value and Satisfaction in the Hotel Industry. *J. Hosp. Leis. Mark.* **1996**, *4*, 5–22.
33. Lockyer, T. The perceived importance of price as one hotel selection dimension. *Tour. Manag.* **2005**, *26*, 529–537.
34. Chen, Z.; Dubinsky, A.J. A conceptual model of perceived customer value in e-commerce: A preliminary investigation. *Psychol. Mark.* **2003**, *20*, 323–347.
35. Duman, T.; Mattila, A.S. The role of affective factors on perceived cruise vacation value. *Tour. Manag.* **2005**, *26*, 311–323.
36. Chan, E.S.W.; Wong, S.C.K. Hotel selection: When price is not the issue. *J. Vacat. Mark.* **2006**, *12*, 142–159.
37. Ye, Q.; Li, H.; Wang, Z.; Law, R. The Influence of Hotel Price on Perceived Service Quality and Value in E-Tourism: An Empirical Investigation Based on Online Traveler Reviews. *J. Hosp. Tour. Res.* **2012**, *38*, 23–39.
38. Lovelock, C.H.; Wirtz, J.; Keh, H.T.; Lovelock, C.H. *Services Marketing in Asia: Managing People, Technology, and Strategy*; Prentice Hall: Singapore, 2002.
39. Ariffin, A.A.; Maghzi, A. A preliminary study on customer expectations of hotel hospitality: Influences of personal and hotel factors. *Int. J. Hosp. Manag.* **2012**, *31*, 191–198.
40. Sweeney, J.C.; Soutar, G.N. Consumer perceived value: The development of a multiple item scale. *J. Retail.* **2001**, *77*, 203–220.
41. Briggs, S.; Sutherland, J.; Drummond, S. Are hotels serving quality? An exploratory study of service quality in the Scottish hotel sector. *Tour. Manag.* **2007**, *28*, 1006–1019.
42. Sargeant, A.; Mohamad, M. Business Performance in the UK Hotel Sector—Does it Pay to be Market Oriented? *Serv. Ind. J.* **1999**, *19*, 42–59.

43. Tsang, N.; Qu, H. Service quality in China's hotel industry: A perspective from tourists and hotel managers. *Int. J. Contemp. Hosp. Manag.* **2000**, *12*, 316–326.

44. Choi, T.Y.; Chu, R. Determinants of hotel guests' satisfaction and repeat patronage in the Hong Kong hotel industry. *Int. J. Hosp. Manag.* **2001**, *20*, 277–297.

45. Lockyer, T. Hotel cleanliness-how do guests view it? Let us get specific. A New Zealand study. *Int. J. Hosp. Manag.* **2003**, *22*, 297–305.

46. Hsieh, L.; Lin, L.; Lin, Y. A service quality measurement architecture for hot spring hotels in Taiwan. *Tour. Manag.* **2008**, *29*, 429–438.

47. Kuo, Y.; Wu, C.; Deng, W. The relationships among service quality, perceived value, customer satisfaction, and post-purchase intention in mobile value-added services. *Comput. Hum. Behav.* **2009**, *25*, 887–896.

48. Chiang, C.; Lee, L. An Examination of Perceived Value Dimensions of Hotel Visitors: Using Exploratory and Confirmatory Factor Analyses. *J. Int. Manag. Stud.* **2013**, *8*, 167–174.

49. Mayer, R.C.; Davis, J.H.; Schoorman, F.D. An Integrative Model of Organizational Trust. *Acad. Manag. Rev.* **1995**, *20*, 709–734.

50. Lee, M.K.O.; Turban, E. A trust model for consumer internet shopping. *Int. J. Electron. Commer.* **2001**, *6*, 75–91.

51. Singh, J.; Sirdeshmukh, D. Agency and Trust Mechanisms in Consumer Satisfaction and Loyalty Judgments. *J. Acad. Mark. Sci.* **2000**, *28*, 150–167.

52. Bijlsma-Frankema, K.; Woolthuis, R.K. *Trust under Pressure: Empirical Investigations of Trust and Trust Building in Uncertain Circumstances*; E. Elgar: Cheltenham, UK, 2005.

53. Lee, J.; Back, K. Reexamination of attendee-based brand equity. *Tour. Manag.* **2010**, *31*, 395–401.

54. Manhas, P.S. *Sustainable and Responsible Tourism: Trends, Practices and Cases*; PHI Learning Private Limited: New Delhi, India, 2012.

55. Chen, J.; Dibb, S. Consumer trust in the online retail context: Exploring the antecedents and consequences. *Psychol. Mark.* **2010**, *27*, 323–346.

56. Kim, J.U.; Kim, W.J.; Park, S.C. Consumer perceptions on web advertisements and motivation factors to purchase in the online shopping. *Comput. Hum. Behav.* **2010**, *26*, 1208–1222.

57. Gretzel, U.; Yoo, K.H. Use and Impact of Online Travel Reviews. In *Information and Communication Technologies in Tourism 2008*; Springer: Vienna, Austria, 2008; pp. 35–46.

58. Ye, Q.; Law, R.; Gu, B. The impact of online user reviews on hotel room sales. *Int. J. Hosp. Manag.* **2009**, *28*, 180–182.

59. Elwalda, A.; Lü, K.; Ali, M. Perceived derived attributes of online customer reviews. *Comput. Hum. Behav.* **2016**, *56*, 306–319.

60. Ladhari, R.; Michaud, M. eWOM effects on hotel booking intentions, attitudes, trust, and website perceptions. *Int. J. Hosp. Manag.* **2015**, *46*, 36–45.

61. Pavlou, P.A.; Gefen, D. Building Effective Online Marketplaces with Institution-Based Trust. *Inf. Syst. Res.* **2004**, *15*, 37–59.

62. Li, J.; Liu, F. A Proposed Framework of eWOM and eTrust in Online Hotel Booking: The Influence of an e-Intermediary. In Proceedings of the 2011 International Conference on Management and Service Science, Wuhan, China, 12–14 August 2011.

63. Jarvenpaa, S.L.; Tractinsky, N.; Saarinen, L. Consumer Trust in an Internet Store: A Cross-Cultural Validation. *Inf. Technol. Manag.* **2000**, *1*, 45–71.

64. Bilgihan, A.; Nusair, K.; Okumus, F.; Cobanoglu, C. Applying flow theory to booking experiences: An integrated model in an online service context. *Inf. Manag.* **2015**, *52*, 668–678.

65. Zhao, X.; Wang, L.; Guo, X.; Law, R. The influence of online reviews to online hotel booking intentions. *Int. J. Contemp. Hosp. Manag.* **2015**, *27*, 1343–1364.

66. Chin, W.W. How to Write up and Report PLS Analyses. In *Handbook of Partial Least Squares*; Springer: Berlin/Heidelberg, Germany, 2010; pp. 655–690.

67. Chin, W.W. The partial least square approach to structural equation modeling. In *Modern Method for Business Research*; Marcoulides, G.A., Ed.; Lawrence Erlbaum: Mahwah, NJ, USA, 1998; pp. 150–170.

68. Hair, J.F. *Multivariate Data Analysis*; Prentice Hall: Upper Saddle River, NJ, USA, 1998.

69. Aznar, J.; Sayeras, J.; Galiana, J.; Rocafort, A. Sustainability Commitment, New Competitors' Presence, and Hotel Performance: The Hotel Industry in Barcelona. *Sustainability* **2016**, *8*, 755.

CHAPTER 3

Price or Convenience: What Is More Important for Online and Offline Bookings? A Study of a Five-Star Resort Hotel in Taiwan

Yi-Man Teng[1], Kun-Shan Wu[2] and Che-Yi Chou[2]

[1]*College of Commerce, Yango University, Fuzhou 350015, China*

[2]*Department of Business Administration, Tamkang University, Taipei 25137, Taiwan*

ABSTRACT

Low price or convenience? What is more important for online and offline bookings? For the sustainable development of the hospitality industry, it is necessary to know the opinions of customers about their online/offline hotel booking experiences. This study aimed to predict the customers' online/offline booking behavior toward a resort hotel in Taiwan by adapting the marketing mix elements. We first designed and executed a detailed questionnaire involving approximately 300 respondents from a five-star hotel in Taiwan, used hypothesis testing to extract important factors from the data, and finally used logistic regression of these factors to predict the customer choices effectively. The study results show that the majority of the customers believe that booking hotel services online provides for a broader choice, offers more discounts and more privacy than available while booking offline, and is cheaper, faster, and more reliable and convenient. The outcomes of logistic regression confirm that "broad choice," but not "low price" has the most significant impact on the customers booking a resort accommodation online or offline. Furthermore, the results of the analysis of variance (ANOVA) show that the younger customers (under the age of 45) and those with university degrees are significantly more likely to make the reservations online for a resort. The findings and the recommendations can provide valuable inputs to the resort industry practitioners in Taiwan for improving the online booking services.

Keywords: *resort hotel; 7Ps marketing mix elements; logistic regression; ANOVA*

INTRODUCTION

Nowadays, innovative development and a wide array of access to information have changed the way people travel [1]. Scholars have indicated that the tourism industry was one of the first to be affected by the Internet [2]. Syed and Suroso [3] have also asserted that tourism has been a sector that has recently progressed rapidly with the use of e-commerce or m-commerce. With the growth of Information and Communication Technologies (ICT) and the Internet, tourism products can now be directly purchased on the Internet, more specifically, through Online Travel Agencies (OTAs) or provider-owned websites [4]. The technology most influential in changing the behavior of tourists has been ICT [5], which has transformed the tourism industry globally [6]. According to Statista 2019, in 2016 the global online travel sales worldwide amounted to 564.87 billion U.S. dollars. It was projected to be 755.94 billion U.S. dollars in 2019 [7].

For decades, more and more consumers have been booking hotel accommodations on hotel websites directly [8] or through OTAs [9]. Among travel products, the top purchases that consumers make online are hotel accommodation bookings [10]. The easy access to the Internet makes reserving hotel accommodation possible with the press of a button on a person's electronic device [9].

Mills and Law [11] have asserted that the Internet has changed tourist service users' behavior. Consumers seek information on hotels, travel, and other facilities on the Internet rather than depending on traditional travel agencies. [5]. When consumers book hotel accommodation online, they now have access to several booking channels, namely the OTAs and the hotels' websites. OTAs play a main role in the vast Internet market of hospitality transactions [9]. Hotels try to utilize the Internet to its full potential, including for online marketing, regardless of the type of hotel [12]. Research shows that websites alone do not attract potential or current guests for sure [13]. Hotels relying on booking opportunities through their websites find it hard to attract potential customers worldwide. In recent years, the coexistence of hotels and OTAs has fallen on hard times. Along with the rising market share of OTAs, the commissions of OTAs have increased too, leading to decreased profitability for hotels; OTAs have become a double-edged sword for hotels [14]. The relationship is now both of a competitive and a cooperative spirit, even though hotels still expect to increase their exposure through multiple channels of OTAs. Worldwide, tourists browse OTA websites first and visit the hotel websites later on, looking for more specific information. This worked fairly well when the hotels paid large commissions (15–30%). From the Statista 2019 report on the revenue of online gross travel bookings worldwide, revenues have risen from 340 billion U.S. dollars in 2011 to 567 billion U.S. dollars in 2017, an increase of almost 66.7% [15].

Hotel website quality is a strong predictor of eTrust and consumers' online booking intentions [3,16]. While the proportion of online hotel bookings is increasing, hotel marketers need to understand the determinants of customers' online hotel booking intentions. There is an increasing number of papers dealing with consumers' intentions to book hotel accommodations online, emphasizing their trust and commitment [16,17,18,19,20], ease of use and interactive ability of the websites [21], website features and updates [19,22,23,24], hotel response times [25,26,27], online hotel ratings [28,29], price fairness perception [30,31], and the consumer demographics and their behavioral trends [32,33]. Most research studies on online hotel bookings also deal with social influence, reviews, and the phenomenon of e-word of mouth [34,35,36,37,38,39,40,41,42].

The results of previous studies concerning price and cost savings prove that lack of additional booking fees and better pricing are benefits of online bookings [17]. Many hotels have been adopting promotional strategies to help in shaping customers' choices [43]. Lien et al. [44] asserted that customers tend to believe that "price" positively affects their online hotel booking intentions. In the competitive environment, "price" is referred to as a heuristic cue that positively influences purchase intentions [45]. Parallel to this view, price discounts enhance the probability that a customer will consider and ultimately book hotel accommodation [46,47]. Overall, price discounts may be a key factor when choosing to book online or offline.

While there are many studies related to online hotel bookings, there is a scarcity of studies looking at the price factor and the integration of e-marketing models in analyzing customers' online hotel booking behavior. Hoteliers compete to offer the best in delivering their services in all of the seven realms of the service marketing mix, comprising the 7Ps—product, price, place, promotion, people, process, and physical evidence [48]. The 7Ps marketing mix is a conceptual framework that highlights the principal decisions marketing managers make while configuring their offerings to the customers' needs [48]. Prior studies have adopted part of the 7Ps marketing mix elements to evaluate customers' intentions or preferences on online hotel booking, such as product [3], price [31], promotion [49], place [50], people response [26,27,28], process [27], and physical evidence [51]. However, there is a lack of studies using the 7Ps marketing mix elements to better understand the complete picture of the changes in the hotel accommodation reservation journey. Therefore, this study used the 7Ps marketing mix elements to classify customers' online/offline booking considerations based on the type of hotel known as resorts. As far as we could find, no literature has discussed the online booking behavior intentions of customers for resorts.

To fill the gap in the literature, this study aimed to (1) study whether the 7Ps marketing mix elements could significantly influence the customers to book a resort online or offline; (2) investigate how the differences in customer demographics could influence online hotel reservation behavior.

LITERATURE REVIEW

Booking Hotel Online and Offline

Booking online and offline are both necessary channels in booking hotel methods. Some customers rely on offline booking hotel, such as walk-in, hotel telephone, fax, reservation center, etc. Some customers rely on online booking hotel, such as OTA, Internet, etc.

Online booking facilities enable establishments to sell hotel rooms both through direct distribution (hoteliers) and intermediaries (OTAs). Hazbar, Mohanned, and Patwary [52] have asserted that the Internet is a useful tool for consumers and suppliers for purchasing products and communicating information in the tourism industry. Due to the several advantages offered to the customers, such as convenience, access to a good comparison of the prices [3], low cost [53], and the provision of latest and accurate information [53], the number of online bookings has grown dramatically during recent decades. This new model of sales is focused on reaching many customers, at any day and time, without geographical limits [4]. Many hotels are focusing on increasing their market share through cooperating with OTAs, which shows how important such cooperative ventures are for hotels to leverage their sales [4]. According to Feinstein [54], with 52% of OTA visitors clicking on hotel websites to receive more information on the hotel and what it offers, hotels could take advantage of the opportunity to convert some of the traffic into direct bookings.

The Influence of Demographic Variables on Booking Online and Offline

Bonn, Furr, and Suskind [55] have pointed out that while higher household incomes and higher education levels showed significant effects on the online booking behavior of customers, gender did not have any considerable impact. Kim and Kim [56] suggested that highly educated people over the age of 30, who recorded more weekly Internet usage, were more likely to make reservations using the Internet, from their study of eight hotels in Korea. They verified that the demographic profiles of the visitors, such as their educational backgrounds, incomes, and ages, and the results showed different correlations related to their online booking intentions for five-star hotels in Macau [32]. The authors also found that those who continued to make more offline bookings tended to be male, older, less educated, and to have lower incomes. Besides that, the study asserted that online and offline users were two different groups of consumers. Further, the study analyzed the effect of gender on brand image, price, trust, and value for online hotel booking, although the results showed no significant differences between the males and the females regarding their purchase intentions [57]. According to the above discussion, the following hypothesis is proposed.

Hypothesis 1 (H1). *Customers' decision to book hotel accommodation online or offline differs according to demographics variables.*

Hypothesis 1 (H1a). *Customers' decision to book hotel accommodation online or offline differs according to customers' gender.*

Hypothesis 1 (H1b). *Customers' decision to book hotel accommodation online or offline differs according to customers' age.*

Hypothesis 1 (H1c). *Customers' decision to book hotel accommodation online or offline differs according to customers' income.*

Hypothesis 1 (H1d). *Customers' decision to book hotel accommodation online or offline differs according to customers' level of education.*

Hotel Booking Behavior Based on the 7Ps Marketing Mix Elements

Hotel marketing product and service planning, communication, and delivery are generally based on the marketing mix elements of the 7Ps (product, price, place, promotion, personnel, process, and physical evidence) [58,59]. Therefore, adoption of marketing mix elements for hotel booking would be relevant and useful for top management and marketers in the hotel industry.

1. Product refers to the product or service that enterprises hope to sell. The rooms provided to the travelers to stay for a while is the main product of a hotel [60]. The purchase of a hotel room includes the guest room, fitness center, pool, restaurants, valet, concierge, housekeeping services, etc. [61]. Hotels cater to different market segments and each of these segments has different requirements. For example, a leisure guest on a family trip looks for recreational and wellness facilities of the hotel. In contrast, a business traveler gives importance to factors like proximity to business centers, and facilities like video conferencing and good in-room Internet connectivity [62]. Thus, the broad choice of hotel rooms, hotel brands, and other available travel products has led to an increased trend to attract potential customers [3,63]. These studies also demonstrated that, if customers wanted a broad selection, they would typically book online. As the above literature [3,63] discussed, with the significance of hotel broad choice, it is assumed that broad choice is the representative factor concerning the product in this study.
2. Price refers to the amount a consumer pays for the good or service [60]. The hotel rate codes and packages are defined keeping in mind attracting or impressing customers [62]. The reference prices of the hotel will be revealed to the customers while shopping online [64]; they could then form a perception of product prices by comparing the prices offered with the reference price on other shopping websites. When measured on a comparative basis, price has a direct and positive effect on the customers' overall satisfaction or their intention to return and purchase a product online [65]. In addition, research indicated that low price was the most significant factor determining whether customers book hotel accommodation online or offline [53,66]. They also demonstrated that, if customers wanted lower prices, they would typically book online. In this study, it is also assumed low price is an important factor whether customers book a hotel online or offline.
3. Place (distribution) refers to the accessibility of the products to the consumers. For the hotel sector, place refers to how the service is provided to travelers. Generally, the place to build a hotel is selected for strategic reasons, such as near a tourist attraction, city, or business center. Usually, online booking provides easy accessibility at any time and any place that may influence consumer purchasing behavior. Alipour, Hajaliakbari, and Javanbakht [67] confirmed that a company website was more like a counter in a retail store, giving people access to the products or services they wanted. This allowed the customers to have the convenience of finding the various elements related to their trips on the same website they booked their hotel accommodations on online [68]. To echo the literature [68], concerning the prominence factor of "convenience" while booking a hotel, we put forward "booking convenience" to represent place (distribution) in this study.

4. Promotion is the way companies communicate to the target customers. The promotion mix includes advertising, public relations, sales promotion, word-of-mouth promotion, and personal selling and telemarketing [61]. Using advertisements on travel websites related to the location of a hotel is a kind of promotion strategy for hotels. Promotion could also mean directly advertising to past clients using social media and press releases [60]. Nevertheless, generally speaking, the discount amount remained the most attractive factor for the customers. In line with previous views, in this study, we put forward "discount allowance" to represent the factor of promotion.
5. People refer to those individuals involved in the delivery of services directly or indirectly [60]. People belonging to hotels interact with the customers and include those in the job roles of receptionist, doorkeeper, concierge staff, manager, recreation center staff, gym staff, waiter, spa staff, etc. Customer satisfaction is directly linked to the experiences of these people who provide the service to the customers. Lee and Cheng [53] and Chow [63] indicated that "reliable service" was one of the significant factors determining whether customers booked hotel accommodations online or offline. In line with previous views, in this study, we put forward "reliable service" to represent the factor of people.
6. Process refers to the flow of activities, mechanisms, and procedures that happen when the consumers and the establishment interact with each other [60]. When the process is more convenient, the customer is more likely to be attracted and retained [69]. Several of the existing studies demonstrated that the customers perceived the hotel or OTA website to be easy to use, and this had a significant impact on their intention to book offline or online [18,61,70]. In addition, Chow [63] also indicated that the "speed of booking process" was an important factor determining whether customers booked the resort services online or offline. Chow [63] also demonstrated that, if the customers wanted the reservations to be made quickly, they would typically book online. To reply to the above scholars' view, we put forward "process speed" to represent the factor of process.
7. Physical evidence has a profound impact on customers' impressions [71]. It refers to the external environment while customers are using the purchased services [72]. Physical evidence is also called the service environment, and is related to the appearance and style of the physical surroundings and other elements encountered by the customer while being served from the establishment [73]. Physical evidence is also important for online booking websites because it conveys to the customer an external image of the website [23,74,75]. Furthermore, Chow [63] indicated that privacy protection was a significant factor determining whether customers booked the resort accommodations online or offline. To echo the literature [63], concerning the prominent factor of "privacy protection" while booking a hotel, we put forward "privacy protection" to represent physical evidence in this study.

Based on the above discussion, the following hypotheses are proposed.

Hypothesis 2 (H2). *The 7Ps marketing mix elements are as important to the customers who booked the services mostly offline as to those who booked them mostly online.*

Hypothesis 2 (H2a). *Broad choice of product is as important to the customers who booked the services mostly offline as to those who booked them mostly online.*

Hypothesis 2 (H2b). *Low price is as important to the customers who booked the services mostly offline as to those who booked them mostly online.*

Hypothesis 2 (H2c). *Booking convenience of place (distribution) is as important to the customers who booked the services mostly offline as to those who booked them mostly online.*

Hypothesis 2 (H2d). *Discount allowance of promotion is as important to the customers who booked the services mostly offline as to those who booked them mostly online.*

Hypothesis 2 (H2e). *Reliable service of people is as important to the customers who booked the services mostly offline as to those who booked them mostly online.*

Hypothesis 2 (H2f). *Process speed is as important to the customers who booked the services mostly offline as to those who booked them mostly online.*

Hypothesis 2 (H2g). *Privacy protection of physical evidence is as important to the customers who booked the services mostly offline as to those who booked them mostly online.*

METHODOLOGY

Sample and Procedure

An empirical study was conducted using purposive sampling of customers who visited the five-star resort hotel in Taipei City, Taiwan. The questionnaires were distributed by the researchers together with the hotel reception staff in the resort lobby. Researchers followed the advice of Roscoe [76] and Sekaran and Bougie ([77] pp: 296–297) based on rules of thumb in determining the sample size. Sample sizes larger than 30 and less than 500 are appropriate and the sample size should be several times (preferably 10 times or more) larger than the number of variables in multivariate study (including multiple regression analysis). Based on this consideration and the rule of thumb, the minimum sample size of the current study is more than 22 (22 × 10) or equal to 220.

A total of 350 questionnaires were distributed, after excluding 50 responses, which answered "no" to the filtering question "Have you stayed at a resort in the last year?" From the 300 recovered samples, after deducting 34 invalid samples, 266 were found to be valid samples, with an adequate sample recovery rate of 88.7%.

Measurement Instruments

The research instrument was reviewed with reference to previous studies and revised and supplemented according to the objectives of this study. For this study, the questionnaire involved three parts. The first part covered questions related to the 7Ps marketing mix elements as generalized from a study by Lee and Cheng [53] and tried to assess the participants' perceived degrees of importance with regard to the seven elements, such as broad choice, low price, booking convenience, discount allowance, reliability of the services, process speed, and privacy protection. All the 7Ps marketing mix elements were measured using a 7-point Likert-type scale (where 1 = extremely unimportant and 7 = extremely important). The questions in the second part were again generalized to include the 7Ps marketing mix elements to assess the perceived degrees of satisfaction of the participants when booking hotel accommodations online or offline. All the 7Ps marketing mix elements were measured using a 7-point Likert-type scale (where 1 = strongly disagree and 7 = strongly agree) (See Appendix A). The third part covered questions related to the demographic variables, including gender, age, monthly income, education level, and occupation, to gather the respondents' demographic profiles.

Data Analysis Process

Firstly, this study used the analysis of variance (ANOVA) and a post-hoc testing procedure to investigate the differences in demographic influences on online hotel reservation behavior. Secondly, it applied a paired-samples *t*-test to explore the mean difference of satisfaction when booking hotel accommodations online as against offline. Lastly, it used a logistic regression model to help the resort predict whether a customer would book the accommodation online or offline based on his/her evaluation of the seven predictive variables.

RESULTS AND DISCUSSIONS

Respondent Profiles

The demographic profiles of the respondents are shown in Table 1. The distribution included 68.4% female and 31.6% male respondents; the majority of the respondents were aged between 36 and 45 (48.5%), or below 35 (33.9%); 48.9% had monthly incomes of 30,001–50,000 NT$; about 45.1% of the respondents held an undergraduate degree, and 80.1% were employed full-time.

The Importance of Seven Predictors While Choosing between the Booking Options

According to the explanation of marketing mix in Section 2.3 above, the elements of 7Ps marketing mix have an impact on whether customers book a hotel online or offline. To identify whether a customer would use an online or an offline channel to book a resort accommodation, we considered the importance given to the seven factors (broad choice, low price, booking convenience, discount allowance, reliability of the service, process speed, and privacy protection) by the customers as predictor variables. Their mean, standard deviation, and Cronbach's alpha values are shown in Table 2. It is found that, while the most important factor is "reliability of the services," the least important one is "low price." In addition, it is noted that the Cronbach's alpha value is 0.757, indicating the reliability of the results.

Deviation in Online Booking Behavior Intentions by Demographic Characteristics

One of the objectives of this study was to determine if there were significant differences across the respondents' demographic characteristics with respect to their online hotel accommodation reservation intentions. The results of the

Table 1. *Demographic profile of respondents.*

Variables	*Frequency*	*Percentage (%)*
Gender		
Male	84	31.6
Female	216	68.4
Age		
≤35	90	33.9
36–45	129	48.5
46–55	32	12.0
≥56	15	5.6
Monthly income		
<=30,000 NTD	7	2.6
30,001–50,000 NTD	130	48.9
50,001–100,000 NTD	63	23.7
>=100,001 NTD	32	12.0
I'd rather not tell	34	12.8
Education level		
Junior college or below	39	14.7
University	120	45.1
Graduate school	107	40.2
Occupation		
Self-employed	26	9.8
Full-time employed	213	80.1
Part-time employed	6	2.3
Other	21	7.9

Table 2. *Mean and standard deviation of the seven predictors.*

Factors of Booking	**Mean**	**SD**	**Cronbachs'α**
Broad choice	6.20	1.003	
Low price	6.16	1.106	
Booking convenient	6.66	0.644	
Discount allowance	6.29	0.858	0.757
Reliable services	6.71	0.764	
Process speed	6.50	0.793	
Privacy protection	6.67	0.713	

ANOVA and post-hoc (multiple comparison) tests on the demographic variables are presented in Table 3.

The results show that gender did not have any significant effect on the customers' online booking behaviors/intentions (T-value = 1.494, $p > 0.05$) from Table 3. As a result, H1a is not supported. These findings echo those of Bonn et al. [55] and Lien et al. [44]. Next, they display that age has a significant effect on customers' online booking behaviors/intentions (F-value = 9.605, $p < 0.01$). Accordingly, the results support H1b. In addition, by performing the post-hoc test, it can be seen that the respondents under the age of 45 were significantly more likely to make

Table 3. *Variation in online booking behavior intentions by demographic characteristics.*

Variables	Booking Online Intentions
Gender	
Male	7.75
Female	7.07
***t*-test**	**1.494**
Age	
≤35	8.02 [c]
36–45	7.60 [b]
46–55	5.22 [a]
≥56	4.47 [a]
F-test	**9.605 ****
Monthly income	
<=30,000 NTD	4.43 [a]
30,001–50,000 NTD	6.35 [b]
50,001–100,000 NTD	9.11 [c]
>=100,001 NTD	6.22 [b]
F-test	**12.347 ****
Education level	
Junior college or below	6.63
University	8.16 [b]
Graduate school	6.11 [a]
F-test	**9.208 ****

Note: ** denotes $p < 0.01$; a,b,c: The mean difference is significant at the p, 0.01 level in post-hoc tests.

reservations online. This implies that the consumers who booked their accommodations online tended to be younger, a finding similar to that of Qi et al. [32]. Moreover, Table 3 shows that the level of monthly income has a significant effect on the customers' online booking behaviors/intentions (F-value = 12.347, $p < 0.01$). As a result, H1c is supported. Besides, after the post-hoc test, it can be found that the respondents with a monthly income between 50,001 and 100,000 NT$ were significantly more likely to make the reservations online. Lastly, Table 3 also indicates that education level has a significant effect on customers' online booking behaviors/intentions (F-value = 9.208, $p < 0.01$). As result, H1d is supported. By performing the post-hoc test, it was found that respondents with a university degree were significantly more likely to make the bookings online.

As the above results, which support H1b, H1c, and H1d, show, customers' decisions to book hotel accommodation online or offline differ according to customers' age, monthly income, and educational level. However, the results do not support H1a; as the above results show, H1 was only partially supported.

Mean Difference of Satisfaction When Booking Hotel Accommodations Online as against Offline

For each of the factors of broad choice, low price, convenience, discount, reliability of the services, speed, and privacy, each respondent provided his/her ratings for online and offline bookings, and a paired samples *t*-test was conducted. The analysis of the paired-samples *t*-test identified a statistically significant difference between the satisfactions of booking hotel online and offline, with the confidence level of 0.01 (Table 4), which confirms the difference between online and offline customer satisfaction in 7Ps mixed marketing. Among them, the gap in satisfaction of border choice was the largest, and that of privacy protection was the smallest. In addition, the research has shown that customers tended to agree that online booking provided a broader choice, more discounts, and more privacy, was cheaper, faster, and more convenient, and offered more reliable services than offline booking.

Table 4. *Paired samples t-test for mean difference.*

Variables	Paired Sample Difference (Online–Offline)				t	*p*-Value
	Mean	SD	95% Confidence Interval			
			Lower	Upper		
Broad choice	2.098	2.305	1.820	2.376	14.846	0.000 **
Low price	1.741	2.458	1.444	2.037	11.549	0.000 **
Booking convenient	1.827	2.621	1.511	2.143	11.370	0.000 **
Discount allowance	1.726	2.205	1.459	1.992	12.761	0.000 **
Reliable services	0.714	2.040	0.468	0.961	5.712	0.000 **
Process speed	1.380	2.579	1.068	1.691	8.725	0.000 **
Privacy protection	0.342	2.130	0.085	0.599	2.620	0.009 **

Note: ** denotes $p < 0.01$.

Predicting the Customer's Booking Channel

The study used logistic regression to predict whether customers would book their accommodations online or offline, based on how they valued the seven aforementioned variables. It was also noted that how and what the customers perceived/expected about the characteristics and functions of online versus offline booking could influence their choices of a booking channel in the future [78].

Firstly, Table 5 provides details of the correlation between the variables and the percentages of online purchases. It is found that "broad choice" has the strongest positive correlation to purchasing online ($r = 0.676$, $p < 0.001$), and also that purchasing online is positively related to factors like booking convenience, process speed, reliability of the services, low prices, and discount allowance (coefficients ranging from 0.109 to 0.405), separately (based on the significance level $\alpha = 0.01$). However, purchasing online is not related to the factor "privacy protection" ($r = 0.120$, $p > 0.05$). Among the predictors, the strongest correlations are with two factors, namely, "low price" and "discount allowance" ($r = 0.570$, $p < 0.01$). However, there appears to be no multi-collinearity as we do not see any substantial correlation between predictor variables based on the criterion that none of the Pearson's correlations (r) are over 0.9 [79]. This implies that the set of variables used in this study can reasonably predict online resort accommodation bookings.

Table 5. *Correlation matrix.*

	Percentage Purchased Online	Broad Choice	Low Price	Booking Convenient	Discount Allowance	Reliable Services	Process Speed	Privacy Protection
Percentage purchased online	1							
Broad choice	0.676 ***	1						
Low price	0.235 ***	0.168 **	1					
Booking convenient	0.405 ***	0.404 ***	0.428 **	1				
Discount allowance	0.169 **	0.142 *	0.570 **	0.455 ***	1			
Reliable services	0.301 ***	0.174 **	0.203 **	0.412 ***	0.182 **	1		
Process speed	0.367 ***	0.372 ***	0.303 **	0.576 ***	0.342 ***	0.441 ***	1	
Privacy protection	0.120 #	0.240 ***	0.250 **	0.344 ***	0.147 *	0.336 ***	0.463 ***	1

Note: *** denotes $p < 0.001$; ** denotes $p < 0.01$; * denotes $p < 0.05$; # denotes $p < 0.1$.

Secondly, it is found from Table 6 that broad choice (Wald value = 46.872, $p < 0.01$), reliability of the services (Wald value = 6.387, $p < 0.05$), process speed (Wald value = 3.990, $p < 0.05$), and privacy protection (Wald value = 7.785, $p < 0.01$) are the four significant factors determining whether customers book online or offline. That means the hypotheses H2a, H2e, H2f and H2g are supported. Among these, "broad choice" has the most significant impact on customers' booking decisions. That result is similar to the prior study that greater diversity of hotel rooms, hotel brands, and other available travel products results in an increased tendency of attracting potential consumers [22,68]. "Broad choice" plays a prominent role in customer online and offline booking hotel. However, that result is quite different with Kim and Kim [56]; their study suggested the significant factors that affected online reservation intention in both the online group and the non-online group were convenience, safety, and price. Next, process speed also has a significant influence on consumers' intentions toward online hotel reservations. These findings echo those of [18,61,63,70]. Moreover, privacy protection has a significant influence on consumers' intentions toward online hotel reservations. The findings of this study are in line with the findings of [63].

On the one hand, other predictor variables do not play a significant role in customers' selection of an online booking channel. That means hypotheses H2b, H2c, and H2d are not supported. This implies that price does not significantly influence consumers' intentions toward online hotel reservations. The finding is inconsistent with prior studies [53,66]. The reason may be that the study subjects are five-star resort hotel guests; they may not pay so much attention to the price factor when booking online or offline. Moreover, booking convenience does not significantly influence consumers' intentions toward online hotel reservations. This finding is inconsistent with [68]. Further, discount allowance does not significantly influence consumers' intentions toward online hotel reservations. The findings of this study are in line with the findings of [63]. The reason may be that the five-star resort hotel with the object of this study has little difference in discount allowance whether online or offline.

In addition, Table 7 depicts the predicted numbers of respondents who might book more online or offline as against the observed numbers. The overall accuracy of this model to predict whether or not potential customers would book online is 81.2%. As the above results, the H2 was partially supported.

Table 6. *Logistic regression between online booking and 7P dimensions.*

Variables	B	S.E.	Wald	*p*-Value	Exp (B)
Broad choice	1.644	0.240	46.872	0.000 **	5.174
Low price	0.215	0.186	1.333	0.248	1.239
Booking convenient	0.249	0.351	0.505	0.477	1.283
Discount allowance	0.199	0.256	0.605	0.437	1.220
Reliable services	0.601	0.238	6.387	0.011 *	1.825
Process speed	0.608	0.304	3.990	0.046 *	1.836
Privacy protection	−0.807	0.289	7.785	0.005 **	0.446
−2 Loglikehood = 200.962					
Cox & Snell R-square = 0.408					
Nagelkerke R-square = 0.565					

Note: ** denotes $p < 0.01$; * denotes $p < 0.05$.

Table 7. *Model discrimination.*

	Predicted		
Observed	More Offline	More Online	Total
More offline	62	28	90
More online	22	154	176
Classification accuracy	68.9%	87.5%	266
Overall accuracy		81.2%	

Note: Cut value = 0.5 to determine more online or more offline.

CONCLUSIONS

This study is an analysis of customers' online/offline booking behavior toward a resort and can be used in system analysis in developing online booking facilities for the hospitality industry. While there is a significant increase in the number of users who book their hotel accommodations directly on the hotel websites or OTAs now, for the sustainable development of the hospitality industry, it is necessary to know the opinions of travelers about their online hotel booking experiences and behaviors.

The results of this study highlight the implications for improving online booking facilities in the resort market context. Firstly, it is evident that "broad choice" is an important factor helping customers determine whether to book a resort accommodation online or offline. However, according to Lee and Cheng [53], "broad choice" is not significant for determining booking channel selection behavior in the airline industry. While the rooms are the core products for the hotel industry, the resorts offer much more than rooms, for example, multi-style restaurants, bars, and cafes, spa and fitness, conference, speakerphone with voicemail service, etc. Thus, the broad choice of hotel rooms along with other available travel products could result in an increased tendency of attracting potential customers [3].

Therefore, the resort hoteliers, generally catering to different market segments, would need to take care of the different requirements of these segments to influence the booking choices positively.

Secondly, from the logistic regression between the online bookings and the 7P dimensions, it is found that broad choice, reliability of the services, process speed, and privacy protection are the four significant factors determining whether customers book resort accommodations online or offline. "Low price" does not necessarily stimulate online bookings, and it is found that customers considered promotional price cuts analogous to low service quality [80,81]. As a result, customers are more likely to avoid a hotel offering promotional pricing but providing good quality, reliable service, and broad choice while booking online.

Thirdly, the results of the demographic effect analysis show that gender did not have any significant effect on customers' online booking behavior/intentions. Younger customers (<45 years of age) and those with a university degree were more significantly found to make online bookings. This could imply developing market segment strategies accordingly. The resort hoteliers may consider selecting middle and younger aged customers with higher education as their target demographic groups for online promotions.

As a whole, this study reflects the importance of 7Ps marketing mix elements to help the hoteliers gain a more significant competitive advantage in the market. To acquire a competitive advantage, while customer booking online, hotel reservation systems facilitate the collection of information on customer characteristics and online behavior. That information provides hoteliers with the ability to build customer databases and implement customized promotional activities that meet different groups' specific needs in order to delight and incentivize customers, while also protecting the privacy of sensitive guest information, such as direct mail and the sending of electronic hotel newsletters, promotional hotel package products and greeting cards for different holidays and birthdays for different market segments.

Several limitations are present in this study that also provide fertile grounds for further research. To begin with, one limitation is that only one resort was reviewed in this study, leaving scope for a future survey with a broader area of examination. There may be other factors related to consumers' decisions to use online and offline hotel booking for different types of resorts. In a future study, the survey should include at least three resorts so that it can recognize and indicate more factors that influence consumers' decisions for different resort types, such as all-inclusive resort, beach and lake resort, golf resort, luxury resort, and mountain resort. Secondly, this research did not consider cross-cultural issues. Referring to suggestions of Liu et al. [82], there will be potential differences in attitude between Chinese and Western tourists towards various hotel room reservation policies. In future studies, comparative studies from different countries could make a valuable contribution to the body of knowledge. Third, as a prior study [83] evidenced, guests' reviews show a positive effect on hotel purchasing intention; the stream of research on word-of-mouth cannot be ignored in future hotel booking research. Lastly, as the analysis focuses only on the study of online and offline hotel bookings in one resort in Taiwan, generalization of the study results may not be applicable.

Author Contributions

K.-S.W., Y.-M.T., and C.-Y.C. formulated the study, analyzed the collected data and wrote the article. All authors confirmed the final manuscript. All authors have read and agreed to the published version of the manuscript.

APPENDIX A

Table A1. *Variable descriptions.*

Descriptions	Responses
Q1. What percentage of air tickets do you purchase online?	Please use a 10-point scale, where 1 means "0–10%", 2 means "11–20%", and 10 means "90–100%."
Q2. How important is the broadest choice (i.e., displaying full rates and related information from all nearby hotels) to you?	Possible answers ranging from [1]-Extremely unimportant to [7]-Extremely important.
Q3. How important is finding the lowest price to you?	
Q4. How important is booking convenient to you?	
Q5. How important is discount allowance to you when booking the hotel?	
Q6. How important is reliable service to you?	
Q7. How important is the speed of the booking process to you?	
Q8. How important is privacy protection when booking the hotels?	
Q9.Do you agree that you are provided with all possible choices when booking online?	Possible answers ranging from [1]-Strongly disagree to [7]-Strongly agree.
Q10.Do you agree that you are provided with all possible choices when booking offline?	
Q11. Do you agree that you are getting the lowest price when booking online?	
Q12. Do you agree that you are getting the lowest price when booking offline?	
Q13.Do you agree that you are getting the more convenient when booking online?	
Q14. Do you agree that you are getting the more convenient when booking offline?	
Q15. Do you agree that you are getting the more discount when booking online?	
Q16. Do you agree that you are getting the more convenient when booking offline?	
Q17. Do you agree that online booking provides reliable service?	
Q18. Do you agree that offline booking provides reliable service?	
Q19. When booking online, how satisfied are you with the speed of the booking process?	
Q20. When booking offline, how satisfied are you with the speed of the booking process?	
Q21. When booking online, how satisfied are you with the privacy protection?	
Q22. When booking offline, how satisfied are you with the privacy protection?	

REFERENCES

1. Pitoska, E. E-Tourism: The Use of Internet and Information and Communication Technologies in Tourism: The Case of Hotel Units in Peripheral Areas. Available online: https://ssrn.com/abstract=2289872 (accessed on 11 February 2020).
2. Standing, C.; Tang-Taye, J.P.; Boyer, M. The impact of the Internet in travel and tourism: A research review 2001–2010. *J. Travel Tour. Mark.* **2014**, *31*, 82–113.

3. Syed, A.A.; Suroso, J. Factors affecting consumers' decision for E-Hotel booking. *ComMIT J.* **2018**, *12*, 111–123.

4. Da Silva, G.L.; Filho, L.M.; Júnior, S.M. Analysis of the perception of accommodation consumers on the use of online travel agencies (OTAs). *Revista Brasileira de Pesquisa em Turismo* **2019**, *13*, 40–57.

5. Crnojevac, I.H.; Gugić, J.; Karlovčan, S. eTourism: A comparison of online and offline bookings and the importance of hotel attributes. *J. Inform. Organ. Sci.* **2010**, *34*, 41–54.

6. Buhalis, D.; Law, R. Progress in information technology and tourism management: 20 years on and 10 years after the Internet—The state of eTourism research. *Tour. Manag.* **2008**, *29*, 609–623.

7. Statista. Digital Travel Sales Worldwide from 2014 to 2020. 2019. Available online: https://www.statista.com/statistics/499694/forecast-of-online-travel-sales-worldwide/ (accessed on 9 February 2020).

8. Jeong, M.; Oh, J.; Gregoire, M. Conceptualizing web site quality and its consequences in the lodging industry. *Int. J. Hosp. Manag.* **2003**, *22*, 161–175.

9. Ivanov, I.; Atanasova, I. Hotel Reservations Via Online Travel Agency Booking.com. Eu Dimensions of the "Best Price" Clause. CBU International Conference Proceedings. 2019. Available online: https://ojs.journals.cz/index.php/CBUIC/article/view/1354/2027 (accessed on 9 February 2020).

10. Cassedy, K. Know your Online Customer: Forrester Research Creates Technographics. 2002. Available online: https://www.hospitalitynet.org/news/4010740.html (accessed on 9 February 2020).

11. Mills, J.E.; Law, R. *Handbook of Consumer Behavior, Tourism, and the Internet*; Haworth Hospitality Press: Binghamton, NY, USA, 2004; ISBN 0-7890-2599-X.

12. Baloglu, S.; Pekcan, Y.A. The website design and Internet site marketing practices of upscale and luxury hotels in Turkey. *Tour. Manag.* **2006**, *27*, 171–176.

13. Kasavana, M.L. eMarketing: Restaurant websites that click. *J. Hospit. Leisure. Market.* **2001**, *9*, 161–178.

14. Xue, P. Hotel Online Booking Decisions Based on Price Complexity, Alternative Attractiveness, and Confusion. Master's Thesis, The University of Guelph, Guelph, ON, Canada, 2019. Available online: https://atrium.lib.uoguelph.ca/xmlui/bitstream/handle/10214/15936/Xue_Pengsongze_201905_Msc.pdf?sequence=1&isAllowed=y (accessed on 9 February 2020).

15. Statista. Revenue of Online Gross Travel Bookings Worldwide 2011–2017. 2019. Available online: https://www.statista.com/statistics/238852/online-travel-bookings-worldwide/ (accessed on 9 February 2020).

16. Wang, L.; Law, R.; Guillet, B.D.; Hung, K.; Fong, K.C. Impact of hotel website quality on online booking intentions: eTrust as a mediator. *Int. J. Hosp. Manag.* **2015**, *47*, 108–115.

17. Sparks, B.A.; Browning, V. The impact of online reviews on hotel booking intentions and perception of trust. *Tour. Manag.* **2011**, *32*, 1310–1323.

18. Agag, G.; El-Masry, A.A. Understanding the determinants of hotel booking intentions and moderating role of habit. *Int. J. Hosp. Manag.* **2016**, *54*, 52–67.

19. Li, L.; Peng, M.; Jiang, N.; Law, R. An empirical study on the influence of economy hotel website quality on online booking intentions. *Int. J. Hosp. Manag.* **2017**, *63*, 1–10.

20. Agag, G.; Khasan, M.; Colmekcioglu, N.; Almamy, A.; Alharbi, N.S.; Eid, R.; Shabbir, H.; Abdelmoety, Z.H.S. Converting hotels website visitors into buyers: How online hotel web assurance seals services decrease consumers' concerns and increase online booking intentions. *Inf. Technol. People* **2019**, *33*, 129–159.
21. Abdullah, D.; Kamal, S.B.M.; Azmi, A.; Lahap, J.; Bahari, K.A.; Din, N.; Pinang, C.P. Perceived website interactivity, perceived usefulness and online hotel booking intention: A structural model. *Malays. J. Consum. Fam. Econ.* **2019**, *21*, 45–57.
22. Liu, J.N.; Zhang, E.Y. An investigation of factors affecting customer selection of online hotel booking channels. *Int. J. Hosp. Manag.* **2014**, *39*, 71–83.
23. Bilgihan, A.; Bujisic, M. The effect of website features in online relationship marketing: A case of online hotel booking. *Electron. Commer. Res. Appl.* **2015**, *14*, 222–232.
24. Kamal, S.B.M.; Abdullah, D.; Nor, N.M.; Ngelambong, A.; Bahari, K.A. Hotel booking websites and their impact on e-satisfaction and e-loyalty: Analysis on utilitarian and hedonic features. *Int. J. Acad. Res. Bus. Soc. Sci.* **2018**, *8*, 160–177.
25. Casado-Díaz, A.B.; Andreu, L.; Beckmann, S.C.; Miller, C. Negative online reviews and webcare strategies in social media: Effects on hotel attitude and booking intentions. *Curr. Issues Tour.* **2018**, *23*, 418–422.
26. Meng, F.; Dipietro, R.B.; Gerdes, J.H.; Kline, S.; Avant, T. How hotel responses to negative online reviews affect customers' perception of hotel image and behavioral intent: An exploratory investigation. *Tour. Rev. Int.* **2018**, *22*, 23–39.
27. Zhang, Z.; Li, H.; Meng, F.; Li, Y. The effect of management response similarity on online hotel booking: Field evidence from Expedia. *Int. J. Contemp. Hosp. Manag.* **2019**, *31*, 2739–2758.
28. Casaló, L.V.; Flavián, C.; Guinalíu, M.; Ekinci, Y. Do online hotel rating schemes influence booking behaviors? *Int. J. Hosp. Manag.* **2015**, *49*, 28–36.
29. Gavilan, D.; Avello, M.; Martinez, G. The influence of online ratings and reviews on hotel booking consideration. *Tour. Manag.* **2018**, *66*, 53–61.
30. Encarnación, M.; Gomez-Borja, M.A.; Mondéjar-Jiménez, J.A. A model to evaluate the effects of price fairness perception in online hotel booking. *Electron. Commer. Res.* **2014**, *14*, 171–187.
31. El Haddad, R.; Hallak, R.; Assaker, G. Price fairness perceptions and hotel customers' behavioral intentions. *J. Vacat. Mark.* **2015**, *21*, 262–276.
32. Qi, S.; Law, R.; Buhalis, D. Who booked five-star hotels in Macau? A study of hotel guests' online booking intention. *J. Hosp. Tour. Manag.* **2013**, *20*, 76–83.
33. Chang, C.M.; Liu, L.W.; Huang, H.C.; Hsieh, H.H. Factors influencing online hotel booking: Extending UTAUT2 with age, gender, and experience as moderators. *Information* **2019**, *10*, 281.
34. Ye, Q.; Law, R.; Gu, B. The impact of online user reviews on hotel room sales. *Int. J. Hosp. Manag.* **2009**, *28*, 180–182.
35. Xie, H.; Miao, L.; Kuo, P.J.; Lee, B.Y. Consumers' responses to ambivalent online hotel reviews: The role of perceived source credibility and pre-decisional disposition. *Int. J. Hosp. Manag.* **2011**, *30*, 178–183.
36. Ladhari, R.; Michaud, M. eWOM effects on hotel booking intentions, attitudes, trust, and website perceptions. *Int. J. Hosp. Manag.* **2015**, *46*, 36–45.
37. Cezar, A.; Ögüt, H. Analyzing conversion rates in online hotel booking: The role of customer reviews, recommendations and rank order in search listings. *Int. J. Contemp. Hosp. Manag.* **2016**, *28*, 286–304.

38. Chan, I.C.C.; Lam, L.W.; Chow, W.C.; Fong, L.H.N.; Law, R. The effect of online reviews on hotel booking intention: The role of reader-reviewer similarity. *Int. J. Hosp. Manag.* **2017**, *66*, 54–65.
39. Confente, I.; Vigolo, V. Online travel behaviour across cohorts: The impact of social influences and attitude on hotel booking intention. *Int. J. Tour. Res.* **2018**, *20*, 660–670.
40. Hwang, J.; Park, S.; Woo, M. Understanding user experiences of online travel review websites for hotel booking behaviours: An investigation of a dual motivation theory. *Asia Pac. J. Tour. Res.* **2018**, *23*, 359–372.
41. Manes, E.; Tchetchik, A. The role of electronic word of mouth in reducing information asymmetry: An empirical investigation of online hotel booking. *J. Bus. Res.* **2018**, *85*, 185–196.
42. Danish, R.Q.; Ali, H.F.; Shahid, R.; Nadeem, K. Impact of online consumer reviews on hotel booking intentions: The case of Pakistan. *Eur. Sci. J.* **2019**, *15*, 144–159.
43. Lee, S.H.; Croes, R.; Rivera, M. Exploring the role of human judgment in making discount decisions in the lodging industry. *J. Hosp. Financ. Manag.* **2015**, *23*, 45–62.
44. Lien, C.H.; Wen, M.J.; Wu, K.L. Online hotel booking: The effects of brand image, price, trust and value on purchase intentions. *Asia Pac. Manag. Rev.* **2015**, *20*, 210–218.
45. Yoon, S.; Oh, S.; Song, S.; Kim, K.K.; Kim, Y. Higher quality or lower price? How value-increasing promotions affect retailer reputation via perceived value. *J. Bus. Res.* **2014**, *67*, 2088–2096.
46. Christou, E. Exploring online sales promotions in the hospitality industry. *J. Hosp. Mark. Manag.* **2011**, *20*, 814–829.
47. Chang, A.Y. A study on the effects of sales promotion on consumer involvement and purchase intention in tourism industry. *Eurasia J. Math. Sci. Technol. Educ.* **2017**, *13*, 8323–8330.
48. Zeithaml, V.A.; Bitner, M.J.; Gremler, D.D. *Services Marketing: Integrating Customer Focus Across the Firm*; McGraw Hill: London, UK, 2012.
49. Morales, T. Increasing Direct Booking in Hotels. Bachelor's Thesis, University of Applied Science, Haaga-Helia, Helsinki, Finland, 2017.
50. Mellinas, J.P.; Nicolau, J.L.; Park, S. Inconsistent behavior in online consumer reviews: The effects of hotel attribute ratings on location. *Tour. Manag.* **2018**, *71*, 421–427.
51. Baek, J.; Ok, C.M. The power of design: How does design affect consumers' online hotel booking? *Int. J. Hosp. Manag.* **2017**, *65*, 1–10.
52. Hazbar, A.H.A.; Mohanned, A.A.; Patwary, A.K. An Empirical Study of Factors Influencing Hotel Customers' Online Booking Intention. 2019, Volume 5, pp. 1–17. Available online: http://hesj.org/ojs/index.php/hesj/article/view/40/38 (accessed on 9 February 2020).
53. Lee, Z.H.; Cheng, K. Predictors of customer preference for online versus offline air travel booking. *Tour. Rev. Int.* **2009**, *13*, 183–200.
54. Feinstein, E. OTA's vs. Direct Hotel Bookings: Which is the Leading Trend for 2018? Available online: https://www.traveldailynews.com/post/otas-vs-direct-hotel-bookings-which-is-the-leading-trend-for-2018 (accessed on 9 February 2020).
55. Bonn, M.A.; Furr, H.L.; Suskind, A.M. Using the Internet as a pleasure travel planning tool: An examination of the sociodemographic and behavioral characteristics among Internet users and nonusers. *J. Hosp. Tour. Res.* **1998**, *22*, 303–317.

56. Kim, W.G.; Kim, D.J. Factors affecting online hotel reservation intention between online and non-online customers. *Int. J. Hosp. Manag.* **2004**, *23*, 381–395.
57. Lin, H.F. The impact of website quality dimensions on customer satisfaction in the B2C e-commerce context. *Total Qual. Manag. Bus. Excell.* **2007**, *18*, 363–378.
58. Jeong, M.; Lambert, C.U. Adaptation of an information quality framework to measure customers' behavioral intentions to use lodging Web sites. *Int. J. Hosp. Manag.* **2001**, *20*, 129–146.
59. Loo, P.T.; Leung, R. A service failure framework of hotels in Taiwan: Adaptation of 7Ps marketing mix elements. *J. Vacat. Mark.* **2018**, *24*, 79–100.
60. Expert Program Management. Service Marketing Matrix: The 7P's of Marketing. Available online: https://expertprogrammanagement.com/2018/03/services-marketing-mix-7-ps/ (accessed on 11 February 2020).
61. Bhargav, S. A study on marketing mix of hospitality industry. *Int. J. Manag. IT Eng.* **2017**, *7*, 253–265.
62. Setupmyhotel. 2019. Available online: https://setupmyhotel.com/train-my-hotel-staff/sales-and-marketing/285-marketing-mix.html (accessed on 11 February 2020).
63. Chow, C.Y. Analysis on the Influencing Factors of Online Verse Offline Hotel Reservation. Master's Thesis, Tamkang University, New Taipei City, Taiwan, 2018.
64. Kim, H.W.; Xu, Y.; Gupta, S. Which is more important in Internet shopping, perceived price or trust? *Electron. Commer. Res. Appl.* **2012**, *11*, 241–252.
65. Jiang, P.; Rosenbloom, B. Customer intention to return online: Price perception, attribute-level performance, and satisfaction unfolding over time. *Eur. J. Mark.* **2005**, *39*, 150–174.
66. Wong, J.; Law, R. Analysing the intention to purchase on hotel websites: A study of travellers to Hong Kong. *Int. J. Hosp. Manag.* **2005**, *24*, 311–329.
67. Alipour, M.; Hajaliakbari, F.; Javanbakht, N. The impact of web-marketing mix (4s) on development of tourism industry in Iran. *Int. J. Bus Soc. Sci.* **2011**, *2*, 267–274.
68. O'connor, P.; Piccoli, G. Marketing hotels using global distribution systems revisited. *Cornell Hotel Restaur. Adm. Q.* **2003**, *44*, 105–114.
69. Kushwaha, G.S.; Agrawal, S.R. An Indian customer surrounding 7P's of service marketing. *J. Retail. Consum. Serv.* **2015**, *22*, 85–95.
70. Ozturk, A.B.; Bilgihan, A.; Nusair, K.; Okumus, F. What keeps the mobile hotel booking users loyal? Investigating the roles of self-efficacy, compatibility, perceived ease of use, and perceived convenience. *Int. J. Inf. Manag.* **2016**, *36*, 1350–1359.
71. Kranias, A.; Bourlessa, M. Investigating the relationship between service quality and loyalty in Greek banking sector. *Procedia Econ. Financ.* **2013**, *5*, 453–458.
72. Nouri, B.A.; Soltani, M. Evaluating the effect of tourism marketing mix on buying holiday homes in Cyprus. *Int. J. Bus. Adm.* **2015**, *6*, 63–74.
73. Klaus, P. EXQ: A multiple-item scale for assessing service experience. *J. Serv. Manag.* **2012**, *23*, 5–33.
74. Hong, W.; Thong, J.Y.L.; Tam, K.Y. The effects of information format and shopping task on consumers' online shopping behavior: A cognitive fit perspective. *Manag. Inf. Syst.* **2004**, *21*, 149–184.
75. Chiu, C.M.; Wang, E.T.G.; Fang, Y.H.; Huang, H.Y. Understanding customers' repeat purchase intentions in B2C e-commerce: The roles of utilitarian value, hedonic value and perceived risk. *Inf. Syst. J.* **2014**, *24*, 85–114.

76. Roscoe, J.T. *Fundamental Research Statistics for the Behavioral Sciences*, 2nd ed.; Holt, Rinehart and Winston: New York, NY, USA, 1975.

77. Sekaran, U.; Bougie, R. *Research Methods for Business: A Skill-Building Approach*, 5th ed.; John Wiley & Sons: Haddington, UK, 2010.

78. Schiffman, L.G.; Kanuk, L.L. *Consumer Behavior*, 9th ed.; Prentice Hall: Englewood Cliffs, NJ, USA, 2006.

79. Hair, J.F.; Anderson, R.E.; Tatham, R.L.; Black, W.C. *Multivariate Date Analysis*, 5th ed.; Prentice-Hall: Englewood Cliffs, NJ, USA, 1998.

80. Yang, W.; Zhang, L.; Mattila, A.S. Luxe for less: How do consumers react to luxury hotel price promotions? The moderating role of consumers' need for status. *Cornell Hosp. Q.* **2016**, *57*, 82–92.

81. Hu, X.; Yang, Y. Determinants of consumers' choices in hotel online searches: A comparison of consideration and booking stages. *Int. J. Hosp. Manag.* **2019**.

82. Liu, W.; Guillet, B.D.; Xiao, Q.; Law, R. Globalization or localization of consumer preferences: The case of hotel room booking. *Tour. Manag.* **2014**, *41*, 148–157.

83. Mauri, A.G.; Minazzi, R. Web reviews influence on expectations and purchasing intentions of hotel potential customers. *Int. J. Hosp. Manag.* **2013**, *34*, 99–107.

CHAPTER 4

Predicting Conversion Rates in Online Hotel Bookings with Customer Reviews

Liang Tang[1], Xi Wang[2] and Eojina Kim[3]

[1]*Apparel, Events, and Hospitality Management, College of Human Sciences, Iowa State University, Ames, IA 50011, USA*

[2]*Culture, Creativity and Management, School of Culture and Creativity, BNU-HKBU United International College, Zhuhai 519085, China*

[3]*Hospitality and Tourism Management, Pamplin College of Business, Virginia Tech, Blacksburg, VA 24061, USA*

ABSTRACT

E-commerce in the hospitality and tourism field has already ranked No. 2 among all online shopping categories worldwide. However, customers' visits to a hotel booking website cannot guarantee the generation of sales, while the conversion rate is regarded as the indicator that effectively assesses the e-commerce website performance. This study aimed to investigate the influential factors of conversion rates from both affective content and the communication style of customer's online reviews. The affective content was evaluated with eight emotional dimensions (i.e., joy, sadness, anger, fear, trust, disgust, anticipation, and surprise) in Plutchik's emotion wheel, and the communication style perspective was assessed with linguistic style matching (LSM). In total, 111,926 customer reviews from 641 hotels in five cities in the U.S. were collected for the analysis. Results indicated that LSM and four emotions have significant impacts on hotel conversion rates. This research contributes to the knowledge body of customers' conversion behaviors on hotel booking websites and offers pertinent practical implications.

Keywords: *conversion rate; e-commerce in hospitality; hotel booking; Plutchik's emotion wheel; linguistic style matching*

INTRODUCTION

The emergence of e-commerce has restructured marketing activities in the hospitality and tourism industry since the digital realms overhauled customers' purchase patterns [1,2]. Based on customers' claimed purchasing, e-commerce in the hospitality and tourism field ranked No. 2 among all online shopping categories worldwide in 2018 [3]. Specifically, hotel reservations contributed the most and accounted for 39% of all the e-bookings in the hospitality and tourism industry [4]. Similar to the e-retailers in other manufacturing and service industries, hoteliers have made tremendous marketing efforts by improving website traffic on e-commerce channels [5]. However, a big gap exists between the numbers of lookers and bookers on hotel booking websites [6,7]. Previous academic studies have mostly focused on the impact of the content and design of e-commerce websites on customers' behavioral intentions rather than actual booking patronage due to the challenges of data collection [8,9]. But behavioral intentions cannot exactly predict actual behavior [10]. Therefore, it is crucial to investigate how to convert lookers to actual bookers on e-commerce websites (rather than just having the intention of booking) [11]. The look-to-book ratio is termed as the conversion rate (CR), which is used to differentiate between the numbers of browsers on an e-commercial platform and the number of customers who actually buy online. CR is a key indicator of an e-commerce website's performance [12]. The average CR of hotel booking websites is only 2.2%, with the top 20% of hotels at 5.6% and the bottom 20% of hotels at 0.3% [13]. Even a marginal increase in CR could lead to a considerable growth in sales [14]; thus, how to improve CR on booking websites is of the utmost important for hoteliers.

Despite the importance of CR, limited studies on this topic have been found in the general business's e-commerce discipline [15,16], and even fewer in the hospitality and tourism field. To the knowledge of the present authors, Cezar and Ogut [11] and Horan et al. [12] were the only two studies in this field. The variables in these two studies are exclusively "quantitative surrogates" on internet bookings (e.g., review rating and tourism volume). However, controversy exists around the predictive outcome of these numerical quality diagnostics on customers' attitudes and behaviors (e.g., assessment of review helpfulness, and conversion behavior) on e-commerce websites [17,18,19]. For example, previous studies identified the contrasting effect of the same "quantitative surrogate" on an attitudinal or behavioral variable (e.g., the influence of hotel star ratings on room sales is positive in Ye et al. [20] but negative in Ye et al. [21]). Thus, some scholars suggested that natural language reviews should be given more attention [22,23], as indicated by Xu [24] that "online customer textual reviews contain rich information about customers' consumption experience, which reflect their perceptions of the detailed attributes of product and service quality." The precise and emotion-charged information expressed by language cannot be replaced with a "quantitative surrogate" [25]. Since the enriched content of textual reviews boosts information and emotional communications between reviewers and readers, it shows a greater capability for predicting readers' feelings and actions [26].

In the same vein, the present authors explored CR as a measure of customers' conversion behavior from the perspective of textual reviews. Furthermore, Ludwig et al. [27] suggested that "new insights into the customer review phenomenon can be derived from studying the semantic content and style properties of verbatim customer reviews to examine their influence." Thus, the present study analyzed textual reviews from the two perspectives of semantic content and linguistic style.

A focal element of semantic content is emotion. Emotion depicts innate or intuitive moods in contrast with rationale or knowledge. Emotions in textual reviews have been widely investigated as an antecedent of customers' attitudes (e.g., satisfaction and review helpfulness) or behavioral intentions [25,28,29]. One-dimensional scalability (positive vs. negative) has been mostly adopted in previous studies [26,30]. However, Pfister and Bohm [31] argued that the multiple dimensions (e.g., anger and trust) underlying either positive or negative emotions have distinct origins, denotations, and appraisals. Plutchik's wheel is a four-dimensional circumplex with eight basic emotions, intensities, opposites, and combinations, which allow researchers to explore complicated emotional systems of customers in depth [25]. Furthermore, the eight basic emotional dimensions in Plutchik's wheel, as subjective reactions (e.g., trust), are expected to result in behavioral reactions (e.g., groom generated by trust), which further predict survival functions (e.g., mutual support generated by groom) [32]. The distinct survival functions initiated by subjective reactions (i.e., basic emotions) indicate that the eight basic emotions embedded in reviews may generate impacts on CR at distinct extents. Such information is crucial for industry practitioners to improve CR via strategically presenting reviews addressing different emotions (e.g., ranking and filter) on e-commerce websites. To the knowledge of the present authors, Ludwig et al. [27], as the only study that investigated the relationship between affection and CR, adopted the one-dimensional scalability of affection (i.e., positive vs. negative). To take one step further, the present study examined how CR is impacted by the eight aspects (i.e., joy, sadness, anger, fear, trust, disgust, anticipation, and surprise) of Plutchik's emotional wheel, which is a cornerstone emotional framework in psychology.

Besides semantic content, linguistic style features of online reviews generate substantial influences on readers' comprehension and perception [33]. Coordination is required in human communication. Each participant regulates his/her own presentation of ideas and opinions in the conversation to strengthen mutual attractions and improve shared comprehension [34]. One of the critical strategies for such a regulation is language mimicry. Linguistic style matching (LSM) is defined as an algorithm to automatically evaluate language mimicry with the adoption of functional words [35]. According to the similarity-liking premise proposed by Byrne et al. [36], greater LSM potentially leads to a stronger bond between the parties, which is a predictor of their attitudes and behaviors. Therefore, LSM of the review bundle for a specific hotel was assessed as a diagnostic cue for CR (i.e., as a behavioral construct) in the current study.

The purpose of the present study is to investigate the influential factors of CR on an individual hotel booking website from the affective content (emotion) and communication style (LSM) aspects. The specific objectives of the research include: (1) assessing the impact of eight individual emotional dimensions (i.e., Plutchik's wheel) embedded in reviews on CR, and (2) examining the impact of

LSM embedded in reviews on CR. The researchers selected www.booking.com as the investigation site since it is ranked as the No. 1 hospitality e-commerce and hotel booking website across the world by Bramblett [37]. Furthermore, this website offers real-time browsing and booking statuses for an individual hotel listing, which are required for counting CR. CR examined in the present study is a crucial indicator of website visitors' patronage behaviors, leading to hotels' revenue. Thus, our innovative assessment of CR's determinant factors from semantic content and linguistic style not only paves a new research venue, but it also generates far-reaching implications in the hospitality and tourism industry.

LITERATURE REVIEW

Conversion Rate and Information Processing Theory

The conversion rate (CR) on an e-commerce website is defined as the percentage of browsing on a website that ends with a purchase within a specific time window [38]. For example, if 100 visitors browse an e-commerce website and one of them places an order, the CR for the site is 1%. A high CR refers to a great percentage of customer patronages on the site on each visit, while a low CR means that most visitors browse the website without generating sales [15].

Previous studies on the topic of CR could be classified into four streams. The first stream examined the impact of website design on CR. Examples of website features assessed in the past research were composed of promotion (e.g., discount policy), quality (e.g., luxury products) [39], and usability factors [40]. The second stream was to establish the CR prediction mechanism with machine learning and other mathematical models by scholars in computer science [41,42]. The third stream was to address the importance of customers' previous e-shopping experience on CR. For example, Moe and Fader [16] tested how CR is influenced by customers' past visit experiences, whereas Li and Kannan [43] investigated the carryover and spillover effects of previous website visits on CR. The last and widely ignored stream was to examine how recommendation systems and textual reviews impact CR. The majority of previous studies in this stream focused on recommendation systems. For example, Ghose and Yang [44] and Rutz and Bucklin [45] confirmed the relationship between the rank order of a listing among customers and CR. To the knowledge of the present authors, very sporadic research investigated how textual reviews influence CR on an e-commerce website. The work of Ludwig et al. [27] is such an example with the study setting of www.Amazon.com.

The relationship between textual reviews and CR could be explained with information processing theory. Information processing theory describes an individual's learning process, which covers four steps including input, processing, storage, and output [46]. Humans receive input about our surroundings through our sensory organs (e.g., eyes and ears), perform analysis on information both cognitively and affectively, store information either in short-term or long-term memory, and present the results as an output [47]. Particularly, language as a means for expressing cultural values is crucial in the design and content of the messages that senders convey [48]. When receivers are familiar with the language used in the message, they are inclined to perceive less risk, identify higher usability, and generate greater satisfaction [49].

Language expressed either orally or textually (i.e., input in the information processing theory) has been widely proven in the psychology discipline to generate robust explanative and predictive impacts on an individual's behavior (i.e., output in the information processing theory), and such a linkage has been applied in different fields (e.g., education, marketing, and community service) to improve communication effectiveness [50,51,52]. In the same vein, textual reviews as the input of language have been proven to influence customers' behaviors (e.g., recommendations to others, patronage, and CR) as output in the information processing theory [53]. Specifically, Schindler and Bickart [54] suggested that textual reviews should be deciphered through the basic word categorizations of content (e.g., adjective) and communication styles (e.g., functional words). The justifications for including emotion (i.e., as one content component) and language style matching (i.e., as one communication-style component) as the determinant variables of CR are presented in the "Emotions" section and the "Linguistic Style Matching (LSM)" section.

Customer Review Emotion

Emotion is defined as a neural circuit, feedback mechanism, and feeling status that activates and structures cognitions and behaviors [55]. Emotion is either intrapersonal or interpersonal. The intrapersonal emotion depicts an individual's internal affections, whereas the interpersonal emotion represents the external detectable articulation of affections in the interactive communications [56]. The emotional representation in textual reviews emphasizes the interpersonal dimension [57].

Previous studies of the e-commerce in the hospitality and tourism field predominantly adopted a dichotomy of emotions: positive vs. negative [26,30,58]. An assumption behind these studies is that all emotional states are naturally sorted as either positive or negative. However, this presumption is not always tenable since ample evidence supports the idea that an individual's choice does not confirm to simple scalability [59]. By realizing the dichotomy's limitation, sporadic efforts were made to investigate more specific emotional dimensions in user-generated content [28,60,61]. The present study examines the eight dimensions of Plutchik's emotional wheel, with the rationale explained in the next subsection.

Multi-Dimensional Emotional Framework

A multi-dimensional approach has been advanced to feature discrete emotions in the psychology discipline [32,62,63]. Specifically, the Geneva emotional model (GEM) was proposed by Scherer et al. [63] GEM covers 10 positive dimensions and 10 negative ones. Fredrickson et al. [64] created a modified differential emotions scale (mDES). The mDES includes a 10-item positive emotion subscale and an 8-item negative emotion subscale. Ekman generated six fundamental emotion aspects: joy, anger, disgust, sadness, fear, and surprise [62]. Plutchik enriched Ekman's framework by adding two more emotional dimensions, adding trust and anticipation, and mapped the eight basic emotional aspects on a wheel [32]. The eight basic emotional aspects are revealed with four contrasting pairs: sadness–joy,

Table 1. *Sample words of Plutchik's wheel.*

Emotional Dimensions	Sample Words
Anger	annoying, battle, complaint, dispute
Anticipation	attempt, countdown, develop, expected
Disgust	abject, contamination, defective, falsity
Fear	afraid, barbarian, cautionary, defend
Joy	abundant, beautiful, charmed, delicious
Sadness	abortive, badly, embarrass, fell
Surprise	amaze, occasional, quickness, rapid
Trust	accountable, believed, cohesive, deputy

fear–anger, disgust–trust, and surprise–anticipation. The word examples in each emotional dimension are shown in Table 1.

As shown in Figure 1, each emotional dimension belongs to either positive sentiment (represented with "+" category) or negative sentiment (represented with "–" category) has a different intensity, which is shown vertically on each

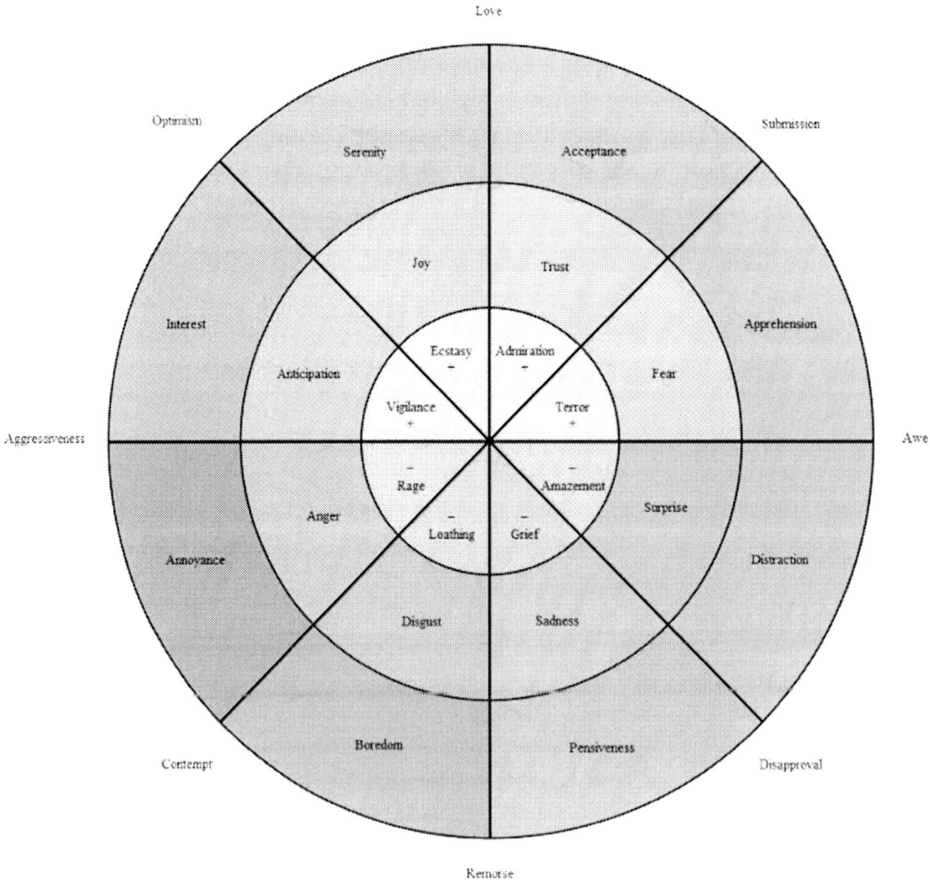

Figure 1. *Emotional wheel (Revised based on Plutchik's emotional wheel).*

spoke. Specifically, presented by the fluctuation of the color and saturation, the emotional intensity is indicating increases from the outer edge to the center. For example, anger serves as one of the eight emotional dimensions. A lower extent of anger is annoyance on the outer edge, whereas a greater extent of anger is rage in the center of the wheel. A dyad emotion sits between any two adjacent spokes, which rises out of the respective pairs of basic emotions. For example, anger and anticipation, as two foundational emotional dimensions, are mixed to generate aggressiveness. Plutchik also indicated that tertiary feelings exist that are a combination of three or more basic emotions, which are not shown in the emotional wheel [65].

In the context of e-commerce, the emotional representation in textual reviews emphasizes the interpersonal dimension [57]. Wang et al. suggested that "in the interpersonal communication context, affective cues provided by the communicator could evoke automatic affective reactions of the recipient, which need the recipient's few processing resources, occur rapidly, and assist in the formation of attitude and behavior" [25]. Therefore, the sentiment cue embedded in a review could transfer to the mood or feeling of a reader, which predicts his/her purchase behavior [27]. In the present context, emotion in a textual review is particularly used to predict conversion behavior (i.e., CR). Based on the previous discussions, we propose that the four emotional dimensions at the positive extreme of Plutchik's wheel have positive impacts on CR, while the four emotional dimensions at the negative extreme have negative impacts on CR within the e-commerce context.

Hypothesis 1. *Joy embedded in reviews has a positive impact on CR.*

Hypothesis 2. *Anger embedded in reviews has a positive impact on CR.*

Hypothesis 3. *Trust embedded in reviews has a positive impact on CR.*

Hypothesis 4. *Anticipation embedded in reviews has a positive impact on CR.*

Hypothesis 5. *Sadness embedded in reviews has a negative impact on CR.*

Hypothesis 6. *Fear embedded in reviews has a negative impact on CR.*

Hypothesis 7. *Disgust embedded in reviews has a negative impact on CR.*

Hypothesis 8. *Surprise embedded in reviews has a negative impact on CR.*

Linguistic Style Matching (LSM)

Communication accommodation theory (CAT) is a foundational psychology theory of interpersonal or intergroup communications [34]. Communication accommodation refers to adjustments or changes made in any type of communication (e.g., verbal, text, and posture) in order to gain approval from the receiver, enhance communication effectiveness, and establish a positive social identity [66]. The purpose of CAT is to suggest a communicative adjustment strategy for the sender and to predict how the receiver perceives, assesses, and responds to the sender [67]. A core strategy of CAT is convergence, which refers to adjusting the communicative behavior to be consistent with one and another [68].

Table 2. *LSM categories and sample words.*

Category	Examples
Personal pronouns	I, he, she
Impersonal pronouns	anyone, everyone, other
Articles	a, an, the
Conjunctions	as, if, when
Prepositions	across, between, for
Auxiliary verbs	can, do, become
High-frequency adverbs	extremely, hence, indeed
Negations	don't, doesn't, no
Quantifiers	all, every, few

In verbal and written communication, such a convergence is represented as LSM. Language style shows the features of language expressions under the assistance of subjective and objective considerations. Specifically, LSM suggests that an individual is inclined to match his/her linguistic style to pursue synchronization with other parties [33]. LSM is an algorithm designed for assessing the extent of synchronization between two parties as it relates to the use of functional words [35]. The nine categories and their corresponding example words are provided in Table 2.

Community members show interest in playing "so-called language games... in which members adhere to the collective's style of conversing to demonstrate their affiliation" [69]. An e-commerce website for a specific product category (e.g., books, and hotels) could be viewed as an online community of customers who share a common interest or goal [70]. Chung and Pennebaker suggested that high LSM in the reviews written by customers could promote harmony and form a common identity on the website [71]. Moreover, Liu and Liu [72] indicated the following: in an online environment, the process of reading reviews essentially is a language exchange process, just using another form of verbal communication. Therefore, the LSM will have an impact on the result of the exchange. The LSM, or degree of synchronization between two conversants in terms of their use of function words, also has behavioral implications (p. 571).

Many previous studies have proven the crucial role of LSM in textual communication between individuals in online settings [27,33]. For example, Wang et al. indicated that the LSM of customer online review has significant effects and shows the convergence in the restaurant industry, which assists readers' diagnosticity of the review [25]. To take the idea even further, we aimed to test how LSM impacts conversion behavior. Accordingly, the hypothesis was created below.

Hypothesis 9. *LSM embedded in reviews has a positive impact on CR.*

METHODOLOGY

Data Collection

Data were legally collected from www.booking.com with the Datatool scraping software, which followed the guidance of the Institutional Review Board at the authors' affiliated university. Data scraping was completed 14–29 January 2020.

Previous studies on CR usually collected data for one week [73,74]. However, to obtain a more precise result, we collected data for 16 days. Data were collected in July because it is a peak season for traveling with a higher volume of both visiting number and booking number than other seasons.

The study sample included the hotels at six cities among the best tourism destinations in the U.S. [75]. The six cities across diverse regions (North, South, Northeast, Northwest, Southeast, and Southwest) included Chicago, Houston, New York City, San Francisco, Orlando, and Las Vegas. We further set two screening criteria. The first criterion was to only keep hotels among different property types (e.g., motels and B&Bs). The second criterion was to remove the default review with no actual content (i.e., a statement shown as "there are no comments available for this review"). After screening unqualified ones, 641 hotels and 111,926 corresponding customer reviews remained for further analysis. The number of hotels and corresponding customer reviews in each of the cities' studies were 96(14,413), 101(5,717), 107(18,119), 107(22,736), 159(22,010), and 71(28,931), respectively.

Variables

As for the dependent variable of hotel website's conversion rate, since the data were collected for 16 days, the average daily webpage visiting number and booking number for each hotel were used to compute CR. The original information of the booking number on www.booking.com only shows on a daily basis (i.e., "xx times of booking during past 24 h"). However, the online booking status is dynamic, which means the information of the booking times showing on the website is always changing. Therefore, consistent with the approaches used in Cezar and Ogut [11], we collected the booking number on a 2 h basis and then took the average of them within a 24 h period from 12:00 a.m. to 11:59 p.m. to represent the daily information of CR. The formula of CR is demonstrated below.

$$hotel\ conversion\ rate = \frac{hotel\ booking\ number}{hotel\ webpage\ visiting\ number} \tag{1}$$

As for the independent variables, both customer review emotional dimensions and LSM were computed based on the online review contents. Developed by Pennebaker, LIWC can help identify emotional and structural components in diverse textual contexts, such as online review content of e-commerce. LIWC proposes to calculate the percentage of each word, and then indicates a specific value score for a certain measured category [76].

Taking advantage of LIWC, the independent variable of LSM was calculated with the following four steps. In the first step, the LIWC was used to compute the score for each of the nine functional word categories. In the second step, the nine scores for the corresponding nine components of functional words generated by LIWC were further used in the following formula [35]. The formula is illustrated with the example of the functional word category "articles".

$$LSM_{art} = 1 - [(art_1 - art_G) \div (art_1 + art_G + 0.0001)] \tag{2}$$

In the formula, art_1 indicates the percentage of "articles" in a specific customer review, while art_G represents the overall percentage of "articles" in the remaining reviews within the same group. Step three was to generate the LSM score of a customer review by calculating the average of all the individual LSM scores for the corresponding nine components of functional words. The LSM score of an individual review ranged from 0 to 1. The higher LSM score means there is a greater extent of LSM [77].

Meanwhile, regarding the eight emotional dimensions, since the default dictionary of LIWC only covers three specific emotions (anxiety, anger, and sadness) [76], the Word–Emotion Association Lexicon (EmoLex) developed by the National Research Council Canada was further imported into LIWC. The EmoLex was used to identify the eight emotional dimensions of Plutchik's emotional wheel, and then calculate the value score of every individual emotional dimension related to the customer's online review contents [78].

Five control variables were directly extracted from the website, including distance from a hotel to the city center, hotel room rate, hotel star rating, risk-free cancellation policy, and high-demand status. The cities (i.e., Chicago, Houston, New York City, San Francisco, Orlando, and Las Vegas) were used as the dummy variable. In order to calculate the dependent variable of CR, we collected the webpage visiting number and booking number for each of the 641 hotels. Descriptive statistic results of all the variables—the dependent variable, the independent variables, and the control variables—are present in Table 3.

Table 3. *Descriptive statistic results of the variables.*

Variable	Mean	Median	S.D.	Min	Max	Range
CR	0.389	0.357	0.105	0.004	0.891	0.888
Anger	1.724	0.000	3.991	0.000	75.000	75.000
Anticipation	3.321	1.790	4.906	0.000	60.000	60.000
Disgust	1.617	0.000	4.234	0.000	75.000	75.000
Fear	1.074	0.000	3.051	0.000	75.000	75.000
Joy	4.904	3.030	6.465	0.000	80.000	80.000
Sadness	1.638	0.000	3.503	0.000	75.000	75.000
Surprise	1.672	0.000	3.722	0.000	50.000	50.000
Trust	5.203	3.450	6.458	0.000	80.000	80.000
LSM	0.501	0.530	0.236	0.010	0.940	0.930
Distance from a hotel to the city center	3.060	1.100	4.121	0.066	19.300	19.234
Hotel room rate	139.2876	129	87.2025	29	849	820
Hotel star rating	2.9576	3.0000	0.9338	0	5	5
Risk-free cancellation policy	0.6290	1.0000	0.4831	0	1	1
High-demand status	0.6546	1.0000	0.4755	0	1	1

Beta Regression Analysis

Beta regression was used for data analysis, considering CR as the dependent variable, ranging from 0 to 1. Although ordinary least squares (OLS) can be generally used in most regression analyses, beta regression is especially designed for modeling rate and proportion variables [79]. Compared to traditional OLS, beta regression can avoid generating a fit value beyond the lower and upper bounds between 0 and 1. Additionally, beta regression eliminates the inefficient effect of estimators caused by the standard error [11]. In beta regression, the coefficient associated with a variable refers to the change in log-odds of the target outcome (e.g., "success rate" or "retention rate"). To take the emotional dimension of anticipation as an example, if the estimated log-odds of anticipation is 0.02, the odds for CR should change by 1.0202 times (i.e., exp (0.02) = 1.0202). That is to say, with 1-unit increase in anticipation, the estimated odds of CR would increase by 2.02%.

RESULTS

Multicollinearity effects were tested for the assumption of beta regression as step one. The correlations between all the variables were examined first. CR was correlated with all the independent and control variables, except LSM and anticipation. Since there are some multicollinearity effects, the variance influence factor (VIF) for all the variable pairs were checked. VIF ranged from 1.17 to 6.52, which were satisfactory rates. Overall, the multicollinearity effects were insignificant in the model, which satisfied the prerequisite of beta regression.

A twofold beta regression analysis was conducted in the present study. In the first step, regression analysis was only applied to all control variables in order to have a clear understanding of shadow effects. According to Table 4, the hotel room rate, risk-free cancellation policy, and high-demand status control variable showed a positive influence on the dependent variable CR, whereas distance from a hotel to the city center, hotel star rating, city of Houston, and city of New York had negative influences on the dependent variable. The Pseudo R-squared of the control variable's regression model was 0.17.

Table 4. *Beta regression result and comparison.*

	Model with Only Control Variables					Research Model				
Variable	Estimate	Std. Error	z Value	Pr(>|z|)		Estimate	Std. Error	z Value	Pr(>|z|)	
(Intercept)	−0.69	0.12	−5.70	0.00	***	−0.70	0.18	−3.92	0.00	***
Distance from a hotel to the city center	−0.02	0.01	−2.67	0.01	**	−0.01	0.01	−1.98	0.04	**
Hotel star rating	−0.10	0.03	−3.32	0.00	***	−0.06	0.02	−2.46	0.01	**
Hotel room rate	0.00	0.00	−3.63	0.00	***	−0.01	0.00	−2.00	0.04	**
Risk-free cancellation policy	0.25	0.05	4.61	0.00	***	0.06	0.04	1.38	0.17	
High-demand status	0.34	0.06	6.08	0.00	***	0.17	0.04	3.98	0.00	***
City_Houston	−0.23	0.11	−2.08	0.04	**	−0.08	0.08	−1.02	0.31	
City_LasVegas	0.04	0.10	0.39	0.69		0.14	0.08	1.85	0.06	
City_NewYorkCity	−0.18	0.09	−1.95	0.05		−0.03	0.07	−0.48	0.63	
City_Orlando	−0.07	0.11	−0.63	0.53		0.07	0.08	0.81	0.42	
City_SanFrancisco	−0.02	0.10	−0.16	0.88		−0.05	0.07	−0.69	0.49	
LSM						0.71	0.26	2.78	0.01	***
Anger						−0.04	0.01	−5.57	0.00	***
Anticipation						0.02	0.01	2.17	0.03	**
Disgust						−0.02	0.01	−3.68	0.00	***
Fear						0.01	0.01	1.00	0.32	
Joy						−0.02	0.02	−1.18	0.24	
Sadness						0.01	0.01	1.19	0.24	
Surprise						0.01	0.02	0.55	0.58	
Trust						0.03	0.01	2.06	0.04	**

** $p < 0.05$; *** $p < 0.01$; Research model's Pseudo R-squared increased from 0.17 to 0.52.

In the second step, we explored the effect of all focal variables of interests in the present study. After including the independent variables of interest (i.e., LSM and eight emotional dimensions), the Pseudo R-squared increased from 0.17 to 0.52. It indicated that the model fit was significantly increased 35% after introducing the independent variables of customer review emotion and LSMs. With the $p < 0.01$ and the log likelihood of 670.90, the overall model fit of the beta regression analysis was acceptable.

Referring to the details presented in Table 4, four out of the eight emotional dimensions showed significant impacts on CR. Specifically, anticipation ($\beta = 0.02$; $p = 0.03$) and trust ($\beta = 0.03$; $p = 0.04$) had positive influences on CR, which meant that with an increase of both anticipation and trust emotions expressed in the customer reviews, there would also be an increase of hotel CR. Anger ($\beta = -0.04$; $p < 0.01$) and disgust ($\beta = -0.02$; $p < 0.01$) had negative influences on CR, that is to say, with an increase in either anger or disgust emotion contained in customer reviews, the hotel CR would also suffer with a significant decrease. As it relates to the linguistic style of customer reviews, LSM ($\beta = 0.71$; $p = 0.01$) had a positive effect on CR, which indicated that with a greater extent of LSM, the hotel CR would increase.

The results of the control variables aligned with the previous literature [11]. Based on the results of the research model, the high-demand status of a hotel ($\beta = 0.17$; $p < 0.01$) had a significantly positive impact on CR. However, the distance from a hotel to the city center ($\beta = -0.01$; $p = 0.04$), hotel star rating ($\beta = -0.06$; $p = 0.01$), and hotel room rate ($\beta = -0.01$; $p = 0.04$) had significantly negative impacts on CR. No significant difference could be identified among cities. The current study also conducted a robustness check with OLS, which showed consistent results for the beta regression analysis.

DISCUSSION AND IMPLICATIONS

Theoretical Implications

The present study contributes to the extant research on customer behavior by exploring the effect of semantic content and LSM on online booking website and e-commerce platform of the hospital and tourism industry; meanwhile, it extends the extant literature in four important ways. First, the present research is a pioneer that investigates the influence of review content on CR from the perspectives of semantic content and LSM. Previous studies have primarily investigated readers' attitudes and behavioral intentions as consequences of checking reviews. For example, Radojevic et al. examined customer reviews on www.TripAdvisor.com and confirmed that hotel attributes and customers' characteristics most powerfully influenced customer satisfaction [80]. However, the present study focuses on CR, as it is an actual behavioral outcome that needs more attention from scholars. While the study of Ludwig et al. was the only existing one on this topic, it examined the effect of only the dichotomy of emotions (i.e., positive vs. negative) and LSM on the CR of book sales on www.Amazon.com [27]. Our research took Ludwig et al.'s idea further and deeper, particularly in e-commerce context of the hospitality and tourism field. This analysis followed the classic CR calculation precure by aggregating transaction level data, and although, along with the calculation, there may exist some systemic errors, the analysis results statistically confirmed the dynamic influences of LSM and four of the eight emotions on CR. LSM showed a positive impact on CR in the present study, which is consistent with Ludwig et al. [27].

Established based on the information processing theory, the present study also made significant contributions of the academical applications of the information processing theory in the e-commerce field. In the analysis, besides stating a plain truth of influence of the language style and language structure from online reviews, it further provided an in-depth consideration on both cognitive and affective contents (LSM and emotions) of customer reviews. With the purpose of improving the effectiveness of the communication, the results of the present study consolidated the theorical foundation of the information processing theory and, in addition, verified the distinctive effects of the customer's language expression on their corresponding behavior intention in the business and communication contexts as well.

Third, the present study is one of the pioneer studies to examine the effect of how individual emotional dimensions influence CR. In particular, the present study extends the extant literature on emotions and customer behavior by exploring the effects of various aspects of emotions on CR. Among the eight individual emotional categories of Plutchik's framework [32], CR is positively influenced by anticipation and trust and negatively influenced by anger and disgust. The results indicated that individual emotional dimensions have distinct impacts on CR.

Specifically, anticipation conveys a reviewer's perception on the future. It simulates a forthcoming situation into the affective present as an individual "evolves" into the anticipated state [81]. Thus, the readers could generate resonance with a reviewer's aspiration of the hotel, which accordingly leads to CR. Trustworthiness is the foundation for readers to use the information of reviews to guide their behavior [82]. The honest and responsible image of a hotel conveyed in reviews could strengthen readers' confidence of their future experience at the hotel. Accordingly, trust shows a positive influence on CR.

Anger and disgust are two emotional dimensions in reviews that are mostly used to depict service failures [25]. When service failure happens, reviewers may express anger and disgust in online reviews to depict the disappointing consumption experience [58]. It could be explained with prospect theory. Prospect theory indicates that individuals give more weight to perceived gains versus perceived losses [83]. The present study confirmed that anger and disgust, which depict service failures in reviews, discouraged prospective customers from making a purchase (i.e., CR). The results are consistent with Wang et al., who indicated that both anger and disgust expressed in reviews are helpful for the perceptions of readers [25].

Analysis conducted in the present study provided the in-depth understanding on the conversion rate of hotel booking website. For instance, according to the results, the emotion of anger was identified with more of an intensive effect than disgust, even though both of them were identified with the negative impacts. In the same manner, the trust emotion was identified with more of an intensive effect than anticipation. The beta regression specially selected for the data analysis targeting to analyze the rate/ratio variable with an upper and lower bounds between 0 and 1, which ensures an accurate evaluation of the regression outcome for those intendent variables of interests.

Joy and sadness do not show significant impacts on CR. The writings of joy and sadness from business experiences are easily exaggerated, or even fabricated as fake or spam reviews [25,28]. Thus, joy and sadness expressed in reviews may generate mixed and insignificant impacts on readers' decision making (i.e., CR). Fear shows an insignificant impact on CR for lodging reservations.

Words in the category of fear (e.g., terror, and firearms) are primarily relevant to physical and psychological safety. In extremely rare situations, a hotel locates itself in a dangerous community or area. In other words, safety is almost a "pre-assumption" for most of the hotels. Thus, fear as an expression of unsafety in reviews cannot arouse echoes among readers, which further shows an insignificant influence on CR. Another emotional dimension that has an insignificant impact on CR is surprise. Surprise depicts a psychological status caused by an unexpected event. By analyzing its sample words (e.g., occasional, sudden, and unexpected), surprise may indicate a neutral, pleasing, or unpleasing experience, which is different from travel plans [84]. Considering the mixed nature of the unexpected experience, it is reasonable that the surprise expressed in reviews insignificantly impacts readers' CR.

Fourth, the present study adds to the literature of emotions by shedding light on the interpersonal role of emotions. Previous studies on the role of emotions on customer behavior have focused on an intrapersonal dimension of emotion within an individual customer [58,85]. However, the interpersonal nature of emotion has been widely overlooked. In the view of the significance effect of the intrapersonal perspective in this study, these dimensions should be accounted for when analyzing customers' emotions. With the popularity of e-commerce, the interpersonal role of emotion has been strengthened [57] since the sentiment cues expressed in a review could ignite affective responses in readers and consequently influence their attitudes and behaviors [25,28]. The present study contributes to understanding the interpersonal role of emotion.

Last, beyond the influence of the website features in the context of customer reviews, the present study underscores the important role of textual reviews. The limited studies on CR [11,12] in the context of customer reviews have emphasized website features (e.g., utility), leaving textual reviews sporadically discovered. To bridge these gaps, we contribute to the emerging research body on CR by examining textual reviews from both the content and linguistic style perspectives. In the hospitality and tourism field, we show, for the first time, how individual emotional dimensions and LSM play roles cognitively and affectively in shaping CR.

Practical Implications

The findings from the present study also provide insightful implications for industry practitioners who aim to increase CR for online retailers since customers increasingly utilize online reviews in making their hotel-booking decisions. First, the online travel agencies wishing to increase CR may be motivated to understand the drivers of CR. Due to the rapid growth of user-generated content and increasing usage of online reviews across a wide variety of online travel agencies, it would be vital to identify the predictors of CR. This can be done by analyzing customer sentiment and LSM, using the vast amount of real-time data. The findings from the present study suggest that industry practitioners could develop guidance for reviewers, especially elite reviewers, to express their views, as the linguistic nature of reviews ultimately influences CR in the e-commerce.

Second, not all of the eight emotional dimensions in reviews are persuasive enough to influence customers' purchase decisions. Thus, online travel agencies are advised to develop the criteria for ranking reviews in the recommendation system, considering the individual emotional dimensions, especially those that have significant impacts on prospective customers' conversion behavior. Currently for most online travel agencies, one of the primary review ranking criteria is customer rating (i.e., numerical rating from high to low or from low to high). The emotional analysis of textual reviews related to the four specific dimensions (i.e., anticipation, trust, disgust, and anger) could be incorporated into mathematic models of deciding the review rankings together with the overall numerical rating of the business. The industry practitioners are advised to evaluate their performance with our model, which is capable of predicting CR by taking into account sentiments and language matching along with online hotel booking features.

Third, hotel practitioners are also advised to examine specific emotional dimensions embedded in reviews. Accordingly, they could detect "whether the customers are happy with, dissatisfied with, losing trust in, or angry with their product or a particular feature of the product" [78]. The analysis of affective content from customer reviews, especially those with any of the four emotional dimensions that predict future customers' conversion behavior, could offer hotels an "emotion-aware system" to understand customers' feelings, discover their reasonings, and recover from service failures. Furthermore, the result of the present study also gives industry practitioners guidance on how to choose endorsement/compliment messages on the official websites of hotels. Specifically, the positive reviews that convey anticipation and trust are more convincing than those that convey joy, since they influence prospective customers' patronage decisions.

Fourth, LSM could be viewed as the analysis of linguistic style under a microscope. It is a creative approach to decode the underlying thinking procedure that results in readers' conversion behavior. A unique advantage of utilizing LSM to predict CR is to eliminate non-disruptive and lesser biases by comparing with self-reporting (e.g., post-review surveys with readers). When a hotel conveys similar thinking styles in the communicative messages with its customers, customers are inclined to generate feelings of intimacy and psychological synchrony. Thus, we suggest that in hotels' marketing and promotional materials (e.g., responses to reviewers' comments on third-party e-commerce or review websites), industry practitioners should adopt the functional words and word patterns demonstrating high-extent LSM with reviews, which is expected to enhance persuasion effectiveness.

Author Contributions

Conceptualization, L.T.; Methodology, X.W.; Software, X.W.; Validation, L.T. and E.K.; Formal Analysis, X.W.; Investigation, L.T. and E.K.; Resources, X.W.; Data Curation, X.W.; Writing—Original Draft Preparation, L.T. and X.W.; Writing—Review and Editing, L.T. and X.W.; Visualization, X.W.; Supervision, L.T.; Project Administration, X.W.; Funding Acquisition, X.W. All authors have read and agreed to the published version of the manuscript.

REFERENCES

1. Ali, F. Hotel website quality, perceived flow, customer satisfaction and purchase intention. *J. Hosp. Tour. Technol.* **2016**, *7*, 213–228.

2. Heung, V.C. Barriers to implementing E-commerce in the travel industry: A practical perspective. *Int. J. Hosp. Manag.* **2003**, *22*, 111–118.

3. Grynberg, J. Nielsen Explores Consumers' Connected Lives in Global E-Commerce Survey: 53% of the Global Population is Online. 2018. Available online: https://www.portada-online.com/2018/12/10/nielsen-explores-consumers-connected-lives-in-global-e-commerce-survey/ (accessed on 12 February 2019).

4. Eventforte. Hospitality Online: Internet Travel & Hotel Booking Statistics. 2018. Available online: https://eventforte.com/hospitality-online-statistics.html (accessed on 22 February 2018).

5. Gupta, R. Driving Traffic and Lifting Bookings o Hotel Brand Websites. 2012. Available online: https://www.eyefortravel.com/distribution-strategies/driving-traffic-and-lifting-bookings-hotel-brand-websites (accessed on 21 February 2019).

6. Chatterjee, P.; Wang, Y. Online comparison shopping behavior of travel consumers. *J. Qual. Assur. Hosp. Tour.* **2012**, *13*, 1–23.

7. Zhang, Z.; Liang, S.; Li, H.; Zhang, Z. Booking now or later: Do online peer reviews matter? *Int. J. Hosp. Manag.* **2019**, *77*, 147–158.

8. Ongsakul, V.; Ali, F.; Wu, C.; Duan, Y.; Cobanoglu, C.; Ryu, K. Hotel website quality, performance, telepresence and behavioral intentions. *Tour. Rev.* **2020**, *76*, 681–700.

9. Wang, L.; Law, R.; Guillet, B.D.; Hung, K.; Fong, D.K.C. Impact of hotel website quality on online booking intentions: eTrust as a mediator. *Int. J. Hosp. Manag.* **2015**, *47*, 108–115.

10. Wong, J.K.; Sheth, J.N. Explaining intention-behavior discrepancy-a paradigm. *Adv. Consum. Res.* **1985**, *12*, 378–384.

11. Cezar, A.; Ögüt, H. Analyzing conversion rates in online hotel booking: The role of customer reviews, recommendations and rank order in search listings. *Int. J. Contemp. Hosp. Manag.* **2016**, *28*, 286–304.

12. Horan, P.; McCarthy, P.; Frew, A. Analysis of the Volume, Value and Conversion Performance of a National Destination Marketing System Website. 2002, pp. 77–86. Available online: https://citeseerx.ist.psu.edu/viewdoc (accessed on 21 February 2018).

13. Boss, J. The Real Talk on Hotel Website Conversion Rates. Available online: https://www.fastbooking.com/newsfeeds/the-real-talk-on-hotel-website-conversion-rates (accessed on 21 February 2018).

14. Sismeiro, C.; Bucklin, R.E. Modeling purchase behavior at an e-commerce web site: A task-completion approach. *J. Mark. Res.* **2004**, *41*, 306–323.

15. Ayanso, A.; Yoogalingam, R. Profiling retail web site functionalities and conversion rates: A cluster analysis. *Int. J. Electron. Commer.* **2009**, *14*, 79–114.

16. Moe, W.W.; Fader, P.S. Dynamic conversion behavior at e-commerce sites. *Manag. Sci.* **2004**, *50*, 326–335.

17. Chen, P.-Y.; Wu, S.; Yoon, J. The impact of online recommendation and consumer feedback on sales. In Proceedings of the International Conference on Information Systems, New York, NY, USA, 6–8 August 2004; pp. 711–724.

18. Hu, X.; Yang, Y. What makes online reviews helpful in tourism and hospitality? A bare-bones meta-analysis. *J. Hosp. Mark. Manag.* **2021**, *30*, 139–158.
19. Yang, Y.; Park, S.; Hu, X. Electronic word of mouth and hotel performance: A meta-analysis. *Tour. Manag.* **2018**, *67*, 248–260.
20. Ye, Q.; Law, R.; Gu, B. The impact of online user reviews on hotel room sales. *Int. J. Hosp. Manag.* **2009**, *28*, 180–182.
21. Ye, Q.; Law, R.; Gu, B.; Chen, W. The influence of user-generated content on traveler behavior: An empirical investigation on the effects of e-word-of-mouth to hotel online bookings. *Comput. Hum. Behav.* **2011**, *27*, 634–639.
22. Amatulli, C.; De Angelis, M.; Stoppani, A. Analyzing online reviews in hospitality: Data-driven opportunities for predicting the sharing of negative emotional content. *Curr. Issues Tour.* **2019**, *22*, 1904–1917.
23. Hu, Y.H.; Chen, Y.L.; Chou, H.L. Opinion mining from online hotel reviews—A text summarization approach. *Inf. Process. Manag.* **2017**, *53*, 436–449.
24. Xu, X. Examining the relevance of online customer textual reviews on hotels' product and service attributes. *J. Hosp. Tour. Res.* **2019**, *43*, 141–163.
25. Wang, X.; Tang, L.; Kim, E. More than words: Do emotional content and linguistic style matching matter on restaurant review helpfulness? *Int. J. Hosp. Manag.* **2019**, *77*, 438–447.
26. Zhao, Y.; Xu, X.; Wang, M. Predicting overall customer satisfaction: Big data evidence from hotel online textual reviews. *Int. J. Hosp. Manag.* **2019**, *76*, 111–121.
27. Ludwig, S.; De Ruyter, K.; Friedman, M.; Brüggen, E.C.; Wetzels, M.; Pfann, G. More than words: The influence of affective content and linguistic style matches in online reviews on conversion rates. *J. Mark.* **2013**, *77*, 87–103.
28. Luo, Y.; Tang, R. Understanding hidden dimensions in textual reviews on Airbnb: An application of modified latent aspect rating analysis (LARA). *Int. J. Hosp. Manag.* **2019**, *80*, 144–154.
29. Luo, Y.; Xu, X. Predicting the helpfulness of online restaurant reviews using different machine learning algorithms: A case study of yelp. *Sustainability* **2019**, *11*, 5254.
30. Cheng, M.; Jin, X. What do Airbnb users care about? An analysis of online review comments. *Int. J. Hosp. Manag.* **2019**, *76*, 58–70.
31. Pfister, H.R.; Böhm, G. The multiplicity of emotions: A framework of emotional functions in decision making. *Judgm. Decis. Mak.* **2008**, *3*, 5–17
32. Plutchik, R. *The Psychology and Biology of Emotion*; Harper Collins College Publishers: Palatine, IL, USA, 1994.
33. Taylor, P.J.; Thomas, S. Linguistic style matching and negotiation outcome. *Negot. Confl. Manag. Res.* **2008**, *1*, 263–281.
34. Giles, H.; Coupland, N. *Language: Contexts and Consequences*; Open University Press: Milton Keynes, UK, 1991.
35. Ireland, M.E.; Pennebaker, J.W. Language style matching in writing: Synchrony in essays, correspondence, and poetry. *J. Pers. Soc. Psychol.* **2010**, *99*, 549.
36. Byrne, D.; Clore, G.L.; Smeaton, G. The attraction hypothesis: Do similar attitudes affect anything? *J. Personal. Soc. Psychol.* **1986**, *51*, 1167–1170.
37. Bramblett, R. Best and Worst Hotel Booking Sites. 2019. Available online: https://www.frommers.com/slideshows/819303-best-and-worst-hotel-booking-sites (accessed on 22 February 2019).

38. Zhou, M.; Ding, Z.; Tang, J.; Yin, D. Micro behaviors: A new perspective in e-commerce recommender systems. In Proceedings of the Eleventh ACM International Conference on Web Search and Data Mining, Los Angeles, CA, USA, 5–9 February 2018; pp. 727–735.

39. Di Fatta, D.; Patton, D.; Viglia, G. The determinants of conversion rates in SME e-commerce websites. *J. Retail. Consum. Serv.* **2018**, *41*, 161–168.

40. Kuan, H.-H.; Bock, G.-W.; Vathanophas, V. Comparing the effects of website quality on customer initial purchase and continued purchase at e-commerce websites. *Behav. Inf. Technol.* **2008**, *27*, 3–16.

41. Hu, D.J.; Hall, R.; Attenberg, J. Style in the long tail: Discovering unique interests with latent variable models in large scale social e-commerce. In Proceedings of the 20th ACM SIGKDD International Conference on Knowledge Discovery and Data Mining, New York, NY, USA, 24–27 August 2014; pp. 1640–1649.

42. Wu, X.; Bolivar, A. Predicting the conversion probability for items on C2C ecommerce sites. In Proceedings of the 18th ACM Conference on Information and Knowledge Management, Hong Kong, China, 2–6 November 2009; pp. 1377–1386.

43. Li, H.; Kannan, P.K. Attributing conversions in a multichannel online marketing environment: An empirical model and a field experiment. *J. Mark. Res.* **2014**, *51*, 40–56.

44. Ghose, A.; Yang, S. An empirical analysis of search engine advertising: Sponsored search in electronic markets. *Manag. Sci.* **2009**, *55*, 1605–1622.

45. Rutz, O.J.; Bucklin, R.E. *A Model of Individual Keyword Performance in Paid Search Advertising*; Yale University and University of California: Rochester, NY, USA, 2007.

46. LaBerge, D.; Samuels, S.J. Toward a theory of automatic information processing in reading. *Cogn. Psychol.* **1974**, *6*, 293–323.

47. Miller, G.A.; Galanter, E.; Pribram, K.H. *Plans and the Structure of Behavior*; Adfo Books: Amsterdam, The Netherlands, 2013.

48. Straub, D.; Loch, K.; Evaristo, R.; Karahanna, E.; Srite, M. Toward a theory-based measurement of culture. *J. Glob. Inf. Manag.* **2002**, *10*, 13–23.

49. Alcántara-Pilar, J.M.; Blanco-Encomienda, F.J.; Armenski, T.; Del Barrio-García, S. The antecedent role of online satisfaction, perceived risk online, and perceived website usability on the affect towards travel destinations. *J. Destin. Mark. Manag.* **2018**, *9*, 20–35.

50. Gong, F.; Gage, S.J.L.; Tacata, L.A., Jr. Helpseeking behavior among Filipino Americans: A cultural analysis of face and language. *J. Community Psychol.* **2003**, *31*, 469–488.

51. Petersen, I.T.; Bates, J.E.; D'Onofrio, B.M.; Coyne, C.A.; Lansford, J.E.; Dodge, K.A.; Pettit, G.S.; Van Hulle, C.A. Language ability predicts the development of behavior problems in children. *J. Abnorm. Psychol.* **2013**, *122*, 542–557.

52. Van Vaerenbergh, Y.; Holmqvist, J. Speak my language if you want my money: Service language's influence on consumer tipping behavior. *Eur. J. Mark.* **2013**, *47*, 1276–1292.

53. Zhang, K.Z.; Zhao, S.J.; Cheung, C.; Lee, M.K. Examining the influence of online reviews on consumers' decision-making: A heuristic–systematic model. *Decis. Support Syst.* **2014**, *67*, 78–89.

54. Schindler, R.M.; Bickart, B. Perceived helpfulness of online consumer reviews: The role of message content and style. *J. Consum. Behav.* **2012**, *11*, 234–243.

55. Dienstbier, R.A. The role of emotion in moral socialization. In *Emotion Cognition and Behavior*; Izard, C., Kagan, J., Zajonc, R.B., Eds.; Cambridge University Press: New York, NY, USA, 1984; pp. 484–513.

56. Martínez-Iñigo, D.; Totterdell, P.; Alcover, C.M.; Holman, D. Emotional labour and emotional exhaustion: Interpersonal and intrapersonal mechanisms. *Work. Stress* **2007**, *21*, 30–47.

57. Lee, M.; Jeong, M.; Lee, J. Roles of negative emotions in customers' perceived helpfulness of hotel reviews on a user-generated review website: A text mining approach. *Int. J. Contemp. Hosp. Manag.* **2017**, *29*, 762–783.

58. Kim, E.; Tang, R. Rectifying failure of service: How customer perceptions of justice affect their emotional response and social media testimonial. *J. Hosp. Mark. Manag.* **2016**, *25*, 897–924.

59. Lichtenstein, S.; Slovic, P. (Eds.) *The Construction of Preference*; Cambridge University Press: New York, NY, USA, 2006.

60. Martin, L.; Sintsova, V.; Pu, P. Are influential writers more objective? An analysis of emotionality in review comments. In Proceedings of the 23rd International Conference on World Wide Web, Seoul, Korea, 7–11 April 2014; pp. 799–804.

61. Rahmani, K.; Gnoth, J.; Mather, D. A psycholinguistic view of tourists' emotional experiences. *J. Travel Res.* **2019**, *58*, 192–206.

62. Ekman, P. An argument for basic emotions. *Cogn. Emot.* **1992**, *6*, 169–200.

63. Scherer, K.R.; Shuman, V.; Fontaine, J.R.J.; Soriano, C. The GRID meets the Wheel: Assessing emotional feeling via self-report. In *Components of Emotional Meaning: A Sourcebook*; Fontaine, J.R.J., Scherer, K.R., Soriano, C., Eds.; Oxford University Press: Oxford, UK, 2013; pp. 281–298.

64. Fredrickson, B.L.; Tugade, M.M.; Waugh, C.E.; Larkin, G.R. What good are positive emotions in crisis? A prospective study of resilience and emotions following the terrorist attacks on the United States on September 11th, 2001. *J. Personal. Soc. Psychol.* **2003**, *84*, 365.

65. Plutchik, R. The nature of emotions: Human emotions have deep evolutionary roots, a fact that may explain their complexity and provide tools for clinical practice. *Am. Sci.* **2001**, *89*, 344–350.

66. Gallois, C.; Giles, H. Communication Accommodation Theory. In *The International Encyclopedia of Language and Social Interaction*; John Wiley & Sons: Boston, MA, USA, 2015; pp. 159–176.

67. Dragojevic, M.; Gasiorek, J.; Giles, H. Communication accommodation theory. In *Encyclopedia of Interpersonal Communication*; Berger, C.R., Roloff, M.L., Eds.; Blackwell/Wiley: Hoboken, NJ, USA, 2016; Volume 1, pp. 176–196.

68. Giles, H.; Willemyns, M.; Gallois, C.; Anderson, M.C. Accommodating a new frontier: The context of law enforcement. In *Social Communication*; Fiedler, K., Ed.; Psychology Press: New York, NY, USA, 2007; pp. 129–162.

69. Fayard, A.L.; DeSanctis, G. Enacting language games: The development of a sense of 'we-ness' in online forums. *Inf. Syst. J.* **2010**, *20*, 383–416.

70. Gruss, R.; Kim, E.; Abrahams, A. Engaging restaurant customers on facebook: The power of belongingness appeals on social media. *J. Hosp. Tour. Res.* **2020**, *44*, 201–228.

71. Chung, C.; Pennebaker, J.W. The psychological functions of function words. *Soc. Commun.* **2007**, *1*, 343–359.

72. Liu, X.; Liu, C. A Study on the Effect of Language Style Matching of a Review and the Whole Reviews on Perceived Customer Review Helpfulness. In Proceedings of the Wuhan International Conference on e-Business, Wuhan, China, 26–28 May 2017; pp. 570–579.

73. Lu, Q.; Pan, S.; Wang, L.; Pan, J.; Wan, F.; Yang, H. A practical framework of conversion rate prediction for online display advertising. In Proceedings of the ADKDD 17, Halifax, NS, Canada, 14 August 2017; pp. 1–9.

74. Tallis, M.; Yadav, P. Reacting to variations in product demand: An application for conversion rate (cr) prediction in sponsored search. In Proceedings of the 2018 IEEE International Conference on Big Data (Big Data), Seattle, WA, USA, 10–13 December 2018; pp. 1856–1864.

75. Touropia. 25 Best Places to Visit in the USA. 2015. Available online: https://www.touropia.com/best-places-to-visit-in-usa (accessed on 3 November 2018).

76. Pennebaker, J.W.; Boyd, R.L.; Jordan, K.; Blackburn, K. *Development and Psychometric Properties of LIWC-2015*; University of Texas at Austin: Austin, TX, USA, 2015.

77. Gonzales, A.L.; Hancock, J.T.; Pennebaker, J. Language style matching as a predictor of social dynamics in small groups. *Commun. Res.* **2010**, *37*, 3–19.

78. Mohammad, S.; Turney, P.D. Crowdsourcing a word-emotion association lexicon. *Comput. Intell.* **2013**, *29*, 436–465.

79. Cribari-Neto, F.; Zeileis, A. Beta regression in R. *J. Stat. Softw.* **2010**, *34*, 1–24.

80. Radojevic, T.; Stanisic, N.; Stanic, N. Inside the rating scores: A multilevel analysis of the factors influencing customer satisfaction in the hotel industry. *Cornell Hosp. Q.* **2017**, *58*, 134–164.

81. Vuust, P.; Frith, C.D. Anticipation is the key to understanding music and the effects of music on emotion. *Behav. Brain Sci.* **2008**, *31*, 599–600.

82. Chang, K.C. Examining the effect of tour guide performance, tourist trust, tourist satisfaction, and flow experience on tourists' shopping behavior. *Asia Pac. J. Tour. Res.* **2014**, *19*, 219–247.

83. Kahneman, D.; Tversky, A. Prospect theory: An analysis of decision under risk. In *Handbook of the Fundamentals of Financial Decision Making: Part I*; World Scientific: Singapore, 2013; pp. 99–127.

84. Reisenzein, R. Exploring the strength of association between the components of emotion syndromes: The case of surprise. *Cogn. Emot.* **2000**, *14*, 1–38.

85. Lam, W.; Chen, Z. When I put on my service mask: Determinants and outcomes of emotional labor among hotel service providers according to affective event theory. *Int. J. Hosp. Manag.* **2012**, *31*, 3–11.

CHAPTER 5

Investigating Multiple Devices Used in the Hotel Reservation Process

Chieh-Heng Ko

Department of Hospitality Management, College of Tourism and Hospitality, Da-Yeh University, Taiwan.

ABSTRACT

With the growing ownership of multiple technology devices, and the contribution of mobile travel bookings to the overall travel market, it is critical to investigate the hotel searching and booking process for different device users. This research investigates four categories of device users via a survey with 383 respondents, in the context of search behaviour and information sources used. The results reveal that search engines and family and friends are the most frequently used information sources while the personal computer (PC) is the most used device for both searching and booking. However, there is a significant difference in how these device users engage with information sources, specifically online travel agents (OTAs) and search engines. Furthermore, device users favor one device and are unlikely to switch devices during the search process.

Keywords: *Hotel Reservation, Smartphone, Multi Devices, Channel Management*

INTRODUCTION

With the increasing ownership of multiple devices, and the expansion of smartphone and tablet ownership among the travel population, the assumption that online travel planning was performed on a personal computer or laptop may no longer be justified [1]. More recently, Google and Ipsos MediaCT [2] reported travel planning was increasingly performed on multiple screens, and activities started on one device could be transferred, repeated or completed on another screen.

The proliferation of smartphones and tablets now extends when and where customers engage with content. Heggestuen [3] stated that 22% of the global population now own smartphones, 20% own PCs (desktops and laptops), and 6% own tablets. Consumers select the combination of devices that best meets their needs and wants and increasingly smartphones are the device of choice for consumers, while tablets are gradually replacing traditional PCs.

Meanwhile, there has been a dramatic increase in information and booking channels available for customers [4]. Hotel customers use an extensive range of information through various channels such as search engines, comparison websites, supplier sites, and online travel agents (OTAs). An OTA, such as Expedia.com or Booking.com specializes in offering planning sources and booking capabilities from suppliers such as airlines, hotels and cruise companies who may also have their own sites, referred to as supplier sites [5]. Though research has been conducted on these channels and has clearly identified the most used information sources, they tended to focus specifically on travelers and destinations [6], and there is little investigation of the specific hotel booking context that often entails a lengthy, complex booking process [7]. Google and Ipsos MediaCT [2] also reported that travelers planned journeys in micro-increments and switched between devices during the booking process.

Given the accelerating adoption of smartphones and tablets, the growing ownership of multiple devices, the contribution of mobile travel bookings to the overall travel market, and the reported different behaviors between smartphone and tablet users, it is imperative to investigate the hotel booking process for different device users. By examining the devices and information channels, this study will contribute not only to the literature but also to practice. The main contribution to the literature will be in examining the booking process and information channel behaviors for various device users. Despite the growing importance of multiple device use, there has been limited, academic or empirical research, especially at the critical stages of information search and booking. Related studies examined some aspects of device usage in travel but failed to investigate the synergies between various devices and emerging information channels. Thus, this research aims to fill the gap and investigate the range of multi-use devices with the information sources and booking processes used. It contributes to our understanding of the information search behavior for a range of device users, not just the solitary examination of mobile use. Thus it includes PC users, smartphone users, tablet users, and traditional landline phone users. This research will also contribute to managerial practice in a number of ways, for example, to inform the design of content for specific devices and promote responsive websites for consumers. It further answers a call by previous researchers [8] that further research on devices "should extend beyond the focus on functionalities... the dialectic worldview suggests that the opposite side of the phenomenon (i.e. the non-use of smartphones) is also critical for a comprehensive understanding of the phenomenon" (p. 25).

Eriksson [9] identify and categorize segments of mobile users by ownership, frequency or usage. However, in our research we use the device/s to categorize users in order to give a wider perspective of all commonly used devices and ensure that mobile and fixed devices are therefore included as information search still depends on both online and offline modes. Fesenmaier, Xiang, Pan, and Law [10] have identified the five most frequently used information sources, search engines,

OTAs, suppliers' sites, review sites, and friends and family and these channels will be examined here. The over-arching research question is, Are there significant differences in the use of devices in information searching and in the hotel booking process? In particular, three sub-questions will be addressed in this study:

1) Do device users use information sources differently?
2) When we compare PC users against other device users, do they use information sources differently?
3) When comparing PC users against other device users, do they use these devices differently?

LITERATURE REVIEW

Information Sources and Multiple Devices

Information sources are composed of internal and external sources [11]. Internal sources are dependent on personal experiences and knowledge and external sources tend to be commercially based and market-dominated. The Internet is now the most important external source of information for travel planning and hotel booking [10]. Customers search and consult information sources prior to booking accommodation more frequently than other travel related products [6]. Fesenmaier et al. [10] rank travel-related websites in the following order in terms of sources of information, that is, general search engines, suppliers' sites, OTAs, friends and family, review sites, destination sites, general travel sites, travel search engines, travel guidebook sites, community sites, newspaper/magazine sites, consumer content generates sites, and social networking sites. Verma, Stock, and McCarthy [12] state that travellers use different websites during different stages, with search engines more important at the beginning of information search, while review sites, suppliers' and OTA sites are essential during the comparing and considering stage. Suppliers and OTA sites are more important at the booking stage. Anderson [13] reports that, among suppliers' site bookers, 75% have previously visited OTAs and 83% visited search engine sites before booking. Google dominates the search engine market with 92.8% of the European market [14]. Though the search engines are not information sources as such, they are tools for finding information and thus play a mediating role for consumers in the search process.

Multiple Devices and Booking

These multiple devices are characterized by certain features and functions. The PC (desktop and laptop) is less portable but has a physical keyboard and more storage capacity. It is supported by a range of business software that is compatible with certain accepted protocols and standards. The tablet format is specifically designed for graphic display and ease of reading, though the virtual keyboard uses up half the display, resulting in less functionality when typing. The smartphone is portable, versatile and accessible virtually anywhere. A smartphone combines cellular phone, Internet access, e-mail, music and movie player, camera and camcorder, GPS navigation system and several built-in applications, with versions for iPhone, Android, BlackBerry and Windows Phone [2]. Smartphones and tablets are used more for leisure purposes and PCs (desktop and laptops) are more task or work based. The traditional landline phone has limited capacity to transmit and store voice messages whereas laptops, tablets, and smartphones are computing devices with distinct benefits and disadvantages.

Hotel booking behavior patterns also vary widely between devices and activities. Google and Ipsos Media CT [2] report that, during the online research process, 88% of travel search is performed on PCs/tablet, compared to 27% smartphone. Hotel bookings are mostly completed on PCs/tablets (81%) in preference to smartphones (21%) with post purchase sharing divided between PCs/tablets (57%) and smartphones (50%). Furthermore, both tablets and smartphones have unique functions in the travel purchasing process [2]. Walsh [15] reports that even though tablet users also own smartphones, they tend to use tablets to select destinations, for shopping and booking. Google and Ipsos Media CT [2] reported smartphone sales tend to be smaller in value or simpler transactions, involving last-minute hotel stays or car rental, while tablet sales tend to be larger transactions involving longer trips.

Mobile and Travel-Specific Technologies

Increasingly, mobile technology adoption is characterized by the use of "smartphones" and "tablets". Smartphones and tablets support ubiquitous computing, contextual computing, pervasive computing, ubiquitous connectivity to the Internet, and integration of various sensors [16]. Smartphones have changed tourist behaviors, information needs, decision making, and experience documenting and sharing [16]. The portable nature of smartphones and tablets have prompted researchers to investigate both pre-trip and during trip traveler behaviors [9]. The perceived benefits of using mobile technology have been explored by several researchers [17] and include ubiquity, convenience, immediacy, personalization, information access, pragmatism, money savings, innovation, planning capacity, and entertainment. Similarly, investigation of the perceived barriers to use mobile technology during the trip have been widely examined and focus on high entry costs, usage costs, security issues, poor technology capability, and lack of relevant services [9].

Other researchers have addressed some behavioral characteristics and different contexts in the use of mobile technology devices. For example, Peres, Correia, and Moital [18] investigated intention to use and habitual use and MacKay and Vogt (2012) have explored specific contexts such as examining the "spillover" theory to explain the adoption of mobile technology devices from everyday life and use. Most researchers highlight the next wave of innovation will come from the accelerating growth of applications and the capacity of mobile technology [19]. Though these studies provide insights into device user behavior, they fail to examine specific device use for explicit tasks in the hotel booking process.

Segmenting the Device Market

Okazaki et al. [20] identified segments of mobile user as; savvies, planners, opportunists, and low-techs. These segments differ in their mobile usage patterns, and perceived benefits of mobile internet usage. Alternatively, MacKay and Vogt [21] used IT equipment ownership and frequency of Internet use to categorize respondents. Eriksson (2014) focused on activities conducted on mobile devices and identified five segments; allrounders, bookers, checkers, info-seekers, and non-users. PCs remain highly relevant to all travel activities, including search, reserve, pay, change/cancel, check-in, and reflect. Yet, smartphones and tablets are increasingly used for these activities, such as change/cancel, check-in [9]. Given the accelerating adoption of mobile devices, and the "spillover" effect of IT use, more research is needed in identifying behavioral aspects of multiple devices users, including mobile service users [9].

The hotel booking process has become even more complex, including multiple points of contact while consumers revert to a wide and diverse range of information sources on a variety of devices, which makes the context of hotels a unique phenomenon worthy of study. In our research, we use the device/s to segment the market and users in order to provide a specific investigation of the commonly used devices in the hotel booking process. Explicitly, Wang et al. [19] recommend future research should focus on the influence of mobile devices on travel planning. Furthermore, Lamsfus et al., [16] argued that the widely accepted and researched technology acceptance model (TAM) could be enhanced by considering the importance of incorporating the specificity of technology characteristics and usage contexts.

METHODOLOGY

The goal of this study is to identify the relationships between multiple device users, information searching and the final hotel booking. The research design is predominately quantitative in this investigation. The use of multiple devices in hotel booking and information searching is the context under examination and this goal can be examined best through a survey method [22]. Thus this study employed a survey instrument to investigate the range of devices used in the information searching and booking stages of the hotel room. The devices investigated in this study are PCs (laptop and desktop), smartphones, tablets, and traditional phones. The information sources, as identified by previous researchers are; search engines, OTAs, suppliers' sites, review sites, and friends and family.

Research Instrument

Whittaker [8], Walsh [15] have variously identified the several devices and information sources used in the buying process. From this established research, we developed a three-part, structured questionnaire for this study. In the first part, the respondents were asked to refer to their most recent hotel reservation and identify the devices used to search and the device used to make the final booking. Respondents indicated their various use of devices in four close-ended, dichotomous format questions. For the device used in the final booking, respondents selected only one of the four devices. In the second part, respondents indicated which five information sources were used as sources in their pre-trip planning by responding to five close-ended, dichotomous format questions.

Instrument Administration

A convenience, purposive sample was drawn from within Switzerland as there are identifiable respondents that match the required profile. The data collection was conducted from October 2017 till January 2018 and administered by email. The sample frame included email contacts from our own institution and known multi-device users who had recently participated in the hotel booking process. After recruitment of this initial set of participants, a snowball technique was used where the initial seed respondents were asked to refer the survey by email to others who share the same multi-device use, and specifically to give a more diverse variety of respondents [23]. All instructions were included in the questionnaire. Snowball sampling is a non-probability sampling technique and used in hard to reach populations, such as multi-device users who are engaged in a specific activity, in this case booking a hotel room [24].

There were 403 returned questionnaires with 383 usable results. Based on our over-arching research question and three main research questions postulated, the data was analyzed using descriptive statistics, chi-square tests, and multinomial logit regression. The demographic data and frequencies are presented in percentages in tables. Chi-square is used to investigate the significant differences between device users and information sources. Multinomial logit regression allows the comparison between the reference group (the PC users) and other categories (tablet users, smartphone users, and phone users), individually. Multinomial logit regression is used to compare device users' information sources and to compare the multiple uses of devices. The results are presented in the tables below.

RESULTS

Eriksson [9], MacKay and Vogt [21] and Okazaki et al. [20] used IT equipment ownership and frequency of Internet use to categorize respondents. Here, the device used to make the hotel booking is used to categorize respondents into four segments, specifically, PCs users, tablet users, smartphone users, and (traditional) phone users.

As shown in Table 1, respondents use a wide range of channels as information sources for hotel pre-purchase decisions. Search engines were used by 64% of respondents, representing the information source with the highest usage. This is followed by family and friends (58%), suppliers' sites (54%), OTAs (45%), and review sites (42%).

Table 2 presents the usage of information sources by multiple device users. Each row is one of the five information sources. Each column represents a category of device users. For example, general search engines are used by 68% of PC users, 59% of tablet users, 48% of smartphone users, and 52% of phone users. Also, within the PC user group, 68% use general search engines, 58% use family and friends, 54% use suppliers' sites, 49% OTA sites, and 44% review sites.

Table 2 indicates different behaviors among device users. Smartphone users are most likely to consult family and friends as sources of information, as are the traditional phone users. Tablet users, by contrast, are most likely to consult OTAs and search engines compared to other sources. To confirm if these differences are statistically significant, chi-square tests have been conducted.

Table 3 shows the results from the chi-square tests. It is evident that from the information source perspective, that there is a significant difference between device users in their use of general search engines and OTAs.

Table 1. *Information sources used.*

Information sources	All
General search engine	64%
Family and friends	58%
Suppliers' sites	54%
OTAs	45%
Review sites	42%

Table 2. *Information sources by category of device users.*

Information sources	PC users	Tablet users	Smartphone users	Phone users
General search engines	68%	59%	48%	52%
Family and friends	58%	45%	64%	62%
Suppliers' sites	54%	41%	52%	58%
OTAs	49%	59%	20%	25%
Review sites	44%	45%	28%	33%

Table 3. *Chi-square test results e comparing device users' information sources.*

Information sources	Chi square value[a]
General search engine	7.85***
Family and friends	2.06 (n.s.)
Suppliers' sites	1.83 (n.s.)
OTAs	18.76***
Review sites	4.68 (n.s.)

***Significant at $p < 0.05$ level, n.s. not significant. [a]Chi square critical value: 7.815.

Multinomial logit regression was applied to investigate the differences in the use of information sources. The first multinomial logit regression compares three categories of device users (tablet, smartphone, and phone) with PC users, in terms of how they use information sources. As presented in Table 4, the coefficients for the intercept and OTAs are significant. Negative coefficients can be interpreted as less likely to occur, while positive coefficients are more likely. Specifically, compared to PC users, smartphone and traditional phone users are less likely to use OTA sites.

Table 5 presents the usage of devices by device users during the search process. Each row is one of the four devices. Each column represents a group of device users. For example, the PC is used by 98% of PC users, 73% of tablet users, 64% of smartphone users, and 71% of phone users. Also, of the PC user group, 98% use PCs, 23% use tablet, 25% use smartphones, and 22% use phones. This table indicates that PC users are comparatively low users of other devices, while other users tend to employ several devices.

To test different behaviors among device users, we conducted a multinomial logit regression. The second multinomial logit regression compared the three

Table 4. *Multinomial logit results e comparing device users' information sources.*

Group	Intercept	Search engine	Family and friends	Supplier sites	OTA sites	Review sites
Tablet/PC	2.1148***	0.4884*	0.4538*	0.3517 (n.s.)	0.4337*	0.0961 (n.s.)
Smartphone/PC	1.7645***	0.3923 (n.s.)	0.1900 (n.s.)	0.1339 (n.s.)	1.1898***	0.2035 (n.s.)
Phone/PC	1.2049***	0.3819*	0.0907 (n.s.)	0.1111 (n.s.)	0.9131***	0.0923 (n.s.)

**Significant at p < 0.05 level, *Significant at p < 0.1 level, n.s. not significant.

Table 5. *Device used in the search process by device users.*

Device	PC users	Tablet users	Smartphone users	Phone users
PC	98%	73%	64%	71%
Tablet	23%	64%	16%	21%
Smartphone	25%	41%	60%	12%
Phone	22%	9%	28%	60%

Table 6. *Multinomial logit results e comparing the use of devices.*

Group	Intercept	PC	Tablet	Smartphone	Phone
Tablet/PC	0.8648***	2.5711***	1.7198***	0.2730 (n.s.)	1.3398***
Smartphone/PC	0.5090 (n.s.)	2.7654***	0.7262*	1.2325***	0.5077*
Phone/PC	0.5610*	3.0523***	0.1776 (n.s.)	1.4272***	1.9684***

**Significant at p < 0.05 level, *Significant at p < 0.1 level, n.s. not significant.

groups of device users with PC users on their use of different devices in the search process. The results from the second multinomial logit regression are presented in Table 6. This table indicates that customers have a preferred device to search. Tablet users prefer their tablets to search while smart-phone and phone users remaining loyal to their phones. It also shows that compared to PC users, all three other groups of users are less likely to use PCs to search, and more likely to use their preferred devices to search. Furthermore, compared to PC users, tablet users are less likely to use their phones, while traditional phone users are less likely to use smartphones. Additionally, the smartphone users are less likely to use tablets and more likely to use phones, though these findings are only significant at 0.1 level.

DISCUSSION AND IMPLICATIONS

This paper investigates the range of devices used in the hotel booking process, the information sources used by device users and compares behaviors among device users.

As shown in Table 2, although PCs remain the most used device in the search process, tablets, smartphones and phones also are used by about one-quarter of respondents. This confirms that when searching for hotel accommodation, travelers do adopt a multi-device approach. Nonetheless, PCs remain highly relevant in the search process, as reported by Eriksson [9] and Google and Ipsos MediaCT [2]. Respondents return to their PCs (74%) and traditional phones to make the final hotel booking. In this study, 13% of travellers used phones to book hotel rooms, similar to results reported by Schegg et al. [25]. These findings confirm the importance of accessible content through multiple devices, as well as having the appropriate staff to respond to phone enquires and bookings.

In terms of information sources used in the hotel booking context, the importance of search engines, friends and family, supplier sites, OTAs, and review sites are comparable to results from other researchers [2] [11]. It is noteworthy that friends and family remain a major influence and this traditional information source is still a key part of the booking decision. This finding supports research by Kim, Lehto, and Morrison [17] [26].

The dominance of search engines is highlighted here, as travelers consult search engines on a regular basis in their daily lives, and extend their use of search engines to conduct their hotel accommodation search, referred to as the "spillover effect" [19] [21]. The introduction of Google HotelFinder and Google Carousel may also promote the use of Google as a more detailed source of information to inform hotel bookings. OTA sites are also being extensively used as information sources. The variety of hotel selections, comparability, user-friendliness of the site and mobile-friendly content offered by OTAs may contribute to their popularity.

Table 5 shows that various device users use search engines and OTA sites differently. In Table 6, the multinomial logit results further indicate that compared to PC users, smartphone and phone users are less likely to use OTA sites. To a certain extent, compared to PC users, both tablet and phone users are less likely to use search engines. These findings indicate that investing resources to improve search engine results and OTA ranking results may satisfy only PC users, but may prove somewhat redundant for the other device users.

Table 5 and Table 6 clearly demonstrate that, for devices used in the search process, users have their preferred devices, and they are significantly less likely to use other devices. In comparison to PC users, all other device users are less likely to use PCs. This finding confirms that the assumption that all web interactions are mainly taking place between users on PCs is no longer valid [15]. Furthermore, these findings also confirm tablet and smartphone users have different behaviors [2]. Tablets and smartphones have smaller screens, can present fewer results per screen, and are more challenging for users to input data. Despite these constraints, tablet and smartphone users still prefer to conduct their hotel search on these devices.

Hotel managers need deep insights into the devices that their customers are most likely to use, ensuring relevant content is available on those devices, thus giving a consistent online experience. This study highlights that customers have different device preferences in both the search process and booking, and these preferences must be accommodated when deploying digital marketing strategies to increase visibility and bookings. It is crucial that hoteliers do not assume that PC/laptop users are their typical customers and thus design content and website information architecture based solely on desktop use. Although most reservations may come from PCs, customers tend to search on several different devices before the final booking and thus tracking users across multiple devices would provide more accurate information about the customer journey. It would also provide a seamless experience for the customer; though tracking across a variety of browsers, applications and networks remains a challenge. Whatever the device used, hotel websites and preferred channels must be "responsive", that is, able to detect the device in use and convert the website experience to the functionalities of the device. As smartphone and phone users are less likely to use OTA sites, this presents problems for hotels that have relied on OTAs and the "billboard effect" (Anderson, 2011) to generate visibility. Hotels need to be present on the channels where smartphone users are more likely to be "looking" and "comparing" before "booking". Hoteliers should also be aware of the specific barriers preventing customers from booking through smartphones and tablets.

Though mobile bookings are still relatively low compared to other channels, smartphone and tablets are used increasingly to share information. Google and Ipsos MediaCT [2] reported that customers demand download speed, design customized to device, and compatibility from mobile devices. Hoteliers need to ensure that their content and web presence 'fits' the screen size(s) of these devices to enhance the usability at any stage during the booking process. Furthermore, they must provide customized content that communicates the hotel's value proposition on mobile channels/devices/partners, particularly at the information searching stage. Given the increasing switching behavior [2], this content must be consistent across all channels and devices, to retain customers and minimize confusion. This will require vigilance and investment in content and channel management from hotel marketers.

Search engines are the most important information sources, despite not being the content owners. This magnifies the importance of search engine optimization (SEO) of the hotel's website. Search engine result pages (SERPS) are further limited in size on tablets or mobile phones. As customers become more mobile, SEO on smaller screens will present increasing challenges of visibility, already a problem for individual hotels where the big players like Booking.com and Tripadvisor, dominate search engine results. As hotel search is dominated by Google [2], this creates further obstacles for hotel marketers, as Google changes its algorithm and limits the search result presentation by including paid hotel links on the first SERP, along with a Google map marking the hotel locations. In addition, Google has developed Google Hotel Finder and Google Carousel, which further intensifies the competition for visibility. Hoteliers should manage their Google Business accounts to improve their visibility on search engines, Google Hotel Finder, Google Carousel, and Google Maps. In addition, hotels need to work with either OTAs or customer reservation systems (CRSs) to deliver real-time rates and availabilities on Google Hotel Finder.

Though a simple proposition, hotel marketers must remain aware that most information sources serve a dual purpose, providing information but also serving as booking channels [27]. It is therefore important to track the consumption path and map key customer touch points in order to determine which channels are critical and convert information seekers to hotel bookers. This means that hotels must invest in more sophisticated customer tracking by using 'cookies' or agencies that will gather this critical information and inform channel investment. As customers migrate and switch to different channels and devices, it is critical to remain in their consideration set at the information seeking stage.

CONCLUSIONS

This research contributes to the existing literature by linking the devices used in the hotel search process with information sources and channels. Device users have their preferred devices and are less likely to use other devices. Furthermore, there is a significant difference in the way device users use OTAs and search engines. The results indicate that hoteliers should implement a multi-channel distribution management system across devices, taking into account different devices and the information criteria and formats that could be used to reach customers.

Our results confirm that market-dominated sources, which are the search engines and OTAs, have a dominant position in the marketing of hotels. Hotel marketers need to effectively manage both easily managed channels, such as their own site, and more complex channels, such as OTAs and review sites. Given that friends and family continue to be an important source of information for hotel bookings, it remains critical to have effective customer relationship management incentives for guests to promote the hotel in a positive manner. Hotel marketers should provide accurate and appealing information, across different channels, to facilitate customers' decision making. In addition, hoteliers should leverage their brand sites to have direct contact with potential customers.

There were several limitations of this study. First, a convenience, Swiss-based, partly student sample, makes generalization to a wider population limited and the bias inherent in the sampling approach prevents inference to the general population. Secondly, the survey was based upon a recalled hotel booking, which differs from an actual hotel booking, where there is greater risk involved and more scrutiny given to booking requirements and pre-requisites. Nonetheless, it provides an insight into the changing role of channels and the multiple uses of devices for hotel room bookings.

Future research should explore the customer's level of attachment to their preferred devices and the specific nature of the "spillover effect" from everyday life to travel and particularly hotel bookings [19] [21]. Further research is also needed to investigate and explain why different device users have different preferences in the use for their devices, and use search engines differently. Though Eriksson [9] identified barriers to use mobile technology during trips, this does not explain the lack of mobile hotel bookings, with the exception of "same day" reservations. Investigation to identify these specific barriers to mobile bookings would provide insights for all information providers and booking channel operators. OTAs are more advanced in developing applications (apps), yet smartphone users in this study prefer other sources than OTAs and their apps. This is critical information for hotel marketers who must decide where to invest their marketing budget, develop apps and invest in smartphone friendly platforms and strategic partners.

In addition, this research focuses on hotel bookers' search behavior. Future research should investigate hoteliers' actual channel management practices and identify if alignment exists between hotel booking behavior and hoteliers' channel management. Lastly, previous researchers argue that Technology Acceptance Model is limited in explaining technology adoption behavior, and advocate research that could focus on monitoring the actual behavior [16], and investigate the barriers to use and carefully consider other ways to segment users [9]. This research partially addresses these issues as we investigate device users and differentiate information sources from the booking process.

REFERENCES

1. Walsh, C.S. (2017) Mobile to Represent over One Quarter of U.S. Online Travel Market by 2018. http://www.phocuswright.com/research_updates/mobile-to-represent-over-one-quarter-of-us-online-travel-market-by-2018
2. Google and Ipsos MediaCT (2014) The 2014 Traveler's Road to Deci-sion. https://www.thinkwithgoogle.com/consumer-insights/2014-travelers-road-to-decision/
3. Heg-gestuen, J. (2013) One in Every 5 People in the World Own a Smartphone, One in Every 17 Own a Tablet. Business Insider. https://www.businessinsider.com.au/smartphone-and-tablet-penetration-2013-10
4. Murphy, H. and Chen, M.M. (2014) Online Information Sources Used in Hotel Bookings: Examining Relevance and Recall. *Journal of Travel Research*, **55**, 523-536. https://doi.org/10.1177/0047287514559033
5. Benckendorff, P.J., Sheldon, P.J. and Fesenmaier, D.R. (2014) Social Media and Tourism. In: *Tourism Information Technology*, 2nd Edition, 120-147. https://doi.org/10.1079/9781780641850.0120
6. Jun, S.H. and Vogt, C.A. (2013) Travel Information Processing Applying a Dual-Process Model. *Annals of Tourism Research*, **40**, 191-212. https://doi.org/10.1016/j.annals.2012.09.001
7. Filieri, R. and McLeay, F. (2014) E-WOM and Accommodation an Analysis of the Factors That Influence Travelers' Adoption of Information from Online Reviews. *Journal of Travel Research*, **53**, 44-57. https://doi.org/10.1177/0047287513481274
8. Wang, D., Xiang, Z. and Fesenmaier, D.R. (2014) Adapting to the Mobile World: A Model of Smartphone Use. *Annals of Tourism Research*, **48**, 11-26. https://doi.org/10.1016/j.annals.2014.04.008
9. Eriksson, N. (2014) User Categories of Mobile Travel Services. *Journal of Hospitality and Tourism Technology*, **5**, 17-30. https://doi.org/10.1108/JHTT-10-2012-0028
10. Fesenmaier, D.R., Xiang, Z., Pan, B. and Law, R. (2011) A Framework of Search Engine Use for Travel Planning. *Journal of Travel Research*, **50**, 587-601. https://doi.org/10.1177/0047287510385466
11. Jacobsen, J.K.S. and Munar, A.M. (2012) Tourist Information Search and Destination Choice in a Digital Age. *Tourism Management Perspectives*, **1**, 39-47. https://doi.org/10.1016/j.tmp.2011.12.005
12. Verma, R., Stock, D. and McCarthy, L (2012) Customer Preferences for Online, Social Media, and Mobile Innovations in the Hospitality Industry. *Cornell Hospitality Quarterly*, **53**, 183-186. https://doi.org/10.1177/1938965512445161

13. Anderson, C.K. (2011) Search, OTAs, and Online Booking: An Expanded Analysis of the Billboard Effect. *Cornell Hospitality Report*, **11**, 4-10.
14. Rosoff, M. (2014) Here's How Dominant Google Is in Europe. https://www.businessinsider.com/heres-how-dominant-google-is-in-europe-2014-11
15. Walsh, C.S. (2016) Mobile Travel Strategy Shakeup Ahead as Tablet Adoption Nears 50%. http://www.phocuswright.com/research_updates/mobile-travel-strategy-shakeup-ahead-as-tablet-adoption-nears-50s
16. Lamsfus, C., Wang, D., Alzua-Sorzabal, A. and Xiang, Z. (2014) Going Mobile Defining Context for On-the-Go Travelers. *Journal of Travel Research*, **54**, 691-701.
17. Kim, D.Y., Park, J. and Morrison, A.M. (2008) A Model of Traveller Acceptance of Mobile Technology. *International Journal of Tourism Research*, **10**, 393-407. https://doi.org/10.1002/jtr.669
18. Peres, R., Correia, A. and Moital, M. (2011) The Indicators of Intention to Adopt Mobile Electronic Tourist Guides. *Journal of Hospitality and Tourism Technology*, **2**, 120-138. https://doi.org/10.1108/17579881111154236
19. Wang, D., Park, S. and Fesenmaier, D.R. (2012) The Role of Smartphones in Mediating the Touristic Experience. *Journal of Travel Research, 51*, 371-387. https://doi.org/10.1177/0047287511426341
20. Okazaki, S., Campo, S., Andreu, L. and Romero, J. (2014) A Latent Class Analysis of Spanish Travelers' Mobile Internet Usage in Travel Planning and Execution. *Cornell Hospitality Quarterly, 56*, 191-201.
21. MacKay, K. and Vogt, C. (2012) Information Technology in Everyday and Vacation Contexts. *Annals of Tourism Research*, **39**, 1380-1401. https://doi.org/10.1016/j.annals.2012.02.001
22. Collis, J. and Hussey, R. (2009) Business Research: A Practical Guide for Undergraduate and Postgraduate Students. 3rd Edition, Palgrave Macmillan, Basingstoke.
23. Chang, H.H. and Chen, S.W. (2008) The Impact of Online Store Environment Cues on Purchase Intention: Trust and Perceived Risk as a Mediator. *Online Information Review*, **32**, 818-841. https://doi.org/10.1108/14684520810923953
24. Gabor, M.R. (2007) Types of Non-Probabilistic Sampling Used in Marketing Research, Snowball Sampling. *Management & Marketing (Bucharest)*, **3**, 80-90.
25. Schegg, R., Stangl, B., Fux, M. and Inversini, A. (2013) Distribution Channels and Management in the Swiss Hotel Sector. Springer, Heidelberg Berlin, 554-565. https://doi.org/10.1007/978-3-642-36309-2_47
26. Litvin, S.W., Goldsmith, R.E. and Pan, B. (2008) Electronic Word-of-Mouth in Hospitality and Tourism Management. *Tourism Management*, **29**, 458-468. https://doi.org/10.1016/j.tourman.2007.05.011
27. O'Connor, P. and Frew, A.J. (2002) The Future of Hotel Electronic Distribution: Expert and Industry Perspectives. *The Cornell Hotel and Restaurant Administration Quarterly*, **43**, 33-45. https://doi.org/10.1016/S0010-8804(02)80016-7

CHAPTER 6

Hotel Overbooking and Cooperation with Third-Party Websites

Yufeng Dong and Liuyi Ling

School of Management, University of Science & Technology of China, Jinzhai Road 96, Hefei 230026, China

ABSTRACT

Hotels cooperate with third-party websites to enhance their competitive position and attain sustainable development in the era of e-commerce. Furthermore, hotel managers overbook to hedge against last-minute cancellations and customer no-shows. This paper discusses pricing and overbooking strategies of a hotel in the context of cooperation with multiple third-party websites and analyzes how these strategies influence the cooperation process. The increase in profits resulting from the overbooking strategy is also examined. A model of a Stackelberg game between the hotel and third-party websites and a Nash game among the third-party websites are developed to analyze the process. Results indicate that the compensation coefficient has a slight influence on hotel pricing strategy, but causes a sharp decrease in overbooking level. As the hotel demands to lessen the probability of denying under higher compensation rate, the third-party websites would exert less sales effort to reduce the demand of online customers. Results also show that under a given market demand, hotel effort only serves to redistribute market shares among the hotel and third-party websites, without influencing hotel pricing and overbooking decisions. Specifically, the market shares of the third-party websites decrease in the effort level of the hotel resulting from an increase in the hotel market share. Finally, in the numerical example where one hotel and two websites are analyzed, hotel overbooking strategy improves hotel profit by 4.20%, whereas profit improvements for Websites 1 and 2 are as high as 5.26% and 5.21%, respectively. Managerial implications of the study are also provided.

Keywords: *pricing; overbooking; online distribution; hotel; third-party website*

INTRODUCTION

In the hospitality industry, some customers may cancel their reservations before the target date or fail to show up without prior notification [1,2]. Unlike tangible goods, hotel rooms are perishable [3,4,5]; that is, when a reservation is suddenly cancelled, it is difficult to obtain a customer to occupy the hotel room in time. Consequently, hoteliers lose income if the hotel room becomes unoccupied. This distinguishing characteristic results in a zero salvage value to hotel rooms, because unoccupied rooms do not generate any revenue for hoteliers and cannot be reflected in the inventory for future use [6,7]. On the other hand, managing hotel rooms incurs a high fixed cost but a relatively low variable cost, leading to considerable marginal profits for hoteliers [7,8]. By contrast, hotels suffer heavy revenue loss from last-minute cancellations and customer no-shows.

Hotels reduce this loss by adopting overbooking strategy to ensure full room occupancy and to maintain a high occupancy rate [9,10,11]. Overbooking is defined as selling more rooms than hotel capacity, which is performed when a certain number of booked customers are anticipated to cancel or not to show up [12]. As a functional component of revenue management application, overbooking generates as high as 20% of the total revenue opportunity for hotels [13,14].

The occupancy rates of hotel rooms will increase because of overbooking [15]. However, if the number of customers with last-minute cancellations and no-shows is extremely small, the number of arrivals may exceed hotel capacity. When hotels cannot accommodate all arrivals at a target date, they will suffer losses because of compensation for the inconvenience of denied customers, loss of goodwill, and operating constraints [14,16]. Hence, determining the balance between the benefits and harm in implementing overbooking strategy is important. This study aims to address this issue.

Grönroos [17] stresses the significance of service marketing in the marketing area and gives a cutting-edge interpretation on the service marketing theory. Due to the changes in the world economy and business practice, services dominate the modern economies of the world, and Zeithaml *et al.* [18] suggest that mangers should consider service marketing as a competitive business imperative. In recent decades, the online distribution channel becomes prevalent and indispensable in the promotion of goods and services in the service industry [19,20,21,22]. Hotels facing intense competition will certainly embrace prevalent online booking requirements. In the process, they cooperate with third-party websites, such as Orbitz, Expedia, and eLong, to broaden their market demand. Specially, many hotels are unknown to the public and turn to well-known third-party websites to promote room selling. These third-party websites enable customers to search for different information on their trips and aid them in choosing the most suitable goods or services. Third-party websites also allow control for customers in the selection process and provide convenience. Therefore, hotels should cooperate with third-party websites to widen the market and enhance their competitive position, thereby ensuring their sustainable development [23,24].

Many studies have been conducted on hotel overbooking strategy [25,26] or cooperation between hotels and third-party intermediaries [27,28,29,30]. The present paper develops a model to explore hotel pricing and overbooking strategies in the context of the cooperation between a hotel and multiple third-party websites. Hadjinicola and Panayi [31] observe that overbooking at the hotel level generates more cost savings than at each tour operator level when the hotel cooperates with multiple tour-operators. Thus, the present paper considers hotel room capacity as a whole, and formulates a single overbooking strategy for the hotel instead of multiple overbooking strategies for each third-party website separately. A Stackelberg game model is developed to explore the cooperation process between the hotel and third-party websites, while a Nash game is built among multiple third-party websites to describe their competitiveness on limited hotel rooms. The profit improvement for the hotel and third-party websites by overbooking strategy is then analyzed. This study seeks to answer the following questions: (1) What are the equilibrium decisions on hotel pricing and overbooking strategies and the effort level for the third-party websites? (2) What are the effects of compensation paid to a denied customer, demand fluctuation, hotel effort, and room capacity on optimal decisions? (3) How does the overbooking strategy of the hotel influence the cooperation process with the third-party websites? (4) How much profit improvement does a hotel overbooking strategy bring to the hotel and third-party websites?

Results presented in this paper are constructive. First, the compensation coefficient is observed to have a slight effect on optimal room rate, but causes a sharp decrease in the overbooking level because the hotel anticipates reducing the risk of over-sale. On the other hand, along with the increase in compensation coefficient, the third-party websites exert less effort in room sales to attract fewer customers as the hotel demands to lessen the probability of denying. Second, given the market demand, hotel effort will affect market shares of the hotel and cooperative third-party websites, but not hotel pricing and overbooking strategies. Specifically, the market shares of the third-party websites decrease in hotel effort level because of an increase in the market share of the hotel. Third, overbooking strategy brings profit increases of 5.26% and 5.21% for Websites 1 and 2, respectively, in the numerical example, but only 4.20% for the hotel. Therefore, third-party websites benefit more from the overbooking policy than the policy implementer, namely, the hotel. However, third-party websites that exert more effort to make sales do not always benefit more from the overbooking strategy.

The rest of paper is structured as follows: Section 2 reviews previous literature on the overbooking strategy in hotels and their cooperation with third parties, and addresses the research gap between previous studies and this paper. Section 3 describes the problem of hotel overbooking and cooperation with multiple third-party websites. A mathematical model is built and equilibrium solutions are derived. In Section 4, a numerical study is conducted to illustrate the effects of parameters on optimal decisions and profits. Section 5 explores how the overbooking strategy improves profits. Finally, Section 6 concludes this paper, provides some managerial implications, and highlights directions for future research.

LITERATURE REVIEW

Hotel Overbooking Strategy

Overbooking has long been a crucial lever for hotel revenue management [16,32,33,34]. Rothstein [35] is the first to develop a mathematical model to determine hotel overbooking level, and he suggests that hotel managers set overbooking limits at various decision points prior to the target date and optimize the overbooking problem by adjusting these limits. Ivanov [36] analyzes how optimal overbooking limits will change when a new booking request is received for a specific date, given the guaranteed and nonguaranteed reservations rate, which provides hotel managers with a simple operable methodology to control their room inventory when the guaranteed/nonguaranteed bookings ratio changes. Liberman and Yechiali [37] establish optimal overbooking level by maximizing the net profit of the hotel manager. In their paper, overbooking decisions are formulated by comparing the inventory level of confirmed reservations and the number of new requests. Toh [38] proposes a model that helps hotel managers to establish optimal booking levels systematically by balancing the opportunity cost of empty rooms with the adverse consequences of over selling. Toh and Dekay [39] also emphasize the importance of that balance in setting customer service levels to solve hotel overbooking problems. Koide and Ishii [40] maximize expected total sales by allowing customers paying the regular rate to make cancellations but not those with discounted rates. Therefore, the expected total sale is proved to be unimodal on the number of overbooking, indicating that the expected total sale is concave in the number of overbooking and the unique optimal overbooking level is obtained. Talluri and Van Ryzin [41] outline overbooking as one of the most successful revenue management practices. They build static as well as dynamic overbooking models to maximize the total volume of sales by balancing the negative effects of denying service against the rewards of increased sales.

In the hotel industry, one inventory class may be used as a substitute to satisfy the demand of another, which is known as an upgrade or a downgrade. Karaesmen and van Ryzin [42] discuss the overbooking problem by considering multiple reservations and inventory classes and jointly determine overbooking levels for the reservation classes.

Unlike the previous studies mentioned above, the present study develops a mathematical model to determine optimal overbooking levels by maximizing hotel revenue considering stochastic cancellation of customers in the context of cooperation with third-party websites. A similar study is conducted by Hadjinicola and Panayi [31]. However, their paper merely states that the overbooking strategy at the hotel level generates more cost savings than at the tour operator level by the method of data analysis. Obtaining the optimal overbooking level or monitoring the cooperation process between the hotel and tour operators is not performed in their paper.

Cooperation with Third-Party Websites

Online distribution channels enhance the promotion of goods and services in the service industry [19,21,22], among which OTA is one of the most important intermediaries and serves as web supermarket in air, hotels, rental car, and cruise lines marketing [43]. Medina-Muñoz and García-Falcón [24] seek to identify the determinants of successful relationships between hotels and travel agencies and claim that for a hotel, collaborating with other entities is the most cost-effective method for extending sales and marketing effort. Ling *et al.* [44] develop a pricing model between small- and medium-sized hotels and a third-party website, considering that these hotels are not likely to run websites of their own because of high costs. Beritelli [45] presents evidence on how to choose cooperative actors in tourism destinations. Huang *et al.* [46] outline how tour operators contribute to a tourism supply chain composed of multiple hotels and travel agencies. A number of other studies explore the cooperation between service providers and third parties from the perspective of a strategic alliance but not to the individual level [28,29,30].

All these studies emphasize the important role of third parties in hotel room marketing. However, third-party websites compete severely with hotels on customer source, which causes a problem of conflict of distribution channel for hotels [47,48]. Therefore, Xu *et al.* [49] optimize room allocation between hotels and third-party websites by first setting online-exclusive rooms for third-party websites, and then allowing the hotel to decide whether to accept additional requests from the website to maximize its profit. Lee *et al.* [50] examine the hostile relationship between OTAs and hotels taking the example of Choice Hotels International and Expedia.com and suggest hotel avoid overreliance on OTAs. In our paper, the hotel and cooperative third-party websites make effort independently to encourage customers to book rooms from their own distribution channels.

The present paper analyzes the cooperation and competition relationship between the hotel and multiple third-party websites simultaneously, and explores the effect of hotel decision on that of third-party websites.

PROBLEM STATEMENT

This paper discusses the cooperation problem between one hotel and n third-party websites. To distribute its rooms online and widen its online market, the hotel cooperates with n third-party websites on room sales. Considering some customers cancel their reservations very late or just do not show up at the target date without notifying the hotel, the hotel adopts an overbooking strategy and determines its overbooking level by taking account into stochastic cancellations of customers. The hotel is examined in terms of its overbooking level and room rate, whereas third-party websites are examined in terms of their sales effort.

Cooperation between the Hotel and Third-Party Websites

A hotel with C identical rooms cooperates with n third-party websites on room booking service to improve its occupancy rate. Under this cooperation, the hotel has two types of customers: *t-customer* who books a room by phone, in person, or through the hotel's own website and *w-customer* who books a room through third-party websites. The hotel conducts price parity among all selling parties as a strategy to attract customers [27]. Price parity means that hotels charge the same room rate p per day to all customers from different distribution channels.

No booking fees are charged when making reservations. The variable cost of each occupied room is c, while the fixed cost of the hotel is F.

In this study, the agency model is applied in the cooperation between the hotel and third-party websites, in which the hotel pays a commission rate to third-party websites for each room sold [4,50,51]. The room inventory of hotels is usually not transparent to third-party websites under the agency model. In practice, the commission is usually given as a percentage of the room rate [27], that is, $\omega_i = \theta_i p$, $i = 1,2,\ldots,n$, and θ_i differs according to third-party websites.

The total demand of the hotel, including that of t-customers and w-customers, is denoted as D, where D is given as $D = a - bp + \varepsilon$. The expected part of the demand is influenced by room rate p, whereas stochastic component ε is independent of room rate. Random variable ε is distributed continuously with probability density function $f(\varepsilon)$ and cumulative distribution function $F(\varepsilon)$.

As the hotel and third-party websites have the same customer market, they compete with each other on customer resources and exert sales effort to encourage customers to book rooms through their own ordering system [52]. For example, some hotels offer special services, such as breakfast for t-customers only. Third-party websites, on the other hand, provide customers with various travel information, which is highly convenient for the customers. Ctrip, the largest online travel agency in Mainland China, also provides cash back to w-customers who check-in successfully [52]. The effort levels of the hotel and website i are denoted respectively as e_0 and e_i, $i = 1,2,\ldots,n$. Consequently, the market shares of the hotel and website i are calculated respectively as $e_0/(e_0 + \Sigma e_i)$ and $e_i/(e_0 + \Sigma e_i)$, as shown in Figure 1. The effort will incur a cost of $h(e_0)$ and $h(e_i)$ to the hotel and third-party websites i, respectively. According to [52,53,54,55], effort cost is increasingly convex with effort level. Therefore, we assume that the effort cost for the hotel and website i is $ke_0^2/2$ and $ke_i^2/2$, respectively, where $k > 0$ is the investment coefficient.

Overbooking and Expected Profits

Some customers suddenly cancel their bookings at the last minute or do not show up on the target date without notifying the hotel because of some personal reasons such as a change in the trip or work schedule update. Hence, to improve its occupancy rate, the hotel implements an overbooking strategy and sets an overbooking level of l, which is defined as the number of accepted room bookings beyond hotel capacity. Consequently, $C + l$ room bookings can be accepted at most by the hotel. Integrate all customers as a whole and its show-up rate is denoted as β, where $\beta \in [\beta_1, \beta_2]$, and its probability density function and cumulative distribution function are $g(\beta)$ and $G(\beta)$, respectively. This assumption is widely applied in academic research and does not influence the results [56]. Therefore, $\beta(C + l)$ customers will show up at the hotel reception on the target date if $C + l$ customers make room reservations.

However, the overbooking strategy of the hotel may lead to over sales [14]. When the number of arriving customers on the target date exceeds room capacity, some will be denied check-in. Hence, to prevent bad publicity through word of mouth and maintain a good reputation, the hotel will attempt to placate the denied customers through various means [41]. For instance, hotels would recommend the denied customers to other hotels that can accommodate them or provide a free one-night stay on a future date. In this study, the hotel provides each denied customer with a compensation rate $v = rp$, which increases with room rate, and r is compensation coefficient.

With the overbooking policy, the expected demand of the hotel x, which includes both t- and w-customers, is given as follows. First, when the number of room bookings is smaller than room capacity, that is, $D \le C$, the hotel accepts all bookings and βD arriving customers are accommodated on the target date. Second, when the number of room bookings is within the range of C to $C + l$, *i.e.*, $C < D < C + l$, the hotel accepts all room bookings, and βD customers arrive on the target date. The hotel accommodates all customers if $\beta D \le C$; otherwise, $\beta D - C$ are denied. Third, when the number of room bookings is greater than $C + l$, the hotel only accepts $C + l$ room bookings. The hotel accommodates all $\beta(C + l)$ customers on the target date if $\beta(C + l) \le C$; otherwise, $\beta(C + l) - C$ of the bookings are denied. Thus, the expected demand for the target date is given as

$$x = \underset{\varepsilon,\beta|D\le C}{E}[\beta D] + \underset{\varepsilon,\beta|C<D<C+l}{E}\left[\min\{\beta D, C\}\right] + \underset{\varepsilon,\beta|D\ge C+l}{E}\left[\min\{\beta(C+l), C\}\right] \quad (1)$$

where $D = a - bp + \varepsilon$.

The expected demand of the third-party website i is given as

$$x_i = xe_i \big/ \left(e_0 + \sum e_i\right),\ i = 1, 2, \ldots, n \quad (2)$$

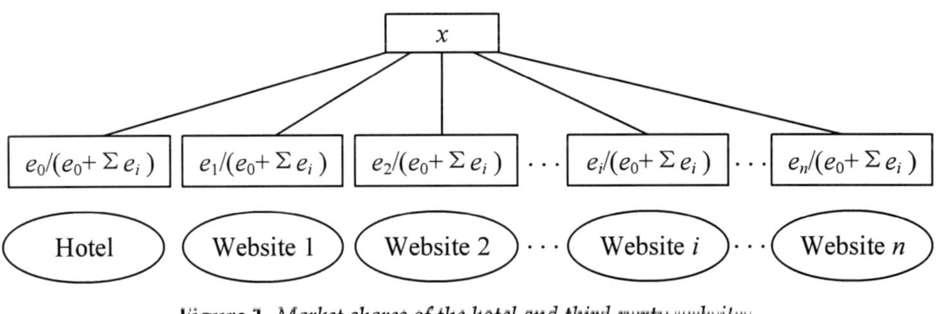

Figure 1. *Market shares of the hotel and third-party websites.*

As the expected demands are observed, the expected profit of the hotel is realized as follows:

$$\pi_0 = (p-c)x - \sum \omega_i x_i - v\left(\underset{\varepsilon,\beta|C<D<C+l}{E}[\beta D - C]^+ + \underset{\varepsilon,\beta|D\ge C+l}{E}\left[\beta(C+l) - C\right]^+\right) - ke_0^2/2 - F \quad (3)$$

where $D = a - bp + \varepsilon$. The first part is revenue obtained from accommodated customers. The second part represents total commission paid to third-party websites. The third part is total compensation fee paid to denied customers. The fourth and fifth parts represent effort cost and fixed cost, respectively.

The expected profit of third-party website i is given as

$$\pi_i = \omega_i x_i - ke_i^2/2,\ i = 1, 2, \ldots, n \quad (4)$$

Optimal decisions for a hotel will be affected by various factors, such as seasons, weathers, or even social activities [8,57], however, this model can be applied for various hotels with diverse capacities by assuming a fixed demand function.

RESULTS AND DISCUSSION

Solution Methodology

This section discusses the optimal solution for the cooperation problem described previously. The interaction between the hotel and third-party websites is modeled as a Stackelberg game, which is used to describe the competitive relationship between two or more members. The member who acts first to make decisions is known as the leader, and the one who acts according to the leader's decisions is known as the follower [58,59]. In recent years, the Stackelberg game has been widely adopted in the service industry to depict the cooperative relationship between services providers and their partners [52,60,61]. For example, Huang *et al.* [62] apply this game theory to analyze the relationship between two hotels and a travel agency and study impacts of different power structures on room rate. In the present study, the hotel is the leader and n third-party websites are the followers. In providing room reservation service cooperatively, the hotel first determines its room rate and overbooking level. Then commission rates paid to the third-party websites are given because commission rate is θ_i percentage of the room rate. Subsequently, the third-party websites determine their sales effort according to the commission rates. The Nash game is played among n third-party websites, which is used to describe the competitive relationship of members who act simultaneously [63]. The multiple websites compete for finite room capacity and determine their effort levels.

The sequence of events involved in the cooperation between the hotel and third-party websites are as follows:

Step 1: The hotel determines overbooking level l and room rate p.

Step 2: Third-party website i determines effort level e_i according to commission rate $\omega_i = \theta_i p$.

Step 3: The hotel and third-party websites accept room bookings.

Step 4: The hotel accommodates all arriving customers on the target date when its capacity is sufficient; otherwise, some of the arriving customers are denied and are provided a compensation rate of v.

The optimal decisions can be obtained through *backward induction*, with which the followers' decisions are analyzed first and then the leader's decisions are obtained. First, for a given l and p, website i maximizes its profit by solving $\max_{e_i} \pi_i$. From the first-order condition of Equation (4) on e_i, the unique effort level of website i is given by

$$\omega_i x\left(e_0 + \sum_{j \neq i} e_j\right) = k e_i \left(e_0 + \sum e_i\right)^2, \quad i = 1, 2, \ldots, n \tag{5}$$

Second, with knowledge of the website's reaction to its decisions, the hotel maximizes its profit by determining the optimal overbooking level and room rate (l^*,p^*) by solving the following problem:

$$\max_{(l,p)} \pi_0 = (p-c)x - \sum \omega_i x_i - v\left(\underset{\varepsilon,\beta|C<D<C+l}{E}[\beta D - C]^+ + \underset{\varepsilon,\beta|D\geq C+l}{E}\left[\beta(C+l)-C\right]^+ \right) - \frac{k}{2}e_0^2 - F$$

$$s.t. \begin{cases} D = a - bp + \varepsilon \\ x = \underset{\varepsilon,\beta|D\leq C}{E}[\beta D] + \underset{\varepsilon,\beta|C<D<C+l}{E}\left[\min\{\beta D, C\}\right] + \underset{\varepsilon,\beta|D\geq C+l}{E}\left[\min\{\beta(C+l), C\}\right] \\ x_i = xe_i \big/ \left(e_0 + \sum e_i\right),\ i = 1,2,\ldots,n \\ \omega_i x\left(e_0 + \sum_{j\neq i} e_j\right) = ke_i\left(e_0 + \sum e_i\right)^2,\ i = 1,2,\ldots,n \end{cases} \tag{6}$$

By solving the above problem, the optimal overbooking level l^* and room rate p^* of the hotel are obtained. Substitute them into Equation (5), the optimal effort levels of the third-party websites are then calculated. Consequently, the optimal profits of the hotel and website are obtained as π_i^* and π_i^*, respectively. However, since distributions of customer demand and show-up rate are not known, a closed-form solution of the model cannot be obtained. A numerical example is shown in the next subsection to illustrate the optimal solutions.

Numerical Experiments

This section conducts numerical analysis of one hotel and two third-party websites based on the mathematical model constructed in Section 3 and the solution methodology given in Section 4.1. The hotel determines the room rate and overbooking level by maximizing its profit. As $\omega_i = \theta_i p$, commission paid to website i is given once the room rate is determined. Website i, $i = 1,2$, then determines its effort level with its maximal profit. The numerical example illustrates the equilibrium solutions in previous sections and provides insights into hotel pricing and overbooking strategies while under an agreement with cooperative third-party websites.

For convenience, and without affecting the findings, the show-up rate of customers β is uniformly distributed over [0.8,1], while ε follows a normal distribution with mean value $\mu = 0$ and standard deviation $\sigma = 45$. Other values of basic parameters are given in Table 1. Based on the these values of parameters, optimal pricing and overbooking strategies of the hotel and optimal effort levels of the third-party websites can be calculated through simulations with a genetic algorithm using Matlab 2011b (® 7.13.0.564). The details can be found in Table 2.

The results in Table 2 indicate that to maximize its occupancy rate, the hotel will overbook 13 rooms in anticipation of last-minute cancellations and no-shows of customers. Furthermore, a higher commission rate $(\theta_2 > \theta_1)$ will result in a higher effort level from the website $(e_2 > e_1)$. In this example, Website 2 exerts more effort on room sales and obtains higher market share $(x_2 > x_1)$ and consequently a richer profit $(\pi_2 > \pi_1)$.

Table 1. *Values of parameters.*

Parameters	n	C	c	F	a	b	e_0	θ_1	θ_2	k	r
Values	2	150	15	4000	500	3.2	30	0.12	0.15	1	1

Note: n = the number of websites; C = room capacity; c = variable cost of each occupied room; F = fixed cost of the hotel; a = total demand of the market; b = price elastic coefficient; e_0 = effort level of the hotel; θ_i = commission coefficient for website i, i = 1, 2; k = investment coefficient. a and b are calculated from array $(p,E[D])=(100,180)$ and $(p,E[D])=(150,20)$.

Table 2. *Optimal decisions and profits.*

p	l	e_1	e_2	ω_1	ω_2	x	x_1	x_2	π_0	π_1	π_2
107	13	17.65	20.73	12.84	16.05	126.73	32.71	38.41	6035.9	264.2	401.7

Note: p = room rate; l = overbooking level set by the hotel; e_i = effort level of website i; ω_i = commission rate paid to website i; x = expected demand of the hotel; x_i = market share of website i; π_0 = profit of the hotel; π_i = profit of website i, i = 1,2.

A sensitivity analysis is conducted to further address the effects of parameters on decisions and profits of the hotel and third-party websites. Practical implications are analyzed based on the results obtained. Based on basic values in Table 1, Table 3 depicts the effects of compensation coefficient on optimal decisions, while Table 4 shows the effects of fluctuations in customer demand. Table 5 illustrates the effects of hotel effort level on optimal solutions. Table 6 shows the effects of room capacity.

Table 3 indicates that compensation coefficient does not have significant effect on hotel pricing strategy. However, the overbooking level decreases sharply when the compensation coefficient increases because the hotel attempts to reduce the expected demand to lessen the necessity to pay compensation fees to denied

Table 3. *Effects of compensation coefficient on decisions and profits.*

r	p	l	e_1	e_2	ω_1	ω_2	x	x_1	x_2	π_0	π_1	π_2
0.5	106	20	17.78	20.88	12.72	15.90	129.55	33.55	39.39	6136.3	268.7	408.4
1	107	13	17.65	20.73	12.84	16.05	126.73	32.71	38.41	6035.9	264.2	401.7
1.5	107	10	17.59	20.66	12.84	16.05	125.95	32.46	38.12	5980.9	262.1	398.5
2	107	8	17.54	20.60	12.84	16.05	125.34	32.26	37.89	5945.9	260.4	396.0
2.5	107	7	17.51	20.57	12.84	16.05	125.00	32.15	37.76	5921.5	259.5	394.6

Table 4. *Effects of demand fluctuations on decisions and profits.*

δ	p	l	e_1	e_2	ω_1	ω_2	x	x_1	x_2	π_0	π_1	π_2
25	107	13	18.22	21.38	12.84	16.05	133.83	35.04	41.11	6618.3	283.9	431.2
35	107	13	17.94	21.06	12.84	16.05	130.29	33.88	39.76	6327.6	274.0	416.5
45	107	13	17.65	20.73	12.84	16.05	126.73	32.71	38.41	6035.9	264.2	401.7
55	106	13	17.39	20.42	12.72	15.90	124.63	31.95	37.54	5746.5	255.3	388.3
65	106	13	17.10	20.09	12.72	15.90	121.15	30.83	36.23	5465.7	246.0	374.2

customers. On the other hand, along with the increase in compensation coefficient, the third-party websites will lower their effort levels although commission rates paid by the hotel remain unchanged.

Table 4 indicates that fluctuations in total demand have a slight effect on pricing and overbooking strategies of the hotel but a strong effect on hotel profit because a larger deviation in customer demand results in smaller expected demand for the hotel. Thus, lower expected demand leads to lower hotel profit. As customer demand fluctuates violently, the third-party websites exert a lower effort level in room sales. Hence, the third-party websites also obtain lower profits.

Table 5 shows that under a given market demand, the effort level of the hotel redistributes market shares among the hotel and third-party websites but has no effect on hotel pricing and overbooking strategies. The hotel gains a larger market share by exerting more sales effort, which in reverse leads to a smaller market share for the third-party websites. Thus, the profit of the hotel increases, whereas that of the websites decreases.

Table 5. *Effects of hotel effort level on decisions and profits.*

e_0	p	l	e_1	e_2	ω_1	ω_2	x	x_1	x_2	π_0	π_1	π_2
20	107	13	18.64	21.63	12.84	16.05	126.73	39.20	45.48	6089.2	329.5	496.0
25	107	13	18.15	21.20	12.84	16.05	126.73	35.75	41.74	6081.0	294.3	445.3
30	107	13	17.65	20.73	12.84	16.05	126.73	32.71	38.41	6035.9	264.2	401.7
35	107	13	17.15	20.24	12.84	16.05	126.73	30.02	35.43	5955.8	238.4	363.8
40	107	13	16.66	19.74	12.84	16.05	126.73	27.63	32.75	5842.1	216.0	330.7

As shown in Table 6, a hotel with a larger room capacity will set a lower room rate to increase customer demand and then improve room occupancy rate. The hotel also tends to set a higher overbooking level to reduce the number of unoccupied rooms, resulting in an increase in expected demand. Effort levels of the third-party websites increase with room capacity for the same reason. Hence, the expansion in room capacity will increase profits for the hotel and third-party websites.

Table 6. *Effects of room capacity on decisions and profits.*

C	p	l	e_1	e_2	ω_1	ω_2	x	x_1	x_2	π_0	π_1	π_2
130	111	12	16.73	19.67	13.32	16.65	111.46	28.08	33.02	5168.3	234.1	356.3
140	109	12	17.20	20.21	13.08	16.35	119.03	30.37	35.69	5621.6	249.3	379.2
150	107	13	17.65	20.73	12.84	16.05	126.73	32.71	38.41	6035.9	264.2	401.7
160	105	14	18.06	21.19	12.60	15.75	134.27	35.01	41.09	6411.7	278.1	422.6
170	103	15	18.42	21.61	12.36	15.45	141.66	37.27	43.71	6749.9	290.9	441.9

EXTENSION: PROFIT IMPROVEMENT BY OVERBOOKING STRATEGY

This section explores profit improvement for the hotel and n third-party websites based on the overbooking strategy. As a benchmark, the scenario in which the overbooking strategy is not adopted by the hotel is set. In the benchmark, the hotel determines its optimal room rate by maximizing its profit. Once room rate is determined, the commission rates paid to the third-party websites are also obtained. Subsequently, the websites determine their effort levels with their maximal profits.

The expected demand of the benchmark scenario is given as

$$x^B = \underset{\varepsilon,\beta|D\le C}{E}[\beta D] + \underset{\varepsilon,\beta|D>C}{E}[\beta C]$$

where $D = a - bp^B + \varepsilon$.

The market share for third-party website i is obtained as

$$x_i^B = x^B e_i^B / \left(e_0 + \sum e_i^B\right),\ i = 1,2,\ldots,n$$

According to the cooperation problem described in Section 3, the expected profits of the hotel and third-party website i, without the overbooking strategy, are given as follows:

$$\pi_0^B = \left(p^B - c\right)x^B - \sum \omega_i^B x_i^B - ke_0^2/2 - F,\ \pi_i^B = \omega_i^B x_i^B - k\left(e_i^B\right)^2/2,\ i = 1,2,\ldots,n$$

where $\omega_i^B = \theta_i p^B$, $i = 1,2,\ldots,n$.

The solving process is similar to that described in Section 4.1. First, given the hotel room rate, third-party website i determines its effort level as

$$\omega_i^B x^B \left(e_0 + \sum_{j\neq i} e_j^B\right) = ke_i^B\left(e_0 + \sum e_i^B\right)^2,\ i = 1,2,\ldots,n \tag{7}$$

Second, with knowledge of the decision of third-party website i, the hotel determines its optimal room rate by solving the following problem:

$$\max_{p^B} \pi_0^B = \left(p^B - c\right)x^B - \sum \omega_i^B x_i^B - ke_0^2/2 - F$$

$$s.t.\begin{cases} D = a - bp^B + \varepsilon \\ x^B = \underset{\varepsilon,\beta|D\le C}{E}[\beta D] + \underset{\varepsilon,\beta|D>C}{E}[\beta C] \\ x_i^B = x^B e_i^B / \left(e_0 + \sum e_i^B\right),\ i = 1,2,\ldots,n \\ \omega_i^B x^B\left(e_0 + \sum_{j\neq i} e_j^B\right) = ke_i^B\left(e_0 + \sum e_i^B\right)^2,\ i = 1,2,\ldots,n \end{cases} \tag{8}$$

By solving this problem, the optimal room rate is obtained. Substitute it into Equation (7), the optimal effort levels of the third-party websites can be calculated. Then the optimal profits of the hotel and third-party website i are given as π_0^{B*} and π_i^{B*}, respectively. The improved profits due to the overbooking strategy for the hotel and third-party website i are denoted as $\Delta\pi_0 = \pi_0^* - \pi_0^{B*}$ and $\Delta\pi_0 = \pi_i^* - \pi_i^{B*}$, respectively.

A numerical example is displayed to illustrate optimal results in the benchmark and to enable a better understanding of the model. One hotel and two third-party websites are considered, and the basic values of other parameters are identical to those given in Table 1. The optimal decisions of the hotel and third-party websites as well as profit improvement based on overbooking strategy are shown in Table 7.

Table 7. *Profit improvement based on overbooking strategy.*

—	p	e_1	e_2	x	x_1	x_2	π_0	π_1	π_2
Benchmark scenario	108	17.25	20.27	120.82	36.23	42.58	5792.5	251.0	381.8
Overbooking scenario	107	17.65	20.73	126.73	38.31	45.00	6035.9	264.2	401.7
Profit improvement	—	—	—	—	—	—	4.20%	5.26%	5.21%

Table 7 reveals the following findings. First, with overbooking strategy, the expected demand is larger than that in the benchmark scenario. In other words, overbooking strategy increases hotel demand. Second, an overbooking strategy improves the profits of the third-party websites, with a higher proportion at 5.26% for Website 1 and 5.21% for Website 2 than that of the hotel at only 4.20%. This result can be attributed to the third-party websites bearing no risk of over sale caused by overbooking, whereas the hotel has to pay a compensation fee to each denied customer. Finally, third-party websites that exert more effort to make sales do not always benefit more from the overbooking strategy. In the numerical example, Website 2 who exerts more effort in room sales only achieves an improvement of 5.21% in profit, which is lower than 5.26% for Website 1.

CONCLUSIONS

Hotels adopt overbooking strategy to accept more room bookings to hedge against last-minute cancellations and no-shows at the price of a compensation fee paid to denied customers, and cooperate with third-party websites to attract more customers at the price of commission. This study investigates pricing and overbooking strategies of a hotel in cooperation with multiple third-party websites by discussing cooperation and competition relationship between the hotel and third-party websites simultaneously. We also explore the effect of a hotel overbooking strategy on this cooperation process.

This study concludes with several important findings. First, compensation coefficient has a slight effect on hotel pricing decision. However, with the increase of compensation coefficient, the hotel will set a lower overbooking level to reduce the risk of over sale. As a result, the third-party website would exert lower effort level in room sales along with the increase of compensation coefficient. Second, under a given market demand, the effort level of the hotel will not affect its pricing and overbooking strategies and results only in a redistribution of the market shares among the hotel and third-party websites. Along with the increase in hotel effort level, the market shares of the third-party websites will decrease resulting from an increase in hotel market share. Third, by adopting overbooking strategy, the hotel achieves more profit improvement than the website (243.4 for the hotel, *versus* 13.2 for Website 1 and 19.9 for Website 2). Nevertheless, a hotel overbooking strategy increases the profits of Websites 1 and 2 by a proportion of 5.26% and

5.21%, respectively, but only 4.20% for the hotel. Due to the fact that the third-party websites are not responsible for over sale caused by overbooking, they benefit more from this strategy than the hotel. Results also show that cooperative websites getting richer commission and exerting more sales effort do not always benefit more from the overbooking strategy of hotels.

The conclusions obtained yield significant management implications for hotels and third-party websites. First, over sale caused by overbooking will harm customer's goodwill, cause revenue loss to hotels and damage a hotel's reputation [14,64]. Consequently, hotels should make an appropriate overbooking strategy by considering the expense of compensating denied customers. The present paper indicates hotels how to determine the optimal overbooking level under given compensation to denied customers. To placate denied customers, hotels should give priority to them or provide them with free stay in the future to compensate them. Second, as hotels cooperate with third-party websites on room reservation, they inevitably compete with each other on the customer source because of the same customer market [48]. Therefore, both hotels and third-party websites should exert more efforts to encourage customers to make reservation directly through their own distribution channels. For example, hotels can make marketing effort by providing breakfast to h-customers only to encourage them to book rooms through their brand website. Alternatively, some third-party websites (such as Ctrip in Mainland China) offer cash back to customers who make room reservations through their webpage and check in successfully. Finally, as shown in the numerical example, larger room capacity and higher room rate of the cooperative hotels will result in a richer profit for the third-party websites. Thus, third-party websites should cooperate with luxury and large-scale hotels to earn more profits.

This study is limited in several aspects, on which future studies could focus. First, the demand for hotels change over time in actual settings, and dynamic programming may be a desirable method to address this problem. Second, a non-performance penalty imposed on the hotel is discussed; that is, the hotel pays compensation fees to denied customers for their inability to accommodate them. However, imposing early departure and no-show penalties on customers are other effective methods to hedge against last-minute cancellations and no-shows, and improve occupancy rate. Finally, all hotel rooms are assumed identical in this study. Different types of rooms may be considered for future research, and an upgrade or downgrade strategy may also be effective in increasing the total occupancy rate of hotels.

ACKNOWLEDGMENTS

Thank the anonymous reviewers for constructive suggestions, which improves the quality of the paper. This work was supported by the National Natural Science Foundation of China under Grant 71271197; the Foundation for Innovative Research Groups of the National Natural Science Foundation of China under Grant 71121061; and the Foundation for International Cooperation and Exchange of the National Natural Science Foundation of China under Grant 71110107024. We appreciate Yanhua Chen, who is from Department of Biostatistics, School of Public Health and Health Professions-University at Buffalo for English corrections.

Author Contributions

Liuyi Ling proposed the idea and conceived the experiments; Yufeng Dong developed the model, performed the experiments, analyzed the data and wrote the paper. Both authors have read and approved the final manuscript.

REFERENCES

1. Bitran, G.R.; Mondschein, S.V. An application of yield management to the hotel industry considering multiple day stays. *Oper. Res.* **1995**, *43*, 427–443.
2. Chatwin, R.E. Continuous-time airline overbooking with time-dependent fares and refunds. *Transp. Sci.* **1999**, *33*, 182–191.
3. Easingwood, C.J. New product development for service companies. *J. Prod. Innov. Manag.* **1986**, *3*, 264–275.
4. Vargo, S.L.; Lusch, R.F. The four service marketing myths remnants of a goods-based, manufacturing model. *J. Serv. Res.* **2004**, *6*, 324–335.
5. De Chernatony, L.; Dall'Olmo Riley, F. Experts' views about defining services brands and the principles of services branding. *J. Bus. Res.* **1999**, *46*, 181–192.
6. Tang, K.; Zairi, M. Benchmarking quality implementation in a service context: A comparative analysis of financial services and institutions of higher education. Part I: financial services sector. *Total Qual. Manag.* **1998**, *9*, 407–420.
7. Ladany, S.P. Optimal market segmentation of hotel rooms—The non-linear case. *Omega* **1996**, *24*, 29–36.
8. Guo, X.; Ling, L.; Yang, C.; Li, Z.; Liang, L. Optimal pricing strategy based on market segmentation for service products using online reservation systems: An application to hotel rooms. *Int. J. Hosp. Manag.* **2013**, *35*, 274–281.
9. Klophaus, R.; Pölt, S. Airline overbooking with dynamic spoilage costs. *J. Revenue Pricing Manag.* **2007**, *6*, 9–18.
10. Mauri, A. Yield management and perceptions of fairness in the hotel business. *Int. Rev. Econ.* **2007**, *54*, 284–293.
11. Barth, J.E. Yield management: Opportunities for private club managers. *Int. J. Contemp. Hosp. Manag.* **2002**, *14*, 136–141.
12. Koennevig, M.; Media, D. What Does Overbooked at a Hotel Mean? Available online: http://traveltips.usatoday.com/overbooked-hotel-mean-108088.html (accessed on 13 April 2015).
13. Mauri, A.G. *Hotel Revenue Management: Principles and Practices*; McGraw-Hill: Milan, Italy, 2012.
14. Vinod, B. Unlocking the value of revenue management in the hotel industry. *J. Revenue Pricing Manag.* **2004**, *3*, 178–190.
15. Zhang, X.; Wang, P.; Wang, Y.; Wang, G. Regulatory Focus and Recovery Fit in Airline Overbooking. In Proceedings of the 2010 IEEE International Conference on Industrial Engineering and Engineering Management (IEEM), Macao, China, 7–10 December 2010; pp. 758–761.
16. Hwang, J.; Wen, L. The effect of perceived fairness toward hotel overbooking and compensation practices on customer loyalty. *Int. J. Contemp. Hosp. Manag.* **2009**, *21*, 659–675.

17. Grönroos, C. *Service Management and Marketing: Customer Management in Service Competition*, 2nd ed.; John Wiley & Sons Ltd.: Chichester, UK, 2000; pp. 24–25.
18. Zeithaml, V.A.; Bitner, M.J.; Gremler, D.D. *Services Marketing: Integrating Customer Focus across the Firm*, International ed.; McGraw-Hill Education: Singapore, 2006.
19. Garcés, S.A.; Gorgemans, S.; Sánchez, A.M.N.; Pérez, M.P. Implications of the Internet—An analysis of the Aragonese hospitality industry, 2002. *Tour. Manag.* **2004**, *25*, 603–613.
20. Gregory, S.; Breiter, D. Leveling the playing field: E-marketing's impact on lodging operations. *J. Hosp. Leis. Mark.* **2001**, *7*, 45–60.
21. Kim, D.J.; Kim, W.G.; Han, J.S. A perceptual mapping of online travel agencies and preference attributes. *Tour. Manag.* **2007**, *28*, 591–603.
22. Theodosiou, M.; Katsikea, E. Antecedents and performance of electronic business adoption in the hotel industry. *Eur. J. Mark.* **2012**, *46*, 258–283.
23. Ma, C. E-collaboration: A universal key to solve fierce competition in tourism industry? *Int. Bus. Res.* **2009**, *1*, P65.
24. Medina-Muñoz, D.; García-Falcón, J.M. Successful relationships between hotels and agencies. *Ann. Tour. Res.* **2000**, *27*, 737–762.
25. Ivanov, S. Optimal Overbooking Limits for a 3-Room Type Hotel with Upgrade and Downgrade Constraints. Available online: http://ssrn.com/abstract = 2190042 (accessed on 18 August 2013).
26. Noone, B.M.; Lee, C.H. Hotel overbooking: The effect of overcompensation on customers' reactions to denied service. *J. Hosp. Tour. Res.* **2011**, *35*, 334–357.
27. Toh, R.S.; Raven, P.; DeKay, F. Selling rooms: Hotels *vs.* third-party websites. *Cornell Hosp. Q.* **2011**, *52*, 181–189.
28. Jamal, T.B.; Getz, D. Collaboration theory and community tourism planning. *Ann. Tour. Res.* **1995**, *22*, 186–204.
29. Chathoth, P.K.; Olsen, M.D. Strategic alliances: A hospitality industry perspective. *Int. J. Hosp. Manag.* **2003**, *22*, 419–434.
30. Byrd, E.T. Stakeholders in sustainable tourism development and their roles: Applying stakeholder theory to sustainable tourism development. *Tour. Rev.* **2007**, *62*, 6–13.
31. Hadjinicola, G.C.; Panayi, C. The overbooking problem in hotels with multiple tour-operators. *Int. J. Oper. Prod. Manag.* **1997**, *17*, 874–885.
32. Baker, T.K. New Approaches to Yield Management: Comprehensive Overbooking/Allocation Heuristics for the Hotel Industry. Available online: http://sunzi.lib.hku.hk/ER/detail/hkul/2993390 (accessed on 18 August 2013).
33. Lambert, C.U.; Lambert, J.M.; Cullen, T.P. The overbooking question: A simulation. *Cornell Hotel Restaur. Adm. Q.* **1989**, *30*, 14–20.
34. Weatherford, L.R.; Bodily, S.E. A taxonomy and research overview of perishable-asset revenue management: Yield management, overbooking, and pricing. *Oper. Res.* **1992**, *40*, 831–844.
35. Rothstein, M. Hotel overbooking as a markovian sequential decision process. *Decis. Sci.* **1974**, *5*, 389–404.
36. Ivanov, S. Dynamic overbooking limits for guaranteed and nonguaranteed hotel reservations. *Tour. Today* **2007**, *7*, 100–108.

37. Liberman, V.; Yechiali, U. On the hotel overbooking problem—An inventory system with stochastic cancellations. *Manag. Sci.* **1978**, *24*, 1117–1126.
38. Toh, R.S. An inventory depletion overbooking model for the hotel industry. *J. Travel Res.* **1985**, *23*, 24–30.
39. Toh, R.S.; Dekay, F. Hotel room-inventory management: An overbooking model. *Cornell Hotel Restaur. Adm. Q.* **2002**, *43*, 79–90.
40. Koide, T.; Ishii, H. The hotel yield management with two types of room prices, overbooking and cancellations. *Int. J. Product. Econ.* **2005**, *93–94*, 417–428.
41. Talluri, K.T.; van Ryzin, G.J. *The Theory and Practice of Revenue Management*; Springer Science & Business Media: New York, NY, USA, 2006.
42. Karaesmen, I.; van Ryzin, G. Overbooking with substitutable inventory classes. *Oper. Res.* **2004**, *52*, 83–104.
43. Vinod, B. Distribution and revenue management: Origins and value proposition. *J. Revenue Pricing Manag.* **2009**, *8*, 117–133.
44. Ling, L.; Guo, X.; Liang, L. Optimal pricing strategy of a small or medium-sized hotel in cooperation with a web site. *J. China Tour. Res.* **2011**, *7*, 20–41.
45. Beritelli, P. Cooperation among prominent actors in a tourist destination. *Ann. Tour. Res.* **2011**, *38*, 607–629.
46. Huang, Y.; Song, H.; Huang, G.Q.; Lou, J. A Comparative Study of Tourism Supply Chains with Quantity Competition. *J. Travel Res.* **2012**.
47. Buhalis, D. Relationships in the distribution channel of tourism: Conflicts between hoteliers and tour operators in the Mediterranean region. *Int. J. Hosp. Tour. Adm.* **2000**, *1*, 113–139.
48. Myung, E.; Li, L.; Bai, B. Managing the distribution channel relationship with e-Wholesalers: Hotel operators' perspective. *J. Hosp. Market. Manag.* **2009**, *18*, 811–828.
49. Narasimhan, K. Service management and marketing: Customer management in service competition. *Manag. Serv. Qual.* **2009**, *19*, 629–630.
50. Lee, H.A.; Guillet, B.D.; Law, R. An examination of the relationship between online travel agents and hotels: A case study of Choice Hotels International and Expedia.com. *Cornell Hosp. Q.* **2013**, *54*, 95–107.
51. Tso, A.; Law, R. Analysing the online pricing practices of hotels in Hong Kong. *Int. J. Hosp. Manag.* **2005**, *24*, 301–307.
52. Guo, X.; Zheng, X.; Ling, L.; Yang, C. Online coopetition between hotels and online travel agencies: From the perspective of cash back after stay. *Tour. Manag. Perspect.* **2014**, *12*, 104–112.
53. Huang, Z.; Li, S.X. Co-op advertising models in manufacturer-retailer supply chains: A game theory approach. *Eur. J. Oper. Res.* **2001**, *135*, 527–544.
54. Little, J.D. Aggregate advertising models: The state of the art. *Oper. Res.* **1979**, *27*, 629–667.
55. Taylor, T.A. Supply chain coordination under channel rebates with sales effort effects. *Manag. Sci.* **2002**, *48*, 992–1007.
56. Kasilingam, R.G. An economic model for air cargo overbooking under stochastic capacity. *Comput. Ind. Eng.* **1997**, *32*, 221–226.
57. Fernández-Morales, A.; Mayorga-Toledano, M.C. Seasonal concentration of the hotel demand in Costa del Sol: A decomposition by nationalities. *Tour. Manag.* **2008**, *29*, 940–949.

58. Osborne, M.J.; Rubinstein, A. *A Course in Game Theory*; MIT Press: Cambridge, MA, USA, 1994.
59. Gibbons, R. *Game Theory for Applied Economists*; Princeton University Press: Princeton, NJ, USA, 1992.
60. Dong, Y.; Ling, L.; Guo, X. Travel package modeling: Optimal bidding strategy of tour operator to cooperative hotels. *Asia Pac. J. Tour. Res.* **2013**, *19*, 1–24.
61. Guo, X.; He, L. Tourism supply-chain coordination: The cooperation between tourism hotel and tour operator. *Tour. Econ.* **2012**, *18*, 1361–1376.
62. Huang, Y.; Wang, K.; Huang, G.Q. Price Competition under Different Power Structures of Hotels and Travel Agency in Tourism Supply Chain. Available online: http://www.aicit.org/AISS/ppl/AISS3319PPL.pdf (accessed on 18 August 2012).
63. Guo, X.; Ling, L.; Dong, Y.; Liang, L. Cooperation contract in tourism supply chains: The optimal pricing strategy of hotels for cooperative third party strategic websites. *Ann. Tour. Res.* **2013**, *41*, 20–41.
64. DeKay, F.; Yates, B.; Toh, R.S. Non-performance penalties in the hotel industry. *Int. J. Hosp. Manag.* **2004**, *23*, 273–286.

CHAPTER 7

Forecasting Hotel Room Occupancy Using Long Short-Term Memory Networks with Sentiment Analysis and Scores of Customer Online Reviews

Yu-Ming Chang[1,2], Chieh-Huang Chen[1], Jung-Pin Lai[1], Ying-Lei Lin[1] and Ping-Feng Pai[1,3]

[1]*PhD Program in Strategy and Development of Emerging Industries, National Chi Nan University, Nantou 54561, Taiwan*

[2]*Department of Culinary Arts and Hotel Management, Hung Kuang University, Taichung 43302, Taiwan*

[3]*Department of Information Management, National Chi Nan University, Nantou 54561, Taiwan*

ABSTRACT

For hotel management, occupancy is a crucial indicator. Online reviews from customers have gradually become the main reference for customers to evaluate accommodation choices. Thus, this study employed online customer rating scores and review text provided by booking systems to forecast monthly hotel occupancy using long short-term memory networks (LSTMs). Online customer reviews of hotels in Taiwan in various languages were gathered, and Google's natural language application programming interface was used to convert online customer reviews into sentiment scores. Five other forecasting models—back propagation neural networks (BPNN), general regression neural networks (GRNN), least square support vector regression (LSSVR), random forest (RF), and gaussian process regression (GPR)—were employed to predict hotel occupancy using the same datasets. The numerical data indicated that the long short-term memory network model outperformed the other five models in terms of forecasting accuracy. Integrating hotel online customer review sentiment scores and customer rating scores can lead to more accurate results than using unique scores individually. The novelty and applicability of this study is the application of deep learning techniques in forecasting room occupancy rates in multilingual comment scenarios with data gathered from review text and customers' rating scores. This study reveals that using long short-term memory networks with sentiment analysis of review text and customers' rating scores is a feasible and promising alternative in forecasting hotel room occupancy.

Keywords: *sentiment analysis; online reviews; long short-term memory networks; forecast; hotel room occupancy*

INTRODUCTION

Business performance management is significant for enterprises in any industry, especially in the tourism and hotel industry, because of the fixed service products in terms of content and quantity. When a room passes the sales time point, a fixed cost is paid. However, no more sales can be made, which directly affects the company's revenue and operating performance. Therefore, the prediction and management of occupancy are important. Hotel performance management is usually composed of two aspects—revenue management and cost control. The discipline of revenue management includes two strategic levers, namely duration control and demand-based pricing [1]. Research on hotel needs consists of two major categories. One category involves developing new methods to improve the accuracy of demand prediction. This type of research usually employs many alternative forecasting models to predict travel or hotel demand and compares forecasting performance. The other category involves determining hotel needs and the relationship between needs. Existing econometric models are applied to quantify the impact of demand factors using demand elasticity analysis [2].

A variety of factors influence hotel operating performance. In the past, historical sales data have been used to analyze demand patterns and trends in addition to hotel factors, such as geographic locations, hotel facilities, service quality, and marketing activities. Recently, with the rise of online booking platforms, customers' behavior patterns in searching and choosing hotel accommodations have changed. When online customers choose a hotel, they target the date and area. Then, they filter out hotel information that meets their needs on the basis of the accommodation options provided by the online travel agent booking website. Finally, when determining accommodation, previous customer reviews tend to be an influential factor. Thus, more studies are using customer online comment analysis as the subject of hotel management research. The Tourism Bureau of the Ministry of Transportation in Taiwan pointed out some statistical indicators ranking the operating performance of hotels, such as total revenue, annual occupancy rate, annual average price, and the annual average price of saleable rooms. The revenue of tourist hotels usually comes from the guest room and catering departments. However, the consumer reviews on the booking websites are mainly for guests' consuming experience of hotel accommodation. Thus, hotels' total operating incomes are not appropriate for further analysis. Furthermore, differences in total operating income and average house prices may be caused by the number of operating rooms, locations, and decoration equipment. Therefore, this study employed hotel room occupancy rates as a criterion for evaluating hotel operating performance. The rest of this study is organized as follows: Section 2 discusses the literature, Section 3 briefs long short-term memory networks, Section 4 introduces the proposed forecasting architecture for hotel room occupancy, Section 5 depicts the numerical results, and Section 6 presents the conclusions.

RELATED LITERATURE

Online Customer Reviews Analysis

Recently, Online Travel Agencies (OTAs) have emerged, and customers can search, compare prices, and make online reservations through various platforms. Customer reviews thus have been increasingly important sources providing informative data for customers when making purchasing decisions. Three directions can be categorized in the literature of online customer reviews. The first category involves using statistical analysis or hypothesis testing. Salehan and Kim [3] employed correlation analysis to investigate review text and sentiments. The study provided insights regarding the reviews' impact on potential customers. De Pelsmacker et al. [4] used the number of reviews and review valence to analyze occupancy and revenue per available room. This study revealed that review volume and review valence influenced room occupancy and revenue per available room, respectively. Furthermore, hotel locations and room quality are the two most essential terms of review comments. Anagnostopoulou et al. [5] used statistical methods to analyze the impact of online customer reviews on financial profitability. It was reported that positive comments were significantly related to hotel financial performance. Liu et al. [6] employed customers' reviews to analyze distributions of domestic and international customers' hotel ratings. This study pointed out that domestic travel, international travel, language, and culture had a statistically significant impact on hotel preference and satisfaction. The second category involves employing data-driven approaches to explore the relationship between customers' reviews and hotel performance. Fernandes et al. [7] used a cross-industry standard process for data mining to investigate the influences of online reviewers' comments on restaurant performance. Phillips et al. [8] utilized a partial least squares path method to examine the influences of positive and negative reviews on revenue per available room. This study concluded that "stars" and percentages of positive comments had a critical impact on revenue per available room. The third category uses sentiment analysis tools, such as a sentiment dictionary, to understand online customer reviews and the impact of reviews. Morente-Molinera et al. [9] indicated that the users' opinions were usually unstructured, and users were used to expressing opinions in their own ways. This study employed fuzzy ontology to homogenize information; therefore, subjective and unformatted information could be handled. Hu et al. [10] used standardized coefficients to analyze the interrelationship between ratings, sentiments, and sales rankings. The study reported that ratings did not have a significant impact on sales directly but did have an indirect impact through sentiments. Zhang et al. [11] utilized a majority decision algorithm and a stochastic gradient descent technique to classify sentimental orientations of WeChat texts. The numerical results indicated that the presented method outperformed the other four machine learning approaches.

In the previous three categories of studies mentioned, descriptive statistics, hypothesis testing, correlation analysis, cluster analysis, and regression analysis were employed by studies to analyze the influence of customers' online reviews on hotel performance. Some investigations focused on exploring the relationship between emotional words and ratings. However, predictions of hotel performance, such as room occupancy, have not been conducted.

Occupancy Rate Forecast

First, for the online data sources employed for occupancy rate predictions, Li et al. [12] pointed out that online data utilized to forecast hotel room occupancy includes Baidu Index [13], Google Trends [14], web traffic volume-Google Analytics [15,16], and Twitter tweets and retweets [17]. Second, the approaches employed in forecasting hotel room occupancy are depicted as follows. Aliyev et al. [18] analyzed time series data and applied the fuzzy c-means clustering algorithm to forecast hotel occupancy rates. Ampountolas [19] investigated hotel daily demand in a U.S. metropolitan city. The attributes used included temperature, holidays, and hotel ranking. The results indicated that a seasonal autoregressive integrated moving average with exogenous variables model was superior to the other forecasting models. Zhang et al. [20] forecasted hotel occupancy in Charleston, South Carolina, USA using weekly data. The authors reported that for the mid-term prediction of hotel stays in tourist destinations, the revised model provided more accurate prediction results than the original EEMD-ARIMA (ensemble empirical mode decomposition–autoregressive integrated moving average) model. Ginindza and Tichaawa [21] studied hotel occupancy rates in the kingdom of Swaziland using the factors of Airbnb room occupancy rates, foreign visitor arrival numbers, unemployment rates, and exchange rates with statistical approaches. The numerical result showed a positive relationship between the hotel occupancy rates and Airbnb room occupancy rates. Fiori and Foroni [22] integrated historical and advanced booking methods into a combination of prediction models. The results revealed that the proposed model had a practical impact on the design and implementation of effective demand-side policies for hotels. Assaf and Tsionas [23] proposed two Bayesian compression methods and applied them in the hotel occupancy rate forecasting. This study indicated that the presented Bayesian compression models outperformed the other forecasting alternative models in terms of forecasting accuracy in all forecast horizons. Al Shehhi and Karathanasopoulos [24] employed the adaptive network fuzzy interference system to forecast hotel room prices in the Gulf Cooperation Council region. The authors claimed that forecasting results provided by the proposed adaptive network fuzzy interference system were superior to the other three forecasting models in terms of forecasting accuracy. Zhang et al. [25] used deep neural networks to predict the occupancy and prices of hotels on weekdays and peak days. The numerical results indicated that deep neural network models could significantly outperform the other seven models, including time-series forecasting models and machine learning models. Sánchez-Medina and Eleazar [26] employed artificial neural networks with genetic algorithms to forecast booking cancellations. The designed method could reach an accuracy of 98 percent and was significantly superior to the other three forecasting techniques in terms of forecasting accuracy. Wang and Duggasani [27] designed two long- and short-term memory models to predict the daily booking volume of hotels by data of arrival dates, booking dates, and the day of the week. The proposed method could improve the forecasting accuracy by about three percent compared with the best results generated by the other six machine learning methods. Huang and Zheng [28] proposed using the agglomeration effect combined with the attention mechanism and Bayesian optimization algorithm to predict the daily demand of hotels with agglomeration effects. The results showed that the proposed model was helpful in increasing hotel revenue management by decreasing the gap between the potential demand and available capacity. Das et al. [29] used a light gradient boosting machine to predict demand with seasonality using historical booking data. In this study, customer booking patterns and potential trends in the booking curve were investigated. Then, daily, monthly, and holiday occupancy were predicted. The experiment results revealed that the light gradient boosting machine could generate more accurate forecasting results than the other five forecasting methods, including the time-series techniques. Lee et al. [30] proposed a combined neural network framework architecture with time series booked data and seasonal components to predict accommodation demand. It was reported that the designed model could generate more accurate forecasting results than the other time-series methods. Phumchusri and Ungtrakul [31] developed an artificial neural networks model to forecast daily hotel demand in Thailand. The numerical results showed that artificial neural networks could obtain more accurate forecasting results than the other forecasting models employed in the study.

According to the review of related literature, deep learning techniques have not been broadly explored in predicting hotel room occupancy rates. Furthermore, most of the previous research on online customer sentiment analysis has focused on reviews in English, apparently lacking multilingual comment content. Thus, this study collected daily and monthly research data from Internet crawling and government databases, and it used long short-term memory networks to forecast hotel room occupancy using sentiment analysis of review text and consumers' rating scores in multilingual comment content. The other five machine learning forecasting approaches were used to conduct predictions with the same datasets to compare forecasting performance.

LONG SHORT-TERM MEMORY NETWORKS

Long short-term memory networks are extended algorithms that improve the gradient vanishing problems in the recurrent neural networks when processing long sequences. They save essential information for a long time so that earlier information can be associated with current tasks. Long short-term memory networks provide fusion memory units, allowing the network to update hidden units on the basis of new information before learning. Thus, they are especially able to remember the most important information for future tasks. In addition, long short-term memory networks can select the tanh function as an activation function, which is a stable method that is beneficial in regression problems. Figure 1 shows the neural network architecture of long short-term memory networks. There are many variants in use called bidirectional long short-term memory networks. The cell or memory area of long short-term memory networks is composed of the input gate, forget gate, output gate, and cell state. The forget gate controls whether the memory should be cleared or how much information is entered into the next cell's memory. The input gate controls whether the input value enters the memory. On the other hand, the output gate controls whether the updated value should be output to the next layer of networks. These layers all operate in a specific way, of which three gates control all additions or deletions of the unit state. The long short-term memory network calculation is from the input sequence x, represented by Equation (1):

$$x = (x_{t-1}, x_t, x_{t+1}..., x_{t+n}) \tag{1}$$

to the output sequence y, denoted by Equation (2).

$$y = (y_{t-1}, y_t, y_{t+1}..., y_{t+n}) \tag{2}$$

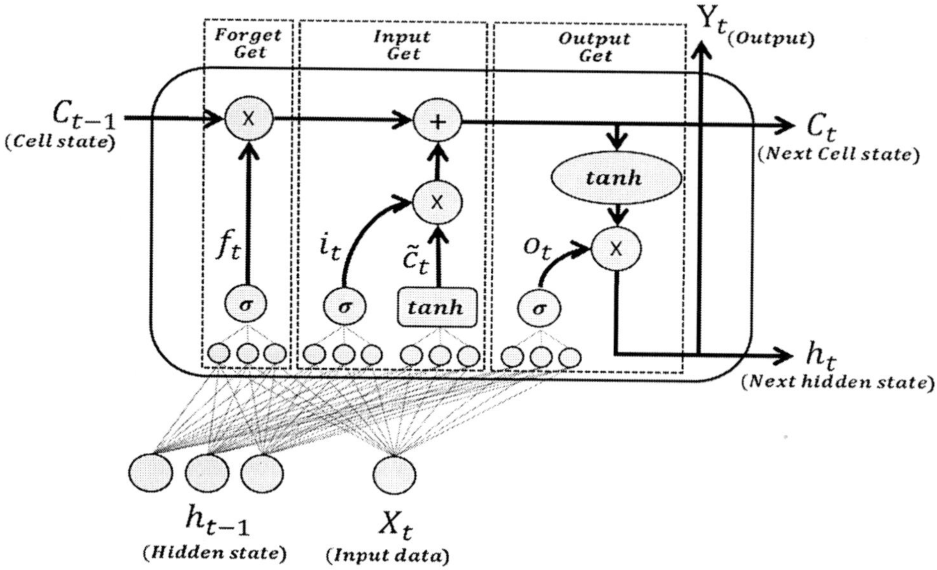

Figure 1. *A long short-term memory network's neural network architecture.*

For mapping, the first step is to input the activation vectors i_t and $\tilde{c}_t$, represented by Equations (3) and (4), respectively.

$$i_t = sigmoid(W_i[x_t, h_{t-1}] + b_i) \tag{3}$$

$$\tilde{c}_t = tanh(W_c[x_t, h_{t-1}] + b_c) \tag{4}$$

The sigmoid represents the activation function and maps the variable to values between zero and one, where W is the weight matrix, and b is the bias, $\tilde{c}_l$ is created by each tanh layer, and the forgetting gate f_t is created by Equation (5).

$$f_t = sigmoid(W_f[x_t, h_{t-1}] + b_f) \tag{5}$$

$\tilde{c}_t$ and f_t are employed to generate the new state of the memory cell C_t, which can be expressed by Equation (6):

$$C_t = i_t\tilde{c}_t + f_tc_{t-1} \tag{6}$$

The cell state vector C_t is utilized to calculate the output gate o_t, which is illustrated in Equation (7).

$$o_t = sigmoid(W_o[x_t, h_{t-1}] + b_o) \tag{7}$$

Finally, the output vector h_t of long short-term memory networks is determined by Equation (8).

$$h_t = tanh(c_t)o_t \tag{8}$$

The output gate uses the cell state and activation vector to calculate the output, and the weight matrix is used in the training phase to learn with the bias vector. The long short-term memory network architecture has been successful and effective in dealing with vanishing gradient problems [32,33,34,35].

THE PROPOSED HOTEL OCCUPANCY FORECASTING ARCHITECTURE

Figure 2 shows this study's proposed forecasting architecture for hotel room occupancy. The designed architecture uses the customer-generated experience content on the official database and online travel agent reservation websites to predict monthly hotel room occupancy rates in Taiwan. In particular, three parts are included in the framework, namely data collection, data preprocessing, and model testing. For the data collection, data of hotel lists and reviews of customers were gathered. In the data preprocessing stage, multilingual customer reviews were converted into sentiment scores, and the rating scores and sentiment scores were scaled into ranking variables. Then, the counts of variables were accumulated according to monthly data and mapped into the room occupancy in the next month. Finally, data were split into a training dataset and a testing dataset for modeling and performance evaluation of forecasting models.

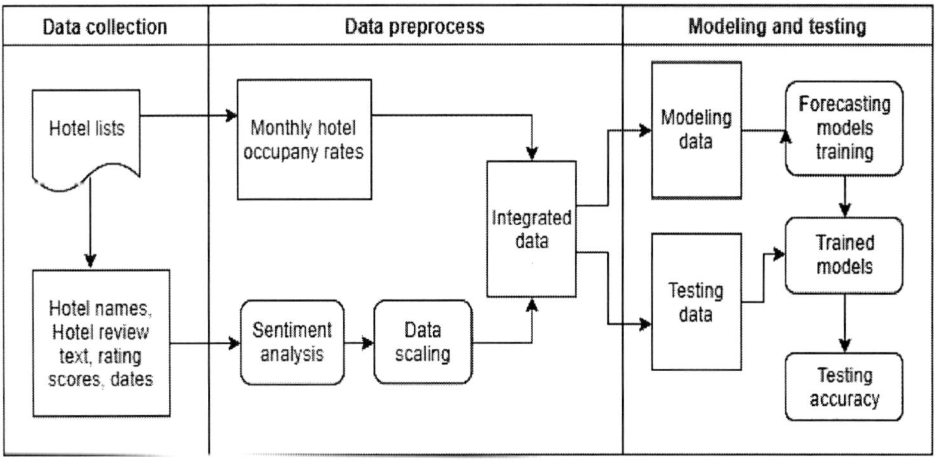

Figure 2. *The proposed hotel room occupancy forecasting architecture.*

Data Collection

This study collected data from the booking website Booking.com (accessed on 27 April 2021) and the Taiwan travel and accommodation website taiwanstay.net.tw, which is commissioned by the Tourism Bureau of the Ministry of Transportation of Taiwan. The customer hotel database provided by the Tourism Bureau contained monthly data, such as revenue, average room prices, occupancy rates, number of employees, etc. Hotels with room occupancy rates and customer reviews on the Booking.com (accessed on 27 April 2021) website were collected for this study. The datasets were based on the customer hotel database listed by the tourism bureau and text crawled from the booking website, including customers' online rating scores and comments. Figure 3 depicts the data collection flow of this study. The monthly data collection period was from July 2017 to December 2019. In total, 53 hotels with 1590 hotel data on the booking website were crawled. The customer review page obtained from the Booking.com (accessed on 27 April 2021) website is illustrated in Figure 4. The data of the hotels contain multiple customer review entries, including overall satisfaction scores for consumption experiences as well as positive and negative customer comments.

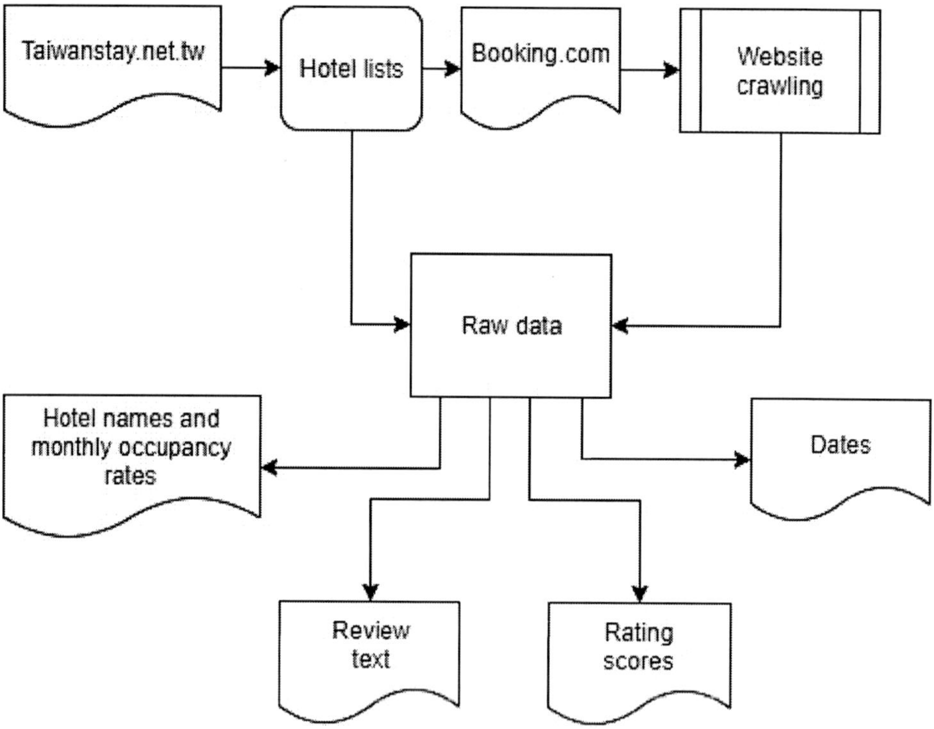

Figure 3. *Data collection process.*

Data Preprocessing

In this study, online customer reviews gathered from websites were processed using the natural language application programming interface developed by Google (https://cloud.google.com/natural-language?hl = zh-tw (accessed on 27 April 2021)) to generate sentiment scores. Multilingual sentiment analysis was

Figure 4. *Customer review content data items.*

performed in this study. Google's natural language application programming interface is based on machine learning theory. It has developed and provided user-friendly functions and interfaces for coping with multilingual sentiment analysis. Some of its successful applications have been reported [36,37]. Figure 5 shows the flow chart of thc sentiment analysis generated from customer reviews. Online customer reviews are divided into positive and negative reviews. Therefore, this study separately calculated the sentiment scores of positive and negative comments and integrated the scores. Then, online customer reviews were converted to sentiment scores. Table 1 lists data collected from the booking websites and the results of sentiment analysis. R_s refers to the customers' rating scores, whereas P_s and N_s refer to positive and negative sentiment scores, respectively, obtained from the comments. In addition, the term Lang. refers to the language categories of the customer reviews.

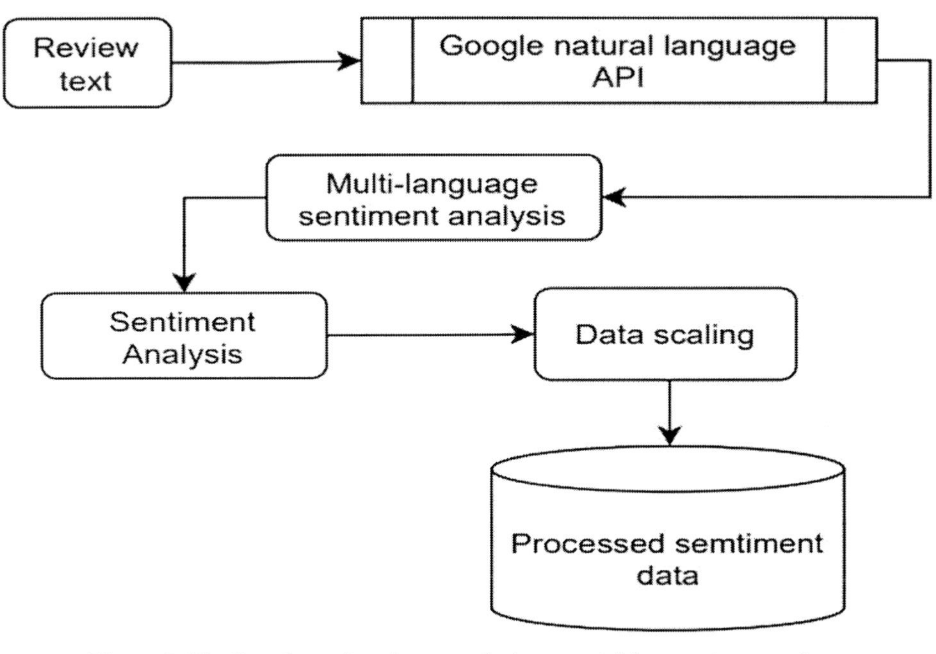

Figure 5. *The flow chart of sentiment analysis generated from customer reviews.*

Table 1. *Sentiment analysis in multilingual comment content.*

R_s	Positive Reviews	Negative Reviews	P_s	N_s	Lang.
9.2	Clean, spacious room.	Corridors leading to room could ...	0.9	−0.8	en
7.5	ロケーション抜群	施設が古い	0.9	−0.9	ja
7.9	交通特别方便，捷运出来 ...	空调声音略有点大	0.9	−0.4	zh
9.6	중앙역 바로 맞은 편이라 ...	특별한 것은 없음.	0.8	−0.4	ko
7.1	Hotel très bien placé, ...	C'est dommage qu'un si grand	0.9	−0.3	fr
10	ทำเลดีมาก. สดวก	บางครั้งน้ำร้อนไม่ค่อยพอ	0.8	−0.2	th
7.9	Ein sehr großes und ...	Es waren sehr kalte und ...	0.8	−0.3	de
7.9	La habitación era muy	El desayuno tenía poca oferta ...	0.3	0	es
7.9	早餐好吃，但是幾乎沒什麼 ...	衛浴設備過度老舊	0.2	−0.7	zh-Hant

For use in further analysis, this study transformed the sentiment analysis of the review text and customers' rating scores into ranking data. The sentiment scores of Google's application programming interface were between −1 and 1. The greater the positive value, the higher the positive sentiment. Conversely, the greater the negative value, the higher the negative sentiment. Thus, the study divides sentiment scales into seven ranks, as shown in Table 2. In Table 2, the fourth rank is "more than or equal to −0.1 and less than 0.1". This rank includes a sort of "neutral" state. Negative reviews contain both important aspects and minor issues with respect to various ranks, with scores from −0.1 to −1. Customers' ratings, illustrated in Table 3, are based on the hotel ratings of the booking website. Table 3 reflects major or minor issues collected from customers in terms of six ranks provided by booking systems with scores from 0 to 10. Then, by integrating Table 2 and Table 3, Table 4 illustrates the sample datasets employed in this study. To compare the performance of the sentiment analysis of the review text, customers' rating scores, and the combined data of customers' rating scores in forecasting monthly hotel occupancy rates, three datasets are illustrated in Table 5.

Table 2. *Sentiment scales.*

Rank	Abbreviations	Boundaries
1	X_1	less than −0.7
2	X_2	more than or equal to −0.7 and less than −0.4
3	X_3	more than or equal to −0.4 and less than −0.1
4	X_4	more than or equal to −0.1 and less than 0.1
5	X_5	more than or equal to 0.1 and less than 0.4
6	X_6	more than or equal to 0.4 and less than 0.7
7	X_7	more than or equal to 0.7

Table 3. *Customer rating scales.*

Rank	Abbreviations	Boundaries
1	X_8	less than or equal to 6.9
2	X_9	between 7.0 and 7.9
3	X_{10}	between 8.0 and 8.4
4	X_{11}	between 8.5 and 8.9
5	X_{12}	between 9.0 and 9.4
6	X_{13}	more than or equal to 9.5

Table 4. *All independent variables and monthly occupancy rates.*

X_1	X_2	X_3	X_4	X_5	X_6	X_7	X_8	X_9	X_{10}	X_{11}	X_{12}	X_{13}	Y (%)
3	3	1	2	3	2	7	0	2	0	1	3	5	56.23
5	10	3	1	4	6	20	5	4	2	2	3	15	86.20
2	5	0	1	2	3	11	1	1	0	1	1	11	45.13
5	7	3	1	4	5	12	4	7	1	2	1	9	64.90
2	2	1	0	2	1	6	2	2	0	1	1	4	67.35
0	1	0	0	1	0	1	0	0	2	0	2	0	11.96
3	4	2	0	2	4	14	3	5	1	2	3	9	74.91
0	2	0	0	0	2	1	0	0	0	0	2	3	77.18
4	7	3	1	2	4	14	1	3	0	8	5	8	60.81
5	7	5	0	8	8	16	3	4	5	8	2	13	66.00
1	2	0	1	0	0	5	3	0	1	0	0	2	19.31

Y (%) = monthly occupancy rates.

Table 5. *The three divided datasets used in this study.*

	Content of Data	Variables
Dataset I	sentiment analysis of review text	X_1–X_7
Dataset II	customers' rating scores	X_8–X_{13}
Dataset III	sentiment analysis of review text and customers' rating scores	X_1–X_{13}

Modeling and Testing

The data are divided into two datasets—a modeling dataset and a testing dataset. The modeling dataset with 1272 data included monthly data from July 2017 to June 2019, whereas the testing dataset with 318 data consisted of monthly data from July 2019 to December 2019. The modeling dataset was employed to train forecasting models, and the testing dataset was used to evaluate the performance of forecasting models. Figure 6 illustrates the modeling dataset and the testing dataset. A one-month-ahead forecasting policy was used in this study. Therefore, data gathered from the booking website in a given month were employed to predict hotel room occupancy rates in the next month.

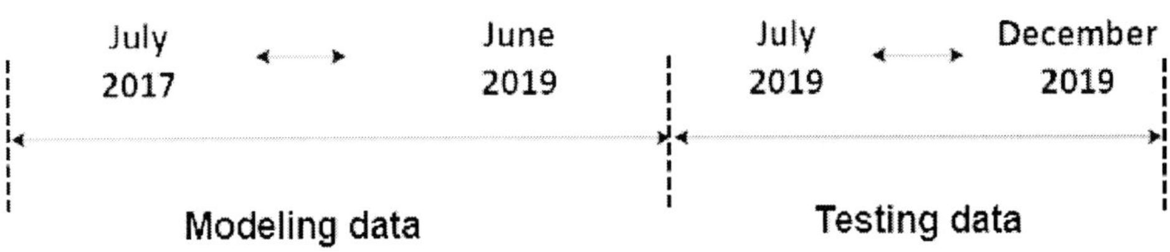

Figure 6. *The modeling dataset and the testing dataset.*

NUMERICAL RESULTS

In this study, six forecasting models were used to predict hotel room occupancy rates. The long short-term memory network model used in this study contained 61 neurons. The time step, batch size, and epoch were 1, 72, and 100, respectively. For the structure of backpropagation neural networks, one hidden layer with 10 hidden nodes was used. Table 6 lists the parameters used by the forecasting models in this study. Two indices—mean absolute percentage error (MAPE) and root mean square error (RMSE), expressed as Equations (9) and (10)—were employed to measure the performance of the forecasting models. Table 7 shows two

Table 6. *Parameters of forecasting models.*

Model	Parameters	Dataset I	Dataset II	Dataset III
LSTM	Learning rate	0.020	0.029	0.016
	Beta_1	0.725	0.883	0.900
	Beta 2	0.812	0.913	0.997
	Decay	0.023	0.012	0.004
BPNN	Learning rate	0.900	0.200	0.100
	Momentum	0.500	0.800	0.800
GRNN	Spread	0.100	0.200	0.900
LSSVR	γ	480	500	350
	σ	1	50	100
RF	Number of trees	1000	1100	1050
	Minimum number of samples to split	2	4	4
	Minimum number of samples at a leaf node	1	2	3
	Maximum depth	50	54	60
GPR	Kernel bounds	[−11,11]; [−11,11]	[−16,16]; [−11,11]	[−18,18]; [−11,11]

Table 7. *Measurements of forecasting accuracy by six models with different datasets.*

Datasets	Measurements	Models					
		LSTM	BPNN	GRNN	LSSVR	RF	GPR
Dataset I	MAPE (%)	16.618	17.391	20.254	19.449	21.747	22.447
	RMSE	13.221	14.698	17.364	16.494	18.753	22.043
Dataset II	MAPE (%)	16.883	17.898	20.721	19.062	20.777	25.296
	RMSE	13.494	15.177	18.139	16.876	17.210	25.673
Dataset III	MAPE (%)	16.416	17.006	19.717	18.905	21.471	21.049
	RMSE	13.076	13.826	17.197	16.401	17.946	20.624

measurements of forecasting accuracy generated by six models with three datasets. In terms of forecasting accuracy, it was indicated that long short-term memory network models could generate superior forecasting accuracy compared with the other five forecasting models. According to the numerical results in Table 7, it can be observed that using sentiment analysis of review text and customers' rating scores in forecasting models can yield more accurate results than using unique data of sentiment analysis of review text or customers' rating scores only. Thus, in this study, hybrid data were recommended for hotel room occupancy forecasting. Figure 7, Figure 8 and Figure 9 plot the absolute error values of hotel occupancies provided by the forecasting models with three datasets. A boxplot was used to plot the error values. The boxplot provides a clear data distribution map when there is a large number of values in the visual representation [38].

$$\mathrm{MAPE}(\%) = \frac{100}{N}\sum_{t=1}^{N}\left|\frac{Y_t - F_t}{Y_t}\right| \tag{9}$$

$$\mathrm{RMSE} = \sqrt{\frac{\sum_{t=1}^{N}(Y_t - F_t)^2}{N}} \tag{10}$$

where N is the number of forecasting periods, Y_t is the real value at period t, and F_t is the forecasting value at period t. In addition, the Wilcoxon signed-rank test [39] was performed to examine the significance of the accuracy improvement of the LSTM models. Table 8 illustrates the results of the Wilcoxon signed-rank test with $\alpha = 0.025$. The results indicated that the LSTM models statistically and significantly outperformed the other five forecasting models.

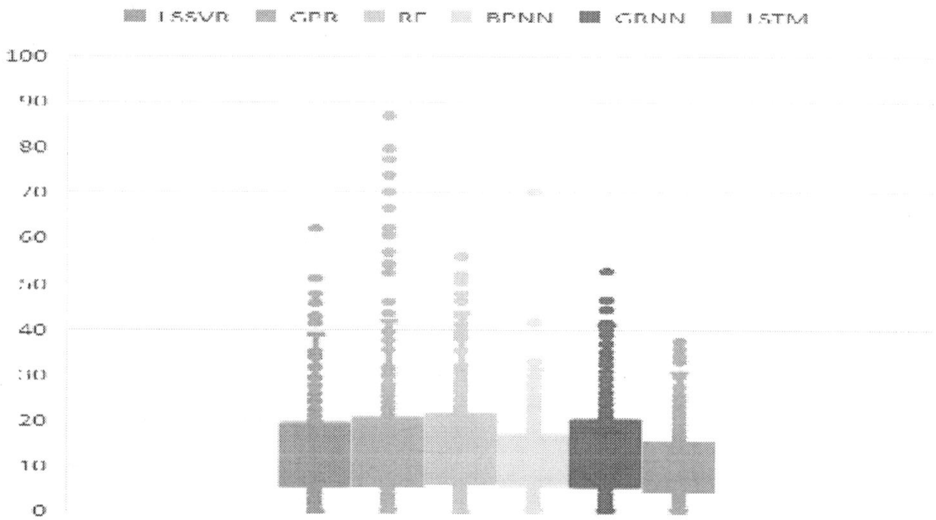

Figure 7. *Absolute errors with sentiment analysis of review text.*

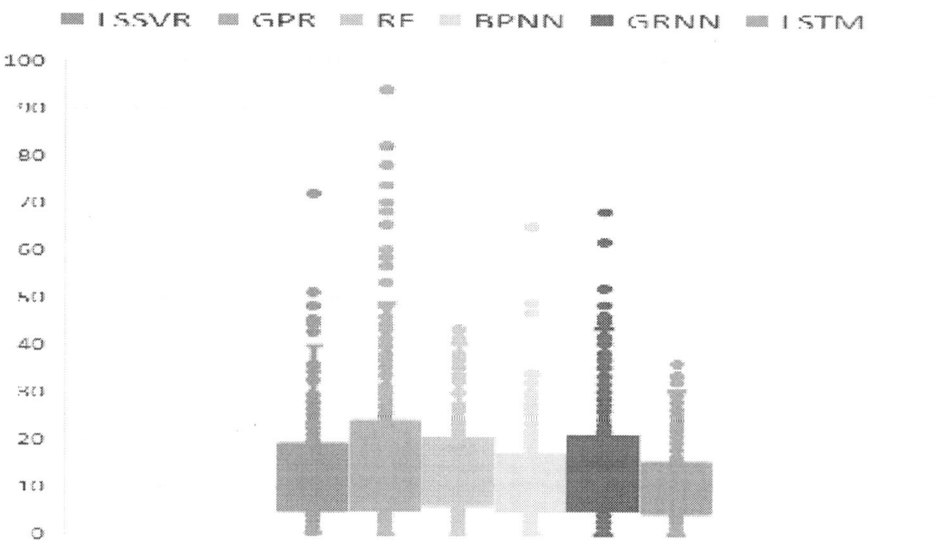

Figure 8. *Absolute errors with customers' rating scores.*

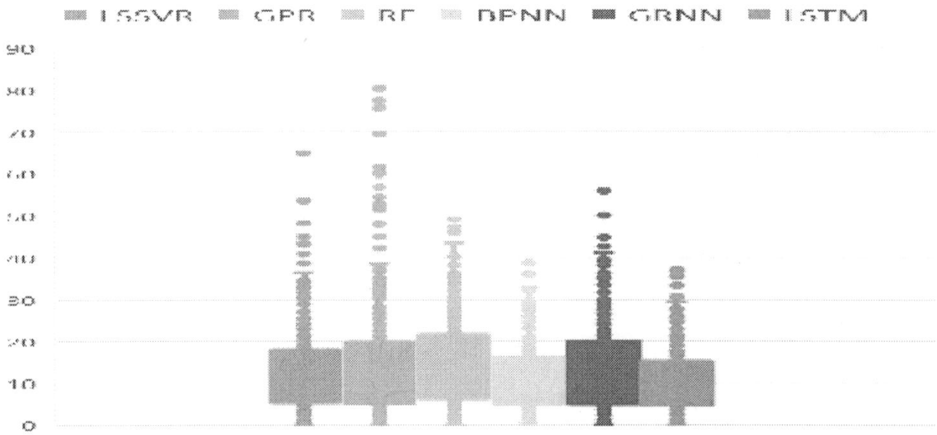

Figure 9. *Absolute errors with sentiment analysis of review text and customers' rating scores.*

Table 8. *The results of the Wilcoxon signed-rank test with $\alpha = 0.025$.*

Dataset	Measurements	LSTM vs.				
		LSSVR	**BPNN**	**GRNN**	**GPR**	**RF**
Dataset I	Z Value	4.042	3.296	4.534	7.507	5.903
	Significance	Yes	Yes	Yes	Yes	Yes
	Positive number	184	188	185	206	192
	Negative number	134	130	133	112	126
Dataset II	Z Value	3.821	3.327	4.204	5.545	5.315
	Significance	Yes	Yes	Yes	Yes	Yes
	Positive number	184	177	180	193	195
	Negative number	134	141	138	125	123
Dataset III	Z Value	4.065	2.783	3.164	3.849	6.052
	Significance	Yes	Yes	Yes	Yes	Yes
	Positive number	194	174	178	179	198
	Negative number	124	144	140	139	120

CONCLUSIONS

Because of the expansion of online travel agent booking systems, the collection of customers' opinions on accommodations has become more diversified. Customers' online rating scores and review text in booking systems have become major sources that gather customers' experiences; hence, they are essential influences to forecast hotel occupancy. This study used three datasets—a sentiment analysis of review text, customers' rating scores, and combined data of customers' rating scores—to predict the monthly hotel occupancy rates with a one-month-ahead forecasting policy. Besides, multilingual comment contents were included in this study. Six forecasting models—LSTM, BPNN, GRNN, LSSVR, RF, and GPR—were utilized to deal with the same dataset. The numerical results indicated that the long short-term memory network model could provide more accurate hotel occupancy forecasting rates than the other five models in three datasets. In addition, the hybrid data of the sentiment analysis of review text and customers' rating scores produced the most accurate results among all forecasting models.

For future studies, more detailed data, such as attributes of hotels and customers, can be added as input data for forecasting models. The hotel attributes include international type, customer type, location, the number of rooms, and prices. The customer attributes possibly consist of gender, nationality, and stay type. The sentiment analysis and comparison according to clusters of different countries and the study of site-specific peculiarities could be paths for future study. With more detailed data, forecasting models are able to provide more informative data for hotel management and decision-making. In addition, the hotel room occupancy used in this study was gathered from public sectors that do not provide bed and breakfast room occupancy data. Bed and breakfast room occupancy data, mostly used for the AirBnB system, could be another possible direction for further study to examine the performance of the proposed hotel room occupancy forecasting architecture. Finally, because the COVID-19 crisis affected hotel room occupancy, the data collected in the COVID-19 period is a challenging topic worthy of future investigation.

Author Contributions

Conceptualization, P.-F.P.; data curation; Y.-M.C., C.-H.C. and J.-P.L.; formal analysis, Y.-M.C. and P.-F.P.; methodology, Y.-M.C. and P.-F.P.; software, C.-H.C., J.-P.L. and Y.-L.L.; visualization, Y.-M.C., J.-P.L. and Y.-L.L.; writing—original draft preparation, Y.-M.C. and P.-F.P.; writing—review and editing, P.-F.P.; funding acquisition, P.-F.P. All authors have read and agreed to the published version of the manuscript.

REFERENCES

1. Kimes, S.E.; Chase, R.B.; Choi, S.; Lee, P.Y.; Ngonzi, E.N. Restaurant Revenue Management. *Cornell Hotel Restaur. Adm. Q.* **1998**, *39*, 32–39.
2. Wu, D.C.; Song, H.; Shen, S. New developments in tourism and hotel demand modeling and forecasting. *Int. J. Contemp. Hosp. Manag.* **2017**, *29*, 507–529.
3. Salehan, M.; Kim, D.J. Predicting the performance of online customer reviews: A sentiment mining approach to big data analytics. *Decis. Support Syst.* **2016**, *81*, 30–40.
4. De Pelsmacker, P.; van Tilburg, S.; Holthof, C. Digital marketing strategies, online reviews and hotel performance. *Int. J. Hosp. Manag.* **2018**, *72*, 47–55.
5. Anagnostopoulou, S.C.; Buhalis, D.; Kountouri, I.L.; Manousakis, E.G.; Tsekrekos, A.E. The impact of online reputation on hotel profitability. *Int. J. Hosp. Manag.* **2020**, *32*, 20–39.
6. Liu, Y.; Teichert, T.; Rossi, M.; Li, H.; Hu, F. Big data for big insights: Investigating language-specific drivers of hotel satisfaction with 412,784 user-generated reviews. *Tour. Manag.* **2017**, *59*, 554–563.
7. Fernandes, E.; Moro, S.; Cortez, P.; Batista, F.; Ribeiro, R. A data-driven approach to measure restaurant performance by combining online reviews with historical sales data. *Int. J. Hosp. Manag.* **2020**, *94*, 102830.
8. Phillips, P.; Zigan, K.; Silva, M.M.S.; Schegg, R. The interactive effects of online reviews on the determinants of Swiss hotel performance: A neural network analysis. *Tour. Manag.* **2015**, *50*, 130–141.

9. Morente-Molinera, J.; Kou, G.; Pang, C.; Cabrerizo, F.; Herrera-Viedma, E. An automatic procedure to create fuzzy ontologies from users' opinions using sentiment analysis procedures and multi-granular fuzzy linguistic modelling methods. *Inf. Sci.* **2018**, *476*, 222–238.
10. Hu, N.; Koh, N.S.; Reddy, S.K. Ratings lead you to the product, reviews help you clinch it? The mediating role of online review sentiments on product sales. *Decis. Support Syst.* **2013**, *57*, 42–53.
11. Zhang, S.T.; Wang, F.F.; Duo, F.; Zhang, J.L. Research on the Majority Decision Algorithm based on WeChat sentiment classification. *J. Intell. Fuzzy Syst.* **2018**, *35*, 2975–2984.
12. Li, X.; Law, R.; Xie, G.; Wang, S. Review of tourism forecasting research with internet data. *Tour. Manag.* **2020**, *83*, 104245.
13. Zhang, B.; Pu, Y.; Wang, Y.; Li, J. Forecasting Hotel Accommodation Demand Based on LSTM Model Incorporating Internet Search Index. *Sustainability* **2019**, *11*, 4708.
14. Pan, B.; Wu, D.C.; Song, H. Forecasting hotel room demand using search engine data. *J. Hosp. Tour. Technol.* **2012**, *3*, 196–210.
15. Pan, B.; Yang, Y. Forecasting Destination Weekly Hotel Occupancy with Big Data. *J. Travel Res.* **2016**, *56*, 957–970.
16. Yang, Y.; Pan, B.; Song, H. Predicting Hotel Demand Using Destination Marketing Organization's Web Traffic Data. *J. Travel Res.* **2013**, *53*, 433–447.
17. Bigne, E.; Oltra, E.; Andreu, L. Harnessing stakeholder input on twitter: A case study of short breaks in Spanish tourist cities. *Tour. Manag.* **2019**, *71*, 490–503.
18. Aliyev, R.; Salehi, S.; Aliyev, R. Development of fuzzy time series model for hotel occupancy forecasting. *Sustainability* **2019**, *11*, 793.
19. Ampountolas, A. Modeling and Forecasting Daily Hotel Demand: A Comparison Based on SARIMAX, Neural Networks, and GARCH Models. *Forecasting* **2021**, *3*, 580–595.
20. Zhang, M.; Li, J.; Pan, B.; Zhang, G. Weekly Hotel Occupancy Forecasting of a Tourism Destination. *Sustainability* **2018**, *10*, 4351.
21. Ginindza, S.; Tichaawa, T.M. The impact of sharing accommodation on the hotel occupancy rate in the kingdom of Swaziland. *Curr. Issues Tour.* **2017**, *22*, 1975–1991.
22. Fiori, A.M.; Foroni, I. Reservation Forecasting Models for Hospitality SMEs with a View to Enhance Their Economic Sustainability. *Sustainability* **2019**, *11*, 1274.
23. Assaf, A.G.; Tsionas, M.G. Forecasting occupancy rate with Bayesian compression methods. *Ann. Tour. Res.* **2019**, *75*, 439–449.
24. Al Shehhi, M.; Karathanasopoulos, A. Forecasting hotel room prices in selected GCC cities using deep learning. *J. Hosp. Tour. Manag.* **2019**, *42*, 40–50.
25. Zhang, Q.; Qiu, L.; Wu, H.; Wang, J.; Luo, H. Deep Learning Based Dynamic Pricing Model for Hotel Revenue Management. In Proceedings of the 2019 International Conference on Data Mining Workshops (ICDMW), Beijing, China, 8–11 November 2019.
26. Sánchez-Medina, A.J.; C.-Sánchez, E. Using machine learning and big data for efficient forecasting of hotel booking cancellations. *Int. J. Hosp. Manag.* **2020**, *89*, 102546.
27. Wang, J.; Duggasani, A. Forecasting hotel reservations with long short-term memory-based recurrent neural networks. *Int. J. Data Sci. Anal.* **2018**, *9*, 77–94.
28. Huang, L.; Zheng, W. Novel deep learning approach for forecasting daily hotel demand with agglomeration effect. *Int. J. Hosp. Manag.* **2021**, *98*, 103038.

29. Das, R.; Chadha, H.; Banerjee, S. Multi-layered market forecast framework for hotel revenue management by continuously learning market dynamics. *J. Revenue Pricing Manag.* **2021**, *20*, 351–367.

30. Lee, M.; Mu, X.; Zhang, Y. A machine learning approach to improving forecasting accuracy of hotel demand: A comparative analysis of neural networks and traditional models. *Issues Inf. Syst.* **2020**, *21*, 12–21.

31. Phumchusri, N.; Ungtrakul, P. Hotel daily demand forecasting for high-frequency and complex seasonality data: A case study in Thailand. *J. Revenue Pricing Manag.* **2019**, *19*, 8–25.

32. Hochreiter, S.; Schmidhuber, J. Long short-term memory. *Neural Comput.* **1997**, *9*, 1735–17808.

33. Fischer, T.; Krauss, C. Deep learning with long short-term memory networks for financial market predictions. *Eur. J. Oper. Res.* **2018**, *270*, 654–669.

34. Hua, Y.; Zhao, Z.; Li, R.; Chen, X.; Liu, Z.; Zhang, H. Deep Learning with Long Short-Term Memory for Time Series Prediction. *IEEE Commun. Mag.* **2019**, *57*, 114–119.

35. Chandra, R.; Jain, A.; Chauhan, D.S. Deep learning via LSTM models for COVID-19 infection forecasting in India. *arXiv* **2021**, preprint. arXiv:2101.11881.

36. White, T.E.; Rege, M. Sentiment Analysis on Google Cloud Platform. *Issues Inf. Syst.* **2020**, *21*, 221–228.

37. Luo, X.; Zimet, G.; Shah, S. A natural language processing framework to analyse the opinions on HPV vaccination reflected in twitter over 10 years (2008–2017). *Hum. Vaccines Immunother.* **2019**, *15*, 1496–1504.

38. Tukey, J.W. *Exploratory Data Analysis*; Addison-Wesley: Boston, MA, USA, 1977; ISBN 978-0201076165.

39. Wilcoxon, F. Individual Comparisons by Ranking Methods. *Biom. Bull.* **1945**, *1*, 80.

CHAPTER 8

The Impact of Hotel Customer Experience on Customer Satisfaction through Online Reviews

Yae-Ji Kim[1] and Hak-Seon Kim[2,3]

[1]*School of Global Studies, Kyungsung University, 309 Suyoungro, Nam-gu, Busan 48434, Korea*

[2]*Wellness & Tourism Big Data Research Institute, Kyungsung University, 309 Suyoungro, Nam-gu, Busan 48434, Korea*

[3]*School of Hospitality & Tourism Management, Kyungsung University, 309 Suyoungro, Nam-gu, Busan 48434, Korea*

ABSTRACT

With the growing popularity of the internet, customers can easily share their experiences and information in online reviews. Consumers recognize online reviews as a useful source of information prior to consumption, and many online reviews influence consumer purchasing decisions. Understanding the customer experience in online reviews is thus necessary to maintain customer satisfaction and repurchase intention for the sustainable development of the hotel business. This study assessed the fundamental selection attributes of customers from online reviews reflecting the hotel customer experience, and investigated their association with customer satisfaction. A total of 8229 reviews were collected from Google travel websites from December 2019 to July 2021. Text mining and semantic network analysis were adopted for big data analysis. Factor and regression analyses were then used for quantitative analysis. Based on linear regression analysis, the Service and Dining factors significantly affected customer satisfaction. Service is a critical selection attribute for customers, and the provision of more particular services is necessary, especially after COVID-19. These results indicate that understanding online reviews can provide theoretical and practical implications for developing sustainable strategies for the hotel industry.

Keywords: *online review; customer experience; customer satisfaction; selection attribute; text mining; semantic network analysis*

INTRODUCTION

When tourists plan to travel and book accommodations, they often search for hotels they have never been to before. Acquisition of hotel information can reduce the risk of choosing poorly. Traditionally, word of mouth (WOM) from friends has been used to reduce risks, and with the popularity of the internet, electronic word of mouth (eWOM) is becoming important [1,2], as consumers begin to trust in WOM transmitted over the internet [3,4]. Commonly, consumers want to express or share their opinions and seek information via digital means [5,6]. Filieri and McLeay [7] found that 96.4% of their respondents (7000) had used the internet as a source of information in the travel planning stage, and 90% referred to other customers' reviews.

Because the characteristics of the service field are not like those for tangible products, it is difficult to determine the actual situation of a hotel until the customer has experienced it [8]. Here, eWOM provides rich data that reflect consumer characteristics and perceptions of service satisfaction. The experience of the service mentioned in eWOM thus implies the main attributes and quality levels of the product or service considered by the customer [9], and eWOM can significantly affect tourists' purchase decisions and the business performance of hotels [10].

Many researchers have conducted surveys to investigate customer satisfaction and hotel selection attributes in the hotel and hospitality industry [11,12,13]. Although the survey method has the advantage of being able to elicit answers to the desired questions, there may be limitations due to factors that might cause measurement errors, such as the form of the questionnaire, the survey term, the response category, and the order of the survey [14]. To address this gap, online review mining was conducted to gain more accurate and detailed customer information through the application of big data analytics in the hospitality sector [15,16,17,18,19]. Filieri and Mariani [16] adopted big data analytics to examine how reviews from different countries evaluate the helpfulness of online reviews. Ban and Kim [19] analyzed user reviews to understand various airline passenger satisfaction attributes using text mining analysis.

However, there are still only limited studies on the online reviews of hotel customers that use big data analytics, explore the factors reflecting customer experiences based on these review data, and then verify the relationship between the extracted factors and customer satisfaction. Therefore, this study sought to derive meaningful implications by analyzing online reviews of hotels and exploring which attributes affected customer satisfaction.

LITERATURE REVIEW

Electronic Word of Mouth

E-commerce has a strategic emphasis for business and consumers, and WOM has been reconceptualized as eWOM since traditional, face-to-face WOM is changing into eWOM, as consumers can obtain information regarding products or services online before making a purchase decision [20,21]. When purchasing intangible products or services, consumers tend to rely more on eWOM for products or services they have not used or experienced before [22], as this helps customers obtain specific information influenced by customers' selection attributes and shared personal experiences, opinions, photos, hotel reviews, and vacation suggestions [23].

Online review websites such as Tripadvisor serve as an essential platform for consumers to share purchasing experiences and express their opinions about products and services [24]. Reviews exchanged among consumers contain information about the user's experience and how that experience is perceived [25], such that customers are more likely to trust eWOM than information provided by sellers [22]. By reading other people's reviews, potential consumers better construct their interpretation of the product and become more aware of the risks to their transactions. Vermeulen and Seegers [26] found that consumers' exposure to online reviews improved the probability of booking a hotel. Stringam, Gerdes, and Vanleeuwen [27] analyzed reviews on Expedia.com, an online travel agency platforms, and found that the overall satisfaction evaluation had a high correlation between recommendation intentions. Ban and Kim [19] analyzed the online reviews on Skytrax.com and quantitatively identified the relationship among six evaluation factors (seat comfort, staff, F&B, entertainment, ground service, and value for money), customer satisfaction, and recommendations.

This study thus investigates customer experience through text-mining analysis of reviews of hotel products, which are representative experience goods greatly affected by online reviews.

Customer Experience and Satisfaction

Customer experience, which means that an individual has experienced the goods or services of a company as a consumer, was first conceptualized by Schmitt [28] as being composed of sensory, emotional, cognitive, behavioral, and relational experiences. Meyer and Schwager [29] defined customer experience as the customers' personal/subjective response to direct/indirect contact with a firm in any form. Customer experience is remembered positively or negatively depending on the customer's situation, which leads to customer satisfaction, and customers who positively evaluate the experience can be said to feel satisfied [29].

Customer satisfaction is a complex experience in the hospitality industry, and assessing what the customer has experienced is complicated [30]. Focusing on customer experience and satisfaction has inevitably increased as the market has changed from a producer-driven market to a buyer-driven one [20]. Customer-satisfaction management is the only strategy that can respond to such market changes. Corporate marketing activities have made it a fundamental goal to focus on customer satisfaction, which, through customer experience, can increase customer loyalty, repurchase intention, positive WOM, and consequently, contribute to higher profitability [31]

Customers prefer and think about hotel selection attributes, which play a critical role in the information search and alternative selection process and is thus a target for evaluating hotel satisfaction and dissatisfaction [32,33]. Identifying the customer's hotel selection attributes is essential for improving service quality and increasing customer satisfaction to gain a competitive advantage [34].

Big Data Analysis

Big data analysis of online-generated data to predict consumer behavior and psychological is an emerging topic in the hospitality industry [19]. It is necessary to extract and convert data from online reviews before analysis, and text mining and semantic network analysis play an important role in big data analysis due to the large and unstructured nature of consumer-generated data. This study employed text analytics to deconstruct numerous customer reviews collected from Google.com, which was followed by semantic network analysis to examine the association with extracted keywords [19,22].

Text mining for knowledge discovery based on text databases was first mentioned by Feldman and Dagan [35], and is the discovery of valuable unknown patterns in text using information retrieval and extraction and natural language processing (NLP) techniques [36]. Text mining involves data collection, data refining, data analysis, a management information system and knowledge generation [37], as shown in Figure 1.

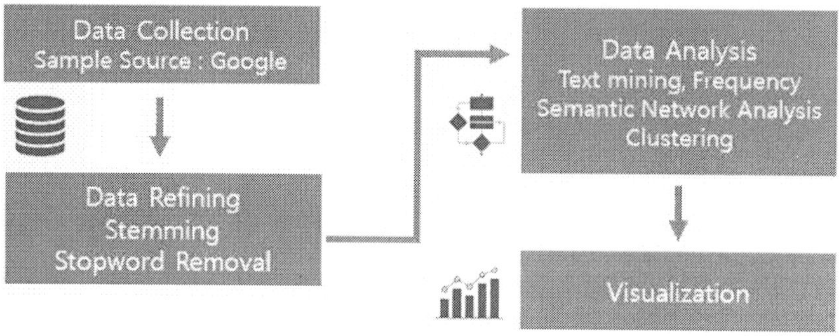

Figure 1. *Text mining process, source Ban and Kim [19].*

When collecting data, researchers identify the type of information they want, clarify concepts, limit the scope of what they want to collect, and familiarize themselves with the characteristics of the keywords. Data refining and preprocessing involves converting unstructured textual data into structured forms. For accurate results, sophisticated pretreatment is essential. As a step to analyze text-based technologies such as information extraction, document summary, and clustering are involved in the next step for analyzing text-based data, and analysis methods suitable for research purposes are then applied to manage information systems at worksites and to accumulate knowledge [19,38].

Text mining for the hospitality industry has recently been the subject of active research. Boo and Busser [8] qualitatively and quantitatively investigated meeting planners' online reviews of destination hotels. The results yielded insights to respond to the online reviews and formed the basis for hotel evaluation criteria. Stepchenkova and Morrison [39] analyzed Russia-related texts on 212 websites, measured Russia's tourist destination image, and identified the differences between US and Russian websites. He, Zha, and Li [40] described an in-depth case study that applied text mining to analyze text on the Facebook and Twitter sites of three pizza chains: Pizza Hut, Domino's Pizza, and Papa John's Pizza, which are representative franchises in the industry. The results confirmed the value of social media competitive analysis and the power of text mining as an effective technique for extracting business value from the vast amount of available social media data. The formation of social issues through SNS (Social Networking Service) is accelerating in various fields. With the development of SNS, network analysis is becoming essential to extract different meanings and concepts inherent in text-based messages and to understand their relational characteristics [41]. Semantic network analysis assesses the structure of a semantic network retrieved according to the given text, and it also explores meaning through the structural relationship of words as message components, rather than lexical units [42].

Semantic network analysis uses individual words to clarify network structure and meaning within a text. Selecting a specific term and repeatedly using it when emphasizing a particular meaning is one method for content analysis of the relationship between words that appear simultaneously in a sentence or paragraph. The core of semantic network analysis is indicating the influence of words, and analysis based on structural identity consists of an index for classifying subgroups based on word similarity [19,30,43].

METHODOLOGY

Data Collection

The data collection procedure for this study is as follows. Hotel reviews were collected from Google Travel (www.google.com/travel), the largest search engine globally. Google hotel reviews include detailed information about the hotel brand used by the customer, the reviewer's ID, review date, comment, rating, and type of trip. Figure 2 shows a specific example from Google Online Reviews. SCTM

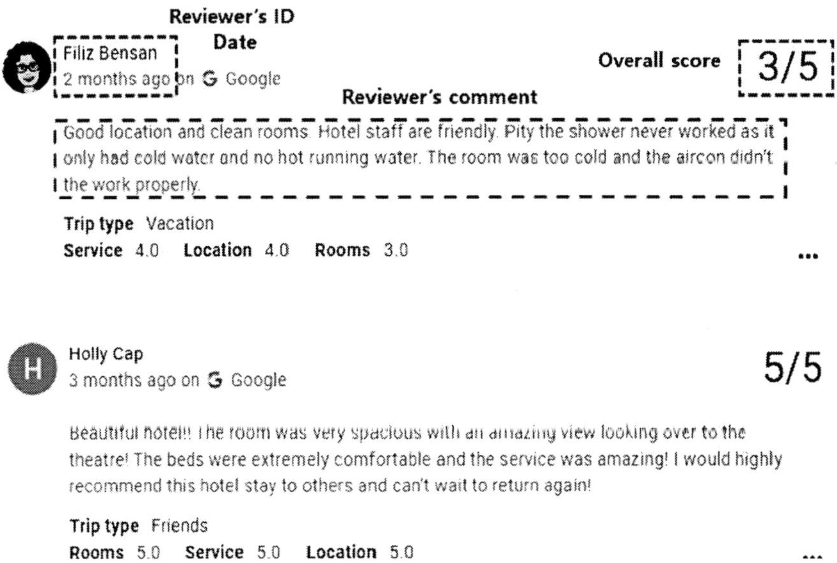

Figure 2. *Screenshot of customer review on Google Travel.*

(Smart Crawling & Text Mining, developed by the Wellness and Tourism Big Data Research Institute at Kyungsung University) and TEXTOM (a big data analysis solution to collect and refine data and generate matrix data) were used to collect and refine online data.

Words were ranked according to the frequency of their occurrence, to analyze the unstructured data. Table 1 shows the 25 recommended hotels and the number of reviews for each hotel. A total of 8448 reviews were collected, and 8229 reviews and 314,813 words were extracted, excluding data that were not readable or had only ratings with no review content. The data collection period was from December 2019, when COVID-19 first appeared, to July 2021, to determine if there were any different implications from a prior study of Ban, Choi, Choi, Lee, and Kim [44], who conducted research using online hotel reviews before the COVID-19 pandemic, making this a longitudinal study.

Table 1. *Number of reviews according to 2021 Hotel ranking source from Tripadvisor website.*

Rank	Hotel	Count	Rank	Hotel	Count
1	Hotel Colline de France	332	14	The Ritz-carlton Macau	155
2	THE OMNIA	158	15	Sukhumvit Park, Bangkok Marriott Executive Apartments	336
3	Sani Dunes	84	16	Hotel Ambiez	72
4	Kandolhu Maldives	45	17	Hamanasi Adventure & Dive Resort, Belize	186
5	ACHTIS HOTEL	65	18	Mint House at 70 Pine NYC	138
6	Mandapa, a Ritz-Carlton Reserve	382	19	Jaya House River Park Hotel	183
7	The Legian Seminyak, Bali	318	20	Gran Hotel Ciudad de México	2064
8	Gardena Grödnerhof Hotel & Spa	52	21	The Hari	210
9	Tulemar Bungalows & Villas	55	22	Waldorf Astoria Amsterdam	225
10	Hacienda Beach Club & Residences	259	23	Corpo Santo Lisbon Historical Hotel	333
11	Club Prive by Rixos Belek	38	24	Villa Rosa Kempinski	2123
12	Chandys Windy Woods 5 Star Resort Munnar	525	25	Tokoriki Island Resort	83
13	Mirihi Island Resort	27		**Total**	**8448**

Data Analysis

The analysis was conducted according to previous studies [19,30,43,44]. Big data analysis was performed in two parts: text mining and semantic network analysis. Factor and linear regression analyses were then used. First, the top 90 most frequent words were extracted through the text mining refining process. The Python-based Natural Language Toolkit was used. A stop word refers to commonly used word (e.g., "the", "a", "an", "in"). The program ignores stop words both when indexing entries for searching and when retrieving them as the result of a search query. Through the refinement process, pronouns, prepositions, and meaningless words were removed, and the generated data included only words related to the hotel experience. The word matrix (word × word) was then deduced. To assess the overall satisfaction with the hotel experience, a distribution of hotel experience evaluations based on the rating score was used, and this 'overall rating' was used as a dependent variable, because the value can be treated as the primary output variable [43].

Second, based on the matrix data, the network of words was visualized using Ucinet 6.0 to clarify the connection structure and connectivity between nodes. Semantic network analysis focused on degree and eigenvector centralities, which are indicators quantified based on the centrality concept arrangement and measurement method. Freeman proposed eigenvector centrality as a measure of the influence of a node in a network [19,30]. Relative weights are assigned to all nodes in the network, based on the idea that connections to high-scoring nodes contribute more to the score of the node in question than an equal number of links to low-scoring nodes [45]. Finally, CONCOR (CONvergence of iterated CORrelation) analysis was conducted to segment the words and acquire the dimensions of hotel customer experience. CONCOR analysis was performed repeatedly to find the connections and relationships between the words and similarity groups by forming clusters including keywords [42]. The results were visualized with Netdraw to provide a more intuitionistic visualization of the segmentation of the top-frequency words used by customers.

Finally, quantitative analysis was performed. By integrating the results of the CONCOR analysis and a comparison of word frequency and centrality, words were selected for further factor and linear regression analyses using dummy variables. Tao and Kim [43] investigated customer experience-related words with the highest explanatory power for customer satisfaction, and conducted a study on words with high frequency. These high-frequency words were ultimately judged to be appropriate because of Freeman's high centrality in demonstrating word relevance and variables focused on revealing communities in combination with key items in the CONCOR results.

Factor analysis was performed to retrieve the main factors affecting hotel customer satisfaction, using 55 out of the 90 top-frequency words. In addition, linear regression analysis, which consisted of four independent variables derived from the factor analysis and overall ratings as a dependent variable, was performed to verify the following hypothesis: The hotel experience shown in the online review can be used to explain customer satisfaction.

RESULTS

Frequency Analysis

The data were transformed from unstructured information such as sentences to structured data such as single words and their corresponding frequency. A total of 314,813 words were collected. After deleting repeated, unnecessary, and low-frequency words, a total of 90 high-frequency words were extracted. Table 2 shows the 90 highest frequency words with Term Frequency-Inverse Document Frequency (TF-IDF). Figure 3 illustrates the network visibility of these 90 top frequency words.

The TF-IDF weight model evaluates how important words inside a document are in text mining. TF-IDF is a value obtained by multiplying TF and IDF, and the higher the score, the less frequently the word appears in other documents and the more frequently it appears in the document considered. A word with a larger TF-IDF value is more likely to determine the topic or meaning of the document to which it belongs, and this can be used as a measure to extract critical keywords. For example, the words indicating the location or included in hotel brand, such as "ciudad" or "mexico", which are second and third in the frequency ranking, have a TF-IDF of 2892 and 2882, respectively, and the TF-IDF rankings are also highly ranked, at third and fourth. Words representing the hotel brand or location were meaningful words in the review data.

Table 2. *Top 90 frequent words with TF-IDF from the online review.*

Rank	Word	Freq.	TF-IDF	Rank	Word	Freq.	TF-IDF	Rank	Word	Freq.	TF-IDF
1	service	2523	4027	31	waldorf	253	908/33	61	option	120	553
2	ciudad	2104	2892/3	32	quality	252	967	62	coffee	120	550
3	méxico	2085	2882/4	33	astoria	243	873/36	63	window	119	564
4	hotel	1244	2899/2	34	family	238	927	64	variety	119	543
5	restaurant	893	2412	35	people	231	907	65	night	118	545
6	resort	798	2303/6	36	guest	223	893	66	moment	115	555
7	place	701	1865	37	hospitality	216	836	67	villa	114	508
8	experience	671	1892	38	luxury	214	863	68	brunch	112	555
9	breakfast	651	1902	39	belgrave	212	791/43	69	thank	102	471
10	locate	620	1792	40	belize	209	794/42	70	holiday	100	471
11	ritz carlton	572	1510/14	41	custom	209	822	71	park	98	470
12	chandys	551	1509/15	42	island	202	834	72	class	97	449
13	staff	544	1595	43	property	198	817	73	entrance	96	473
14	everything	507	1618	44	ambience	194	742	74	city	95	453
15	trip	478	1364	45	dinner	177	733	75	decorate	94	470
16	attention	458	1571	46	reception	175	745	76	Zermatt	94	504/69
17	mandapa	440	1350/18	47	architecture	172	751	77	Tokoriki	93	429/81
18	lisbon	412	1317/19	48	everyone	166	694	78	amenity	92	430
19	serve	402	1228	49	security	155	667	79	conference	90	428
20	france	377	1202/23	50	history	153	703	80	employee	90	446
21	hamanasi	377	1424/16	51	price	151	667	81	bathroom	89	423
22	seminyak	352	1143/25	52	atmosphere	151	657	82	garden	89	431
23	terrace	341	1284	53	manage	150	657	83	elevator	88	438
24	adventure	314	1179	54	drink	146	636	84	world	86	409
25	room	313	1019	55	build	142	643	85	environment	85	408
26	buffet	311	1243	56	food	142	596	86	stay	84	389
27	facility	278	1037	57	accommodate	131	586	87	excellent	84	384
28	residence	276	941	58	view	129	570	88	wait	83	415
29	amsterdam	275	987/28	59	friend	127	573	89	afternoon	82	422
30	hacienda	264	910/32	60	station	121	577	90	balcony	82	404

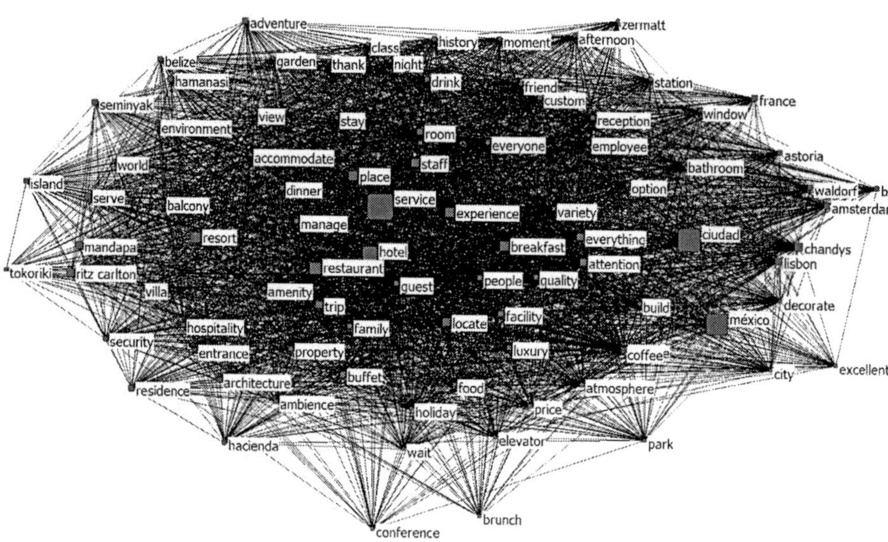

Figure 3. *Keyword visualization.*

It is undeniable but surprising that "service" had the highest frequency, and this implies that, for hotel consumers, a hotel's service is the aspect they mentioned most. There were also words related to service, such as "restaurant", "experience", and "staff", that appeared with high frequency. Referring to the number of online hotel reviews, although the "Gran Hotel Ciudad de México" ranked 20th in the hotel brand among 25 hotels, it recorded the highest number of reviews, at 2064, which suggests that the two words "ciudad" and "mexico" have high web visibility. Words related to location or name of the hotel were also common, such as "ciudad", "ritz carlton", "chandy", "mandapa", "lisbon", and "france", as were words such as "experience", "trip", "adventure", "family", "security", and "price", which could reflect the purpose of the trip.

Semantic Network Analysis

Semantic network analysis identifies the relationship between words and expresses their connection in the network [44]. The centrality of the top 90 most frequent words was calculated, compared with word frequency, and synthesized in Table 3, in which the top 50 most frequent words are described. As a result, words such as "service", "hotel", "restaurant", "experience", and "breakfast" are shown to have both high frequency and high centrality. To a great extent, this indicated that these words were frequently used by online users and are closely associated with other nodes in the semantic network.

Table 3. *Comparison of keyword frequency and centrality analysis.*

	Frequency		Degree		Eigenvector			Frequency		Degree		Eigenvector	
	Freq.	Rank	Coef	Rank	Coef	Rank		Freq.	Rank	Coef	Rank	Coef	Rank
service	2523	1	0.070	1	1.000	1	buffet	311	26	0.012	21	0.242	17
ciudad	2104	2	0.037	3	0.889	3	facility	278	27	0.007	37	0.129	33
méxico	2085	3	0.037	4	0.890	2	residence	276	28	0.004	61	0.048	80
hotel	1244	4	0.036	5	0.569	5	amsterdam	275	29	0.008	33	0.091	48
restaurant	893	5	0.035	6	0.592	4	hacienda	264	30	0.004	62	0.046	82
resort	798	6	0.039	2	0.514	6	waldorf	253	31	0.007	38	0.080	56
place	701	7	0.014	15	0.271	16	quality	252	32	0.010	26	0.181	23
experience	671	8	0.025	7	0.368	9	astoria	243	33	0.007	39	0.076	58
breakfast	651	9	0.024	8	0.392	7	family	238	34	0.011	24	0.163	24
locate	620	10	0.020	10	0.343	10	people	231	35	0.010	27	0.152	27
ritzcarlton	572	11	0.012	18	0.143	29	guest	223	36	0.012	22	0.187	21
chandys	551	12	0.009	28	0.134	31	hospitality	216	37	0.006	43	0.091	49
staff	544	13	0.016	14	0.239	18	luxury	214	38	0.007	40	0.119	39
everything	507	14	0.018	13	0.291	14	belgrave	212	39	0.003	75	0.043	86
trip	478	15	0.020	11	0.307	12	belize	209	40	0.012	23	0.197	20
attention	458	16	0.014	16	0.300	13	custom	209	41	0.009	29	0.186	22
mandapa	440	17	0.012	19	0.138	30	island	202	42	0.007	41	0.094	45
lisbon	412	18	0.008	31	0.152	26	property	198	43	0.008	34	0.127	34
serve	402	19	0.010	25	0.119	38	ambience	194	44	0.003	76	0.052	77
france	377	20	0.008	32	0.146	28	dinner	177	45	0.008	35	0.130	32
hamanasi	377	21	0.024	9	0.375	8	reception	175	46	0.006	44	0.116	40
seminyak	352	22	0.004	60	0.069	64	architecture	172	47	0.005	49	0.123	35
terrace	341	23	0.012	20	0.276	15	everyone	166	48	0.009	30	0.155	25
adventure	314	24	0.019	12	0.310	11	security	155	49	0.004	63	0.058	73
room	313	25	0.013	17	0.198	19	history	153	50	0.005	50	0.123	36

Words such as "place", "facility", and "security" had a relatively lower centrality ranking relative to their high frequency, which suggests that although these words were frequently searched by users, their connection and influence relative to other words is low.

Words such as "room", "adventure", and "dinner" appeared in the opposite distribution, as they do not appear as frequently, while they did strongly relate to other terms with relatively high value. The nodes have great significance in the semantic network because of their strong connection to and influence over other nodes. Figure 4 illustrates the result of the CONCOR analysis. Four sets generated from the semantic network analysis were named based on the notable words and related meaning within the online reviews. Table 4 shows the words grouped in each cluster and the notable words.

The group names—destination, physical environment, service, and trip purpose—reflect the characteristics of the words included in each cluster. The destination cluster includes words related to hotel brands or tour spots (e.g., "France" "waldorf"), as well as general terms such as "locate" or "station". The

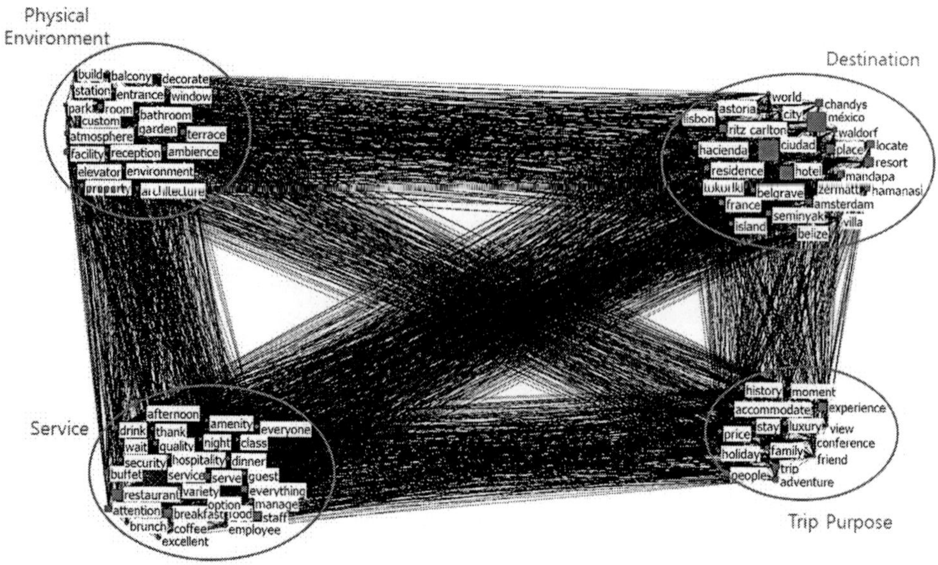

Figure 4. *Visualization of CONvergence of iterated CORrelation analysis.*

Table 4. *Result of CONvergence of iterated CORrelation analysis.*

	Extracted Words	Significant Words
Destination	astoria/residence/france/villa/world/ amsterdam/island/locate/hamansi/station/ lisbon/mexico/hacienda/city/belgrave/chandys/tokoriki/ zermatt/wardorf/mandapa/belize/seminyak/ ciudad/ritzcarlton/hotel/place/resort	residence/hamansi/locate/ chandys/seminyak/resort/ ritz carlton/hotel/place/ciudad/ mandapa/city/hacienda/ mexico/station
Physical Environment	elevator/custom/reception/build/park/ garden/terrace/room/ambience/architecture/ entrance/balcony/bathroom/environment/ window/facility/decorate/atmosphere/property	entrance/property/facility/terrace/ reception/park/architecture/ambience/ room/bathroom/environment/ atmosphere/decorate
Service	buffet/everyone/thank/wait/manage/drink/ serve/service/brunch/employee/night/staff/ quality/variety/food/everything/coffee/ breakfast/excellent/attention/option/amenity/ hospitality/restaurant/dinner/guest/class/ security/afternoon	buffet/thank/brunch/restaurant/ breakfast/food/excellent/staff/quality/ service/attention/security/variety/ hospitality/employee/ everyone/everything
Trip Purpose	conference/history/moment/adventure/ stay/holiday/price/people/accommodate/ friend/family/view/trip/luxury/ experience	conference/adventure/holiday/ price/accommodate/family/friend/ view/trip/experience/stay

physical environment cluster contains words related to facilities, such as "balcony" or "garden". The service cluster contains concepts: food and beverage (F&B) and staff service. F&B contains words such as "buffet" and "restaurant", while staff service includes words such as "attention" and "hospitality", and it is important to note that consumers tend to consider staff service and quality of service when choosing a hotel. The final cluster, trip purpose, contains words relating to purpose such as "conference" and "adventure", as well as including words related to sociality, such as "family" and "friend". After conducting CONCOR analysis, 55 words were used to determine the main factors affecting hotel customer satisfaction.

Factor Analysis

Many measurement variables can be reduced to smaller variables using the varimax rotation process through factor analysis. This study adopted the common factorial criteria for factor extraction. In this study, the standard eigenvalue value is 1.0 or higher, and the factor loading value is 0.400 or higher. Variables loading onto two factors simultaneously were dropped. From the results, 10 key words within four factors contributed 18.458% of all variance, and these were used as the independent variables to derive the key factors affecting customer satisfaction. According to Table 5, the KMO index was above 0.6, indicating a high correlation between related variables. In Bartlett's sphericity test, χ^2 was 84,453.902, with the overall significance of the correlation matrix $p < 0.001$. This means that these data are suitable for exploratory factor analysis. The four factors were named: Service (Factor 1), Physical Environment (Factor 2), Dining (Factor 3), and Location (Factor 4). Factor 1 contains "staff", "quality", and "service", which are related to the core services of the hotel. Factor 2 contains "facility", "environment", and "room", which are related to a tangible part of the hotel. Factor 3 contains "restaurant" and "brunch". Factor 4 consisted of concrete site names, such as "ciudad" and "mexico".

Table 5. *Result of the factor analysis.*

	Words	Factor Loading	Eigen Value	Variance (%)
Service	Staff	0.982	3.214	6.839
	Quality	0.968		
	Service	0.661		
Physical Environments	Facility	0.981	2.199	4.678
	Environment	0.947		
	room	0.654		
Dining	Restaurant	0.943	1.645	3.500
	Brunch	0.893		
Location	Ciudad	0.922	1.617	3.440
	Mexico	0.878		
Total Variance (%) = 18.458				
KMO = 0.671				
Bartlett chi-squared (*p*) = 84,453.902 (*p* < 0.001)				

Linear Regression Analysis

Regression analysis was performed to determine how the independent variables affect the dependent variable. The hotel customer satisfaction rating was used as the dependent variable, and the four hotel customer experience factors were used as the independent variables. The results of refining variables through factor analysis yielded four independent variables—Service (S), Physical Environment (P), Dining (D), and Location (L)—and one dependent variable: Customer Satisfaction (CS). As it can be seen in Table 6, the overall variance explained by the four predictors was 10% ($R^2 = 0.100$), and the standard error of the estimated value was 0.70347. The correlation between the independent and dependent variables was relatively low, because the low frequency of online hotel reviews may not have included any of the four factors affecting customer experience and satisfaction. It is impossible to include all relevant variables in regression analysis to estimate output variables, such as opinion, from text-mining data, so the R^2 value can be low. According to prior studies using regression and factor analyses on online reviews for washing machines and hotels, the R^2 values were 12.5%, and 12%, respectively [30,44]. Here, Service (S, $\beta = 0.027$) and Dining (D, $\beta = -0.021$) are significant at the

$p < 0.05$ and $p < 0.1$ level, respectively. Service (S) is positively related to customer satisfaction, and Dining (D) is negatively related to customer satisfaction. Based on these results, the regression equation can be expressed as follows:

$$CS = 4.733 + 0.019S^{**} + 0.004P - 0.015D^{*} - 0.005L$$

Table 6. *Results of linear regression analysis.*

Model	Unstandardized Coef.		Standardized Coef.	p	t
	B	Std. Error	Beta		
(Constant)	4.733	0.008		0.000	610.319 ***
Service (S)	0.019	0.008	0.027	0.014	2.449 **
Physical Environments (P)	0.004	0.008	0.005	0.620	0.496
Dining (D)	−0.015	0.008	−0.021	0.055	−1.916 *
Location (L)	−0.005	0.008	−0.007	0.521	−0.642

Notes: Dependent variable: Customer Satisfaction (CS); $R^2 = 0.100$; adjusted $R^2 = 0.100$; $F = 2.573$, $p < 0.05$
*** $p < 0.001$, ** $p < 0.05$, * $p < 0.1$.

The Service (S) factor holds the highest standardized coefficients, which means staff service is the essential factor associated with customer satisfaction. The Dining (D) factor was found to negatively influence customer satisfaction, indicating that customers have a negative view of the dining factor, which included words such as restaurant and brunch.

DISCUSSION AND CONCLUSIONS

This study was conducted to assess the customers' experience and satisfaction based on online reviews. Keywords were derived through text mining, and frequency analysis was then performed. The top 90 most frequent words were extracted, and degree and eigenvector centrality analyses were performed to determine the relationship between keywords. CONCOR analysis was then adopted to generate four clusters: destination, physical environment, service, and trip purpose.

These results are similar to those found in a previous study by Ban et al. [44], who named a similar grouping of four clusters—intangible service, physical environment, location, and purpose. Both that study and the present one found factors related to the hotel's essential attributes, which suggests that increasing satisfaction with these attributes is paramount to forming positive eWOM. Overall, this work established that dimensions related to various facilities, location, service, and food and beverage significantly contribute to enhancing hotel customer experience. These findings reaffirm the existing arguments about the complexity and diversity of the hotel experience, which spans various encounters with food and beverage prices, quality, safety, improved service, overall feeling, image, comfortable condition, and location [11]. This work adds to the understanding of customer hotel selection attributes that are a prerequisite for improving service quality and enhancing customer satisfaction to gain a competitive advantage. Additionally, the keywords were visualized by drawing networks and nodes using NetDraw in UCINET 6.0. Factor and linear regression analyses were performed to determine the relationships between extracted factors and customer satisfaction.

This study provides five academic and practical implications based on the research results. For the theoretical implications, this study demonstrates the significance of extending the application area of semantic network analysis. This work extends our knowledge and serves as a benchmark for researchers and stakeholders concerning the factors that provide pleasing outcomes within the hotel context. Given the importance of the hotel sector in the tourism industry, this study empirically explored the hotel experience and satisfaction through big data analysis. Understanding online reviews as an expression of customer experience can help the hotel industry identify key attributes needed to achieve positive repurchase intention and increase revenue. Online reviews provide an efficient way for the hotel industry to collect feedback from hotel customers and discover how to generate positive revisit intention after the experience.

Second, the use of a semantic network analysis provides a valuable tool for exploring customers' comments about their hotel experiences. This method reveals features that explain why customers evaluate their hotel experience positively or negatively. By analyzing customer comments, we can assess the power and meaning of words commonly used by customers when sharing their experiences and how those word choices can inform recommendations through online sources. The power expressed in words contains the customers' expressions and evaluations of their experiences, and serves as a basis for understanding the reality of their experience.

Third, in terms of practical implications, "service" is an important factor influencing customer satisfaction (as in previous studies [46,47]), and a more remarkable result is that customers expect to receive more attentive service during COVID-19. Thus, managers or operators in the hotel industry should pay more attention to maintaining the standard service quality and providing more proactive or extra service to customers during this pandemic. Offering service with warm and sincere hospitality can create positive eWOM and satisfaction, as shown in the following quotations from online reviews: "José Luis and Víctor were always greeting us with a big smile probably one of the best treatment I have had in a hotel" and "The staff is simply amazing! They make every effort to make you feel comfortable and welcome." Appropriate staff service at the service point leads to positive reviews, which then form a positive image of the hotel. There is a need for continuous and systematic education and training to motivate employees with customer-centered thinking.

Fourth, it is noteworthy for hotel operators and managers that dining negatively influences customer satisfaction. One customer mentioned the restaurant and brunch within their review and stated they were not pleased with the dining experience. This indicates that customers using the hotel are paying the same cost as before the pandemic, but they are restricted from using some facilities (such as restaurants) due to COVID-19 or cannot receive regular services. Due to COVID-19, restrictions on restaurants that confine many people into a narrow space are unavoidable, but consideration from the hotel is necessary to ensure that customers do not feel uncomfortable. For example, the hotel could provide a service where customers can eat all the menu offerings from the restaurant in the room. Using a mobile app, the hotel could deliver the food ordered to the room without contacting others. If this exceptional dining service is implemented, it could affect customer satisfaction, revisit intention, and positive WOM. There is need for a service that does not cause inconvenience to customers despite the limited availability of

F&B services due to COVID-19. If the hotel minimizes contact with employees and provides a service that allows the customer to dine in a private space through a delivery service or to order through a mobile app and watch the cooking process on the screen, no problems with hygiene or cleanliness that customers are particularly concerned about with COVID-19 would arise.

Finally, online reviews are a source of information for potential customers to make decisions. Considering that tourism decision making through the internet is rapidly increasing, this study can guide hotel marketing strategy, facility operation, and complaint management through big data analysis of online reviews.

This study has some limitations, and results should be interpreted with caution; these limitations also provide suggestions for future research. First, online reviews were collected from Google, the world's largest search engine. However, there is a possibility that using a specific online channel may not capture all customer preferences, so for representativeness, future samples should be based on analysis of various websites and should use data from many years. Second, it is not easy to understand the additional meaning of words when analyzing their frequency. Future research should adopt the further analysis of positives and negatives, and sentimental analysis could better clarify customer experience and satisfaction. Finally, in this study, reviews of 25 hotels recommended by TripAdvisor were collected from Google Travel and analyzed. However, the quantity of review data collected for each hotel differed widely due to the different sizes, types, and average costs of the hotels considered. Future studies should collect and analyze review data from hotels that share the same characteristics to derive more meaningful research results.

Author Contributions

Y.-J.K. and H.-S.K. designed the research model, analyzed online review data and wrote the paper. All authors have read and agreed to the published version of the manuscript.

REFERENCES

1. Cheung, C.M.; Lee, M.K. What drives consumers to spread electronic word of mouth in online consumer-opinion platforms. *Decis. Support Syst.* **2012**, *53*, 218–225.
2. Park, J.; Hyun, H.; Thavisay, T. A study of antecedents and outcomes of social media WOM towards luxury brand purchase intention. *J. Retail. Consum. Serv.* **2021**, *58*, 102272.
3. Schindler, R.M.; Bickart, B. Characteristics of online consumer comments valued for hedonic and utilitarian shopping tasks. *Adv. Consum. Res.* **2002**, *29*, 428–429.
4. Rosario, A.B.; de Valck, K.; Sotgiu, F. Conceptualizing the electronic word-of-mouth process: What we know and need to know about eWOM creation, exposure, and evaluation. *Acad. Mark. Sci. Rev.* **2020**, *48*, 422–448.
5. Cheung, C.M.; Thadani, D.R. The impact of electronic word-of-mouth communication: A literature analysis and integrative model. *Decis. Support Syst.* **2012**, *54*, 461–470.
6. Khoa, B.T.; Khanh, T. The impact of electronic Word-Of-Mouth on admission intention to private university. *Test Eng. Manag.* **2020**, *83*, 14956–14970.

7. Filieri, R.; McLeay, F. E-WOM and accommodation: An analysis of the factors that influence travelers' adoption of information from online reviews. *J. Travel Res.* **2014**, *53*, 44–57.

8. Boo, S.; Busser, J.A. Meeting planners' online reviews of destination hotels: A twofold content analysis approach. *Tour. Manag.* **2018**, *66*, 287–301.

9. Wang, L.; Wang, X.K.; Peng, J.J.; Wang, J.Q. The differences in hotel selection among various types of travellers: A comparative analysis with a useful bounded rationality behavioral decision support model. *Tour. Manag.* **2020**, *76*, 103961.

10. Nie, R.X.; Tian, Z.P.; Wang, J.Q.; Chin, K.S. Hotel selection driven by online textual reviews: Applying a semantic partitioned sentiment dictionary and evidence theory. *Int. J. Hosp. Manag.* **2020**, *88*, 102495.

11. Lewis, R.C. Isolating differences in hotel attributes. *Cornell Hotel. Restaur. Adm. Q.* **1984**, *25*, 64–77.

12. Chow, K.E.; Garretson, J.A.; Kurtz, D.L. An exploratory study into the purchase decision process used by leisure travelers in hotel selection. *J. Hosp. Mark. Manag.* **1995**, *2*, 53–72.

13. Shanahan, K.J.; Hyman, M.R. An exploratory study of desired hotel attributes for American tourists vacationing in China and Ireland. *J. Vacat. Mark.* **2007**, *13*, 107–118.

14. Groves, R.M.; Lyberg, L. Total survey error: Past, present, and future. *Public Opin. Q.* **2010**, *74*, 849–879.

15. Lee, H.J. Online review analysis on Gyeongbokgung: Using data on tripadvisor.com. *Int. J. Tour. Sci.* **2017**, *32*, 297–318.

16. Filieri, R.; Mariani, M. The role of cultural values in consumers' evaluation of online review helpfulness: A big data approach. *Int. Mark. Rev.* **2021**, *38*, 1267–1288.

17. Mariani, M.; Borghi, M. Environmental discourse in hotel online reviews: A big data analysis. *J. Sustain. Tour.* **2020**, *29*, 829–848.

18. González-Porras, J.L.; Ruiz-Alba, J.L.; Morales-Mediano, J. Customer orientation and e-WOM in the hotel sector. *Int. J. Internet Mark. Advert.* **2021**, *15*, 302–326.

19. Ban, H.J.; Kim, H.S. Understanding customer experience and satisfaction through airline passengers' online review. *Sustainability* **2019**, *11*, 4066.

20. Aakash, A.; Tandon, A.; Gupta Aggarwal, A. How features embedded in eWOM predict hotel guest satisfaction: An application of artificial neural networks. *J. Hosp. Mark. Manag.* **2021**, *30*, 486–507.

21. Verma, S.; Yadav, N. Past, present, and future of electronic word of mouth (EWOM). *J. Interact. Mark.* **2021**, *53*, 111–128.

22. Xiang, Z.; Schwartz, Z.; Gerdes, J.H., Jr.; Uysal, M. What can big data and text analytics tell us about hotel guest experience and satisfaction? *Int. J. Hosp. Manag.* **2015**, *44*, 120–130.

23. Kim, S.; Kandampully, J.; Bilgihan, A. The influence of eWOM communications: An application of online social network framework. *Comput. Hum. Behav.* **2018**, *80*, 243–254.

24. Xiang, Z.; Gretzel, U. Role of social media in online travel information search. *Tour. Manag.* **2010**, *31*, 179–188.

25. De Bruyn, A.; Lilien, G.L. A multi-stage model of word-of-mouth influence through viral marketing. *Int. J. Res. Mark.* **2008**, *25*, 151–163.

26. Vermeulen, I.E.; Seegers, D. Tried and tested: The impact of online hotel reviews on consumer consideration. *Tour. Manag.* **2009**, *30*, 123–127.

27. Stringam, B.B.; Gerdes, J., Jr.; Vanleeuwen, D.M. Assessing the importance and relationships of ratings on user-generated traveler reviews. *J. Qual. Assur. Hosp. Tour.* **2010**, *11*, 73–92.
28. Schmitt, B. Experiential marketing. *J. Mark. Manag.* **1999**, *15*, 53–67.
29. Meyer, C.; Schwager, A. Understanding customer experience. *Harv. Bus. Rev.* **2007**, *85*, 116.
30. Kim, H.S.; Noh, Y. Elicitation of design factors through big data analysis of online customer reviews for washing machines. *J. Mech. Sci. Technol.* **2019**, *33*, 2785–2795.
31. Anderson, E.W.; Fornell, C.; Lehmann, D.R. Customer satisfaction, market share, and profitability: Findings from Sweden. *J. Mark.* **1994**, *58*, 53–66.
32. Kotler, P.; Bowen, P.J.; Makens, J. *Marketing for Hospitality and Tourism*; PrenticeHall: Hoboken, NJ, USA, 1996.
33. Knutson, B.J. Ten laws of customer satisfaction. *Cornell Hotel Restaur. Adm. Q.* **1988**, *29*, 14–17.
34. Verma, V.K.; Chandra, B. Sustainability and customers' hotel choice behaviour: A choice-based conjoint analysis approach. *Environ. Dev. Sustain.* **2018**, *20*, 1347–1363.
35. Loh, S.; De Oliveira, J.P.M.; Gastal, F.L. Knowledge discovery in textual documentation: Qualitative and quantitative analyses. *J. Doc.* **2001**, *57*, 577–590.
36. Hotho, A.; Nürnberger, A.; Paaß, G. A brief survey of text mining. *LDV Forum* **2005**, *20*, 19–62.
37. Fan, W.; Wallace, L.; Rich, S.; Zhang, Z. Tapping the power of text mining. *Commun. ACM* **2006**, *49*, 76–82.
38. Feldman, R.; Sanger, J. *The Text Mining Handbook: Advanced Approaches in Analyzing Unstructured Data*; Cambridge University Press: Cambridge, UK, 2007.
39. Stepchenkova, S.; Morrison, A.M. Russia's destination image among American pleasure travelers: Revisiting Echtner and Ritchie. *Tour. Manag.* **2008**, *29*, 548–560.
40. He, W.; Zha, S.; Li, L. Social media competitive analysis and text mining: A case study in the pizza industry. *Int. J. Inf. Manag. Sci.* **2013**, *33*, 464–472.
41. Esposito, F.; Ferilli, S.; Basile, T.M.; Di Mauro, N. Social networks and statistical relational learning: A survey. *Int. J. Soc. Netw. Min.* **2012**, *1*, 185–208.
42. Wasserman, S.; Faust, K. *Social Network Analysis: Methods and Applications*; Cambridge University Press: Cambridge, UK, 1994.
43. Tao, S.; Kim, H.S. Cruising in Asia: What can we dig from online cruiser reviews to understand their experience and satisfaction. *Asia Pac. J. Tour. Res.* **2019**, *24*, 514–528.
44. Ban, H.J.; Choi, H.; Choi, E.K.; Lee, S.; Kim, H.S. Investigating key attributes in experience and satisfaction of hotel customer using online review data. *Sustainability* **2019**, *11*, 6570.
45. Freeman, L.C.; Roeder, D.; Mulholland, R.R. Centrality in social networks: II. Experimental results. *Soc. Netw.* **1979**, *2*, 119–141.
46. Kim, Y.J.; Kim, H.S.; Kim, H.S. Understanding the effects of COVID-19 on the Starbucks perception through big data analytics: A comparative study. *Culin. Sci. Hos. Res.* **2021**, *27*, 1–14.
47. Ban, H.J.; Kim, H.S. Semantic network analysis of hotel package through the big data. *Culin. Sci. Hos. Res.* **2019**, *25*, 110–119.

CHAPTER 9

Factors Contributing to Staff Turnover in the Hotel Industry: A Literature Review

Shaniekay Codling, Jheanelle Pinnock, Eyonisha Barrett, Shanoya Gayle, Nataki Stephenson, Nikima Sibblies and Gaunette Sinclair-Maragh
University of Technology, Jamaica

ABSTRACT

The purpose of this chapter is to analyze the factors that are contributing to staff turnover in the hotel industry. Staff turnover rate usually affects an organization's performance, productivity and profitability, and can contribute to the loss of assets and resources. This sector of the hospitality and tourism economy was selected for the study as it is deemed to be very demanding and oftentimes overwhelming. In general, the sector is believed to be very stressful especially since the employees have to deal with satisfying the needs and wants of customers and uncertain working conditions. Literature review was used as the methodology for ascertaining the factors that are contributing to staff turnover in hotels. From this review, the chapter identifies that these are both push and pull factors. Push factors are dissatisfactions with the current job which cause employees to seek alternative employment and pull factors are the reasons that attract employees to a new workplace. The chapter concludes that it is important for hotel managers to establish an employee-centric environment with deliberate and effective workplace practices to retain employees. The findings of this study will be very useful in advancing the literature as well as informing hotel practitioners.

Keywords: *staff turnover; hotel industry; staff retention; productivity; hygiene factors; employee-centric environment*

INTRODUCTION

The global economy in the 21st century is driven by three major industries; technology, telecommunication and tourism [1]. Tourism is one of the world's largest and rapidly growing industries [2] and the hospitality industry is a major segment of this global economy [3]. Tourism and in particular, the hospitality industry and sectors are centred on service and according to O'Cass and Sok [4], the employees who are the providers of the service are essential to the overall success of tourism. However, the turnover of employees within this global economic activity is a concern.

Staff turnover is defined as the number of workers who leave an organization and are replaced or rotated with new employees [5]. Zhang [6] further explains that staff turnover refers to the number of persons who voluntarily or involuntarily leave an organization within a specific period. It has been well documented that the level of turnover or in other words the staff turnover rate usually has an impact on organizations. It can in fact contribute to the loss of a company's assets and resources [7].

Ronra and Chaisawat [8] postulate that turnover is one of the key issues in the world's hospitality industry. Narkhede, [9] advances the discourse by stating that staff turnover in the hospitality industry is having an effect on performance, productivity, and profitability. In fact, the turnover rate in the hospitality industry usually averages around 20 to 300 percent annually [10]. It is posited that employee turnover in the hospitality industry is triggered by dissatisfaction, which includes relationships with supervisors, working conditions, work schedules, workload, job content, and salary and benefits [9].

Yazinski [11] posits that staff turnover rate in the industry can be broadly divided into three groups; external factors (e.g. perception of both employment and unemployment rate, and presence of trade union), internal factors (e.g. tenure, education, and gender) and thirdly, work-related factors (e.g. wage, job satisfaction and organizational commitment). Other contributing factors could be narrowed down to employees' expectations of the job, the discrepancy between the job and person, not enough coaching and feedback, minimal growth and career opportunities, stress from being overworked, poor working conditions and job status, whether the individual is fully employed, contracted or seasonally employed [12]. This justifies the claim by Chalkiti and Sigala [13] that there are a plethora of reasons leading to staff turnover in the hospitality industry. It is pointed out that the industry is a very complex one to steer due to its various sub-industries or sectors [14]. In addition, the working environment can be very stressful and overbearing to the staff who have to deal with satisfying the needs and wants of customers as well as dealing with uncertain working conditions [15]. It is therefore imperative to identify the factors that impede staff retention in the industry and subsequently cause staff turnover.

This chapter focuses on staff turnover in the hospitality industry but specific to the hotel category which according to Slattery [16] is one of the free standing hospitality businesses. For the purpose of this study, the term hotel industry will be used throughout the chapter to describe the hotel business which according to Roa and Sahu [17], provides accommodation, meals and other types of services to guests. The hotel industry is chosen for this deductive analysis because it is reported to be a major challenge in this hospitality business [18]. This matter is of great concern in many countries such as in the United Kingdom and Australia [18] as well as small developing island states such as Jamaica [19]. Furthermore, turnover rate in the hotel industry is a worldwide endemic as it is not country-specific [20].

The importance of staffing issues in the hotel industry is driven by the fact that it is service-oriented and highly dependent on the employees [18]. There are several challenges that are encountered when working in the hotel industry to include hard deadlines, long working hours, unexpected interactions with guests and high emotional demands that are accompanied by poor working conditions and low wages [21]. Further study on staff turnover in the hotel industry is imperative in advancing the literature on the matter and informing hotel practitioners of workable and feasible practices to achieve staff retention. According to Davis [22] employee retention is important to the economic advancement of an organization. Replacing employees in the hotel industry can be very costly and is an unhelpful expense due to the fact that it can result in loss of productivity particularly because employers have to train new employees [23]. It is therefore essential that managers seek to grasp a better understanding of staff retention in the hotel industry [22]. Likewise, managers and leaders should strengthen and improve the factors that stimulate employees to stay at the hotel. Having knowledge of these factors; organisational and personal, and instituting appropriate strategies to appreciate employees and stimulate them have the propensity to retain their engagement with the workplace [24] as well as increase their abilities to improve productivity [22]. The purpose of this chapter, therefore, is to analyze the factors contributing to staff turnover in the hotel industry and the subsequent impacts of staff turnover on productivity. The chapter will also propose some strategies that can be implemented by managers to reduce staff turnover in hotels. A review of extant literature will be used as the methodology. This is a plausible approach as according to Xiao and Watson [25], literature review establishes the foundation of academic enquiries.

LITERATURE REVIEW

This review of the literature highlights the factors contributing to staff turnover in the hotel industry as well as the subsequent impact on productivity. This section will also present some strategies to mitigate staff turnover in hotels.

Factors contributing to staff turnover in the hotel industry

Hotels typically regard high turnover as part of the work-group norm and employees tend to believe that they are entering jobs with limited career development opportunities [26]. Aside from the three groups of staff turnover posited by Yazinski [11]; external factors, internal factors and work-related factors, Faz et al., [14] propose that the main contributing factors of staff turnover in the hotel industry are categorized into two subgroups; push factors and pull factors. Push factors are dissatisfactions with the current job and employees then seek alternative employment [27]. Pull factors are those reasons that attract employees to a new workplace [8] The literature will focus on these two categories as indicated in Table 1.

The following information will expand on the factors:

Table 1. *Factors contributing to staff turnover in hotels.*

Push Factors	Pull Factors
Poor relationship	Career advancements
Lack of growth opportunities	Job satisfaction
Job insecurity	Higher salaries
Limited amount of interaction among staff	Benefits and rewards

Push factors contributing to staff turnover in hotels

Poor relationship

Poor relationships are deemed to be the main factor of high staff turnover in the hotel industry [14]. This matter is of significant importance as relationships are discerned as a direct element of an employee's intention to stay at an organization. This is supported by Musa et al., [28] that poor relationships with management and colleagues can result in staff turnover in hotels. In a diverse work setting like the hotel environment where persons travel across the world with the need for accommodation, it is pertinent that employees develop a healthy working relationship as this can be the make or break point for the business [14]. Any strained relationship and discomfort at work can encourage a dissatisfied employee to seek alternative employment in another organization [14].

Employers should show interest in employees' growth so that they create a surrounding where the employees will be enthusiastic and one that will motivate them to remain employed at the organization [14]. It is found that there is a strong dissatisfaction with limited growth opportunities in hotels [29]. The fairness of the promotion process is of significant concern for hotel employees and this can negatively impact employee productivity [30] as well as deter prospective employees [31].

From a gender perspective, it is posited that men tend to have more access to career opportunities than their counterpart [32]. It is also postulated that if women believe that they are unable to move up the ranks in the hotel, then they may leave the organization [33] and this can also impact productivity. Narkhede [9] emphasized that the lack of opportunity for growth in the hotel industry for staff members in their present role is the primary rationale for seeking employment in another organization.

Job insecurity

Etehadi and Karatepe [34] define job insecurity as an employee's concern regarding the stability of their job at an organization. Job insecurity is identified as one of the main contributors to staff turnover [35]. Employees normally feel threatened about their jobs when there is a lack of communication within the organization, particularly during seasonality periods [35]. Akbiyik [36] shares a similar view which suggests that if a hotel decides to reduce the size of its staff based on the uncertainty of its occupancy without informing their employees ahead of time, then this can create a level of mistrust that can lead to high turnover rates.

Job insecurity is crucial because of work-related stress as it activates several emotional reactions among staff members [34]. They further explain that job insecurity can initiate deceitful employees, demotivated staff, decreased productivity as a result of staff demotivation, reduction in employees' emotional wellbeing while on the job, and low job satisfaction that can eventually lead to burnout. Akbiyik [36] adds that job insecurity in the hotel industry influences absenteeism among employees as they are under the impression that they can lose their job at any time. Once an employee displays high rates of absenteeism then the employer will be forced to terminate the staff member for poor work performance which ultimately contributes to staff turnover within the hotel industry [36].

Limited amount of interaction among staff in the hotel

Employee engagement helps to cement organizational culture that promotes unity within the organization [37]. When employees see that there is a positive magnitude of organizational interaction within the business, they are more propelled to display a higher level of interest [38]. Minimal employee interaction could lead to high turnover rates because employees tend to be uninformed of what is taking place within the organization [37].

Kuria et al., [20] highlight that low interaction in the hotel industry can be developed from inadequate transparency among employers and employees or staff and staff. They further indicate that it is a crucial factor for interaction among employees because it helps to influence their decision as to whether they want to stay at the hotel and further their career or leave the organization to seek more suitable development. Fathy [37] posits that a lack of motivation and interaction from an early stage between employers and employees is one of the key factors that lead to staff turnover in the hotel industry. This is because employers failed to develop a strong interaction relationship between employees and as such they are not driven to grow as one within the organization.

Pull factors contributing to staff turnover in hotels

Career advancement

According to Chalkiti & Sigala [13], one of the main factors that lead to high staff turnover rate in several different industries is the lack of career advancement. There is no difference with the hotel industry as McGinley et al. [39] assert that career advancement opportunities in the hotel industry are a conspicuous concern. The opportunity for career development encourages job satisfaction, ensures that employees are successful and enhances their employability (Jugan [40]. If employers do not provide employees with these opportunities there is a high propensity that this will result in great staff turnover [41].

Faz et al., [14], however, caution that the hotel industry is a severely high labour intensive sector that creates numerous competitions between staff members, which decreases the possibilities for career development for other staff members. It is also found that when employees enter the hotel industry they view their employment as short-term and are often of the belief that it is a temporary job opportunity. Subsequently, they are hopeless of any advancement [42]. However, Mwilu [43] on the other hand explains that people seek employment locally and internationally in the hotel industry because of the perceived employment opportunities. Mwilu [43] concludes that people will gravitate more to organizations where they will gain more benefits, thus, the urge of leaving the current organization is very high. Another important point as explained by Narkhede [9] is that, if employees feel that an entity is not fully invested in their career advancement, they will not display any interest in the business development. This is with the view that their efforts will be preoccupied to seek opportunities for growth elsewhere.

Job satisfaction

Rok & Mulej [44] note that job satisfaction is a delightful and positive state of an individual's career advancement which results from a person's job or experience at work. Albattat & Som [12] add that job satisfaction will influence an employee's decision as to whether or not they are to leave their job. Hence, it is likely that job satisfaction will have an impact on employee turnover rates [12].

Several studies have been conducted regarding the relationship between work-related variables and job satisfaction which will ultimately result in employee turnover. For example, a study by Zopiatis et al., [42] in Cyprus highlights that there is a negative relationship between organizational commitment and job satisfaction and this can result in turnover intention.

Davis [22] believes that job satisfaction concentrates mostly on Herzberg's Hygiene Factors. These factors are elements that are correlated to a job that may or may not create satisfaction for employees [45]. The Hygiene Factors take into consideration the environment in which employees do their job and enhance the satisfaction and commitment of the employees. This is supported by Holston-Okae [46] who contends that organizational leaders should meet their employees' hygiene factors to avoid dissatisfactions. This may not immediately lead to job satisfaction or motivation but is a stepping stone.

Higher salaries

Mwilu [43] highlights higher payment packages and technical challenges as pull factors that captivate employees. Dwesini [47] concludes that compensation and rewards are factors that could influence staff turnover in the industry. AlBatta and Som [12] further emphasize that unsatisfactory salaries among intolerant working conditions and poor training could lead to staff turnover. Whenever employers fail to provide employees with favorable salaries, wages or even service charges that are linked to their job function, it is likely to contribute to job turnover. This is supported by [20] who conclude that if organizations do not compensate their workers beneficially it is possible they may encounter high levels of staff turnover by way of the staff leaving for alternate jobs that are higher paying.

Benefits and rewards

Reward systems entail various policies and procedures that are arranged and governed like one [40]. Whenever employees are rewarded it gives them a sense of belonging and makes them feel appreciated by relevant authorities [40]. Rewarding employees allows them to have a better relationship with the organization [48]. This is supported by Jehanzeb et al., [49] who indicate that rewards play a critical role in the retention of employees; it makes them feel wanted and motivates them to continue doing an excellent job. Sageer et al., [50] believes that employees should be rewarded appropriately for their contribution. Rewards are a stepping stone to job satisfaction which leads to a greater probability of the employees remaining within the organization. Jugan [40] suggests that organizations must focus on the extent to which rewards contribute to employee motivation and engagement with the organization and that the factors which determine this degree should be understood. Happy employees represent the organization in the public sphere [50].

Jehanzeb et al., [49] state that rewards have a lasting impression on employees as it communicates how much they are valued within the organization. A survey carried out in hotels in Kisii, Kenya concludes that the lack of fringe benefits encourages persons to leave the organization and this increases the rate of employee turnover [41]. This suggests that whenever an employer is not offering benefits such as sick leave, and education and retirement facilities to the employees, it will result in an increase in the rate of staff turnover [41].

Impacts of staff turnover on productivity

Productivity refers to how effectively and efficiently goods and tasks are carried out. It is further explained as the efficiency in production and is simply measured by the amount of output obtained from a given set of inputs [51]. According to Haenisch [52], productivity in the workplace is detrimental to the success of every organization. Ugoani [53] shares a similar view whilst focusing on the aspect of manpower and determining that employee productivity is a critical factor for the organization to survive financially. Consequently, employers must put specific measures in place for employee performance as it is vital to the success of their business [54]. They should strengthen the work environment to improve employees' performance and productivity as this will ultimately lead to higher profits as well as customer satisfaction and retention [50].

Productivity is used to determine the level of performance of an organization and that decreases with high employee turnover [53]. This was underscored in a study conducted by Ahmad and Scott [18] to determine the issues in managing staff in the front office department. The results were obtained through interviews with managers which showed that staff turnover results in a shortage of staff which causes difficulty in delivering excellent service. The respondents further elaborated that insufficient staff resulted in limited time to interact with staff or complete tasks effectively. These findings reinforce the claim by Siddiqui [54] that the success of a company is ultimately dependent on employees.

Additionally, time must be allocated to train new employees. Fathy [37] elaborates that when hotels replace experienced staff with inexperienced employees, it disrupts the flow of production as time must be allocated on schedules to train the staff on how to properly carry out services and tasks. This also interrupts the time that should be spent catering to the requirements of the guests and this may lead to dissatisfied customers and thus, a decrease in customer retention and ultimately reduced profitability. Hinkin, and Tracey [55] conclude that the hiring and training processes are costs that are associated with turnover.

The hotel industry is service-oriented, therefore, the productivity of the business as it relates to output is measured by the service received by guests. The quality of service conveyed to the guest is a competitive tool and since employees are the ones that deliver the service, it is imperative that they are satisfied and motivated [56]. This is even more important due to the characteristic of service. Service is simultaneous as it is created and consumed at the same time. By way of being perishable, productivity is determined by the number of rooms occupied on a daily basis with the role of the hotel staff being very integral to this matter. For example, the functions of the housekeeping staff or room attendant are critical to the profitability of the hotel [57]. The level of service provided is an indication of guests' satisfaction and whether or not they will stay as well as return the next time.

Using data from 527 hotels within the same chain, Hesford et al., [58] examine how housekeepers and front desk attendants impact revenue and productivity through customer satisfaction. The findings reveal that the tasks carried out by the housekeepers and front desk attendants have significant effect on guest experience. Additional findings reveal that the majority of customer in the budget hotel segment complained about the cleanliness of the rooms. This is the direct responsibility of the housekeeping staff. Poor hospitality and service was also found to be a frequent driver of complaints. This generally refers to guest interactions with the front desk staff. The results indicate that turnover in both positions negatively impacts the customer's experience and satisfaction, and these are some of the main determinants of productivity among hotels.

Notably, hospitality service operations evolve around branded and standardized offerings to customers, therefore, consistent employee performance is a very important element of business strategy [59]. In addition, high staff turnover will lead to higher complaints because of the time it takes to train new employees as well as the loss of key employees. Customer satisfaction, therefore, becomes synonymous with productivity levels in hotels [60]. Hence, if staff turnover is frequent and high, it will disrupt the quality of service [61]. In support, Singh and Amandeep [56] conclude that staff turnover harms the steadiness in the standardization of hotel services.

Moreover, the service will be further impacted as new employees will require time to become as efficient as the previous ones. This was supported by Faz et al., [14] who articulate that a new employee can take up to two years to accomplish the same level of productivity as the previous staff since they have to become knowledgeable of all the necessary skills required to complete their tasks. In addition, the loss of key employees can result in a reduction in both the quality of the service provided and the experience attained by the guest as well as productivity [62]. From a financial perspective, Fathy [37] points out that employee turnover represents 60 percent of the cost of loss productivity.

High staff turnover can also result in disruption of service for other employees and managers resulting in reduced productivity. The disruption in operations redirects managers away from their usual duties of planning, controlling and sales to now training and monitoring new employees. According to Hesford et al., [58], the time that the head housekeeper spends on training new employees pulls them away from inspecting rooms, monitoring the remaining workers and responding to special cleaning requests. Similarly, general managers typically "shadow" a new front desk attendant for the first few shifts. This diverts the manager's effort and attention away from strategic functions such as marketing the property and networking.

METHODOLOGY

This study carefully and systematically reviewed the literature on the factors contributing to staff turnover in the hotel industry; both push and pull, and their consequent impacts on the productivity of hotels. The literature was also reviewed for recommended strategies that are used to mitigate staff turnover in hotels. Literature review is used as the methodology for this study in order to provide a comprehensive review of the literature related to staff turnover in the hotel industry. This is a plausible research technique and is supported by Paul and Criado [63] who postulate that literature review is useful in synthesizing prior studies to strengthen the foundation of knowledge. In addition, Xiao and Watson [25] point out that literature review establishes the foundation of academic enquiries.

Although literature review is usually used as an assessment procedure in nursing settings [64], Snyder [65] proposes that its use as a research method has become more relevant than before, especially in the area of business research. This technique was used by Aziri [66] to examine the subject of job satisfaction and by Ngai [67] to relate on customer service management. It was also used by Brodeur et al., [68] to synthesize insights emerging from a number of studies on the economics of COVID-19. These are all studies in the area of business.

This chapter therefore, examined staff turnover in the hotel industry which is a business research. It was carried out by reviewing research papers in journal articles and book chapters among other sources, for extant literature on the matter. This approach is further recommended by [64]) who posit that effective literature searching is a crucial stage in the process of writing a literature review and that a systematic organized search of the literature that uses available resources is more likely to produce quality work. The review of literature is intended to provide current stance on the subject as well as rationale, positions and discussed ideas [69].

STRATEGIES TO MITIGATE AGAINST EMPLOYEE TURNOVER IN HOTELS

Many hotels face the challenge of high turnover in their organization whether voluntary or otherwise. Hartman and Yrle [70] explains that employees will leave their job even if they are satisfied and conceptualized this voluntary departure as the hobo phenomenon. It is therefore imperative for managers to identify the factors that affect employee turnover and implement appropriate strategies to attain stability in the organization. They need to be aware of their employees' feelings regarding their job functions as well as their satisfaction levels with their working conditions, superiors and peers [71]. Being aware of these factors will allow employers to implement sustainable strategies so as to improve the productivity and efficiency of employees and subsequently influence a reduction in staff turnover. Emphasis and focus should be placed on adequately managing these factors in order to create satisfaction for employees and maintain their interest in working at the organization.

It is important for hotels to conduct an audit of their situation to determine where they are at so that the appropriate strategies can be employed. If they do not have the internal resources to do so, then Ferry [72] recommends that they procure the services of a consulting company to assist them in this regard. As indicated earlier in the chapter by Holtom and Burch [62], the loss of important employees is detrimental to productivity and work quality. Managers need to be cognizant of this matter and implement suitable retention strategies for employees. Some of these strategies include implementing job enrichment plans, promoting job satisfaction, managing hygiene factors, incorporating job embeddedness, including career development and advancement factors, instituting appropriate remuneration, recognition and reward programmes in addition to good training and management. Furthermore, Long and Perumal [73] contend that employees who have little to no intentions to leave an organization have a positive relationship with staff training, compensation or benefits, development of careers in specific areas, performance management, and employee relationships. The following are some of the strategies that can be implemented in large hotels to directly or indirectly reduce staff turnover.

Implement job enrichment plans

The hotel industry leaders need to understand the factors that encourage employees to display high potential in staying with the organization in comparison to them leaving [74]. Managers need to consider job enrichment to avoid high turnover in their organization. This involves designating employees with different types of work without increasing the workload level. Job enlargement can also improve intrinsic motivation for employees and give them more reasons to stay. Onimole [75] contends that when managers provide job enrichment then employees will grasp a deeper interest in doing the work, thus a greater responsibility will be acquired by employees resulting in higher levels of productivity.

Promote job satisfaction

Milman and Dickson [74] proffer that employers should view employees as internal customers of the organization. This can provide important value and create awareness for managers as well as influence the implementation of appropriate strategies to reduce staff turnover. In support, Kim [76] points out that in order to realize a reduction in employee turnover, the human resource management team should conduct internal marketing on employees, focusing on their traits and designing effective programmes for new employees with multiple backgrounds. In addition, Onimole [75] finds that both effective training programs and job satisfaction have a very good relationship. Providing an effective training programme could therefore be a response to reducing the high turnover rate by way of employees being satisfied with their job. Training has proven to be vital in the retention process and in helping to reduce turnover. This is supported by Chen [77] who notes that training of employees influences their retention. When an organization invests in training and development activities it shows that they have placed high importance on employee capacity building. Not only will employees have a sense of being valued but training opportunities will create an emotional tie between employee and employer [78]. Therefore, employees are less likely to leave the organization when they receive the chance to acquire training on the job. Therefore, having a dedicated training procedure to improve employee skills and capabilities have the potential to reduce their intentions to leave.

Stress management is also of importance. McGinley et al. [39] state that there are various ways to deal with stress in the workplaces, which is likely to impact staff turnover intentions. The implementation of task-oriented strategies can cause a reduction in turnover intent and in turn improve on job satisfaction [39]. It is likewise imperative for managers to understand the intentions of their exceptional employees and implement solutions that will increase their desire to stay in the organizations [74]. Lapointe and Vandenberghe [79] summarize that it would be beneficial for managers to put strategies in place to strengthen employee's commitment to the organization and their subsequent satisfaction can possibly reduce turnover rates.

Manage hygiene factors

As indicated earlier in the chapter, job satisfaction concentrates mostly on Herzberg Hygiene Factors and are used to determine employee satisfaction with their job. Examples of such factors are fair pay rate, respect from other workers, salary, incentives and good conditions for work. Other hygiene factors include company policies, supervision, interpersonal relationship and job security. Zhu et al., [80] postulate that the hygiene factors when compared to the motivation factors in the Hertzberg two-factor model (motivation factors and hygiene factors) are more effective in predicting turnover intentions. This means that that will contribute to employee satisfaction which in turn, will reduce high turnover rates.

In essence, the hygiene factors are used to determine employee satisfaction with their job; a high rate of job satisfaction will reduce job turnover intentions. The underlying premise of hygiene factors is that, as long as employees become satisfied, then managers will need to maintain these factors so that they will not resort to dissatisfaction which reduces productivity. In terms of the influence of hygiene factors on productivity, Ogbo et al., [81] find that good working conditions improve employees' productivity. They posit that if working conditions are poor it will create negative impact on employees and as such managers should aim to maintain factors that aid in the increase of productivity. Deri et al., [82] conclude that the hygiene factors of job satisfaction are paramount and managers are to pay attention to them.

Incorporate job embeddedness

Ehrler [83] explains that job embeddedness consists of a range of influences that contribute to an employee's decision to continue with their job. Onimole [75] shares the notion that job embeddedness indirectly reduces high staff turnover costs incurred by the organization. It is therefore important for the hotel organizations to implement activities that can improve job embeddedness and reduce staff turnover.

Embeddedness in the job can create a positive relationship or connection with co-workers. It is determined by the level of co-worker dependency and a sense of belongingness and as such employees will more likely have a long tenure in a company where there is a positive relationship among employees [84]. Employees have a less likely tendency to leave the organization when they are embedded in their job. Ehrler [83] posits that the diversification of employee job embeddedness positively impacts their retention by reducing turnover.

Include career development and advancement factors

Career development as well as advancement opportunities are vital in improving employees' loyalty and retention in the hotel industry [79]. Akyüz et al. [85] assert that if employers desire to reduce the staff turnover rate then they will need to improve the organizational climate and the human resource activities being carried out. The process of molding each employee's career is therefore imperative [86]. This strategy can be a cost saving measure for hotels to save money that would have otherwise been spent on continuously recruiting and training new employees because of turnover.

Offering mentorship to hospitality employees is another great way to mold their careers and keep them empowered and motivated [87]. Mentorship can provide several benefits and opportunities for the personal and professional growth of employees. It is found to be a vital tool in bridging the generation gap and promoting diversity in the workplace as well as transform the organization into a learning one [88]. Mentorship in the workplace is usually carried out by experienced professionals who help in the process of molding other employee's careers and providing the opportunities for them to grow and develop their potential. These mentees will now feel a sense of connection and commitment to the business and its overall success. Hence, managers are to be able to identify opportunities and implement mentorship and training programmes to help and retain young employees. This is despite the claim by Gursoy and Dhar [89], that younger persons will stay in the organization in more cases than the older ones.

Having a formal and structured mentorship programme is recommended [88]. It will facilitate high-quality leader-member relationships. This type of relationship according to Davis [22] will not only engage and inspire employees but will also lead to organizational commitment and lower turnover rates. In essence, hotel managers should be concerned about the growth and development of all employees [29] despite age and gender. As per the latter, they are to remove gender bias perceptions and ensure that programmes are in place to coach female employees in advancing their careers [90]. Overall, managers should provide all employees with opportunities to develop and improve key internal relationships, career advancements and job performance. Employees are comfortable when opportunities to improve themselves arise [89]. Akyüz et al., [85] studied the influences that academic development and organizational climate provides in having healthier organizational commitment which reduces employees' desire to leave the organization. They find that employers that pay special attention to academic development, tasks, and the promotion of improved commitment to the organization recognize that it improves job performance and increases retention rates.

Implement remuneration, recognition and reward programmes

Adequately and fairly remunerating, recognizing and rewarding the efforts and accomplishments of employees are important in staff retention. According to [91] employees tend to develop an emotional bond with the organization and remain an employee when they perceive that the work they have done is appreciated and valued. Long and Perumal [73] point out that employees that are placed on the front-line in the hotel operations are more likely to proportionately receive low salary or rewards, and therefore will be the ones to switch jobs. Rewarding and recognizing these among other employees would make them feel respected, desired and appreciated, resulting in reduced staff turnover rate. However, employees expect to receive recognition and rewards that are established from a fair performance appraisal review [91].

Implement best hiring practices

In order to understand the reasons why employees leave their organization, the human resource management team should hire smartly and implement exit and stay interviews to practice and maintain the communication process [79]. Selecting the right people for the right jobs is one of the most incremental solutions to reducing staff turnover as according to Bin [92] they will be more satisfied and engaged with their jobs. Employees who are not the right fit for a position will be more likely to quit as they may not possess the right skill set, knowledge or even mental ability to tackle that role.

The screening of employees who enter the organization will help employers make better decisions when hiring [39]. Hotel managers should identify the abilities of each employee through the hiring process and according to Sinclair-Maragh et al.; [93], they should foster talent management through coaching, mentorship, motivation and empowerment. Managers should employ effective sourcing strategies as well as maintain, retain and train these employees as it is imperative in the process of improving guest services in the industry. This is supported by Long and Perumal [73] who find that training is vital to the success of any modern organization. They posit that training is the backbone of strategy implementation and the lack of training in critical areas will lead to increased complaints. In providing the necessary conditions to develop the professionalism of employees, managers should consider training them on the job which results in job satisfaction and a reduction in turnover levels [94].

Encouraging communication

Communication between the two parties; managers and employees is paramount. The philosophy and intentions of the hotel should be communicated to the employees to guide them in carrying out their respective tasks [95]. Likewise, employees should be allowed to communicate their potential career path so that they can purposefully envisage their future with the hotel.

Employees should be allowed to identify specific milestones for their achievement and ways in which the employers can use supporting resources to assist them in achieving their goals. The relationship between employees and employers will make it easier for both parties to have a clear, consistent and direct communication about career advancement steps. This will help employees feel more engaged in the organization and increase their job satisfaction, thus, staff turnover rate will be reduced. Sandhya and Kumar [96] conclude that communication between the employee and employer will lead to high levels of employee retention. Communication can also be achieved by way of conducting employee attitudes surveys. This should be aimed at identifying how each employee feel about their role, their intention to stay within the organization and also the goals that they want to achieve in the organization. Care should be taken not to generalize the data collected for human resource management and development strategy implementation [97].

CONCLUSION

The purpose of this chapter is to analyze the factors contributing to staff turnover in the hotel industry and the subsequent impacts of staff turnover on productivity. Additionally, the chapter proposed some strategies that can be implemented by management to reduce staff turnover. The review of literature finds that employee turnover has been a major concern in the hotel industry in several countries despite location. The literature distinguishes two main categories of factors that cause job turnover. The push factors are job-related dissatisfiers such as poor relationships, lack of growth opportunity, job insecurity and limited amount of interaction among staff. Pull factors are those opportunities that attract employees to a new workplace such as career advancements, job satisfaction, higher salaries and benefits and rewards.

Staff turnover needs to be addressed as it can negatively impact productivity. It is important for hotel managers / employers to generate unique and creative solutions to retain employees in the hotels despite the size and location. These include the implementation of job enrichment plans, promotion of job satisfaction, management of hygiene factors, incorporating job embeddedness, including career development and advancement factors, instituting appropriate remuneration, recognition and reward programmes, implementing best hiring practices and encouraging employee-employer communication channel.

Based on the literature review conducted, it is evident that high staff turnover rate is prominent in the hotel industry. It is essential that these managers select the right persons for the respective jobs, foster their abilities and talents, and motivate them in an employee-centric environment. Deliberate and effective workplace practices are therefore recommended.

The findings of this study will be very useful in advancing the literature in the area of staff turnover in the hotel industry and providing relevant information pertaining to people management in that environment. From a practical standpoint, the chapter will be able to inform hotel practitioners of these factors as well as how staff turnover can impact the productivity levels of the hotel. Further studies can be done to empirically assess the factors that are contributing to staff turnover in the hotel industry and the impact of staff turnover on hotel productivity. Future studies can also empirically examine the relationship between hotel productivity and hotel performance.

REFERENCES

1. Behere D. Global tourism and its impact on business. ZENITH International Journal of Business Economics & Management Research. 2018;8(5):73-85
2. De Freitas CR. Tourism climatology past and present: A review of the role of the ISB commission on climate, tourism and recreation. International Journal of Biometeorology. 2017;61(1):107-114
3. Popov LA, Nikolskaya EY, Kosheleva AI, Kobyak MV, Lepeshkin VA. Trends in the development of hotel business in the world and the Russian Federation. International Journal of Applied Business and Economic Research. 2016;14(9):5843
4. O'Cass A, Sok P. An exploratory study into managing value creation in tourism service firms: Understanding value creation phases at the intersection of the tourism service firm and their customers. Tourism Management. 2015;51:186-200
5. Mayhew R. Employee turnover definitions and calculations. Small Business: Managing Employees: Employees. 2018. Retrieved from: https://smallbusiness.chron.com/employee-turnover-definitions-calculations-11611.html [September 25, 2022]
6. Zhang YJ. A review of employee turnover influence factor and countermeasure. Journal of Human Resource and Sustainability Studies. 2016;4(2):85-91
7. Abbasi SM, Hollman KW. Turnover: The bottom line. Public Personal Management. 2000;29(3):333-342
8. Ronra B, Chaisawat M. Factors affecting employee turnover and job satisfaction: A case study of Amari hotels and resorts. Paper Presented at the 3rd International Colloquium on Business & Management (ICBM), Bangkok, Thailand. 2010
9. Narkhede PA. Employee turnover in hospitality industries: A study of service staff. JIMS8M: The Journal of Indian Management & Strategy. 2014;19(3):4-8
10. Demir C, Çolakoğlu Ü, Güzel B. Relationship between employee turnover and the location of hotels: The case of Kuşadası and Izmir in Turkey. Journal of Yasar University. 2007;2(5):477-487
11. Yazinski SK. Job involvement, commitment, satisfaction and turnover: Evidence from hotel employees in Cyprus. Tourism Management. 2009;41:129-140
12. AlBattat ARS, Som APM. Employee dissatisfaction and turnover crises in the Malaysian hospitality industry. International Journal of Business and Management. 2013;8(5):62-71
13. Chalkiti K, Sigala M. Staff turnover in the Greek tourism industry: A comparison between insular and peninsular regions. International Journal of Contemporary Hospitality Management. 2010;22(3):335-359
14. Faz M, Anthonisz A, Dang Y. The impact of staff turnover on a hotel's income statement. White Paper Prepared by TFG Asset Management. 2018. Retrieved from: https://www.researchgate.net/publication/322539791_The_Impact_of_Staff_Turnover_on_a_Hotel's_Income_Statement_White_Paper_prepared_by_TFG_As_ et_Management/citations [September 25, 2022]
15. Kim BP, Murrmann SK, Lee G. Moderating effects of gender and organizational level between role stress and job satisfaction among hotel employees. International Journal of Hospitality Management. 2009;28(4):612-619
16. Slattery P. Finding the hospitality industry. Journal of Hospitality, Leisure, Sport and Tourism Education. 2002;1(1):19-28

17. Roa P, Sahu P. Impact of service quality on customer satisfaction in hotel industry. IOSR Journal of Humanities and Social Science. 2013;18:39-44

18. Ahmad R, Scott N. Managing the front office department: Staffing issues in Malaysian hotels. Anatolia. An International Journal of Tourism and Hospitality Research. 2014;25(1):24-38

19. Adler H, Rigg J. Expatriate hotel general managers in Jamaica: Perceptions of human resource, organizational, and operational challenges. Journal of Hotel and Business Management. 2012;1(1):2169-0286

20. Kuria S, Alice O, Wanderi P. Assessment of causes of labour turnover in three and five star-rated hotels in Kenya. International Journal of Business and Social Science. 2012;3(15):311-317

21. Sampson W, Akyeampong O. Work-related stress in hotel: An analysis of the causes and effects among frontline hotel employees in the Kumasi Metropolis, Ghana. Journal of Tourism and Hospitality. 2014;3(2):127-135

22. Davis OA. Strategies for Low Employee Turnover in the Hotel Industry (Doctoral dissertation, Walden University). Walden University ProQuest Dissertations Publishing; 2018. p. 10788659. Retrieved from: https://www.proquest.com/dissertations-theses/strategies-low-employee-turnover-hotel-industry/docview/2033582016/se-2

23. O'Connell M, Kung MC. The cost of employee turnover. Industrial Management. 2007;49(1):14-19

24. Kyndt E, Dochy F, Michielsen M, Moeyaert B. Employee retention: Organisational and personal perspectives. Vocations and Learning. 2009;2(3):195-215

25. Xiao Y, Watson M. Guidance on conducting a systematic literature review. Journal of Planning Education and Research. 2019;39(1):93-112

26. Davidson MC, Timo N, Wang Y. How much does labour turnover cost? A case study of Australian four-and five-star hotels. International Journal of Contemporary Hospitality Management. 2010

27. Loquercio D. Turnover and retention. In: Ronra B, Chaisawat M, editors. Factors Affecting Employee Turnover and Job Satisfaction: A Case Study of Amari Hotels and Resorts. Paper Presented at the 3rd International Colloquium on Business & Management (ICBM), Bangkok, Thailand. 2010

28. Musa BM, Ahmed I, Bala A. Effect of motivational incentives on staff turnover in hotel industry in Gombe state. Journal of Business and Management. 2014;16(3):36-42

29. El-Said O, Aziz H. Job satisfaction and potential opportunities for career growth among hotel employees: The case of Oman. Tourism and Hospitality Research. 2022;22(4):488-507

30. Russen M, Dawson M, Madera JM. Gender discrimination and perceived fairness in the promotion process of hotel employees. International Journal of Contemporary Hospitality Management. 2021;33(1):327-345

31. Chi CGQ, Wen B, Ouyang Z. Developing relationship quality in economy hotels: The role of perceived justice, service quality, and commercial friendship. Journal of Hospitality Marketing and Management. 2020;29(8):1027-1051

32. Wilkins CL, Wellman JD, Flavin EL, Manrique JA. When men perceive anti-male bias: Status-legitimizing beliefs increase discrimination against women. Psychology of Men and Masculinity. 2018;19(2):282-290

33. Campos-Soria JA, Garcia-Pozo A, Sanchez-Ollero JL. Gender wage inequality and labour mobility in the hospitality sector. International Journal of Hospitality Management. 2015;49:73-82

34. Etehadi B, Karatepe O. The impact of job insecurity on critical hotel employee outcomes: The mediating role of self-efficacy. Journal of Hospitality Marketing & Management. 2018;28(6):665-689

35. Abolade DA. Impact of employees' job insecurity and employee turnover on organisational performance in private and public sector organisations. Studies in Business and Economics. 2018;13(2):6-19

36. Akbiyik B. The association between perceived job insecurity and career commitment in hospitality sector. The role of support at work. Research Journal of Business and Management. 2016;3(1):11-21

37. Fathy E. Issues faced by hotel human resource managers in Alexandria. Egypt. Research in Hospitality Management. 2018;8(2):115-124

38. Holston-Okae BL, Mushi RJ. Employee turnover in the hospitality industry using Herzberg's two-factor motivation-hygiene theory. International Journal of Academic Research in Business and Social Sciences. 2018;8(1):218-248

39. McGinley SP, Hanks L, Line ND. Constraints to attracting new hotel workers: A study on industrial recruitment. International Journal of Hospitality Management. 2017;60:114-122

40. Jugan V. An Investigation into the High Turnover of Employees Within the Irish Hospitality Sector, Identifying What Methods of Retention should be Adopted. (Master of Arts Dissertation). National College of Ireland; 2015

41. Milka W, Kerubo JO, Eunicares L. Factors affecting employee turnover in hospitality establishments in Kisii town, Kenya. Merit Research Journal of Business and Management. 2017;5(1):030-040

42. Zopiatis A, Constanti P, Theocharous AL. Migrant labor in hospitality: The Cyprus experience. International Journal of Hospitality Management. 2014;37:111-120

43. Mwilu MJ. Factors Influencing Employee Turnover in the Hotel Industry in Machakos Town, Machakos County. (Doctoral dissertation). South Eastern Kenya University Digital Repository; 2016. Available from: http://repository.seku.ac.ke/handle/123456789/1920

44. Rok M, Mulej M. CSR-based model for HRM in tourism and hospitality. Kybernetes. 2014;43:346-362

45. Sankar M. Impact of hygiene factors on employee retention: Experimental study on paper industry. Indian Journal of Management Science. 2015;5(1):58-61

46. Holston-Okae BL. Employee Turnover Intentions in the Hospitality Industry (Unpublished doctoral dissertation). Minneapolis, Minnesota, USA: College of Management and Technology, Walden University; 2017

47. Dwesini NF. Causes and prevention of high employee turnover within the hospitality industry: A literature review. African Journal of Hospitality, Tourism and Leisure. 2019;8(3):1-15

48. Victor J, Hoole C. The influence of organisational rewards on workplace trust and work engagement. SA Journal of Human Resource Management (IJM&P). 2017;15(1):1-14

49. Jehanzeb K, Rasheed F, Rasheed A, Aamir A. Impact of rewards and motivation on job satisfaction in the banking sector of Saudi Arabia. International Journal of Business and Social Science. 2012;3(21):272-278

50. Sageer A, Rafat S, Agarwal P. Identification of variables affecting employee satisfaction and their impact on the organization. IOSR Journal of Business and Management. 2012;5(1):32-39

51. Syverson C. What determines productivity? Journal of Economic Literature. 2011;49(2):326 65

52. Haenisch J. Factors affecting the productivity of government workers. SAGE Open. 2012;2(1):1-7. DOI: 10.1177/2158244012441603

53. Ugoani J. Employee turnover and productivity among small business entities in Nigeria. Independent Journal of Management & Production. 2016;7(4):1063-1082

54. Siddiqui MN. Success of an organization is a result of employees performance. Advances in Social Sciences Research Journal. 2014;1(4):179-201

55. Hinkin TR, Tracey JB. The cost of turnover: Putting a price on the learning curve. Cornell Hotel and Restaurant Administration Quarterly. 2000;41(3):14-21

56. Singh D, Amandeep. Impact of employee turnover on the hotel industry- a study of selected hotels of new Delhi. International Journal of Research. 2017;5:153-158

57. Powell PH, Watson D. Service unseen: The hotel room attendant at work. International Journal of Hospitality Management. 2006;25(2):297-312

58. Hesford JW, Malina MA, Pizzini M. Turnover and unit-level financial performance: An analysis of the costs and benefits of voluntary and involuntary turnover in unskilled jobs. Advances in Management Accounting. 2016;26:35-65

59. Bhatti KK, Qureshi TM. Impact of employee participation on job satisfaction, employee commitment and employee productivity. International Review of Business Research Papers. 2007;3(2):54-68

60. Chi CG, Gursoy D. Employee satisfaction, customer satisfaction, and financial performance: An empirical examination. International Journal of Hospitality Management. 2009;28(2):245-253

61. Mohsin A, Lengler J, Aguzzoli R. Staff turnover in hotels: Exploring the quadratic and linear relationships. Tourism Management. 2015;51:35-48

62. Holtom BC, Burch TC. A model of turnover-based disruption in customer services. Human Resource Management Review. 2016;26(1):25-36

63. Paul J, Criado AR. The art of writing literature review: What do we know and what do we need to know? International Business Review. 2020;29(4):101717

64. Timmins F, McCabe C. How to conduct an effective literature search. Nursing Standard. 2005;20(11):41-47

65. Snyder H. Literature review as a research methodology: An overview anD guidelines. Journal of Business Research. 2019;104:333-339

66. Aziri B. Job satisfaction: A literature review. Management Research & Practice. 2011;3(4):77-86

67. Ngai EW. Customer relationship management research (1992-2002): An academic literature review and classification. Marketing Intelligence & Planning (Emerald Group Publishing Limited). 2005;23(6):582-605. DOI: 10.1108/02634500510624147

68. Brodeur A, Gray D, Islam A, Bhuiyan S. A literature review of the economics of COVID-19. Journal of Economic Surveys. 2021;35(4):1007-1044

69. Dunne C. The place of the literature review in grounded theory research. International Journal of Social Research Methodology. 2011;14(2):111-124

70. Hartman SJ, Yrle AC. Can the hobo phenomenon help explain voluntary turnover? International Journal of Contemporary Hospitality Management. 1996;8(4):11-16

71. Lam T, Baum T, Pine R. Study of managerial job satisfaction in Hong Kong's Chinese restaurants. International Journal of Contemporary Hospitality Management. 2001;13(1):35-42

72. Ferry K. Strategy Activation: The Power of Service and Purpose. 2020. Available from: https://www.kornferry.com/insights/this-week-in-leadership/power-service-and-purpose#:~:text=First_link_service_directly_to,a_priority_with_n_the_organization [Retrieved June 2, 2022]

73. Long CS, Perumal P. Examining the impact of human resource management practices on employees' turnover intention. International Journal of Business & Society. 2014;15(1):111-126

74. Milman A, Dickson AMD. Employment characteristics and retention predictors among hourly employees in large US theme parks and attractions. International Journal of Contemporary Hospitality Management. 2015;26:447-469

75. Onimole SO. Work design and job satisfaction. International Journal of Humanities and Social Science. 2015;5(10):202-207

76. Kim N. Employee turnover intention among newcomers in travel industry. International Journal of Tourism Research. 2014;16(1):56-64

77. Chen M. The effect of training on employee retention. International Conference on Global Economy, Commerce and Service Science. 2014;1(2):356-359

78. Memon MA, Salleh R, Baharom MNR. The link between training satisfaction, work engagement and turnover intention. European Journal of Training and Development. 2016;40(6):407-429

79. Lapointe E, Vandenberghe C. Supervisory mentoring and employee affective commitment and turnover. The critical role of contextual factors. Journal of Vocational Behaviour. 2017;98(February 2017):98-107

80. Zhu D, Kim PB, Poulston J. An examination of university student workers' motivations: A New Zealand hospitality industry case study. Journal of Hospitality & Tourism Education. 2020;32(4):206-219

81. Ogbo A, Anthony KA, Kosisochukwu O. An assessment of hygiene maintenance factors effect on employees productivity in Nigerian telecommunication industry. International Research Journal of Management, IT and Social Sciences. 2017;4(1):61-70

82. Deri MN, Zaazie P, Bazaanah P. Turnover intentions among hotel employees in the Accra metropolis of Ghana. African Journal of Hospitality, Tourism and Leisure. 2021;10(1):238-255

83. Ehrler M. Using Job Embeddedness Theory to Improve Employee Turnover. ERE Media; 2018. Retrieved from: https://www.tlnt.com/using-job-embeddedness-theory-to-improve-employee-turnover/ [June 2, 2022]

84. Nicholas A, Mensah O, Owusu O. Stay or leave? Using job embeddedness to explain turn over intention among hotel staff in Ghana. Journal of Management Research. 2016;8(3):13-139

85. Akyüz B, Kaya N, Özgeldi M. The effects of human resource management practices and organizational climate on turnover intention: An empirical study in Turkish banking sector1. IIB International Refereed Academic Social Sciences Journal. 2015;6(17):48

86. Muthukumar E, Vidhya S. Enriching human resources capital through training and development in hotel industries at Coimbatore. International Journal of Emerging Research in Management and Technology. 2015;4(6):85-91

87. Serrat O. Coaching and mentoring. In: Knowledge Solutions. Singapore: Springer; 2017. pp. 897-902

88. Jeong S, Park S. Mentoring in the human resource development context. In: The Wiley International Handbook of Mentoring: Paradigms, Practices, Programs and Possibilities. John Wiley & Sons, Inc. Wiley Online Library; 2020. pp. 45-63

89. Gursoy S, Dhar R. Employee service innovative behavior: The roles of leader member exchange (LMX), work engagement, and job autonomy. International Journal of Manpower. 2016;38:242-258

90. Liu T, Shen H, Gao J. Women's career advancement in hotels: The mediating role of organizational commitment. International Journal of Contemporary Hospitality Management. 2020;32(8):2543-2561

91. Babakus E, Yavas U, Karatepe OM. Does psychological contract on work-family improve employee commitment? Asian Social Science. 2015;11(13):71-83

92. Bin AS. The relationship between job satisfaction, job performance and employee engagement: An explorative study. Issues in Business Management and Economics. 2015;4(1):1-8

93. Sinclair-Maragh G, Jacobs-Gray N, Brown-Roomes N. A case of talent management practices in motivating fast food service employees. Emerald Emerging Markets Case Studies. 2017;7(3):1-16

94. Rane DB. Employee job satisfaction: An essence of organization. Iš: HRM Review. 2011;11(7):10-16

95. Ayupp K, Chung TH. Empowerment: Hotel employees' perspective. Journal of Industrial Engineering and Management (JIEM). 2010;3(3):561-575

96. Sandhya K, Kumar DP. Employee retention by motivation. Indian Journal of Science and Technology. 2011;4(12):1778-1782

97. Rogelberg SG, Luong A, Sederburg ME, Cristol DS. Employee attitude surveys: Examining the attitudes of noncompliant employees. Journal of Applied Psychology. 2000;85(2):284

CHAPTER 10

Applying Revised Gap Analysis Model in Measuring Hotel Service Quality

Yu-Cheng Lee[1], Yu-Che Wang[2], Chih-Hung Chien[3,4], Chia-Huei Wu[5], Shu-Chiung Lu[3,4,11], Sang-Bing Tsai[6,7,8,9] and Weiwei Dong[10]

[1]*Department of Technology Management, Chung-Hua University, Hsinchu, 300, Taiwan*

[2]*Department of Business Administration, Chung-Hua University, Hsinchu, 300, Taiwan*

[3]*PhD Program of Technology Management, Chung-Hua University, Hsinchu, 300, Taiwan*

[4]*Department of Business Administration, Lee-Ming Institute of Technology, Taipei City, 243, Taiwan*

[5]*Department of Tourism and Leisure Management, Yuanpei University of Medical Technology, Hsinchu, 300, Taiwan*

[6]*Zhongshan Institute, University of Electronic Science and Technology of China, Guangdong, 528402, China*

[7]*School of Economics & Management, Shanghai Maritime University, Shanghai, 201306, China*

[8]*Law School, Nankai University, Tianjin, 300071, China*

[9]*School of Business, Dalian University of Technology, Panjin, 124221, China*

[10]*School of Economics and Management, Shanghai Institute of Technology, Shanghai, 201418, China*

[11]*Department of Food and Beverage Management, Lee-Ming Institute of Technology, Taipei City, 243, Taiwan*

ABSTRACTS

Introduction: *With the number of tourists coming to Taiwan growing by 10–20 % since 2010, the number has increased due to an increasing number of foreign tourists, particularly after deregulation allowed admitting tourist groups, followed later on by foreign individual tourists, from mainland China. The purpose of this study is to propose a revised* *gap model to evaluate and improve service quality in Taiwanese hotel industry. Thus, service quality could be clearly measured through gap analysis, which was more effective for offering direction in developing and improving service quality.*

Case description: *The HOLSERV instrument was used to identify and analyze service gaps from the perceptions of internal and external customers. The sample for this study included three main categories of respondents: tourists, employees, and managers.*

Discussion and evaluation: *The results show that five gaps influenced tourists' evaluations of service quality. In particular, the study revealed that Gap 1 (management perceptions vs. customer expectations) and Gap 9 (service provider perceptions of management perceptions vs. service delivery) were more critical than the others in affecting perceived service quality, making service delivery the main area of improvement.*

Conclusion: *This study contributes toward an evaluation of the service quality of the Taiwanese hotel industry from the perspectives of customers, service providers, and managers, which is considerably valuable for hotel managers. It was the aim of this study to explore all of these together in order to better understand the possible gaps in the hotel industry in Taiwan.*

Keywords: *Service quality, HOLSERV, Gap analysis, Gap model, Business management*

BACKGROUND

With the number of tourists coming to Taiwan growing by 10–20 % since 2010, the number has increased due to an increasing number of foreign tourists, particularly after deregulation allowed admitting tourist groups, followed later on by foreign individual tourists, from mainland China. Therefore, the tourism industry has become of greater economic importance, according to the Tourism Bureau statistics of Taiwan. The international tourist industry has experienced significant growth in recent years, and more and more hotels provide exquisite, high-quality and customized service that contributes to a hotel's image and competitiveness in Taiwan (Chen 2013). Thence, the hotel sector within the tourism industry faces more intense global competition than other supply industries. Meanwhile, the rapidly growing number of visitors has increased the workload for hotel employees. Thus, they need to staff sufficient professional employees. However, the hotel industry may face the problem of finding qualified employees to provide services that could meet the standards of foreign tourists. Mei et al. (1999), Tsaur and Lin (2004) and Hooper et al. (2013) stated that one of the most influential factors on customers' perceptions of service quality is the employees. Dedeoğlu and Demirer (2015) stress the factors contributing to hotel service quality are often the services related to employee behavior and tangibles. Tsang (2011) studied the Taiwanese hotel industry and found that success and failure in the service delivery of a hotel largely depends on the attitudes and behaviors of contact employees. Thus, determining how employees perceive the services they deliver becomes critical.

Service quality has been identified as crucial to the hotel industry and is measured to assist managers in making decisions, thus improving overall efficiency and profits. Service quality has gradually been recognized as a key factor in gaining competitive advantage and retaining customers (Callan and Kyndt 2001; Nasution 2016). Currently, Wu and Ko (2013) hotel organizations have difficulties in adequately assessing and improving their service performance from a customers' perspective. They also fail to recognize which factors that customers consider important and when they should best evaluate their hotel experience. Moreover, while most of the studies on the hotel sector in the literature focus mainly on the evaluation of customers for service quality, other stakeholders' (employees' and managers') perceptions have been ignored (Dedeoğlu and Demirer 2015).

Numerous empirical studies have shown that there were considerable differences in expectations of service quality between customers and management in the service industry (Tsang and Qu 2000; Kang and Bradley 2002; Lee et al. 2007; Chen and Chang 2005; Torres et al. 2013; Dedeoğlu and Demirer 2015). Tsang and Qu (2000) evaluated perceptions of service quality in China's hotel industry, from the perceptions of both tourists and managers. Their results indicated that tourists' perceptions of service quality were consistently lower than their expectations and managers overestimated the service delivery. Some studies have shown that front-line employees frequently serve on their way, so it is difficult for management to inspect their behavior (Bowen and Lawler 1992; Schneider and Bowen 1995; Yagil 2002). Dedeoğlu and Demirer (2015) addressed the nature and characteristics of differences in service quality perceptions among customers, managers and employees in the hotel industry. Moreover, Torres et al. (2013) emphasized that studies are required in the field that include the examination of various kinds of feedback (i.e. guests, experts, and operators). The different levels of value provide the need for tourism and hospitality operators to adopt a more comprehensive strategy to collect, analyze, and take appropriate actions. Little empirical research has existed on the evaluation of service quality from the perspective of managers, employees and customers in hotel industry in Taiwan. We believed that management should better understand the customers' expectations that would influence design, development and delivery the service offering. Employees contact with customers should offer consistent quality of services that would attract and maintain customers directly. The evaluation of the service quality should not only base on customers and managers but also employees, consequently that it is able to assess customer needs and wants accurately. Hence, it is essential to understand the perceptions of customers in relation to the perceptions of managers and employees.

Although several researchers (e.g. Carman 1990; Teas 1993) have criticized Parasuraman and et al.' (1985, 1988) gap analysis in measuring customer's service quality perceptions and expectations, it is still the leading measure of service quality (Lam and Woo 1997). However, Gap 5 has functional relationships with Gaps 1–4 in the PZB model, these relationships are problematic due to the individual measurement of a gap cannot be determined by combining the gaps. Therefore, a number of researchers have revised the gap model to focus on Gap 5, Gap 1, and other additional gaps (Jannadi et al. 2000; Tsang and Qu 2000; Chen and Chang 2005; Kang and Bradley 2002; Dedeoğlu and Demirer 2015). Some researchers have confirmed that a revised gap model was relevant to the research scope and effectively evaluated service quality problems which could provide management with important insights. Particularly, Lee et al. (2007) revised the gap model by decomposing service activities and focused on Gap 5, Gap 1, and three identified additional gaps (Gap 8, Gap 9, and Gap 10). Through the revised gap model, Lee et al. (2007) stressed that service quality could be clearly measured through these gap scores, which were more effective for offering direction in developing and improving service quality. This study contributes toward an evaluation of the service quality of the Taiwanese hotel industry from the perspectives of customers, service providers, and managers, which is considerably valuable for hotel managers. Furthermore, the study of various sources of perspectives (i.e. tourists, managers, and employees) is often studied separately in the tourism literature. It was the aim of this study to explore all of these together in order to better understand the possible gaps in the hotel industry in Taiwan.

LITERATURE REVIEW

Service quality literature

The SERVQUAL model is the most widely used instruments to measure the customer satisfaction in various industries and across different countries, developed by Parasuraman et al. 1985, then refined in 1988 and 1991. The model is based on the customer's assessment of service quality, which is a comparison of the expected and the obtain value as well as a consideration of gaps in the process of service provision. The foundation of SERVQUAL instrument was the gap model. The model shown in Fig. 1 identifies five gaps. Gap 1 is the difference between customer expectation and management perceptions of customer expectation, Gap 2 is the difference between management perceptions of customer expectations and service quality specifications, Gap 3 is the difference between service quality specifications and the service actually delivered, Gap 4 is the difference between service delivery and external communication, and Gap 5 is the difference between customer expectation on the service and their perceptions of service performance.

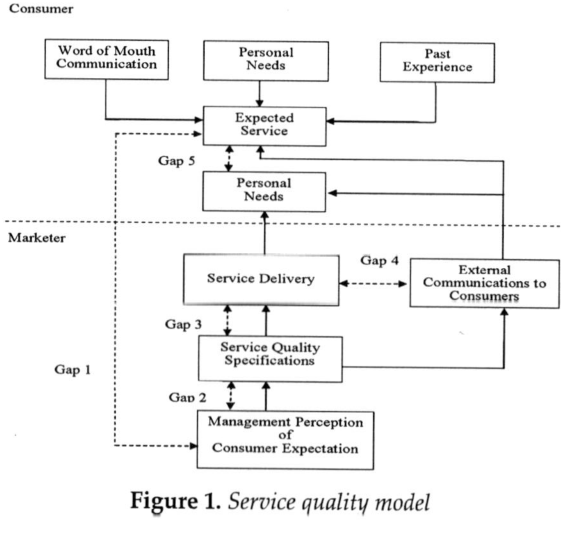

Figure 1. *Service quality model*

Previous studies (Brown et al. 1993; Babakus and Boller 1992; Martin 2003; Han and Baek 2004; Gonzalez et al. 2008; Wei et al. 2011; Stefano et al. 2015) have applied SERVQUAL to measure Gap 5 and Gap 5 has functional relationships with Gaps 1–4 in the PZB model. However, these relationships are problematic because the individual measurement of a gap cannot be determined by combining the gaps.

Application of the Gap model

Luo and Qu (2016) indicated quality of service is more difficult to define, measure, and manage than manufacturing products due to the unique characteristics of services.

Saleh and Ryan (1991) identified the existence of gaps between clients' and management perceptions of attributes of the hotel, and between client expectation and perception of the services offered. Some researchers (Large and Konig 2009; Frederick and Mukesh 2001) designed INTSERVQUAL, an internal service quality measurement scale based on the "gap model" to successfully measure the difference between internal customers' understanding and expectation from frontline service staff. Dedeoğlu and Demirer (2015) indicated while most of the studies on the hotel sector in the literature focus mainly on the evaluation of customers for service quality, other stakeholders' (employees' and managers') perceptions have been ignored. It is argued that the existence of these gaps is a source of dissatisfaction with services provided (Saleh and Ryan 1991). Therefore, numerous of studies have been revised the gap model to focus on Gap 5, Gap 1, and other additional gaps (Jannadi et al. 2000; Tsang and Qu 2000; Chen and Chang 2005; Kang and Bradley 2002; Dedeoğlu and Demirer 2015). Jannadi et al. (2000) investigated four gaps of service quality in the Saudi Consolidated Electric Company in the Eastern Province and revealed that Gap 3 (service performance) was more critical than the others in affecting perceived service quality, making service delivery the main area of improvement. In addition, there was a revised gap model concentrated on Gap 5, Gap 1, and two additional identified gaps (Gap 6 and Gap 7) demonstrated by Tsang and Qu in 2000. Moreover, a conceptual "gaps model" of information technology (IT) service quality was developed by Kang and Bradly in 2002, which identified seven gaps between customers and IT service suppliers. Dedeoğlu and Demirer (2015) addressed the nature and characteristics of differences in service quality perceptions among customers, managers and employees. Torres et al. (2013) emphasized that studies are required in the field that include the examination of various kinds of feedback (i.e. guests, experts, and operators). The different levels of value provide the need for tourism and hospitality operators to adopt a more comprehensive strategy to collect, analyze, and take appropriate actions.

Some researchers have confirmed that a revised gap analysis was relevant to the research scope and effectively evaluated service quality problems which could provide management with important insights. Particularly, Lee et al. (2007) revised the conceptual model by decomposing service activities and focused on Gap 5, Gap 1, and three identified additional gaps (Gap 8, Gap 9, and Gap 10); Although Gap 5 has a functional relationship with Gaps 1–4 in the PZB model (Parasuraman et al. 1985), individual measurement of gap cannot be shown as the combination

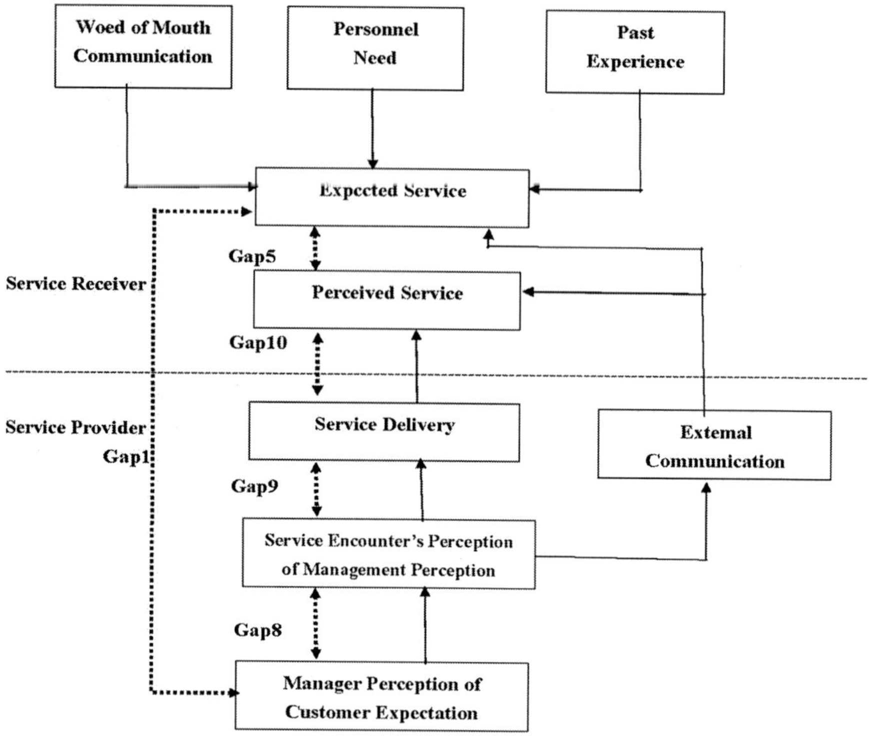

Figure 1. *Revised conceptual model.*
Source: *Adapted from Lee et al. (2007)*

of gaps. Therefore, our studies applied the revised gap model designed by Lee et al. (2007). The structure is shown conveniently identified and service quality could be clearly measured through these gap scores in Fig. 2.

The definitions of Gap 5 and Gap 1 are the same as in the PZB model; Gap 5 is the difference between customer perceptions and expectations, and Gap 1 is the difference between management perceptions and customer expectations. Gap 8 is the difference between management perceptions of customer expectations and service encounter perceptions of management perceptions. Gap 9 is the difference between service encounter perceptions of management perceptions and service delivery. This gap represents the gap of service perceptions through the service delivery process. Gap 10 is the difference between service delivery and the perceived service. The functional relationship can be indicated as follows:

$$\text{Gap } 5 = \text{Gap } 1 + \text{Gap } 8 + \text{Gap } 9 + \text{Gap } 10 \quad (1)$$

The revised conceptual model is another better way to measure gaps of service quality, because it provides a functional relationship that indicates the combination of gaps and the decomposition of service activity. Especially, it offers direction for developing and improving service quality as well (Lee et al. 2007).

Service quality of an international hotel

Despite SERVQUAL's wide use by academics and practicing managers in various industries, a number of studies have questioned the conceptual and operational base of the model (Babakus and Boller 1992; Carman 1990; Teas 1994; Saleh and Ryan 1991). Some researchers suggested that further customization of the scale for the hospitality industry was necessary (Saleh and Ryan 1991). Various measurement scales such as LODGSERV, HOLSERV, LODGQUAL and DINESERV have been developed for service quality evaluation purposes in the tourism industry. LODGSERV (Knutson et al. 1990) and HOLSERV (Mei et al. 1999) are used in the accommodation industry. LODGQUAL (Getty and Thompson 1994) is to assess service quality in the lodging industry while DINESERV (Stevens et al. 1995) is used in the restaurant services sector. Knutson et al. (1990) adapted SERVQUAL dimensions and developed an instrument called LODGSERV. Reliability is the most critical element in LODGSERV. By contrast, Kandampully and Suhartanto (2000) identified customer satisfaction with housekeeping as the only significant factor affecting customer loyalty. Mei et al. (1999) revised SERVQUAL (Parasuraman et al. 1991) to include three dimensions of service quality: employees, tangibles, and reliability. They found that the employee dimension was the best predictor of overall service quality. Dedeoğlu and Demirer (2015) stress the factors contributing to hotel service quality are often the services related to employee behavior and tangibles. In addition, HOLSERV scale more parsimonious and user-friendly than SERVQUAL (Wu and Ko 2013). Moreover, consideration of the type of hotel and the range of facilities available, the HOLSERV instrument is suitable for our study in the hospitality industry in Taiwan, to design service strategies that meet guest expectations.

METHODOLOGY

Questionnaire design and distribution

After a review of the literature, the HOLSERV instrument by Mei et al. (1999) was used to identify and analyze service gaps among the perceptions of tourists, employees and hotel managers. The gap in service quality was measured using the 27 items of the HOLSERV, with a 9-point scale ranging from 1 (completely unfulfilled) to 9 (much fulfillment). The sample comprised three main categories of respondents: tourists; employees, and managers. The first category of the questionnaire was designed to examine the tourists' expectations and perceptions of service quality. The second category of the questionnaire was designed to evaluated managers' perceptions of customer expectations. The third category of the questionnaire was designed to assess employee perceptions of manager perceptions and employee perceptions of perceived service. The target population of the tourist survey was all international tourists who visited hotels in Taipei, Taiwan were chosen for this study.

A total of 382 tourists were invited to complete the questionnaire, and 341 effective samples were obtained (usable response rate of 89.2 %). The gender breakdown of the respondents was 56.3 % male and 43.7 % female. Of the 341 respondents, 255 were tourists, 40 were managers, and 46 were employees.

Demographic profile of the hotel tourists, employees, and managers

The questionnaire survey sites selected for this study were two international hotels in Taiwan. A convenience sampling method was applied. Ultimately, 300 tourists were invited to complete the questionnaire and 255 effective responses were obtained (for a usable response rate of 83.30 %). The sample of tourists contained more males (55.69 %) than females (44.31 %). More than half of the respondents had a university, college, or graduate education. Approximately 55 % of the respondents were professionals, executives, or sales people, and nearly 55 % earned an annual household income of US $32,000 or above. The majority of the respondents (60 %) were aged 21–40 years. Most of the respondents were from the cities of Taipei (55 %), Tainan (15 %), or Taichung (10 %), and the rest of the respondents (20 %) were from other countries.

The target population for the management survey was all supervisors and managers (ranging from the supervisor to the general manager level) who worked in two hotels located in the cities of Taipei and Taichung. The sample size was 40. The sample of managers contained more males (60 %) than females (40 %), and more than 80 % were aged 31–50 years. More than 60 % of the respondents had a university, college, or graduate education. The respondents ranged from supervisors to general managers, and 68 % were departmental managers or supervisors. More than a quarter of respondents worked in the housekeeping department, followed by the front desk (16 %), training (14 %), food and beverage (11 %) and other departments (30 %).

The target population for the employee surveys were from the housekeeping department, front desk, training, food and beverage, and other departments. The sample size was 46. The sample of employees contained more males (56.52 %) than females (43.48 %) and more than 70 % were aged 21–40 years. More than half of the respondents had a university, college, or graduate education.

RESULTS

Gap 5

As noted in Table 1, the results of Gap 5 indicated that, all attributes were negative scores, and there was a significant difference between tourists' actual perceptions and their expectations. And overall service quality provided below tourists' expectation. The biggest gaps were on attributes, 6 "Gives prompt service (−1.048)", 4 "Provides services at the time it promises to do so" (−0.932), 1 "Promises to provide a service and does so" (−0.915), 2 "Shows dependability in handling service problems" (−0.915), and 3 "Performs the service right the first time" (−0.881). Those attributes were the most serious deficiencies which would need pay close attention by managers and make improvement effectively. The overall Gap 5 score was −0.662 which would showed that the overall service quality provided by the hotel in Taiwan would not meet tourists' expectation.

Gap 1

As shown in Table 1, a comparison of managers' perception for tourists' expectation and the tourists' themselves expectation. The result indicted that, the overall

Table 1. *Revised gap scores and functional relationships (Gap 5 = Gap 1 + Gap 8 + Gap 9 + Gap 10)*

Question	Gap 5 TP-TE	Gap 1 MPTE-TE	Gap 8 EPMR-MPTE	Gap 9 EPD-EPMR	Gap 10 TP-EPD
1. Promises to provide a service and does so	−0.915	−1.036	0.767	−0.696	0.050
2. Shows dependability in handling service problems	−0.915	−0.668	0.383	−0.630	0.000
3. Performs the service right the first time	−0.881	−0.891	0.460	−0.500	0.050
4. Provides services at the time it promises to do so	−0.932	−0.377	−0.077	−0.478	0.000
5. Tells guests exactly when the services will be performed	−0.770	−0.555	0.107	−0.522	0.200
6. Gives prompt service	−1.048	−0.750	0.174	−0.522	0.050
7. Always willing to help	−0.811	−0.514	0.125	−0.522	0.100
8. Never too busy to respond to guests' requests	−0.611	−0.877	0.466	−0.500	0.300
9. Instils confidence in guests	−0.610	−0.318	0.036	−0.478	0.150
10. Guests feel safe in the delivery of services	−0.698	−0.500	0.174	−0.522	0.150
11. Guests feel safe and secure in their stay	−0.648	−0.323	−0.053	−0.522	0.250
12. Polite and courteous employees	−0.626	−0.509	0.170	−0.587	0.300
13. Have the knowledge to answer questions	−0.741	−0.559	0.018	−0.500	0.300
14. Have the skill to perform the service	−0.515	−0.736	0.528	−0.457	0.150
15. Gives individual attention	−0.520	−0.650	0.239	−0.609	0.500
16. Deals with guests in a caring fashion	−0.660	−0.500	0.283	−0.543	0.100
17. Has guests' best interests at heart	−0.448	−0.268	0.144	−0.674	0.350
18. Understands guests' specific needs	−0.783	−0.591	0.243	−0.435	0.000
19. Equipment, fixtures and fittings are modern looking	−0.451	−0.814	0.559	−0.496	0.300
20. Facilities are visually appealing	−0.241	−0.427	0.445	−0.609	0.350
21. Neat and professional employees	−0.239	−0.518	0.644	−0.565	0.200
22. Materials are visually appealing	−0.842	−0.873	0.403	−0.522	0.150
23. Fixture and fittings are comfortable	−0.563	−0.514	0.494	−0.543	0.000
24. Equipment and facilities are easy to use	−0.547	−0.468	0.362	−0.391	−0.050
25. Equipment and facilities are generally clean	−0.558	−0.518	0.427	−0.717	0.250
26. Variety of food and beverages meet guests' needs	−0.628	-0.464	0.516	−0.630	−0.050
27. Services are operated at a convenient time	−0.694	−0.518	0.383	−0.609	0.050
Average	−0.662	−0.583	0.312	−0.547	0.156

TE tourist expectation, *TP* tourist perception, *MPTE* managers' perception for tourist s' expectation, *EPMR* employees' perception for managers' requirement, *EPD* employees' perception for delivery

Gap 1 score was −0.583, which would indicated that managers do not have a good understanding of tourist expectation. This finding contrasts with previous studies (Nel and Pitt 1993; Tsang and Qu 2000) but consistent with past research (Choy et al. 1986; Wei et al. 1989).

All 27 attributes were negative and very big. The range from attribute 17 "Has guests' best interests at heart" (−0.268) to attribute 1 "Promises to provide a service and does so" (−1.036) was big variation. The biggest gaps were on attributes, 1 "Promises to provide a service and does so" (−1.036), 3 "Performs the service right the first time" (−0.891), 8 "Never too busy to respond to guests' requests" (−0.877) and 22 "Materials are visually appealing" (−0.873). Therefore, from the results of negative Gap 1 score and big difference, it can be concluded that Gap 1 tend to a major problems related to Gap 5 of service quality in the hotel case.

Gap 8

As noted in Table 1, for the most part, employees' perception for delivery are more than managers' perception for tourists' expectation except attribute 4 "Provides services at the time it promises to do so" (−0.077) and attribute 11 "Guests feel safe and secure in their stay" (−0.053). In addition, the overall Gap 8 score was +0.312, which would indicted that the managers tend to have good communication with employees for understanding tourists' expectation. Hence, Gap 8 is probably not to be a major problem of service quality in the hotel case.

Gap 9

As shown in Table 1, the mean score gaps along each of 27 attributes was calculated for employees' perception of manager's requirement and service delivery by themselves. The result of the overall Gap 9 score for this study was −0.547 and all difference of attributes were negative and very big. The range from attribute 24 (−0.391) to attribute 25 (−0.717), was quite big variation. The biggest gaps were on attributes, 25 "Equipment and facilities are generally clean" (−0.717), 1 "Promises to provide a service and does so" (−0.696), 17 "Has guests' best interests at heart" (−0.674), 2 "Shows dependability in handling service problems" (−0.630) and 26 "Variety of food and beverages meet guests' needs (−0.630)". Accordingly, from the results of negative Gap 9 score and big difference, it also can be concluded that Gap 9 seems one of major problems related to Gap 5 of service quality in the hotel case.

Gap 10

The results of Table 1 show that, for most part, employees believed that their perception for delivery are more than tourists themselves perception except attributes 24 "Equipment and facilities are easy to use" (−0.050) and attribute 26 "Variety of food and beverages meet guests' needs" (−0.050). In addition, the overall gap 10 score was 0.156, which would indicated that the employees tend to have a good understanding of customer expectations. Therefore, from the results of positive gap 10 score, consequently, Gap 10 did not seem to a major problem of service quality in the hotel case as well.

DISCUSSION

This study provided a new measurable instrument and expressed the evaluation results of the service quality gap between expectations and perceptions for tourists, managers, and employees in the hotel industry. Thus, this study identified the gaps (Gap 5, Gap 1, Gap 8, Gap 9, and Gap 10) that could appear from inconsistency in the expectations and perceptions of service quality among tourists, management, and employees and demonstrated how the gaps could be reduced.

An analysis of Gap 5 illustrated how the gaps between customers' perceptions of service quality and their expectations could be reduced. The Gap 5 analysis indicated that tourists' perceptions were consistently lower than their expectations. The overall Gap 5 score was −0.662, which showed that the overall service quality provided by the hotel industry in Taiwan was below tourists' expectations. According to our Gap 5 analysis, the biggest gaps were associated with "gives prompt service," "provides services at the time it promises to do so," and "promises to provide a service and does so." This indicates a problem of reliability and responsiveness in service quality. The negative Gap 5 scores clearly showed that managers in the Taiwanese hotel industry must still improve and enhance its service quality. The Gap 5 analysis was essential because it offered a measurable and useful tool for the management to identify the service problems in the hotel industry in Taiwan. In additional, managers should consistently implement such analysis so that they can further understand the tourists' evaluation process and their consumer experiences and hence meet their expectations more consistently. However, to reduce Gap 5, managers should also concern themselves with the other four gaps (Gap 1, Gap 8, Gap 9, and Gap 10) that contribute to Gap 5. Therefore, this revised gap model offers a method for managers to identify the causes of Gap 5 that can be clearly measured through the gap scores of the hotel industry in Taiwan. According to our results, the functional relationship can be expressed as follows:

$$\text{Gap } 5(-0.662) = \text{Gap } 1(-0.583) + \text{Gap } 8(+0.312) + \text{Gap } 9(-0.547) + \text{Gap } 10(+0.156) \quad (2)$$

Examining Gap 1 was a necessary step that contributed toward the understanding of whether managers accurately perceive tourists' service quality expectations from the Taiwanese hotel industry. The result showed that the overall Gap 1 score was −0.583, indicating that managers do not fully understand customer expectations. Accordingly, given the negative Gap 1 score results and the large difference in expectations and perceptions, we conclude that Gap 1 is one of the major problems of service quality and that it contributes to Gap 5. Moreover, when managers' perception of tourists' expectations is close to the tourists' expectations (Gap 1), the difference in customers' perceptions of service quality and their expectations can be narrowed (Gap 5) as well. Our findings are consistent with those of past studies (Coyle and Dale 1993; Zeithaml et al. 1990; Tsang and Qu 2000) that have argued that managers traditionally have the least contact with customers and are thus unable to understand customer wants accurately. Thus, they might initiate a chain of bad decisions, leading to poor perceived service quality. In improving the service quality (i.e., narrowing Gap 5), managers should re-examine the service delivery process that meets tourists' requirements and wants in the Taiwanese hotel industry. The hotel management should attempt to address marketing research orientation, upward communication, and the quality of management. To gain first-hand knowledge of tourists' expectations and perceptions, senior management should consistently contact tourists and inquire about the actual service delivery. Thus, managers can more accurately fulfill tourists' expectations and provide the desired level of service performance.

Assessing Gap 8 was a critical task that contributed toward knowing whether employees accurately perceive tourists' service quality expectations from the Taiwanese hotel industry. The overall Gap 8 score was 0.312, indicating that the managers did a good job at training or communicating with employees to understand customers' expectations. Hence, Gap 8 was not a primary contributor to Gap 5.

Evaluating Gap 9 was crucial to identifying whether employees followed managers' requirements and were able to perform services at the desired level in the Taiwanese hotel industry. The Gap 9 score in this study was −0.547, indicating a difference between service performance standards and the actual service delivered. Gap 9 often occurred because of some limits, such as poor service attitudes, poorly qualified employees, insufficient service capacity, and inadequate internal communication systems. Because of these constraints, employees could not offer services at the level required by the management. The existence of Gap 9 was related to Gap 1. Moreover, if managers do not fully understand tourists' expectations, employees cannot deliver service adequately. Therefore, to reduce the gap between employees' perceptions of managers' requirements and service delivery, managers in the hotel industry in Taiwan should apply internal investigation systems to evaluate whether their employees can meet the stipulated service standards.

Measuring Gap 10 contributed toward assessing whether employees overestimate whether their service delivery meets tourists' expectations. The overall score in Gap 10 for this study was 0.156, which indicated that employees tended to have a reasonably good understanding of customer expectations. Because of the positive score results, Gap 10 was deemed not to be a primary contributor to Gap 5.

CONCLUSION

This research makes the following three contributions. First, this research develops an evaluation of the service quality of the Taiwanese hotel industry from the perspectives of customers, service providers, and managers, which is considerably valuable for hotel managers. Second, this study explores all of perspectives (i.e. tourists, managers, and employees) together in order to better understand the possible gaps in the hotel industry in Taiwan. This revised gap analysis model can be the reference for related research. Third, the study revealed that Gap 1 (management perceptions vs. customer expectations) and Gap 9 (service provider perceptions of management perceptions vs. service delivery) were more critical than the others in affecting perceived service quality, making service delivery the main area of improvement.

The results of this study also provide a number of managerial contributions. Managers should understand the reason why these differences occur, suggesting that management in the hotel industry spend more time interacting with tourists and conduct internal investigations to assess if their employees are able to meet the service standards, so that the employees willingly provide a good quality of service that benefits hotel operations. Moreover, with the revised gap analysis, managers can effectively prioritize a task to effectively compensate for shortfalls in the provided service. Obviously, managers should eliminate the existence of Gap 1; subsequently, Gap 9 could be reduced. Likewise, if managers do not have a clear perception of customer expectations, employees cannot deliver adequate services. To improve service quality efficiently, managers must be able to identify the priorities of improvements of service attributes especially with limited resources. Finally, the revised gap analysis enable managers to understand the specific attributes that significantly affect service quality and thus enables them to recognize the explicit quality attributes that must be improved and would enhance customer satisfaction within the hotel industry. Overall, this study not only proposes reliable and effective methods but also obviously recognizes which factors that customers consider important as related to management when they should best evaluate their hotel experience. Applying reliable and effective methods for service quality improvement, will lead to a higher level of customer satisfaction and profitability of a firm. In summary, Travel and Tourism is an important economic activity in most countries around the world which not only affect the economic growth but also to increase employment opportunities.

LIMITATIONS AND SUGGESTIONS FOR FUTURE RESEARCH

There are some limitations in this study that must be recognized. First, the international tourist hotels surveyed in this study were small- and medium-sized hotels operating in Taipei. Because Taipei is more modern and well developed than are some other Taiwanese cities, these results might not represent the quality of hotel services across Taiwan. Second, the sample size was quite small (N = 255), employees (N = 46), and managers (N = 40). Future research should collect a larger number of samples and include a more diverse range of tourists, employees, and hotel managers. Third, this study conducted preliminary research into hotel services. Thus, the findings cannot be generalized to other service sectors. Future studies should collect data from different industries, such as banks, airlines, insurance providers, and call centers, to extend the scope of our findings. Fourth, this research was only limited to three-star hotels in Taiwan. Future studies should attempt to examine service quality across different hotel ratings or countries. This may provide an opportunity to compare the quality of service based on different hotel ratings (e.g., four or five-star hotels) or countries. Likely, Luo and Qu (2016) indicated that Westerners were more satisfied with service quality than do Chinese guests. In addition, this research could be applied to different categories, for example three-star, aparthotels, motels, inns and boutique. Finally, the findings of this study were based on a survey. Hence, future studies should apply a qualitative design to obtain an in depth understanding of the perceptions of customers in relation to those of managers and employees.

Authors' contributions

Writing: C-HC; Providing case and idea: Y-CL, Y-CW, C-HW, S-CL; Providing revised advice: S-BT, WD. All authors read and approved the final manuscript.

REFERENCES

1. Babakus E, Boller GW (1992) An empirical assessment of the SERVQUAL scale. J Bus Res 24(3):253–268
2. Bowen D, Lawler EE III (1992) The empowerment of service workers: What, why, how, and when. Sloan Manag Rev 33:31–39
3. Brown TJ, Churchill GA, Peter JP (1993) Improving the measurement of service quality. J Retail 69(1):127–139
4. Callan RJ, Kyndt G (2001) Business travelers' perception of service quality: a prefatory study of two European city centre hotels. Int J Tourism Res 3(4):313–323
5. Carman JM (1990) Consumer perceptions of service quality: an assessment of the dimensions. J Retail 66(1):33–55
6. Chen FY, Chang YH (2005) Examining airline service quality from a process perspective. J Air Trans Manag 11:79–87
7. Chen WJ (2013) Factors influencing internal service quality at international tourist hotels. Int J Hosp Manag 35:152–160
8. Choy DJL, Guan LD, Zhang W (1986) Tourism in PR China. Marketing trends and changing policies. Tour Manag 7(3):197–201
9. Coyle MP, Dale BG (1993) Quality in the hospitality industry: a study. Int J Hosp Manag 12(2):141–153
10. Dedeoğlu BB, Demirer H (2015) Differences in service quality perceptions of stakeholders in the hotel industry. Int J Contemp Hosp Manag 27(1):130–146
11. Frederick AF, Mukesh K (2001) Service quality between internal customers and internal suppliers in an international airline. Int J Qual Reliab Manag 18(4):371–386
12. Getty JM, Thompson KN (1994) A procedure for scaling perceptions of lodging quality. Hosp Res J 18:75–96
13. Gonzalez ME, Mueller RF, Mack RW (2008) An alternative approach in service quality: an e-banking case study. Qual Manag J 15(1):41–59
14. Han SL, Baek S (2004) Antecedents and consequences of service quality in online banking: an application of the SERVQUAL instrument. Adv Consum Res 31:208–214
15. Hooper D, Coughlan J, Mullen MR (2013) The servicescape as an antecedent to service quality and behavioral intentions. J Serv Mark 27(4):271–280
16. Jannadi OA, Assaf S, Maghraby HM, Al-Saggaf HA (2000) Service quality gaps analysis at SCECO-East, Saudi Arabia. J Energy Eng 126(3):116–131
17. Kandampully J, Suhartanto D (2000) Customer loyalty in the hotel industry: the role of customer satisfaction and image. Int J Contemp Hosp Manag 12(6):346–351
18. Kang H, Bradley G (2002) Measuring the performance of IT services: an assessment of SERVQUAL. Int J Account Inf Syst 3:151–164
19. Knutson B, Stevens P, Wullaert C, Patton M, Yokoyama F (1990) LODGSERV: a service quality index for the lodging industry. Hosp Res J 14(2):227–284

20. Lam SK, Woo KS (1997) Measuring service quality: a test-retest reliability investigation of SERVQUAL. J Res Mark Res Soc 39:381–396
21. Large RO, Konig T (2009) A gap model of purchasing's internal service quality: concept, case study and internal survey. J Purch Supply Manag 15:24–32
22. Lee YC, Chen JK, Lin SB (2007) Revised Gap analysis by decomposition of service activities: a case study of information system center. Int J Bus Strategy 8(2):74–98
23. Luo Z, Qu H (2016) Guest-defined hotel service quality and its impacts on guest loyalty. J Qual Assur Hosp Tour 17(3):311–332
24. Martin S (2003) Using SERVQUAL in health libraries across Somerset, Devon and Cornwall. Health Inf Libr J 20(1):15–21
25. Mei AWO, Dean AM, White CJ (1999) Analysing service quality in the hospitality industry. Manag Serv Qual Int J 9(2):136–143
26. Nasution H (2016) Coaligning service quality attributes and its implication to customer value. In: Colin C, Junzhao JM (eds) Looking forward, looking back: drawing on the past to shape the future of marketing. Springer, pp 751–759
27. Nel D, Pitt L (1993) Service quality in a retail environment: closing the gaps. J Gen Manag 18(3):37–56
28. Parasuraman A, Zeithaml VA, Berry LL (1985) A conceptual model of service quality and its implications for future research. J Mark 49(4):41–50
29. Parasuraman A, Zeithaml V, Berry LL (1988) SERVQUAL: a multiple-item scale for measuring consumer perceptions of service quality. J Retail 64(1):12–40
30. Parasuraman A, Zeithaml V, Berry LL (1991) Refinement and reassessment of the SERVQUAL scale. J Retail 67:420–450
31. Saleh F, Ryan C (1991) Analysing service quality in the hospitality industry using the SERVQUAL model. Serv Ind J 11(3):324–345
32. Schneider B, Bowen DE (1995) Winning the service game. Harvard Business School Press, Boston
33. Stefano NM, Casarotto Filho N, Barichello R, Sohn AP (2015) A fuzzy SERVQUAL based method for evaluated of service quality in the hotel industry. Proc CIRP 30:433–438
34. Stevens P, Knutson B, Patton M (1995) "DINESERV: a tool for measuring service quality in restaurants". Cornell Hotel Restaur Adm Q 36(2):56–60
35. Teas RK (1993) Expectations, performance evaluation and customers' perceptions of quality. J Mark 57:18–34
36. Teas RK (1994) Expectations as a comparison standard in measuring service quality: an assessment of a reassessment. J Mark 58(1):132–139
37. Tsang NK (2011) Dimensions of Chinese culture values in relation to service provision in hospitality and tourism industry. Int J Hosp Manag 30(3):670–679
38. Tsang N, Qu H (2000) Service quality in China's hotel industry: a perspective from tourists and hotel managers. Int J Contemp Hosp Manag 12:316–326
39. Tsaur S-H, Lin Y-C (2004) Promoting service quality in tourist hotels: the role of HRM practices and service behavior. Tour Manag 25(4):471–481
40. Torres EN, Adler H, Lehto X, Behnke C, Miao L (2013) One experience and multiple reviews: the case of upscale US hotels. Tour Rev 68(3):3–20
41. Wei L, Crompton JL, Reid LM (1989) Cultural conflicts: experiences of US visitors to China. Tour Manag 10(4):322–332

42. Wei SP, Shih SC, Lin SC, Liu CJ, Lu YW, Chang WL (2011) Primary caregivers satisfaction and its related factors in home health care services. Int J Gerontol 5(2):107–111

43. Wu HC, Ko YJ (2013) Assessment of service quality in the hotel industry. J Qual Assur Hosp Tour 14(3):218–244

44. Yagil D (2002) The relationship of customer satisfaction and service workers' perceived control examination of three models. Int J Serv Ind Manag 13(4):382–398

45. Zeithaml VA, Parasuraman A, Berry LL (1990) Delivering quality service balancing customer perceptions and expectations. The Free Press, New York

CHAPTER 11

Technology-Based Service Encounter—A Study of the Use of E-Mail as a Booking Tool in Hotels

Aihie Osarenkhoe[1], Jotham Mbiito Byarugaba[2], Mabel Komunda Birungi[2], Abednego Feehi Okoe[3], Az-Eddine Bennani[4]

[1]*Department of Business & Economic Studies, Faculty of Education & Economics, University of Gavle, Gavle, Sweden.*

[2]*Makerere University Business School, Kampala, Uganda.*

[3]*University of Professional Studies, Legon-Accra, Ghana.*

[4]*Department of Management & Strategy, Reims Management School, Reims Cedex, France.*

ABSTRACT

Highlighted in this paper, is the extent to which a technological interface that enables customers to produce a service outcome, independent of direct service-employee involvement, is used by hotels of various categories in France. Extant literature has, to date, devoted more attention to the use of interpersonal buyer-seller interactions in the process of creating service outcomes. This paper aims to fill this void by contributing to existing knowledge on customer interactions with technology-based self-service delivery options. An exhaustive sample of 240 hotels located across 120 cities in France constituted the empirical setting. A one-way ANOVA that tested differences between means was used to assess the impact of hotel category (independent variable) on response time (dependent variable) among hotels in France. The findings show that there is significant dissimilarity in responsiveness across the hotel categories. A major implication of these findings for management is that the speed with which enquiries from current and potential customers are responded to is most likely a prelude to providing good quality technology-based buyer-seller interactions to create positive service outcomes using the Internet/e-mail. Major concepts in customer relationship management include the response speed of firms to questions and problems during the service encounter. The main contribution of this study is that it builds on existing literature on interpersonal and technological interfaces.

Keywords: *Hospitality Industry, Leisure and Pleasure Industry, Technology-Based Self-Service Encounter, Information and Communication Technology (ICT)*

INTRODUCTION

Numerous authors [1] [2] underline that the main empirical contributions to the problem of performance have focused mainly on the industrial sector, and subsequently on certain segments in the service sector (banks, retail, insurance). Unfortunately, comparatively little attention has been devoted to the hospitality industry. However, from the 1990s onwards, many studies have applied the performance factors to the hotel sector [3]. For example, Bitner, *et al.* [4], Parasuraman, *et al.* [5] and Osarenkhoe and Bennani [6] highlight the vital role that technology plays in the delivery of services and how it will continue to be a crucial component in customer-firm interactions. These technology-based interactions are expected to become a key criterion for long-term business success [7].

As noted above, there has been unprecedented resurgence of academic as well as practitioner interest in the salient features and dynamics of interpersonal interactions between service providers and customers [9]-[19]. Customer interactions with technological interfaces in hospitality sector, on the other hand, are under researched [4]. Despite the proliferation of customer relationship management enabled technology (self-service technologies, telephone banking, automated hotel checkout, and online investment trading whereby customers produce services for themselves without the assistance of firm employees) firms are increasingly aware that there are barriers to customer adoption and substantial implementation obstacles to be overcome. Some features of hotel businesses and, in particular the presence of three different business areas marked by high intangibility (rooms), the presence of a physical asset (food and beverage) and the typical features of a retail business (shops), coupled with the strong growth recorded by the sector in the past, growing competition and the existence of a high spatial concentration (destinations), make this industry a unique and fascinating research field [20]-[23].

This paper therefore addresses issues regarding the impact that the increasing use of information and communication technology (ICT) in general and electronic means of interaction (a technological interface that enables customers to produce a service independent of direct service employee involvement) in particular has on the process of creating value and the differentiation in service activities in the hospitality industry. The globalization of markets and production has enhanced the propensity of the actors operating in the hospitality business sector to adopt e-mail technology that enables their guests to book and/or to pay for a stay, thus bypassing travel agencies. Still there are large variations in the use of this interface across hotels categories [16]. There can be significant dissimilarities in the response time when using e-mail to communicate with customers.

This paper studies these dissimilarities on the basis of an e-mailing action that encompasses sending a typical room-booking request to French hotels. It analyzes the response time to see how promptly hoteliers reply, and which hotel categories—one-star, two-star, three-star or four-star hotels—use e-mail to answer their customers rapidly. The objective here is to draw up an overview of e-mail as used by hotels in France and to work out whether the response time differs across hotel categories. We begin with an introduction to the theoretical framework in the form of a review of the literature related to the use of ICT and the Internet in the hotel industry. This is followed by a description of the research methodology, a presentation and analysis of the findings, before drawing our conclusions, in addition to the study's contribution to extant literature on the technology-based service encounter.

THEORETICAL BACKGROUND AND HYPOTHESIS

Technology-Based Service Encounter

The world is becoming increasingly characterized by technology-facilitated transactions [9] [16]. Growing numbers of customers interact with technology to create service outcomes instead of interacting with a service firm employee [7] [15]. According to Tosun [24], the characteristics of the firm and industry sector are, however, contributory factors to the extent of adoption and exploitation of information and communication technology by firms to support business processes. The use of ICT has been growing fast in the worldwide hospitality industry. Hoteliers are increasingly adopting the Internet, mainly e-mail and websites, to interact with their guests and provide easier access to customized services.

Buyer-seller interactions during the service encounter have historically taken place on an interpersonal basis [9]-[17]. Recent research has recognized the critical importance of technology in the delivering of services [4] [5] [7] [25]-[27]. In this scenario, the tourism industry might increase the chances of success by exploiting the potentialities of these technologies along with new business practices and strategies. To date, several projects in ubiquitous and context-aware computing have been focused on mobile devices (*i.e.* iPhone, iPod, iPad, pocket PC, etc.) as support for museum and tourism guides [28] [29] in order to retain existing tourists and attract new ones. One of the most efficient tools might be represented by pervasive environments, which have not been thoroughly investigated in the tourism literature.

The increasing competition between regions is forcing the tourism industry to define new strategies in order to improve the position of each area, thus attracting greater tourism flows [30] [31] and enhancing economic advantages [32] [33]. Current research in information and communication technology has a considerable effect on the tourism sector, by providing innovative tools capable, on one hand, of supporting consumers in organizing their holidays and, on the other one, of supplying fast and efficient information on consumer behavior. These innovations compel the sector to develop new marketing and managerial strategies [34]. For instance, according to Chu *et al.* [35], from 1990 to 2000, new websites have been developed, improving the quality of user interaction. In the beginning, Websites were utilized to deliver tourism information such as advertising aimed at promoting tourism attractions.

The Use and Impact of ICT in the Hospitality Industry

According to DiPietro and Wang [36], the lodging industry has, historically, distributed information through print-based media such as brochures, travel planners, or regional guides, and received reservations by mail, phone, and fax. More recently, hotel rooms have been made accessible for booking through global distribution systems (GDS) and through direct access to hotels using central reservation systems (CRS). However, such technologies have been inadequate as customers have traditionally not had access to these systems and travel intermediaries have experienced difficulty and delay in finding and booking appropriate hotels, whereas hotels have incurred high administrative costs to attract and process customer bookings. The emergence of new ICT interfaces presents new opportunities to make these processes more accessible and more efficient [37]. Some suggest that the traditional marketplace interaction is being replaced by a "marketspace" transaction [4] [8]. In this context, e-mail technology is an example of marketspace interactions in which no interpersonal contact is required between the buyer and seller.

E-mail offers a promising tool to help marketers keep in touch with their customers on a regular basis at low cost [14] [38]. The benefits of an active marketer are described in considerable detail in the customer relationship management (CRM) literature, suggesting that marketers can enhance customer loyalty by being active and in regular contact with their customers (see Hansotia [39] and Osarenkhoe and Bennani [13]). In spite of these potential roles for e-mail marketing in building and maintaining customer loyalty, it has only recently started to gain importance in comparative marketing literature and CRM strategies. This is also noted by Reichheld and Schefter [40] (cited in [38]), who discuss how marketers should concentrate efforts on retailing rather than attracting customers on the Internet.

A methodology for assessing ICT productivity impact proposed by Sigala [41] and tested on a dataset of three-star hotels in the UK overcomes these shortcomings. Sigala's findings reveal that productivity gains do not accrue from ICT investments per se, but rather from the full exploitation of its networking capabilities. Martin's

[42] study of e-innovation and Internet impacts on UK hospitality firms looks at six cases in the hospitality sector. Martin's study suggests that the current narrow focus on business growth or on technology alone seen in current initiatives may overlook owners such as those who established an online presence for social and personal purposes but developed business uses alongside these purposes. Where targets are set for increased tourism, Martin notes that the Internet could play a part in developing such growth, if integrated and applied to the context of hospitality firms. Collins *et al.*'s study [43], on the other hand, of a tourist enterprise in the European hotel sector and its utilization of the Internet and perception of online learning systems, aim to demonstrate that ICTs can enable firms to improve their inventory management, strengthen their marketing and communication strategies, and develop their internal business processes. Their survey [44] demonstrates that small and mediumsized tourist firms in the European hotel sector are not utilizing ICT in their businesses to its full potential. These businesses primarily see the Internet as a mechanism for promoting their hotels rather than for interand/ or intra-organizationaland e-commerce purposes.

It can be deduced from the preceding discussion that ICT improves the quality of customer-oriented, personalized service, allows the delivery of e-service, and enhances customer relationships [45]. Some questions, such as the relationship between the client and the supplier, emerge due to the integration of the Internet in company strategies. Because of the use of websites and e-mail, some researchers have reservations about the lack of physical and direct contact between the service provider and his/her customer [46]. This challenges the traditional way of doing business, where customers are served either face to face and/or over the telephone. It allows oneto-one interaction, offers electronic services to customers [40], and makes online relationships possible.

How the Internet Helps the Hotel Industry

The rapid advancement of technology affects practically every industry, and the hotel and service industry is not exempt from this [27] [47]. Previous studies show, in addition, that the firms that provide electronic data interchange (EDI, an electronic communication system that provides standards for exchanging data via any electronic means) offer more services to their customers than firms that do not provide EDI service [5] [48]-[50]. With global and local hotel brands turning to the World Wide Web in order to boost sales and facilitate customer relations, it is easy to see how the industry is evolving along with the Internet [24] [28]. Social networking sites, led by the Facebook phenomenon, are proving to be more and more important for not only hotels but for other businesses as well [32] [34]. With the prevalence and influence of user-generated content such as reviews and other forms of feedback, hotels get the benefit of plugging by way of word-of-mouth [51]. Maintaining relationships with previous clients also becomes easier to handle with a variety of online tools at the hotels' disposal

[51] [52]. There are also websites dedicated to bringing travel services and accommodations straight to the consumers' monitors whether it is through standard personal computer access or through the exponentially growing number of mobile phone Internet users [47] [53]. There are also other utility websites that aid consumers by providing aggregate information, reviews and feedback from numerous sources [52]. Just how big is the impact of online booking for the hotel industry?

According to Van Hoof *et al.* [54], ICT is a major opportunity for the lodging industry, particularly when it comes to marketing and selling room nights. Internet can increase the interaction phenomenon between suppliers and their customers [55]-[57]. As an effective medium for the relationship between guests and hoteliers, it can improve preand after-sales service and enhance customer relationships [45] [58]. Its potential as a means of making reservations is remarkable [9] [51]. More and more people make reservations online and travel seems to be a typical service category sold on the Internet. In the USA, as well as in the European Union, travel services seem to be the most purchased item on the Web. To enhance these key success factors in the hotel industry, some authors believe that hoteliers should invest heavily in more technology focusing on guest services [59]. Kim and Kim [60] postulate that hoteliers should first focus on basic Internet tools such as e-mail. The latter is strategically important for the hospitality industry [19] [47] because, firstly, it enables marketers to experiment with various messages, altering the offer or segmentation to improve outcomes and results. Secondly, compared to conventional direct marketing reply times that can take several weeks, 80% of e-mail messages are answered within a few days [61].

ICT clearly represents the most significant competitive innovation in the hospitality industry throughout the 1990s and beyond [62]. In addition, as transactional costs continue to rise, hotels will need to determine which of the technologies used to develop reservation and distribution channels are the most profitable for them and how they can yield the best results by using these channels. Cooper *et al.* [63] underlined that electronic distribution channels available to hotels have increased dramatically in recent years and, while there are multiple channels, some are obviously minor in terms of their impact and potential. Therefore, selecting the appropriate distribution channels is vital for success, and important if hotel firms want to increase top-line revenues and control overhead costs. Though the range of choice facing hotel executives is vast, e-mail adds another channel that is ubiquitous, cheap, digital, and virtual. Increasing competition has pressured hoteliers into adopting the technology in US [59], Hong Kong [51], Taiwan [64], Thailand [27], Australian [54] and UK [41] luxury class hotels. Pechlaner *et al.* [65] found in their research that e-services are more effective in higher-rated Swiss, Austrian and Italian hotels. Hotels in France, particularly luxury class hotels, should therefore make better use of e-mailing and should provide their customers with high-quality, professional e-service. Responsiveness is the most likely first step in providing this quality e-service using the Internet/e-mail.

Hence the following hypotheses:

H1: E-mail responsiveness is proportional to the number of stars a hotel has: the more stars, the quicker their response.

H2: The richness of the response has a significant impact on the response time.

RESEARCH METHODOLOGY

As for e-tourism, in 2012, between 5.5% (Raffour Interactive) and 14% (TNS Sofres) of active French Internet users purchased their travels online, whereas 14% 24% used the Internet to prepare their travels. According to a French Tourist Board report, the Internet has gained ground compared to the other booking channels. In 2011, the sales turnover for e-tourism in France for the online business-to-customer tourist trade was between 880 million and 1.3 billion EUR. At the end of 2012, online hotel reservations accounted for 3.6% of the total travel market in Europe. 64% of online hotel reservations were made on hotel company websites (Accor.com but also Ryanair.com); 36% were carried out by online intermediaries (such as Expedia and lastminute.com). Table 1 gives the breakdown of French hotels (independent voluntary and integrated chains) according to ownership category. In 2012, there were 11,642 independent hotels and 6575 local chains or multinationals. 63% of all hotels in France are independently owned and 38% are either local chains or multinationals.

The methodological approach adopted consisted of three steps: firstly, a sample of hotels located in France were identified on the Internet. Secondly, those including *.com*, *.fr* or *.net* extensions in their e-mail address and those having their own domain name server (DNS[1]) were browsed. Finally, the replies received within a twomonth period of time were analyzed. A population of hotels with an e-mail address on France Tourism websites was selected. The sample included 240 hotels located in France, the target group, spread out over 120 cities. Two-star hotels were predominant in the sample (Table 2), followed by hotels in the three-star category. These two categories accounted for 86% of the overall target population. Also the limited number (around 4%) of one-star hotels was also noted. E-mails with a booking request were sent to one-, two-, threeand four-star hotels. Written in French, they asked for information about room availability and prices for two adults and two children (16 and 10 years old) for a one-week stay in July, as well as for information on local tourist attractions and excursions and their prices. The e-mails were sent to the selected hotels. The Bcc[2] function enabled us to send multiple e-mails simultaneously while masking this mass mailing for recipients. E-mails that failed to be delivered due to incorrect addresses or to any other problem were not re-sent.

Table 1. *France's tourist hotel 31/12/2012 (Source: French tourist board 2013).*

	Independent hotels	Chains (integrated, franchised, voluntary)
	Number of hotels 31/12/2012	Number of hotels 31/12/2012
0*	1342	796
1*	1505	353
2*	6223	3644
3*	2248	1387
4*	324	395
Total	11642	6575

Table 2. *Breakdown of hotel categories in the sample.*

Hotel Category	1-Star	2-Star	3-Star	4-Star	Not Specified	Total Sent
France	4%	62%	24%	6%	4%	100%

E-mail replies from these hotels were followed-up over a two-month period. On a weekly basis, the received e-mails were analyzed one by one and the information included in them was entered into a database.

RESEARCH FINDINGS AND ANALYSIS

As far as errors are concerned, globally 10% of the sent e-mails were returned as undeliverable due to a faulty address. Of the entire sample (240), 107 hotels replied to the delivered e-mails. More than one in two hotels that replied belonged to the two-star category (Table 3) This shows the domination of this class. It was also noted that the response rate for this category corresponded closely to that of the e-mails sent.

Among the replies, one-star and four-star hotels were under-represented. It was also observed that only a few hotels did not mention their category (around 4%). 66% of the replies received were received within a week (Table 4).

Two and three-star categories are over-represented (55% and 31%, respectively) while one-star (3%) and four-star (7%) hotels are under-represented (Table 3). An analysis of total replies in one day (36) (Table 5), shows that almost 47% (17/36) of two-star hotels, almost 39% (14/36) of three-star hotels, and only 5% (2/36) of oneand four-star hotels reply in one day. Note that 71% of the hotels that respond in under 4 hours are two-star hotels (Table 4). Also only 2% of replies received within a 4-hour time period were from one-star hotels. These results show that the hypothesis that higher category hotels in France show better responsiveness than the lower category hotels is not confirmed. This hypothesis should thus be rejected even if the four-star hotel panel is under-represented in the global sample. Above all, both the two-star and (to a lesser extent) the three-star hotels appear to reply promptly to e-mails received from customers. This could be because of the acute competition within the market segment covered by these categories. The higher category hotels probably assume that their customers belong to the business segment that does not use e-mails to make reservations. Rooms are more likely to be booked by secretaries over the telephone.

Table 3. *E-mail replies according to hotel category.*

Hotels Category	1-Star	2-Star	3-Star	4-Star	Not Specified
France	3%	55%	31%	7%	4%

Table 4. *E-mail replies according to response time (in %).*

	1-Star	2-Star	3-Star	4-Star	Not Specified	Replies per Time Period
<4 hours	2%	71%	14%	9%	4%	39%
1 day	6%	46%	39%	6%	3%	30%
2 days		70%	24%		6%	15%
3 days		66%	17%	17%		5%
4 days		80%	20%			5%
5 days				100%		1%
6 days		67%	33%			3%
7 days		100%				2%
Replies/Category	3%	58%	27%	9%	3%	66%

On the other hand, five binomial variables relating to e-mail responses were created. These variables (room availability, nature of service (half board, full board), local tourist attractions, price of the additional activities, and refer to websites) were coded yes or no and classified into one factor: response richness. The results indicate that more than 93% of hotels provided information about their availability, while only 37.4% specify the nature of service offered (half board or full board). Few hotels (29.9%) provided a description of available activities, and 28% provided references to their own or other websites. Only five hotels provided information about the price of the extra activities. In total, almost 48% of hotels provided references to their own or other websites.

Table 5. *E-mail replies according to response time (actual number).*

	1-Star	2-Star	3-Star	4-Star	Not Specified	Replies per Time Period
1 day	2	17	14	2	1	36
2 days		12	4		1	17
3 days		4	1	1		6
4 days		5	1			6
5 days				1		1
6 days		2	1			3
7 days		2				2
<4 hours	1	32	6	3	2	45
Replies/Category	3	79	28	8	9	137

One-way ANOVA testing differences between means was used to assess the impact of hotel category (independent variable) on response time (dependent variable) for hotels in France. The results of the ANOVA analysis are presented in Table 6. They indicate that no differences were found for response time. That is, hotel category does not have a significant impact on response time (the value is more than 0.05). However, the results in Table 7 suggest a significant impact of the response richness on response time ($p < 0.05$).

Table 6. *One-way ANOVA between hotel category and response time.*

	F ratio	P prob	Significance
Response time	0.843	0.501	Not significant

Table 7. *One-way ANOVA between response richness and response time.*

	F ratio	P prob	Significance
Response time	4.168	0.044	Significant

CONCLUDING REMARKS

This study provides insights on the use of e-mails at customer contact points in hotels in France, for which it found significant dissimilarity in responsiveness across hotel categories. However, our findings differ from the study of Swiss hotels conducted by Pechlaner *et al.* [65]; and Murphy *et al.* [46] in Switzerland. While these previous studies found that being in the high-rated category of hotels influenced technology adoption, thus e-mail usage, they also found that hotels failed to pay much attention to improving customer service. We may note the opposite result obtained for the lower categories, mainly twoand three-star hotels.

The low level of responsiveness to e-mails (an example of marketspace interactions in which no interpersonal contact is required between the buyer and seller during the process of creating the service outcome) demonstrated by hotels of higher categories included in our sample is surprising. Responsiveness is most likely the first step in providing this quality e-service using the Internet/e-mail. One of the major concepts in customer relationship management is the speed at which firms respond to questions and problems during the service encounter. One of the major concepts in customer relationship management is the speed at which firms respond to questions and problems during the service encounter [6]. The customer relationship management literature and direct marketing literature [6] [39] suggest that regular contact with customers helps marketers to enhance customer loyalty. Direct mail is used to crossand up-sell, to increase customers purchasing frequency, and to induce customers to respond and to become involved in a dialogue [38].

The insufficient e-service that we experienced with high category hotels in France could be explained by their lack of interest in the Internet/e-mail-user market segment. This finding seems to be in line with that reported by Sahadev and Islam [27], that the factors influencing a hotel's propensity to adopt ICTs may be broadly divided into location-related and firm-related. The findings also reconcile with the idea shared in extant literature [66], that electronic intermediation tends to "impoverish" service relations, insomuch as the technological interface

can by no means replace the wealth of human interactions on which the creation of value and differentiation of services are based. The objectives that can be expected from the use of e-mailing—a concrete outline of e-service—in the hotel industry have to be formulated in terms of good communication, fine responsiveness, high-quality information and competitiveness.

Our findings in France are probably culturally specific. Elsewhere, the use of the ICT in the lodging industry is growing exponentially, enabling hotels to reconsider the way they do business. Although the lodging sector overall has been slow to adopt ICT compared to other industry sectors [66], many hotel managers are becoming increasingly aware of the potential distribution, promotion, and interactive marketing advantages of the technology. ICT offers several advantages for hotels of all sizes [36], one of which is increased effectiveness due to cost reduction and revenue growth. Another advantage is higher quality customer relationships due to the possibility of personal contact services and dialogue with the customer. For example, customers can answer questions about their personal preferences for rooms and, based on this information, receive services at the hotel that are adapted to these preferences.

MANAGERIAL IMPLICATIONS

The implications of this study for business practice and research are relatively many and straightforward: Although the importance of people in relationship building cannot be emphasized enough, according to Do-naldson and O'Toole [67], technology, particularly information and communication technology, is becoming an important strategic asset for hospitality organizations to improve their organizational performance and strategic competitiveness [66] [68]. As a result, there is a growing significance of the role of technology in enhancing a hospitality organization's competitive advantage, and thus contributing to the success of the organization. In fact, ICT use in the hospitality industry has been changing at a faster rate than at any other time in history. As younger generations become more adept at the use of technology, they want to bring that into their lodging and dining experiences. The decision to adopt and use new technology or technology systems has become so important that many hospitality organizations are transforming their corporate or organization structure to include functions and positions such as taking advantage of technology.

It is now generally agreed [30] [32] [34] [35] that ICT is the single greatest force driving change in the hotel industry and will continue to have dramatic and sweeping implications on how hotels conduct business in the future. Hotels are expected to position themselves strongly on the Internet to take advantage of its distribution capabilities such as reach, content dissemination, feedback collection, interactivity, and one-to-one marketing. Current trends furthermore indicate that this greater involvement in ICT by the industry will increasingly encompass customer-centric approaches to capitalize on the cost structure and long-term potential of the Internet while at the same time differentiating products and building lasting value propositions. For many hospitality organizations, technological advances are at the vanguard of opportunity, yet they represent one of management's biggest challenges. Adopting and using new technology systems and processes entails complicated decisionmaking that requires insight and input from strong research initiatives and organizational commitment.

Social media site such as LinkedIn, Facebook and Twitter have provided us all with great tools to leverage both existing business relationships and also new business relationships. The interference and "noise" created by social media can also have a negative impact on building relationships as more and more people aim for quick or instant results. Social media platforms are merely enablers to support our off-line networking activity. Social media platforms are only one form of communication and should not be used as an excuse to abandon the use other forms of communication. It is essential to have effective strategies to develop meaningful business relationships. Such strategies have to do with what you can do for other people, rather than what others can do for you. Also, never forget about your existing relationships [28] [29] that you may have devoted a great deal of time to cultivating. It is far too easy to let existing business relationships wither and die in the pursuit of new ones.

LIMITATIONS

While the theoretical position developed fits the unique characteristics of the case studied in the industry and country settings, caution should be exercised in generalizing the results of this study beyond this context. A number of important questions warrant continued investigation beyond the evidence of this study. The major concerns are, in our view, that the hotel reservation systems have advanced well beyond email communications in most countries and therefore the findings from this study may not represent a significant contribution to new development/ advancements in the field of e-commerce. Although, this study has certainly added new insights to the specific field of study, we are aware that the contribution is limited. Future research should investigate how the hospitality, travel and tourist industries manage customer relationships. Since customer relationship management emerged as a technology-based customer solution in the mid-1990s, the hospitality industry, and leisure and pleasure industry have until now not been given enough coverage in extant CRM research.

NOTES

1 For example, the DNS included in www.reims-ms.fr is "reims-ms". This one is the property of Reims Management School. In www.wanadoo.fr/company, the DNS is "wanadoo", which belongs to France Telecom.

2 Blind carbon copy.

REFERENCES

1. Chen, C.F. (2007) Applying the Stochastic Frontier Approach to Measure Hotel Managerial Efficiency in Taiwan. *Tourism Management*, **28**, 696-702. http://dx.doi.org/10.1016/j.tourman.2006.04.023

2. Pan, C. (2005) Market Structure and Profitability in the International Tourist Industry. *Tourism Management*, **26**, 845850. http://dx.doi.org/10.1016/j.tourman.2004.04.008

3. Okumus, F. (2002) Can Hospitality Researchers Contribute to the Strategic Management Literature? *International Journal of Hospitality Management*, **21**, 105-110. http://dx.doi.org/10.1016/S0278-4319(01)00033-0

4. Bitner, M.J., Brown, S.W. and Meuter, M.L. (2000) Technology Infusion in Service Encounters. *Journal of the Academy of Science*, **28**, 138-149. http://dx.doi.org/10.1177/0092070300281013

5. Parasuraman, A., Zeithaml, V.A. and Malhotra, A. (2005) "E-S-Qual—A Multiple Item Scale for Assessing Electronic Service Quality. *Journal of Marketing*, **7**, 213-233.

6. Osarenkhoe, A. and Bennani, A.-Z. (2007) An Exploratory Study of Implementation of Customer Relationship Projects. *Business Process Management Journal*, **13**, 139-164. http://dx.doi.org/10.1108/14637150710721177

7. Meuter, M.L., Ostrom, A.L., Roundtree, R.I. and Bitner, M.J. (2000) Self-Service Technologies: Understanding Customer Satisfaction with Technology-Based Service Encounters. *Journal of Marketing*, **64**, 50-64. http://dx.doi.org/10.1509/jmkg.64.3.50.18024

8. Rayport, J.E. and Sviokla, J.J. (1995) Exploiting the Value Chain. *Harvard Business Review*, **73**, 14-24.

9. Cheng, L.C., Gibson, M.L., Carrillo, E.E. and Fitch, G. (2011) A Technology-Centric Framework for Investigating Business Operations. *Industrial Management & Data Systems*, **111**, 509-530. http://dx.doi.org/10.1108/02635571111133524

10. Bettencourt, L. and Gwinner, K. (1996) Customization of the Service Experience: The Role of the Frontline Employee. *International Journal of Services Industry Management*, **7**, 2-20. http://dx.doi.org/10.1108/09564239610113442

11. Yüksel, F., Bramwell, B. and Yüksel, A. (2005) Centralized and Decentralized Tourism Governance in Turkey. *Annals of Tourism Research*, **32**, 859-886. http://dx.doi.org/10.1016/j.annals.2004.09.006

12. Vargo, S.L. and Lusch, R.F. (2004) Evolving to a New Dominant Logic for Marketing. *Journal of Marketing*, **68**, 1-17. http://dx.doi.org/10.1509/jmkg.68.1.1.24036

13. Osarenkhoe, A., Bennani, A. and Lhajji, D. (2006) A study of the Prerequisites for Successful Deployment and Governance of Implementation Process of Technological Innovations. *Asian Journal of Information Technology*, **6**, 1-20.

14. Skinner, C. (2010) Innovation in the Internet Age. *Business Strategy Series*, **11**, 407-411. http://dx.doi.org/10.1108/17515631011093115

15. Chaiprasit, S. and Swierczek, F.W. (2011) Competitiveness, Globalization and Technology Development in Thai Firms. *Competitiveness Review*, **21**, 188-204. http://dx.doi.org/10.1108/10595421111117461

16. Lee, Y.C., Chu, P.Y. and Tseng, H.L. (2011) Corporate Performance of ICT-Enabled Business Process Re-Engineering. *Industrial Management & Data Systems*, **111**, 735-754. http://dx.doi.org/10.1108/02635571111137287

17. Wiengarten, F., Fynes, B., Humphreys, P.K., Chavez, R. and McKittrick, A. (2011) Assessing the Value Creation Process of E-Business along the Supply Chain. *Supply Chain Management: An International Journal*, **16**, 207-219. http://dx.doi.org/10.1108/13598541111139035

18. Winata, L. and Mia, L. (2005) Information Technology and the Performance Effect of Managers' Participation in Budgeting: Evidence from the Hotel Industry. *International Journal of Hospitality Management*, **24**, 21-39. http://dx.doi.org/10.1016/j.ijhm.2004.04.006

19. Sainaghi, R. (2010) Hotel Performance: State of the Art. *International Journal of Contemporary Hospitality Management*, **22**, 920-952. http://dx.doi.org/10.1108/09596111011066617

20. Piccoli, G., Connor, P., Capaccioli, C. and Alvarez, R. (2003) Customer Relationship Management—A Driver for Change in the Structure of the US Lodging Industry. *The Cornell Hotel and Restaurant Administration Quarterly*, **44**, 61-73.

21. Dredge, D. (1999) Destination Place Planning and Design. *Annals of Tourism Research*, **26**, 772-791. http://dx.doi.org/10.1016/S0160-7383(99)00007-9

22. Enright, M.J. and Newton, J. (2004) Tourism Destination Competitiveness: A Quantitative Approach. *Tourism Management*, **25**, 777-788. http://dx.doi.org/10.1016/j.tourman.2004.06.008

23. Ingram, P. and Inman, C. (1996) Institutions, Intergroup Competition, and the Evolution of Hotel Populations around Niagara Falls. *Administrative Science Quarterly*, **41**, 629-658. http://dx.doi.org/10.2307/2393870

24. Tosun, C. (2006) Expected Nature of Community Participation in Tourism Development. *Tourism Management*, **27**, 493-504. http://dx.doi.org/10.1016/j.tourman.2004.12.004

25. Parasuraman, A. (2000) Technology Readiness Index (TRI): A Multiple-Item Scale to Measure Readiness to Embrace New Technologies. *Journal of Service Research*, **2**, 307-320. http://dx.doi.org/10.1177/109467050024001

26. Meuter, M.L., Bitner, M.J., Ostrom, A.L. and Brown, S.W. (2005) Choosing among Alternative Service Delivery Modes: An Investigation of Customer Trial of Self-Service Technologies. *Journal of Marketing*, **69**, 61-83. http://dx.doi.org/10.1509/jmkg.69.2.61.60759

27. Sahadev, S. and Islam, N. (2005) Exploring the Determinants of E-Commerce Usage in the Hotel Industry in Thailand: An Empirical Study. *Information Technology & Tourism*, **7**, 171-180. http://dx.doi.org/10.3727/109830505774297201

28. Pantano, E. and Tavernise, A. (2009) Learning Cultural Heritage through Information and Communication Technologies: A Case Study. *International Journal of Information Communication Technologies and Human Development*, **1**, 68-87. http://dx.doi.org/10.4018/jicthd.2009070104

29. Kemperman, A.D.M., Borgers, A.W.J. and Timmermans, H.J.P. (2009) Tourist Shopping Behaviour in a Historic Downtown Area. *Tourism Management*, **30**, 208-218. http://dx.doi.org/10.1016/j.tourman.2008.06.002

30. Dwyer, L., Edwards, D., Mistilis, N., Roman, C. and Scott, N. (2009) Destination and Enterprise Management for a Tourism Future. *Toursim Management*, **30**, 63-74. http://dx.doi.org/10.1016/j.tourman.2008.04.002

31. Yeoman, I., Brass, D. and McMahon-Beattie, U. (2009) Current Issue in Tourism: The Authentic Tourist. *Tourism Management*, **28**, 1128-1138. http://dx.doi.org/10.1016/j.tourman.2006.09.012

32. Zhang, X., Song, H. and Huang, G.Q. (2009) Tourism Supply Chain Management: A New Research Agenda. *Tourism Management*, **30**, 345-358. http://dx.doi.org/10.1016/j.tourman.2008.12.010

33. Bornhorst, T., Ritchie, J.R.B. and Sheehan, L. (2010) Determinants of Tourism Success for DMOs & Destinations: An Empirical Examination of Stakeholders' Perspectives. *Tourism Management*, **31**, 572-589. http://dx.doi.org/10.1016/j.tourman.2009.06.008

34. Egger, R. and Buhalis D. (2008) eTourism Case Studies: Management & Marketing Issues in eTourism. ButterworthHeinemann, Oxford.

35. Chu, S.C., Leung, L.C., Hui, Y.V. and Cheung, W. (2007) Evolution of E-Commerce Web Sites: A Conceptual Framework and a Longitudinal Study. *Information & Management*, **44**, 154-164. http://dx.doi.org/10.1016/j.im.2006.11.003

36. DiPietro, R.B. and Wang, Y.R. (2010) Key Issues for ICT Applications: Impacts and Implications for Hospitality Operations. *Worldwide Hospitality and Tourism Themes*, **2**, 49-67. http://dx.doi.org/10.1108/17554211011012595

37. Buhalis, D. and Main, H. (2008) Information Technology in Peripheral Small and Medium Hospitality Enterprises: Strategic Analysis and Critical Factors. *International Journal of Contemporary Hospitality Management*, **10**, 198-202. http://dx.doi.org/10.1108/09596119810227811

38. Merisavo, M. and Raulas, M. (2004) The Impact of E-Mail Marketing on Brand Loyalty. *Journal of Product and Brand Management*, **13**, 498-505. http://dx.doi.org/10.1108/10610420410568435

39. Hansotia, B. (2002) Gearing up for CRM: Antecedents to Successful Implementation. *Journal of Database Marketing*, **10**, 121-132. http://dx.doi.org/10.1057/palgrave.jdm.3240103

40. Reichheld, F. and Shefter, P. (2000) E-Loyalty: Your Secret Weapon on the Web. *Harvard Business Review*, **78**, 105114.

41. Sigala, M. (2003) The Information and Communication Technologies Productivity Impact on the UK Hotel Sector. *International Journal of Contemporary Hospitality Management*, **23**, 1224-1245.

42. Martin, L.M. (2004) E-Innovation: Internet Impacts on Small UK Hospitality Firms. *International Journal of Contemporary Hospitality Management*, **16**, 82-90. http://dx.doi.org/10.1108/09596110410519964

43. Collins, C., Buhalis, D. and Peters, M. (2003) Enhancing SMTEs Business Performance through the Internet and E-Learning Platforms. *Education and Training*, **45**, 483-494. http://dx.doi.org/10.1108/00400910310508874

44. Simpson, M.C. (2008) Community Benefit Tourism Initiatives—A Conceptual Oxymoron? *Tourism Management*, **29**, 1-18. http://dx.doi.org/10.1016/j.tourman.2007.06.005

45. Newell, F. (2000) Loyalty.com: Customer Relationship Management in the New Era of Internet Marketing. McGraw Hill Professional, New York.

46. Murphy, J.E., Forrest, J., Wotring, C.E. and Brymer, R.A. (2006) Hotel Management and Marketing on the Internet. *Cornell Hotel and Restaurant Administration Quarterly*, **37**, 70-82. http://dx.doi.org/10.1177/001088049603700322
47. Kim, M.J., Chung, N. and Lee, C.K. (2011) The Effect of Perceived Trust on Electronic Commerce: Shopping Online for Tourism Products and Services in South Korea. *Tourism Management*, **32**, 256-265. http://dx.doi.org/10.1016/j.tourman.2010.01.011
48. Sawabini, S. (2001) EDI and the Internet: Can Two Generations of E-Commerce Coexist. *Journal of Business Strategy*, **22**, 41-43. http://dx.doi.org/10.1108/eb040143
49. Ngai, E.W.T. and Gunasekaran, A. (2004) Implementation of EDI in Hong Kong: An Empirical Analysis. *Industrial Management & Data Systems*, **104**, 88-100. http://dx.doi.org/10.1108/02635570410514124
50. Leonard, L.N.K. and Clemons Davis, C.C. (2006) Supply Chain Replenishment: Before-and-after EDI Implementation. *Supply Chain Management: An International Journal*, **11**, 225-232. http://dx.doi.org/10.1108/13598540610662121
51. Lo, A.S., Stalcup, L.D. and Lee, A. (2010) Customer Relationship Management for Hotels in Hong Kong. *International Journal of Contemporary Hospitality Management*, **22**, 139-159. http://dx.doi.org/10.1108/09596111011018151
52. Osarenkhoe, A. and Bennani, A.Z. (2011) Scandic Hotel Chain in the Baltic—A Case of Strategic Marketing. Emerald Emerging Markets Case Studies, Teaching Case in Marketing Management.
53. Pantano, E. and Naccarato, G. (2010) Entertainment in Retailing: The Influences of Advanced Technologies. *Journal of Retailing and Consumer Services*, **17**, 200-204. http://dx.doi.org/10.1016/j.jretconser.2010.03.010
54. Van Hoof, H., Hubert, B., Hein, F., Ruys, M. and Combrink, C. (1999) The Use of the Internet in the Queensland Accommodation Industry. *Australian Journal of Hospitality Management*, **6**, 11-24.
55. Zettelmeyer, F. (2000) Expanding to the Internet: Pricing and Communications Strategies When Firms Compete on Multiple Channels. *Journal of Marketing Research*, **37**, 292-308. http://dx.doi.org/10.1509/jmkr.37.3.292.18777
56. Alba, J., Lynch, J., Weitz, B., Janiszewski, C., Lutz, R., Sawyer, A. and Wood, S. (1997) Interactive Home Shopping: Consumer, Retailer, and Manufacturer Incentives to Participate in Electronic Market Place. *Journal of Marketing*, **61**, 38-53. http://dx.doi.org/10.2307/1251788
57. Hoffman, D. and Novak, T. (1996) Marketing in Hypermedia Computer-Mediated Environments: Conceptual Foundations. *Journal of Marketing*, **60**, 50-68. http://dx.doi.org/10.2307/1251841
58. Piercy, N.F. (1995) Customer Satisfaction and the Internal Market: Marketing Our Customers to Our Employees. *Journal of Marketing Practice: Applied Marketing Science*, **1**, 22-44. http://dx.doi.org/10.1108/EUM0000000003878
59. Siguaw, J.A., Enz, C.A. and Namiasivayam, K. (2000) Adoption of Information Technology in US Hotels: Strategically Driven Objectives. *Journal of Travel Research*, **39**, 192-201. http://dx.doi.org/10.1177/004728750003900209
60. Kim, H.Y. and Kim, Y.K. (2008) Shopping Enjoyment and Store Shopping Modes: The Moderating Influence of Chronic Time Pressure. *Journal of Retailing and Consumer Services*, **15**, 410-419. http://dx.doi.org/10.1016/j.jretconser.2007.10.003
61. Van Hoof, H. (1998) The Use of the Internet in the US Lodging Industry. *Florida International University Hospitality Review*, **16**, 77-90.

62. Olsen, M.D. (1996) Into the New Millennium: A White Paper on the Global Hospitality Industry. International Hotel Association, Paris.

63. Cooper, C., Scott, N. and Baggio, R. (2009) Network Position and Perceptions of Destination Stakeholder Importance. *Anatolia: An International Journal of Tourism Research,* **20,** 33-45.

64. Chen, M.H. (2010) Interactions between Business Conditions and Financial Performance of Tourism Firms: Evidence from China and Taiwan. *Tourism Management,* **28,** 188-203. http://dx.doi.org/10.1016/j.tourman.2005.11.012

65. Pechlaner, H., Rienzner, H., Matzler, K. and Osti, L. (2002) Response Attitudes and Behavior of Hotel Industry to Electronic Info Requests. In: Wöber, K.W., Frew, A.J. and Hitz, M., Eds., *Information and Communication Technologies in Tourism* 2002, Springer Computer Science, Springer, Vienna, New York, 177-186.

66. Nyheim, P., McFadden, F. and Connolly, D. (2004) Technology Strategies for the Hospitality Industry. Prentice-Hall, Upper Saddle River.

67. Donaldson, B. and Toole, T.O. (2009) Strategic Market Relationship. John Wiley & Sons, Ltd., Chichester.

68. Cilan, C.A., Balaban, E., Coskun, E. and Sharma, D. (2007) An Exploratory Study of Information Technology Utilization and Its Influence on Business Performance of Upscale Hotel Industry in Turkey. *International Journal of Business Strategy,* **7,** 20-43.

CHAPTER 12

Open Innovation Through Customer Satisfaction: A Logit Model to Explain Customer Recommendations in the Hotel Sector

Mónica Méndez Díaz[1] **and Clara Martín Duque**[2]

[1]*Faculty of Law and Social Sciences, Rey Juan Carlos University, Paseo de los Artilleros s/n, 28032 Madrid, Spain*

[2]*Faculty of Commerce and Tourism, Complutense University of Madrid, Av. de Filipinas, 3, 28003 Madrid, Spain*

ABSTRACT

Open innovation allows the hotel industry to create platforms and channels for collaboration with its customers, which results in a better understanding of their tastes and demands. In the current environment, which is full of uncertainty, many companies have seen their profits decrease, and even the permanence of their businesses endangered due to the COVID-19 pandemic. In such an environment, it is even more necessary to take into account the customer's opinion about the service received, since once the customer makes use of the hotel's services, he/she will recommend the hotel to third parties if he/she is satisfied with it. Through customer satisfaction and subsequent recommendations, the hotel thus obtains new clients and retains old ones. This feedback from the client allows for understanding their priorities in order to jointly design a tailor-made service. It is for this reason that this research has been carried out to analyze the service attributes evaluated by customers. In order to achieve the proposed objectives, a survey instrument was used, as well as a longitudinal study procedure applying logistic regression over a period of one year. The descriptive results and the logistic regression show the level of customer satisfaction with the service and the importance given to each of the selected attributes. In this way, the research shows in which areas innovation strategies should be sought. Although the research offers a model composed of five attributes to measure satisfaction through recommendation with a probability of more than fifty percent, it is necessary to take into account the limitations of the current environment due to COVID-19 or the possibility of extending the multidimensionality of the model. It is necessary to continue to work through open innovation platforms to keep contact with the customer and to update the examined attributes in order to obtain customer satisfaction and feedback.

Keywords: *open innovation in tourism; satisfaction; recommendation; hotel*

INTRODUCTION

In recent years, the hotel sector has seen increasing activity in a highly competitive environment [1,2,3]. However, the COVID-19 pandemic has almost completely halted tourism. Many hotels have closed either permanently or temporarily [4]. When tourist activity returns to pre-pandemic levels, the hotel sector will have to regain customers' trust and reinforce their brand [4].

In this sense, innovation is an essential tool for differentiation [5,6,7,8,9]. There are start-ups and SMEs with a leadership culture based on open innovation dynamics [10]. It is of utmost importance to adopt this culture for the management of both new and long-established hotels. This adoption will increase their competitive level and the likelihood of remaining open after the crisis caused by the pandemic.

In order to innovate, however, it is essential to have information about the customer's current needs. Of all the customer information we can collect, recommendation systems have become essential in recent years to retain clients and attract new ones to a hotel [11]. The importance of referral systems for hotels lies in the fact that customers are not only the ones who ultimately decide to stay at a hotel, but also the ones who, through word of mouth, bring new customers to a hotel. In short, the customer is a key source for innovation in the hotel sector [12].

This concept of innovation for service improvement and differentiation is directly related to the concept of open innovation [6]. This space for collaborative customer innovation with the hotel sector is a source of competitive advantage, strengthening customer relationships and loyalty [12].

Collaborative spaces or platforms (social networks, surveys, etc.) are the means through which customers can express their dissatisfaction with the service received. Customers express their satisfaction by recommending the service to third parties [13], and open innovation becomes a key tool for the analysis and study of this recommendation.

In recent research, recommendation variables have been studied from two points of view. On the one hand, there are many studies whose main focus was positive opinions leading to recommendations [14,15]. On the other hand, other studies have analyzed how a set of attributes can influence the customers' opinions which lead to recommendations [16,17,18].

In this study, the authors have analyzed recommendations in relation to a number of customer satisfaction attributes in hotels around the world as an open innovation channel for hotels. Satisfaction and recommendation, as two related constructs, have been analyzed according to the previous scientific literature. In this sense, the research hypothesis seeks to verify whether the recommendation variable can be explained by positive and significant relationships with customer service, cleanliness, facilities, and value for money. This hypothesis has been tested for all quarters.

Thus, the aim of this study is to analyze the responses given by a number of hotel service customers on the perceived satisfaction of a series of attributes and to verify their relationship with the recommendation of the service to third parties. The weights of the different attributes are also analyzed in order to assess which are the most important in the evaluation of customer satisfaction and subsequent recommendation.

The business ecosystem, through platforms such as the one used in this study, obtains numerous responses from customers about the service. In this way, the customer becomes a source of open innovation since, through their collaboration, they transfer their requirements to the business network and allow the latter to create services in line with the customer's expectations. This research processes and analyzes the relationships of these consumer responses.

LITERATURE REVIEW

Open Innovation in the Tourism Sector through Customers and Their Opinions

Business innovation must be flexible and, as Chesbrough [19] points out, companies must be open to the opinions of different stakeholders in order to improve and differentiate their services from those of their competitors [6]. Consequently, the company should break down the barriers that separate it from its environment and open up to the different actors that interact with it in order to gain new knowledge [20].

Despite the relevance of this strategy for the improvement of products and services, most of the research conducted on this topic has focused on the development of products in the manufacturing industry [21]. There are, therefore, few studies that deal with this topic in tourism [12]. The special characteristics of the tourism product (heterogeneity, intangibility, expiration, aggregability) make further research on this specific sector necessary [21].

In the service sector, customers are an external part of the business relationship. Their insights provide unique and valuable information about the hotel service. Their ideas and opinions contribute directly to the creation of competitive strategies. By using customers' knowledge and experiences, hotel establishments can receive innovative ideas [12,22].

These strategies can also help reduce the risk associated with new product launches and increase the company's creativity levels [23,24]. Other authors associate this concept with customer satisfaction and indicate the relevance of innovative systems for increasing customer satisfaction [25].

Business Model for the Creation of Innovative Value through Platforms

The business model is key to the success of innovation, and the company has to identify customer problems and create an innovative value proposition that responds to those problems [26]. The business model has to create innovative processes capable of realizing the value proposition. This business model must be based on openness and collaboration between all parties involved in the business ecosystem [27]. Therefore, there must be continuous communication with suppliers and customers. This communication takes place through networking platforms of suppliers, complementary companies, distributors, promoters, customers, etc. Examples of these digital platforms are those offered by companies such as STR, specialists in benchmarking to improve hotel performance and profitability, or hotel quality for client-company communication.

Through these platforms, the different agents involved can share and evaluate supply and demand in order to have more information and be able to make better business decisions.

There are platforms where tourists can share their experiences and thus become part of the co-creation of activities during the development of new innovations [28], such as WandoExperiences, a digital platform for selling destination experiences. Other platforms allow innovative projects to be shared between administrations. An example of this concept is the smart city.

The regional development impact of these digital platforms is very important. Local businesses in developing countries can benefit from the possibility of using the digital services offered by global platforms. This, together with local knowledge, can be an advantage for locally rooted digital platforms, allowing them to offer services adapted to local demand [29].

Customer Satisfaction: Measurement Models

Understanding the concept of satisfaction is important to guarantee success for any company in the service sector [30,31]. Although there are many definitions of satisfaction, there is no defined theoretical framework. However, there is one issue on which all studies agree, and that is the importance of the customer as the subject that perceives this satisfaction [1,25,32,33,34]. This perception will be conditioned by cognitive and emotional variables [35,36,37], and these variables will be represented by a series of attributes [38,39]. The customer reflects his or her satisfaction with the service received through the perceived quality of these tangible and intangible elements that form part of the hotel service. Within the models for measuring customer satisfaction, we can find studies focused on cognitive or tangible factors, studies that focus on intangible or emotional factors, and multidimensional studies [40]. These dimensions have been measured through different attributes [34,41,42]. One of the most comprehensive approaches is the Northern European approach: a three-dimensional approach that is made up of attributes aimed at measuring technical quality, functional quality, and quality of the result. Technical quality refers to the quality of the physical elements. In the research, the representative attribute for measuring technical quality is the state of the facilities and general cleanliness. Functional quality is the quality of interactions represented by the customer service attribute. Regarding quality of the result, this refers to the final service where the benefits obtained by the clients are measured through the price-quality ratio attribute. Most studies tend to focus more on functional quality than technical, but it is advisable to include both perspectives [43].

The Impact of Customer Satisfaction on the Service Recommendation

Customer loyalty, identified through the recommendation of the product or service, as well as its relationship to satisfaction, has been widely discussed in the specialized literature [37,44,45,46,47]. In the hotel sector, this recommendation is a key factor, fundamentally due to both the difficulty of having the same client evaluating the service before making use of it, as well as its seasonal and perishable nature and the high risk perceived by the client [48].

Many studies explain that the recommendation occurs when the client perceives a service as optimal and experiences a positive emotional response [14,37]. Thus, it should be noted that recommendation is one of the elements that will define a loyal customer [49] and possibly lead to the repurchase of the product or service [17,41]. For a customer to be satisfied, the product must be adapted to his or her needs. In this process, open innovation techniques can help to increase the suitability of the product and therefore customer satisfaction. In this way, we can affirm that open innovation has a positive effect on customer recommendation and customer loyalty [50].

Nonetheless, satisfaction alone is not a guarantee that the customer will recommend the product or service. For this reason, it is important to evaluate what base satisfaction level is needed for a client to recommend it, since there are few studies on this. Reichheld [51] stands out among these studies and establishes that only clients who rate the service between 9 and 10, on a scale of 10, are willing to recommend it. However, this hypothesis is not supported by other authors who indicate that this relationship is not linear [52,53].

The lack of consensus about the relationships between the necessary levels of satisfaction to recommendation leads us to consider the following study. More specifically, a model is proposed consisting of tangible attributes (state of the facilities and cleanliness), intangibles (customer service), and attributes aimed at measuring the result of the service (price-quality). Finally, the recommendation attribute has been included as a way to measure global service satisfaction [41] and customer loyalty [54]. The variables chosen have been used in different research studies (Table 1).

Table 1. *Review of the use of service satisfaction assessment attributes.*

Attribute	Author (Year)
Customer service	Tejada Yánez, 2020 [55]; De la Cruz Vargas, (2017) [56]; Herazo and Huamancayo (2018) [57]; Nunkoo, Teeroovengadum, Ringle, and Sunnassee (2019) [58]; Chumpitaz (2020) [59]
Price	Han and Hyun (2015) [60]; Lima et al. (2017) [61]; Izquierdo, Remigio, Díaz, and Martínez (2020) [62]; Chumpitaz (2020) [59]
Cleanliness	Malik, Akhtar, Raziq, and Agmad (2018) [59]; Nunko et al. (2019) [58]; Chumpitaz (2020) [59]; Izquierdo, Remigio, Díaz, and Martínez (2020) [62]
Facilities	Tefera and Govender (2016) [63]; De la Cruz Vargas (2017) [56]; Herazo and Huamancayo (2018) [57]; Tejada Yánez (2020) [55]
Recommendation	Emir and Kozac (2011) [54]; Raza et al. (2012) [47]; Aguilar-Rojas, Fandos, and Flavián-Blanco (2015) [16]; Han and Hyun (2015) [60]; Le, Nguyen, and Pervan (2020) [64]

According to the previous background, the main goal of this study is to analyze the relationships between a number of attributes (customer services, general cleanliness, facilities, and quality-price ratio) and the recommendation factor taken from the opinions of a large sample of hotel customers after their stay [41,54]. The methodology, statistical analysis, and results are presented in the following sections.

MATERIALS AND METHODS

Participants and Procedure

The data used were derived from the opinions of 165,739 customers during one year (2017) and divided by quarter. Table 2 describes the distribution according to category (number of stars). Four stars was the category with the greatest representation in all quarters. Regarding typology, in all quarters, urban hotels have greater weight than resorts. The surveys were conducted in hotels around the world, although the highest percentage of responses was obtained from guests staying in hotels in Mexico (32.22%), Spain (23.94%), and Brazil (24.3%).

Table 2. *Number of questionnaires and percentages by category, typology, and country.*

Variable/Quarter		First (%)	Second (%)	Third (%)	Fourth (%)
Category	5-star	20.9	19.6	20.5	19.7
	4-star	52.3	53.9	55.9	55.4
	3-star	24.8	24.6	22.2	23.4
	≤2-star	2.0	1.9	1.5	1.5
Typology	Urban	69.5	70.1	67.4	69.8
	Resort	6.8	5.4	7.4	5.3
Country	Mexico	30.1	33.5	31.2	32.2
	Spain	26.0	25.2	23.0	23.3
	Brazil	22.8	21.9	25.4	26.6
Number of questionnaires		33.239	32.871	34.068	32.091

A correlational study was conducted throughout four quarters. The survey was based on an open questionnaire with a non-probability convenience sampling. It was made available to hotel clients at the end of their stay, either as a physical copy or electronically through email. Due to the size of the sample, missing data were removed in all variables. The fieldwork and ethics considerations were managed by the company Hotel Quality (www.hotel-quality.com (accessed on 17 December 2018)) and data were collected in a big database. This company conducted the customer surveys at the end of each quarter, so they in turn provided us with the information on a quarterly basis. In this way, the data were analyzed as they were provided to us. We used the statistical software R in order to analyze the data [65]. The clients filled out the questionnaire voluntarily, no ethical approvals were needed, and there were no rewards for participation in the study.

Instrument

The questionnaire used in this study was structured in two sections. The first part included non-metric variables such as typology (urban or resort), number of hotel stars, and country. In the second one, the customers had to answer to questions about four general attributes: customer services, general cleanliness, facilities, and quality-price ratio. A six-point Likert scale was used to measure customer's opinions, where 1 = very poor, 2 = poor, 3 = fair, 4 = good, 5 = very good, and 6 = excellent. Moreover, the participants had to say if they would recommend (Y = 1) or not recommend (Y = 0) the hotel to future clients. The dependent and independent variables were chosen by the data provider (Hotel Quality).

Analysis

A binary logistic regresion, called "logit", has been applied using the software R. The specific function general lineal model "glm" was employed, where the dependent variables are defined as a binomial parameter (family = binomial). A recommendation is denoted as P(Y = 1) and no recommendation as 1 – P(Y = 1). This statistical procedure is developed in the analysis for which the dependent variable is dichotomous. Thus, X_1, X_2, [...], X_n (n is the number of independent variables) are influential variables for finding Y, and the logistic regression formula is used to learn the probability ratio for recommendation and no recommendation. The logarithm is $LogitP = \alpha + \beta 1X1 + \beta 2X1 + \ldots + \beta m\ Xm$, where m is the number of independent variables X1, X2, X3, and X4, which in this study are: customer service, facilities, cleanliness, and price-quality ratio [66].

RESULTS

Descriptive

Table 3 includes descriptive results: mean, standard deviation, skewness, and kurtosis, for each attribute and quarter. In all cases, the means were over five points (ranging 1–6) and the standard deviation was from 0.89–1.13. Moreover, the dichotomous recommendation variable showed, for each quarter, percentages of: 95% (Y = 1) and 5% (Y = 0) for the first quarter; 94.5% (Y = 1) and 5.5% (Y = 0) for the second quarter; 94.6% (Y = 1) and 5.4% (Y = 0) for the third quarter; and finally, 95% (Y = 1) and 5% (Y = 0) for the fourth quarter.

Table 3. *Descriptive results of the attributes for each quarter.*

Attributes	Quarter	M	SD	Skewness	Kurtosis
Customer service	T 1	5.412	0.8919	−2.222	7.012
	T 2	5.413	0.9048	−2.356	7.813
	T 3	5.414	0.9334	−2.448	8.204
	T 4	5.410	0.9190	−2.452	8.485
Facilities	T 1	5.375	0.8964	−2.100	6.669
	T 2	5.409	0.8937	−2.256	7.467
	T 3	5.390	0.9242	−2.282	7.428
	T 4	5.380	0.9250	−2.212	6.997
Cleanliness	T 1	5.165	1.022	−1.766	4.648
	T 2	5.203	1.009	−1.875	5.248
	T 3	5.184	1.034	−1.830	4.749
	T 4	5.210	0.9990	−1.842	5.034
Price-quality ratio	T 1	5.000	1.133	−1.678	4.059
	T 2	5.025	1.088	−1.608	3.846
	T 3	5.022	1.101	−1.595	3.658
	T 4	5.050	1.098	−1.705	4.244

Results of the Logit Regression for the Four Quarters

Table 4 includes the logistic regression findings for each quarter. For the first quarter, customer services (W = 117.196, $p < 0.01$), facilities (W = 78.578, $p < 0.01$), and price-quality ratio (W = 245.785, $p < 0.01$) were positive and significant. However, cleanliness was not significant (W = 3.208, $p > 0.05$). For the second quarter, all attributes were significant, for instance, customer services (W = 96.086, $p < 0.01$), facilities (W = 51.687, $p < 0.01$), cleanliness (W = 16.049, $p < 0.01$), and price-quality ratio (W = 280.598, $p < 0.01$). For the third quarter, cleanliness was not significant for the regression model (W = 0.852, $p > 0.05$). Customer services (W = 93.628, $p < 0.01$), facilities (W = 92.891, $p < 0.01$), and price-quality ratio (W = 276.039, $p < 0.01$) had a positive and significant relationship with the dichotomous recommendation variable. Finally, for the fourth quarter, all variables had a positive and significant relationship with the dependent variables of the model: customer services (W = 73.447, $p < 0.01$), cleanliness (W = 5.24, $p = 0.022$), facilities (W = 46.206, $p < 0.01$), and price-quality ratio (W = 243.443, $p < 0.01$). These results

Table 4. *Results of the logit regression for each quarter.*

	Variables	B	Wald	Sig.
First quarter	Constant (α)	−8.105	427.194	0.000
	Customer service	0.700	117.196	0.000 **
	Facilities	0.672	78.578	0.000 **
	Cleanliness	0.135	3.208	0.073
	Price-quality ratio	1.049	245.785	0.000 **
Second quarter	α Constant (α)	−7.566	467.709	0.000
	Customer service	0.582	96.086	0.000 **
	Facilities	0.509	51.687	0.000 **
	Cleanliness	0.292	16.049	0.000 **
	Price-quality ratio	0.980	280.598	0.000 **
Third quarter	Constant (α)	−7.787	430.678	0.000
	Customer service	0.645	93.628	0.000 **
	Facilities	0.719	92.891	0.000 **
	Cleanliness	0.069	0.852	0.356
	Price-quality ratio	1.052	276.039	0.000 **
Fourth quarter	Constant (α)	−7.387	375.378	0.000
	Customer service	0.602	73.447	0.000 **
	Facilities	0.532	46.206	0.000 **
	Cleanliness	0.174	5.24	0.022 *
	Price-quality ratio	1.059	243.443	0.000 **

Nagelkerke R^2 for the first quarter = 0.550; Nagelkerke R^2 for the second quarter = 0.519; Nagelkerke R^2 for the third quarter = 0.504, Nagelkerke R^2 for the fourth quarter = 0.534; ** $p < 0.01$; * $p < 0.05$.

show that independent and significant variables of the model have a positive impact on the probability to recommend the hotel. In all quarters, the price-quality ratio variable is, according to the statistical findings, more important than the rest of the attributes. For all quarters, the Nagelkerke R^2 index was 0.51–0.58.

DISCUSSION

According to the results, in all quarters, some of the attributes showed a significant relationship to the recommendation intention of the clients, thus allowing us to partially accept the hypothesis put forward in the research. These results are in agreement with those found by numerous authors who have investigated this relationship [32,55,56,57,67].

Each attribute has a different weight and this conclusion is shared by different authors [68,69,70].

The results of the research reflect how the most important attribute is price-quality ratio in order to explain if the clients would recommend the hotel to another tourist. This conclusion has been reached by several authors, such as Ali et al. [43], Prasetyo et al. [30], and Zagarra et al. [71]. However, cleanliness was not significant in some of the quarters. Due to the pandemic context, these results could be different because new cleanliness measures have been imposed, and this could change the intention of the customer to recommend the hotel in the future. In fact, several authors have identified cleanliness as the clients' most important factor for recommending a service [72,73].

Moreover, customer services and facilities were significant in all quarters as well. These data are consistent with studies by Kim-Soon et al. and Lai and Nguyen [74,75].

Most customers in this sample justify their intention to recommend the hotel according to quality-price ratio, customer services, and facilities. Additionally, some quarters showed cleanliness as an important variable to include in the recommendation model [51].

These results have direct implications for the business ecosystem of hotel establishments. On the one hand, this research confirms the direct and positive relationship between customer satisfaction and recommendation. In this way, it confirms how a customer satisfied with the service received recommends the service to third parties. Therefore, it is essential for managers to know the attributes that lead the consumer to leave the hotel satisfied. Observing the results, the attribute with the greatest weight when it comes to recommending the service is quality-price, so that when it comes to innovating in the search for a business strategy, this attribute must come first, so that hotel management focuses on providing a service whose quality, with respect to the price paid by the consumer, is perceived as high. The results show how companies should look for innovative strategies with respect to the price-quality ratio, since innovating in this area would make a difference in one of the most important aspects for the hotel customer. To this end, it is necessary to work in an environment of collaboration with the rest of the hotel companies, since in order to improve the perception of this attribute it is not only necessary to study the companies in the ecosystem from a competitive perspective (benchmarking), but also from a collaborative perspective.

While price-quality ratio is the attribute with the greatest weight, customer service has positioned itself as the second most important attribute for customer satisfaction. This implies the need to create innovative policies that pursue employee satisfaction so that, in turn, through them, the customer perceives a high-quality service with respect to the treatment received.

On the other hand, this study has implications for the use of platforms as a business model. Hotel service rating platforms, such as the one used in this study, are what allow stakeholders to know the tastes and needs of the customer. This makes it necessary for the hotel business ecosystem to commit to the permanent and continuous use of this type of tool, as it is through them that they are able to connect their businesses with users and other companies. The hotel should encourage its customers to comment on their experience. In this way, the more companies that join a project in which their users can express themselves through a service rating communication platform, the more data they will obtain, and from their analysis they will be able to co-develop innovative services to satisfy the customer. The digital platform providing the data has enabled communication within the hotel business ecosystem. Customers, through their opinions and assessment of attributes when recommending the service, become co-creators of new innovation projects, as indicated by Hernández and Robles [27].

In spite of the results, this study possesses some limitations. First of all, although there is a large sample, the clients were selected through a non-probability sampling method, which could affect the final results. Additionally, the number of clients who would recommend the hotel was larger than the number of clients who would not recommend the hotel. Furthermore, the questionnaire was a self-reporting tool, and it should be taken into account that the participants may have given biased answers. Additionally, logit regression has been applied for all quarters; according to the findings, the statistical procedure could have been applied for all data together, in order to check if the findings were the same or different. The data provided were quarterly, so it was decided to survey the data accordingly. Based on the results obtained, it is decided to carry out an annual analysis with a single logit in the future.

On the other hand, this study was carried out with the attributes chosen by the supplier company. Although these attributes have been widely used throughout the latest research in this field, we believe that there are few attributes, so for future research, measurement models composed of more than four attributes should be used. This fact will be checked in the future with this and other samples and also the effect of imbalance on the data (recommend vs. do not recommend).

Finally, the pandemic context could influence the recommendation opinion of the customers, especially in regard to the importance of the cleanliness attribute, for instance. For these reasons, a possible study in the future should include more attributes in order to know what the hotel recommendation variables are and how the cleanliness measures could change the importance of the model's quality-price ratio. Furthermore, these studies in the current pandemic context should include balanced samples with respect to the recommendation variable [66].

CONCLUSIONS

The logit regression model has shown, on the one hand, the importance of a multidimensional model for the evaluation of satisfaction and, on the other hand, the different weights of each of the attributes. Although the results have shown that the attribute with the highest weight is value for money, it is important to take into account the current pandemic situation, since some attributes such as cleanliness could have acquired greater relevance. Therefore, future research should study consumer evaluations during this crisis and the importance given to the different attributes examined. Future results could show the growing importance of this attribute and the need to develop innovation mechanisms with respect to this attribute.

Companies are currently facing new forms of communication through platforms that allow them to reach their users directly, get to know them in depth, and build loyalty, which means new business opportunities, as well as the generation of innovative ideas that help them to continue to grow and achieve business success. It is of utmost importance that hotels use open innovation platforms to benefit from this customer-company collaboration, as they can identify the degree of customer satisfaction with the service, the elements they examine in the process, and their willingness to recommend. Thus, customer participation in open innovation processes is essential in the industry. Customers are a source of ideas and are the main agents of co-development of the service. This research shows how, in order to customize the hotel service, companies must include the management of an open business model in which the customer is the one who indicates which attributes should be emphasized and how to innovate in these services.

The channel for collecting customer information has made it possible to identify those elements where greater innovation efforts are needed, for example, in relation to the price-quality ratio attribute, so that managers can use this knowledge to develop innovative revenue management policies and strategies to attract new customers and retain existing ones.

This research provides hotel managers with a tool to understand the attributes by which they should seek to innovate. In this way, managers can identify those services they need to improve in order for the customer to be fully satisfied and recommend the service to others. The hotel identifies perceived strengths and weaknesses through the customer, allowing the hotel to focus on improving the sub-optimal part of the service, thereby increasing satisfaction and the likelihood of customers recommending the service. Business leadership based on a culture of open innovation dynamics through the customer will increase the effectiveness of the service quality strategy and management processes, resulting in accelerated business recovery from the pandemic and improved business performance.

Author Contributions

Conceptualization, M.M.D.; methodology M.M.D.; software, M.M.D.; validation, M.M.D.; formal analysis, M.M.D.; investigation, M.M.D.; resources, C.M.D. and M.M.D.; writing—original draft preparation, M.M.D.; writing—review and editing, M.M.D.; visualization, M.M.D.; supervision, M.M.D.; project administration, M.M.D. and C.M.D.; funding acquisition, M.M.D. All authors have read and agreed to the published version of the manuscript.

ACKNOWLEDGMENTS

The authors thank Hotel Quality (www.hotel-quality.com (accessed on 17 July 2018)) for facilitating the database.

REFERENCES

1. Abrudan, I.N.; Pop, C.M.; Lazăr, P.S. Using a General Ordered Logit Model to Explain the Influence of Hotel Facilities, General and Sustainability-Related, on Customer Ratings. *Sustainability* **2020**, *12*, 9302.
2. Nunes, S.; Estevão, C.; Nicolau Filipe, M. Determinant factors of competitiveness in the hotel sector: The case of Portugal. *Compet. Rev.* **2018**, *28*, 122–135.
3. Tussyadiah, I.P.; Zach, F.J. Hotels vs. Peer-to-Peer Accommodation Rentals: Text Analytics of Consumer Reviews. *SSRN Electron. J.* **2015**.
4. Rodríguez-Antón, J.M.; Alonso-Almeida, M.D.M. COVID-19 Impacts and Recovery Strategies: The Case of the Hospitality Industry in Spain. *Sustainability* **2020**, *12*, 8599.
5. Stamboulis, Y.; Skayannis, P. Innovation strategies and technology for experience-based tourism. *Tour. Manag.* **2003**, *24*, 35–43.
6. Chesbrough, H.W. *Open Innovation: The New Imperative for Creating and Profiting from Technology*; First Trade Paper Edición; McGraw-Hill Education Ltd.: New York, NY, USA, 2006.
7. Fagerberg, J.; Godinho, M.M. Innovation and Catching-Up. 2004. Available online: https://smartech.gatech.edu/bitstream/handle/1853/43208/ManuelGodinho_1.pdf?sequence = 1&isAllowed = y (accessed on 17 December 2020).
8. Weiermair, K. Product Improvement or Innovation: What Is the Key to Success in Tourism? 2004. Available online: https://www.researchgate.net/publication/242488511_Product_improvement_or_innovation_what_is_the_key_to_success_in_tourism (accessed on 17 December 2020).
9. Duarte, V.; Sarkar, S. Separating the wheat from the chaff—A taxonomy of open innovation. *Eur. J. Innov. Manag.* **2011**, *14*, 435–459.
10. Yun, J.J.; Zhao, X.; Jung, K.; Yigitcanlar, T. The culture for open innovation dynamics. *Sustainability* **2020**, *12*, 5076.
11. Ramzan, B.; Bajwa, I.S.; Jamil, N.; Amin, R.U.; Ramzan, S.; Mirza, F.; Sarwar, N. An Intelligent Data Analysis for Recommendation Systems Using Machine Learning. 2019. Available online: https://www.hindawi.com/journals/sp/2019/5941096/ (accessed on 17 December 2020).
12. Iglesias-Sánchez, P.P.; Correia, M.B.; Jambrino-Maldonado, C. The Customer as a Source of Open Innovation in the Tourism Sector. In *The Role of Knowledge Transfer in Open Innovation*; Almeida, H., Sequeira, B., Eds.; IGI Global: Hershey, PA, USA, 2019; pp. 158–178.
13. Górska-Warsewicz, H.; Kulykovets, O. Hotel Brand Loyalty—A Systematic Literature Review. *Sustainability* **2020**, *12*, 4810.
14. Akinci, S.; Aksoy, S. The impact of service recovery evaluation on word-of-mouth intention: A moderated mediation model of overall satisfaction, household income and gender. *Tour. Manag. Perspect.* **2019**, *31*, 184–194.
15. Caruana, S.; Schembri, C. The Significance of Electronic Word of Mouth (e-WOM) Content in the Shaping of the Visitor´s Perception of Quality and Value. In *Tourism*

and Culture in the Age of Innovation; Katsoni, V., Stratigea, A., Eds.; Springer Proceedings in Business and Economics: Berlin/Heidelberg, Germany, 2016; pp. 535–550.

16. Aguilar-Rojas, O.; Fandos-Herrera, C.; Flavián-Blanco, C. What may lead you to recommend and revisit a hotel after a service failure instead of complaining? *Int. J. Contemp. Hosp. Manag.* **2015**, *27*, 214–235.
17. Hosany, S.; Prayag, G.; Van Der Veen, R.; Huang, S.; Deesilatham, S. Mediating Effects of Place Attachment and Satisfaction on the Relationship between Tourists' Emotions and Intention to Recommend. *J. Travel Res.* **2016**, *56*, 1079–1093.
18. Perez-Aranda, J.; Guerreiro, M.M.; Da Costa Mendes, J. Predictors of positive reviews on hotels: Hoteliers' perception. *Online Inf. Rev.* **2018**, *42*, 146–160.
19. Chesbrough, H.W. *Open Services Innovation: Rethinking Your Business to Grow and Compete in a New Era*; Illustrated Edición; John Wiley & Sons: Hoboken, NJ, USA; Jossey-Bass: San Francisco, CA, USA, 2011.
20. Laursen, K.; Salter, A. Open for innovation: The role of openness in explaining innovation performance among U.K. manufacturing firms. *Strateg. Manag. J.* **2005**, *27*, 131–150.
21. Aas, T.H. Open Service Innovation: The Case of Tourism Firms in Scandinavia. *J. Entrep. Manag. Innov.* **2016**, *12*, 53–75.
22. Prahalad, C.K.; Ramaswamy, V. Co-opting Customer Competence. 2000. Available online: https://hbr.org/2000/01/co-opting-customer-competence (accessed on 17 December 2020).
23. Aguirre, W.B.P.; Arévalo, M.A.P.; Núñez, L.B.A. Análisis del procesos innovador de las microempresas del área urbana del Cantón Quevedo, Ecuador. *ECA Sinergia* **2017**, *8*, 95–108.
24. Chesbrough, H.W. Bringing Open INNOVATION to Services. 2011. Available online: https://sloanreview.mit.edu/wp-content/uploads/2010/12/a4daa5e156.pdf (accessed on 17 December 2020).
25. Hermawati, A.; Nurwati, N.; Suhana, S.; Machmuddah, Z.; Ali, S. Satisfaction, HR, and Open Innovation in Tourism Sector. *J. Open Innov.* **2020**, *6*, 182.
26. Mäkinen, S.J.; Kanniainen, J.; Peltola, I. Investigating Adoption of Free Beta Applications in a Platform-Based Business Ecosystem. *J. Prod. Innov. Manag.* **2014**, *31*, 451–465.
27. Majava, J.; Kinnunen, T.; Kess, P.; Leviäkangas, P. Spatial Health and Life Sciences Business Ecosystems: Research Frame. *Manag.* **2014**, *9*, 307–322.
28. Hernández, I.J.G.; Robles, F.S. Ecosistemas de negocios a través de plataformas tecnológicas. *Ingenio Y Concienc. Boletín Científico De La Esc. Super. Ciudad Sahagún* **2018**, *5*.
29. Conferencia de Las Naciones Unidas Sobre Comercio y Desarrollo Plataformas Digitales y Creación de Valor En Los Países En Desarrollo: Repercusiones En Las Políticas Nacionales e Internacionales. 2020. Available online: https://unctad.org/system/files/official-document/tdb_ede4d2_es.pdf (accessed on 3 July 2021).
30. Jou, R.C.; Day, Y.J. Application of Revised Importance–Performance Analysis to Investigate Critical Service Quality of Hotel Online Booking. *Sustainability* **2021**, *13*, 2043.
31. Chen, C.M.; Lee, H.T.; Chen, S.H.; Huang, T.H. Tourist behavioural intentions in relation to service quality and customer satisfaction. *Int. J. Tour. Res.* **2011**, *13*, 416–432.
32. Parasuraman, A.; Zeithaml, V.A.; Berry, L.L. Reassessment of expectations as a Comparison Standard in Measuring Service Quality: Implications for Further Research. *J. Market.* **1994**, *58*.

33. Carev, D. Guest Satesfaction and Gest Loyalety Study for Hotel Industry. 2008. Available online: https://scholarworks.rit.edu/theses/508/ (accessed on 17 December 2020).

34. Prasetyo, Y.T.; Tanto, H.; Mariyanto, M.; Hanjaya, C.; Young, M.N.; Persada, S.F.; Redi, A.A.N.P. Factors Affecting Customer Satisfaction and Loyalty in Online Food Delivery Service during the COVID-19 Pandemic: Its Relation with Open Innovation. *J. Open Innov.* **2021**, *7*, 76.

35. Oliver, R. Satisfaction. In *A Beavioral Perspective on the Consumer*; McGraw-Hill: Singapore, 1997.

36. Bigné, E.; Andreu, L. Modelo Cognitivo-Afectivo de La Satisfacción En SERVICIOS de ocio y Turismo. 2004. Available online: https://dialnet.unirioja.es/servlet/articulo?codigo = 1143456 (accessed on 17 December 2020).

37. Sukhu, A.; Choi, H.; Bujisic, M.; Bilgihan, A. Satisfaction and positive emotions: A comparison of the influence of hotel guests' beliefs and attitudes on their satisfaction and emotions. *Int. J. Hosp. Manag.* **2019**, *77*, 51–63.

38. Medina, P.; Salas, J.R.; Sánchez, V.; Álvarez, W.T. Análisis Documental Sobre Calidad y Seguridad Turística En Las Festividades de Tungurahua. 2019. Available online: https://dialnet.unirioja.es/servlet/articulo?codigo = 6836430 (accessed on 17 December 2020).

39. Taylan Dortyol, I.; Varinli, I.; Kitapci, O. How do international tourists perceive hotel quality? *Int. J. Contemp. Hosp. Manag.* **2014**, *26*, 470–495.

40. Argudo-Pesántez, B.L.; Narváez-Zurita, C.I.; Vásquez-Erazo, E.J. Percepción de la Satisfacción del Cliente Externo: Centro Clínico Quirúrgico Ambulatorio Hospital del Día Azogues. *Cienciamatria* **2021**, *7*, 545–574.

41. Baniya, R.; Thapa, P. Hotel Attributes Influencing International Tourists' Satisfaction and Loyalty. *J. Tour. Hosp. Education* **2017**, *7*, 44–61.

42. Ban, H.J.; Choi, H.; Choi, E.K.; Lee, S.; Kim, H.S. Investigating Key Attributes in Experience and Satisfaction of Hotel Customer Using Online Review Data. *Sustainability* **2019**, *11*, 6570.

43. Ali, F.; Hussain, K.; Konar, R.; Jeon, H.M. The Effect of Technical and Functional Quality on Guests' Perceived Hotel Service Quality and Satisfaction: A SEM-PLS Analysis. *J. Qual. Assur. Hosp. Tour.* **2016**, *18*, 354–378.

44. Bowen, J.T.; Shiang-Lih, C. The relationship between customer loyalty and customer satisfaction. *Int. J. Contemp. Hosp. Manag.* **2001**, *13*, 213–217.

45. Kandampully, J.; Suhartanto, D. Customer loyalty in the hotel industry: The role of customer satisfaction and image. *Int. J. Contemp. Hosp. Manag.* **2000**, *12*, 346–351.

46. Oh, H. Service quality, customer satisfaction, and customer value: A holistic Perspective. *Int. J. Hosp. Manag.* **1999**, *18*, 67–82.

47. Raza, M.A.; Siddiquei, A.N.; Awan, H.M.; Bukhari, K. Relationship between Service Quality, Perceived Value, Satisfaction and Revisit Intention in Hotel Indry. 2012. Available online: https://journal-archieves26.webs.com/788-805.pdf (accessed on 17 December 2020).

48. Litvin, S.W.; Goldsmith, R.E.; Pan, B. Electronic word-of-mouth in hospitality and tourism management. *Tour. Manag.* **2008**, *29*, 458–468.

49. Múgica, J.; Berné, C. Direct and Indirect Tourism Online Channels. Do They Have a Different Potential for Customer Loyalty? *Sustainability* **2020**, *12*, 4761.

50. Suwannaporn, P.; Speece, M.W. Assessing new product development success factors in the Thai food industry. *Br. Food J.* **2010**, *12*, 364–386.

51. Reichheld, F. *The Ultimate Question 2.0 (Revised and Expanded Edition): How Net Promoter Companies Thrive in a Customer-Driven World*; Revised and Expanded Edition; Harvard Business Review Press: Boston, MA, USA, 2014.

52. Mittal, V.; Kamakura, W.A. Satisfaction, repurchase intent, and repurchase behavior: Investigating the moderating effect of customer characteristics. *J. Mark. Res.* **2001**, *13*, 31–42.

53. Kumar, P. The impact of performance, cost, and competitive considerations on the relationship between satisfaction and repurchase intention business markets. *J. Serv. Res.* **2002**, *5*, 55–68.

54. Emir, O.; Kozak, M. Perceived Importance of Attributes on Hotel Guests' Repeat Visit Intentions. 2011. Available online: https://hrcak.srce.hr/71005 (accessed on 17 December 2020).

55. Tejada Yáñez, T.M. Experiencia de Marca, Satisfacción y Lealtad de Huéspedes de Hoteles 3 Estrellas de Cadenas Nacionales En Miraflores 2019. 2020. Available online: http://repositorio.usil.edu.pe/bitstream/USIL/9944/1/2020_Tejada%20Y%C3%A1%C3%B1ez.pdf (accessed on 17 December 2020).

56. De La Cruz Vargas, A.D. Calidad de Servicio, Satisfacción y Lealtad, En Los Estudiantes de La Universidad Peruana Unión, 2016. 2017. Available online: https://repositorio.upeu.edu.pe/bitstream/handle/UPEU/1130/Alexander_Tesis_Doctor_2017.pdf?sequence = 5&isAllowed = y (accessed on 17 December 2020).

57. Herazo Pachas, G.; Huamancayo Balarezo, J.A. Relación de La Calidad de Servicio, La Satisfacción y Lealtad de Marca de Los Clientes de Latam En Vuelos Nacionales En El 2017. 2018. Available online: http://repositorio.usil.edu.pe/bitstream/USIL/3925/1/2018_Herazo-Pachas.pdf (accessed on 17 December 2020).

58. Nunkoo, R.; Teeroovengadum, V.; Ringle, C.M.; Sunnassee, V. Service quality and customer satisfaction: The moderating effects of hotel star rating. *Int. J. Hosp. Manag.* **2019**, *91*, 102414.

59. Chumpitaz Prada, Ibrahim Joao La Calidad Del Servicio de Alojamiento y El Nivel de Satisfacción de Los Clientes Del Hotel Camino Real de La Ciudad de Tacna en El Año 2019. 2020. Available online: http://repositorio.upt.edu.pe/bitstream/UPT/1641/1/Chumpitaz-Prada-Ibrahim.pdf (accessed on 17 December 2020).

60. Han, H.; Hyun, S.S. Customer retention in the medical tourism industry: Impact of quality, satisfaction, trust, and price reasonableness. *Tour. Manag.* **2015**, *46*, 20–29.

61. Lima, S.M.; Viana, F.L.E. Criterios Competitivos En Operaciones de Servicios de Hotelería En El Contexto de Online Travel Reviews. 2017. Available online: https://dialnet.unirioja.es/servlet/articulo?codigo = 6328656 (accessed on 17 December 2020).

62. Izquierdo, A.; Remigio, G.; Díaz González, Y.; Martínez Martínez, C.C. Calidad Percibida Por Los Clientes de Los Hoteles de La Provincia Los Ríos, Ecuador. 2020. Available online: https://dialnet.unirioja.es/servlet/articulo?codigo = 7687046 (accessed on 17 December 2020).

63. Tefera, O.; Govender, K. From Servqual to Hotsperf: Towards the Development and Validation of an Alternate Hotel Service Quality Measurement Instrument. 2016. Available online: https://www.researchgate.net/publication/308615186_From_SERVQUAL_to_HOTSPERF_Towards_the_Development_and_Validation_of_an_alternate_Hotel_Service_Quality_Measurement_Instrument (accessed on 17 December 2020).

64. Nguyen, H.T.T.; Nguyen, N.; Pervan, S.; Le, V.H. Development and validation of a scale measuring hotel website service quality (HWebSQ). *Tour. Manag. Perspect.* **2020**, *35*, 100687.

65. R Foundation for Statistical Computing. *R Development Core Team R: A Language and Environment for Statistical Computing*; R Foundation for Statistical Computing: Vienna, Austria, 2008; Available online: http://www.R-project.org (accessed on 17 December 2020).

66. Fernández-Muñoz, J.J.; Moguerza, J.M.; Duque, C.M.; Bruna, D.G. A study on the effect of imbalanced data in tourism recommendation models. *Int. J. Qual. Serv. Sci.* **2019**, *11*, 346–356.

67. Silva-Treviño, J.G.; Macías-Hernández, B.A.; Tello-Leal, E.; Delgado-Rivas, J.G. La relación entre la calidad en el servicio, satisfacción del cliente y lealtad del cliente: Un estudio de caso de una empresa comercial en México. *Ciencia UAT* **2021**, *15*, 85–101.

68. Akbaba, A. Measuring service quality in the hotel industry: A study in a business hotel in Turkey. *Int. J. Hosp. Manag.* **2006**, *25*, 170–192.

69. Gržinić, D. Concepts of Service Quality Measurement in Hotel Industry. 2007. Available online: https://www.researchgate.net/publication/27200641_Concepts_of_service_quality_measurement_in_hotel_industry (accessed on 17 December 2020).

70. Debasish, S.S.; Dey, M.S. Customer Perceptions of Service Quality towards Luxury Hotels in Odisha Using SERVQUAL Model. 2015. Available online: http://www.ijrbsm.org/pdf/v2-i9/1.pdf (accessed on 17 December 2020).

71. Zegarra, M.M.; Mafé, C.R. El valor hedónico como determinante clave de la intención de recompra y de recomendación en el comercio móvil de productos de moda. *UCJC Bus. Soc. Rev.* **2020**, *17*, 54–91.

72. Jiménez-Barreto, J.; Loureiro, S.; Braun, E.; Sthapit, E.; Zenker, S. Use numbers not words! Communicating hotels' cleaning programs for COVID-19 from the brand perspective. *Int. J. Hosp. Manag.* **2021**, *94*, 102872.

73. World Health Organization. Operational Considerations for COVID-19 Management in the Accommodation Sector. 2019. Available online: https://apps.who.int/iris/bitstream/handle/10665/331638/WHO-2019-nCoV-Hotels-2020.1-eng.pdf (accessed on 17 December 2020).

74. Kim-Soon, N.; Ahmad, A.R.; Logeswaary, V. SERVQUAL: Can It be Used to Differentiate Guest's Perception of Service Quality of 3 Star from a 4 Star Hotel. 2014. Available online: https://www.researchgate.net/publication/264707509_SERVQUAL_Can_It_Be_Used_to_Differentiate_Guest's_Perception_of_Service_Quality_of_3_Star_from_a_4_Star_Hotel (accessed on 17 December 2020).

75. Lai, C.-S.; Minh, C.N. Factors Affecting Service Quality, Customer Satisfaction and Loyalty of Mobile Phone Service Providers in Vietnam. 2017. Available online: https://ijoi-online.org/attachments/article/54/FINAL%20ISSUE%20VOL%2010%20NUM%202%20OCTOBER%202017%20-%20SECTION%20A.pdf#page = 75 (accessed on 17 December 2020).

CHAPTER 13

Investigating Key Attributes in Experience and Satisfaction of Hotel Customer Using Online Review Data

Hyun-Jeong Ban[1], Hayeon Choi[2], Eun-Kyong Choi[2], Sanghyeop Lee[3] and Hak-Seon Kim[1]

[1]*School of Hospitality and Tourism Management, Kyungsung University, 309 Suyoungro, Nam-Gu, Busan 48434, Korea*

[2]*Department of Nutrition and Hospitality Management, The University of Mississippi, Oxford, MS 38677, USA*

[3]*Department of Tourism Management, Keimyung University, 1095 Dalgubeol-daero, Dalseo-gu, Daegu 42601, Korea*

ABSTRACT

With the development of social media, customers are sharing their experiences, and it is rapidly spreading as a form of online review. That is why the online review has become a significant information source affecting customers' purchase intention and behavior. Therefore, it is important to understand the customer's experience shown in the online review in order to maintain sustainable customer satisfaction and loyalty. The purpose of this study is to investigate what are the key attributes and the structural relationship of those key attributes. To accomplish this purpose, a total of 6596 hotel reviews were collected from Google (google.com). A frequency analysis using text mining was performed to figure out the most frequently mentioned attributes. In addition, semantic network analysis, factor analysis, and regression analysis were applied to understand the experience and satisfaction of the hotel customer. As a result, the top 99 keywords were divided into four groups such as "Intangible Service", "Physical Environment", "Purpose", and "Location". The factor analysis reduced the dimension of the original 64 keywords to 22 keywords, and grouped them into five factors, which are "Access", "F&B (Food and Beverage)", "Purpose", "Tangibles", and "Empathy". Based on these results, theoretical and practical implications for sustainable hotel marketing strategies are suggested.

Keywords: *customer experience; customer satisfaction; selective attribute; online hotel review; eWOM; big data; semantic network analysis; hospitality marketing*

INTRODUCTION

Nowadays, reviewing a product or service online is common for customers. In the online review, customer leave text comments with a numeric rating to briefly indicate their evaluation of the product or service [1]. The review can be called word of mouth (WOM). In the Internet era, the effect of WOM has been further enhanced in the form of electronic word of mouth (eWOM), and it has developed substantially [2]. The eWOM is a new method to identify the main attributes of service quality from a customer's perspective. The eWOM is the result of a summary of the customer's experience and is usually written voluntarily without any economic cost or external stimulus [3]. This eWOM is used by customers who have experienced a particular service to help other customers make the right choice. Therefore, the experience of the services mentioned in the eWOM implies the main attributes and quality levels of the product or service that the customer considers [4]. Accordingly, online review mining research is actively under way to extract customer information needed to develop new products or improve existing products [5] from online review in various service industries such as medical service, airline [6], dining [7], and hotel [8].

Previously, many studies have focused on identifying key attributes that investigate customer satisfaction with the survey method. Cheng et al. [9] investigated the impact of service recovery dimensions on customer satisfaction and subsequently on customer loyalty in the context of the hotel industry. Nysveen et al. [10] examined the influence of a brand's innovativeness and green image with hotel brand satisfaction. Pizam et al. [11] discussed customer satisfaction and its application to the hospitality and tourism industries. However, the majority of prior studies using the survey method were done a few years ago [12,13,14,15,16]. Nowadays researchers are using the text mining method for analyzing eWOM [4,8,16,17,18,19].

A hotel is an industry in which consumers themselves are the property of the enterprise and engage in production activities through direct contact with the customer. That is why understanding the opinions of customers and their experiences is significant. In addition, the hotel is a special product that combines the tangible product of the facility with the intangible product of human service [20]. Therefore, it is difficult to identify the main attributes because there are so many service attributes and the customer's needs vary depending on the type, purpose of visit, and local characteristics. In view of these characteristics, this study focuses on understanding the customer through online review mining and examines customer experience and satisfaction to find out what key attributes were affecting the customer intention.

LITERATURE REVIEW

Customer Experience and Satisfaction

Customer satisfaction is a complex customer experience in the service industry and can be defined as an evaluation of what the customers have experienced [5]. Understanding what customers expect from a service industry is important in order to provide a standard of comparison against which customers consider an organization's performance regarding the expectation [7]. Service quality can be defined as a customer's overall impression of the relative efficiency of the organization [21]. In addition, customer satisfaction can be defined as an experience made on the basis of a specific service encounter, and it contributes to loyalty, repeat purchase, positive WOM, and ultimately higher profitability [22].

Hotel selection attributes are what a customer considers important among the many attributes a hotel has when choosing a hotel [23]. Hotel selectivity is a determinant that is particularly preferred and considered by the customer and is defined as a target for assessing satisfaction and dissatisfaction [20,24]. Therefore, identifying a customer's hotel selection attributes is part of the effort to improve the quality of service and increase customer satisfaction to gain competitive advantage [25].

Electronic Word of Mouth (eWOM)

eWOM is an Internet-based development in which the delivery of reviews takes place on the Internet [19]. This refers to the online exchange of product information and experience [21]. Unlike WOM, eWOM is very influential to customers as it can be written and edited without the limitations of time and space. Through eWOM, customers share their product reviews with others through social network service (SNS) and online communities regardless of commercial interests. Unlike one-sided advertising, an actual review or specific information from customers with experience is greatly influenced by customers' selection attributes [26]. Through the Internet, people can freely produce and share their experiences and opinions with potential customers at all times.

The service features inseparability where purchases and consumption take place at the same time and intangibility being invisible, unlike ordinary products [27]. Therefore, customers want more specific and practical information to minimize failure. At this time, people will listen to more diverse and specific opinions from a wider group of experienced people through Internet searches, beyond the limited information they get from the people around them [28]. According to Klein [29], this is because customers rely more on the reviews of the actual customers when purchasing experience products than when buying general merchandise. Hu et al. [17] said that online reviews are far more interesting, reflect the best information, and are more reliable than information provided by the company. In other words, customers are more sympathetic to the experiences they have left behind than the promotional information provided by the company. This online review is used as a new source of information for other customers looking for information about the hotel. Accordingly, reviewers will play a role as opinion leaders, whether or not they are meant to be.

Text Mining and Semantic Network Analysis

The text mining refers to discovering unknown useful patterns and knowledge in text using information retrieval, information extraction, and natural language processing techniques [30]. The general process of text mining consists of the steps of data collection, data refining, data analysis, and management information system as shown in Figure 1. Data collection identifies and clarifies the type of information that researchers seek to find. Then, it is important to limit the range of data you want to collect and to be familiar with the characteristics of keywords. The data refining process is the process of converting unstructured text data into structured forms. When the analysis stage is used to analyze text based on technologies such as information extraction, clustering, and categorization, it is utilized as a management information system and accumulated as knowledge [31,32].

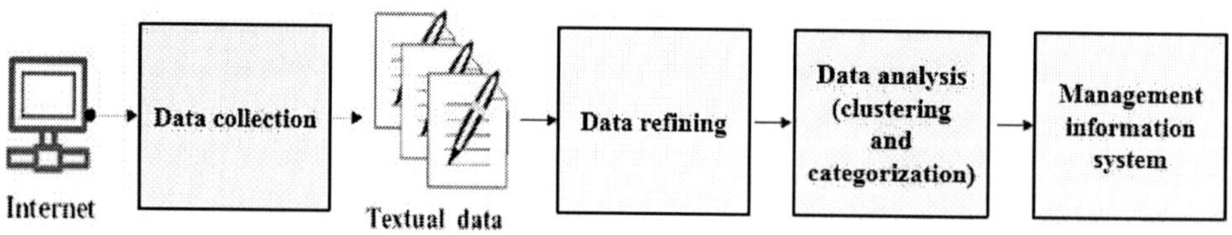

Figure 1. *Text mining process [15].*

Research using text mining in the hospitality industry has been active recently. Joseph and Varghese [33] analyzed user reviews to understand various aspects that drive customer satisfaction using text mining analysis. Hu et al. [17] analyzed 27,864 hotel reviews in New York City, and the results showed that customer complaints for high-end hotels are mainly related to service issues. Kuhzady and Ghasemi [34] used text mining to analyze online hotel reviews for Mazandaran province in Iran. Berezina et al. [35] analyzed the factors of satisfaction and dissatisfaction of U.S. hotel customers, and Philander and Zhong [36] used text mining to analyze customer's feelings about a Las Vegas resort on Twitter.

Semantic network analysis can be described as the use of network analytics techniques based on shared meaning as opposed to paired associations of behavioral or perceived communication links [37,38,39]. In other words, text is coded into a network to identify the structural relationship between words. Semantic network analysis can identify the inherent meaning of the context that has not been revealed. Moreover, it is possible to understand the degree of influence of a particular word through frequency and cluster analysis of words and to analyze how a particular word affects the relationships between groups [40,41]. Semantic network analysis, as a method of quantitative textual analysis, provides an impressive theoretical and methodological foundation with which to describe the semantic nature of the online review [42].

METHODOLOGY

Data Collection

The data collection procedure used in this study was as follow. The first step was to collect the research data. The online hotel reviews were obtained from google.com, which is the largest search engine in the world. That is why it is easy to access and share the online hotel review. The data was collected by web crawling, and the web crawler was written in the Python 2.7. The server operating system was Ubuntu 16.04 LTS from google.com. Several types of data were collected including hotel brands, writer's identification code, written date, overall score, and review as shown in Figure 2. The overall score was defined as the customer satisfaction in this study.

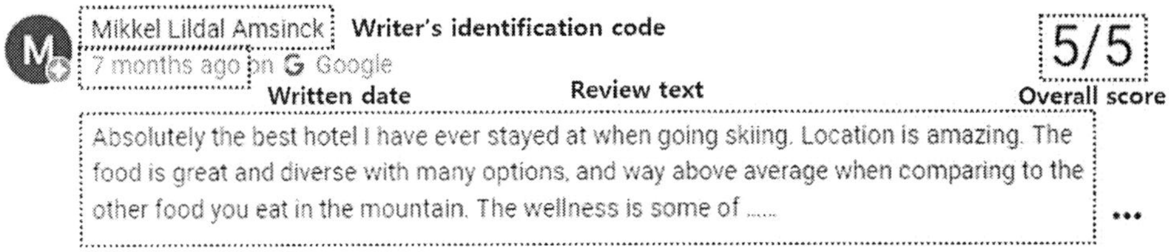

Figure 2. *Google review data screen.*

Initially, 19,332 reviews were collected in top 25 hotels in the world. The ranking information was from TripAdvisor (tripadvisor.com). The top 25 hotels and numbers of reviews are presented in Table 1. After deleting online reviews of languages other than English, there were 6597 online reviews left and a total of 189,571 words were extracted. The period of collected data was for five years from August 2014 to July 2019.

Table 1. *Number of reviews according to hotel brands.*

Rank	Brands	No. of Reviews	Rank	Brands	No. of Reviews
1	Tulemar Bungalows and Villas	181	14	Hotel Amira Istanbul	332
2	Hotel Belvedere	230	15	Hotel 41	217
3	Viroth's Hotel	253	16	Ikos Oceania	449
4	Kenting Amanda Hotel	97	17	Mandapa, a Ritz-Carlton Reserve	466
5	Hotel Alpin Spa Tuxerhof	113	18	Nayara Springs	147
6	French Quarter Inn	339	19	Rosewood Mayakoba	209
7	The Resort at Pedregal	487	20	Valle D'incanto Midscale	77
8	Belmond Palacio Nazarenas	139	21	Hotel Spadai	271
9	Kayakapi Premium Caves	245	22	Constance Prince Maurice	268
10	Hanoi La Siesta Hotel and Spa	278	23	O'Gallery Premier Hotel	377
11	Golden Temple Retreat	220	24	The Nantucket Hotel and Resort	188
12	Quinta Jardins do Lago	170	25	AYADA Maldives	219
13	The Oberoi Rajvilas	625			
	Total/Average			6597/263	

Data Analysis

As for the data analysis of this study, first, the text mining technique was applied to obtain the word frequency from online hotel reviews. The articles, prepositions, and pronouns that are meaningless were excluded, and words that pertained to hotel experience were contained in the refined data. The top 99 frequent words were manually selected after refining the collected data. Furthermore, the distribution of hotel experience evaluation based upon overall satisfaction score was performed to generally ascertain the satisfaction level of hotel experience, and this overall score was used as a dependent variable because its value can be treated as a main output variable. In addition, the word matrix (keywords × keywords) was deduced for further data analysis.

Secondly, the semantic network analysis of these top 99 frequent words was performed using the UCINET 6.0 package with the visualization tool named NetDraw. Furthermore, Freeman's degree centrality and Eigenvector centrality were chosen for illustrating the semantic network. Finally, CONCOR (CONvergence of iterated CORrelation) analysis was conducted to obtain the subgroups of these words so as to understand these interwoven correlations with each other and figure out the facets that customers are interested in.

At last, the results of semantic network analysis were synthesized to select words for further factor analysis and linear regression analysis with a dummy variable. Factor analysis was performed to derive the main factors affecting hotel satisfaction using 64 words out of the 99 top-frequency words, which will be considered as variables for the linear regression analysis. Moreover, the linear regression analysis comprised six independent variables retrieved from the factor analysis and the overall score for each review as a dependent variable was employed to test the hypothesis: The hotel experience represented in online reviews can be used to explain customer satisfaction.

RESULT

Frequency Analysis

To find the words most frequently used in customer reviews, Table 2 listed the top 99 frequent words associated with the hotel experience. The top five words were 'staff', 'service', 'room', 'place', and 'food'. The distribution of frequently used words is shown in Figure 3, and the result of visualizing the network that

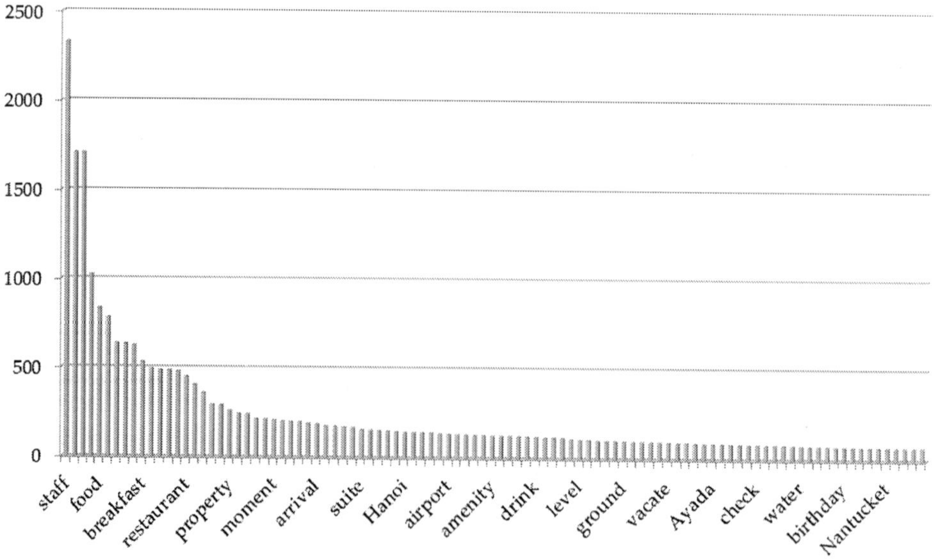

Figure 3. *Distribution of the frequently used words in the hotel online review.*

Table 2. *Top 99 frequent words from the online hotel review.*

Rank	Word	Freq.	Rank	Word	Freq.	Rank	Word	Freq.
1	staff	2332	34	people	168	67	bathroom	99
2	service	1709	35	suite	158	68	price	98
3	room	1708	36	garden	156	69	lake	97
4	place	1024	37	quality	154	70	vacate	96
5	food	835	38	detail	152	71	Quarter	94
6	locate	784	39	city	148	72	street	94
7	resort	640	40	Hanoi	146	73	care	92
8	stay	636	41	class	145	74	part	90
9	view	628	42	holiday	145	75	Ayada	90
10	breakfast	534	43	visit	144	76	reception	90
11	everything	496	44	minute	140	77	walk	87
12	time	488	45	airport	138	78	butler	87
13	night	486	46	home	134	79	Mandapa	86
14	experience	479	47	hospitality	134	80	check	86
15	restaurant	451	48	bar	131	81	kid	85
16	pool	407	49	custom	129	82	distance	85
17	day	362	50	amenity	127	83	manage	84
18	family	295	51	guest	127	84	kind	83
19	star	293	52	wife	127	85	water	81
20	property	264	53	everyone	126	86	thank	79
21	trip	245	54	honeymoon	124	87	concierge	77
22	year	242	55	drink	122	88	heart	77
23	area	216	56	town	120	89	desk	76
24	world	214	57	expectation	120	90	birthday	76
25	moment	210	58	attention	118	91	anniversary	74
26	weekend	204	59	husband	112	92	cave	73
27	spa	203	60	level	110	93	Jaipur	73
28	villa	202	61	boutique	108	94	Istanbul	72
29	facility	192	62	accommodate	105	95	Nantucket	71
30	arrival	190	63	friend	104	96	Amira	71
31	beach	179	64	tour	103	97	notch	71
32	luxury	178	65	ground	101	98	choice	71
33	dining	173	66	team	99	99	Charleston	70

reflects the frequency is Figure 4. There were words describing the food, such as 'food', 'breakfast', 'restaurant', 'dining', 'bar', 'drink' and describing the service, such as 'staff', 'service', 'hospitality', 'care'. Likewise, there were the words related to facility, such as 'room', 'resort', 'view', 'pool', 'spa', 'villa', 'facility', 'beach', 'garden', 'bathroom', 'lake' and the words related to the location or name of the hotel, such as 'place', 'locate', 'Hanoi', 'Quarter', 'Ayada', 'Mandapa', 'distance', 'Jaipur', 'Istanbul', 'Nantucket', 'Amira', 'Charleston'.

Semantic Network Analysis

The semantic network analysis identifies the relationship between words and expresses the connection between them. The centrality and CONCOR analyses of keywords were performed. In the online hotel review, among the top 99 frequent words, the results of an analysis of the degree and eigenvector centrality of the words are described in Table 3.

The degree centrality is a simple centrality measure that counts how many neighbors a node has and refers to the degree to which a word has many connections and becomes central, and the more connections it has, the greater its impact

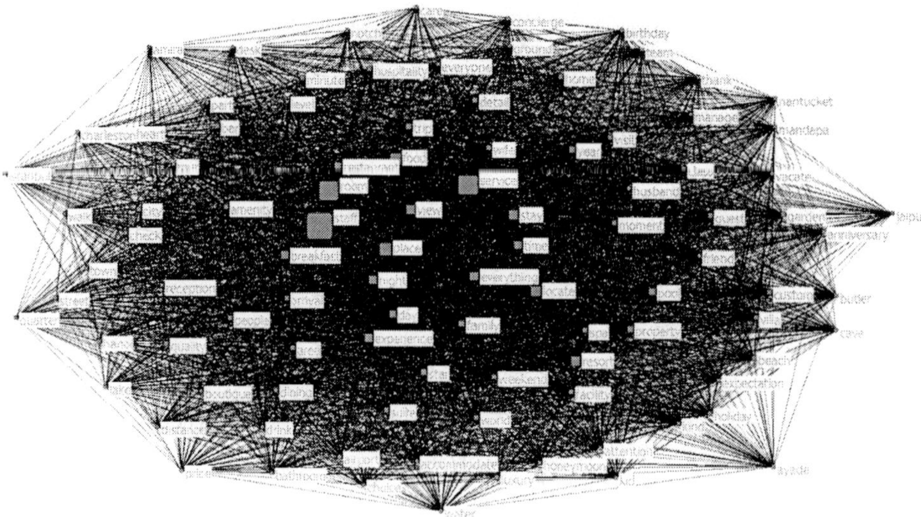

Figure 4. *Keyword visualization of network analysis.*

Table 3. *Comparison of keyword frequency and centrality analysis.*

	Frequency		Degree		Eigenvector			Frequency		Degree		Eigenvector	
	Freq	**Rank**	**Coef.**	**Rank**	**Coef.**	**Rank**		**Freq**	**Rank**	**Coef.**	**Rank**	**Coef.**	**Rank**
staff	2332	1	0.086	1	0.469	1	weekend	204	26	0.009	25	0.052	25
service	1709	2	0.063	3	0.372	3	spa	203	27	0.010	22	0.065	20
room	1708	3	0.070	2	0.425	2	villa	202	28	0.009	26	0.047	33
place	1024	4	0.029	6	0.184	6	facility	192	29	0.008	31	0.055	24
food	835	5	0.036	4	0.240	4	arrival	190	30	0.008	28	0.047	34
locate	784	6	0.031	5	0.222	5	beach	179	31	0.008	30	0.049	29
resort	640	7	0.024	9	0.136	12	luxury	178	32	0.006	42	0.034	51
stay	636	8	0.026	7	0.164	8	dining	173	33	0.007	32	0.048	30
view	628	9	0.025	8	0.154	9	people	168	34	0.007	36	0.040	39
breakfast	534	10	0.023	10	0.176	7	suite	158	35	0.007	34	0.043	36
everything	496	11	0.021	13	0.137	11	garden	156	36	0.007	37	0.044	35
time	488	12	0.021	11	0.126	15	quality	154	37	0.007	35	0.052	26
night	486	13	0.021	12	0.132	14	detail	152	38	0.007	33	0.048	31
experience	479	14	0.017	16	0.105	16	city	148	39	0.006	45	0.038	43
restaurant	451	15	0.020	14	0.139	10	Hanoi	146	40	0.006	39	0.042	37
pool	407	16	0.020	15	0.135	13	class	145	41	0.006	38	0.039	40
day	362	17	0.016	17	0.098	17	holiday	145	42	0.005	55	0.032	55
family	295	18	0.013	18	0.074	19	visit	144	43	0.006	41	0.036	44
star	293	19	0.012	19	0.077	18	minute	140	44	0.006	47	0.032	56
property	264	20	0.010	20	0.061	22	airport	138	45	0.006	46	0.036	45
trip	245	21	0.010	21	0.063	21	home	134	46	0.006	49	0.034	52
year	242	22	0.009	23	0.049	27	hospitality	134	47	0.005	57	0.031	60
area	216	23	0.009	24	0.057	23	bar	131	48	0.006	40	0.042	38
world	214	24	0.008	29	0.047	32	custom	129	49	0.005	52	0.039	41
moment	210	25	0.008	27	0.049	28	amenity	127	50	0.006	48	0.039	42

on other words and the more dominant it can be [43]. The eigenvector centrality extends the concept of connective centrality by considering not only the number of words connected, but also how important a connected relationship is. Thus, it is a useful indicator for finding the most influential central node in the network

[44]. It is sometimes used to measure a node's influence in the network. It performs matrix calculations to determine adjustments.

The result is that 'staff', 'service', 'room' recorded top in both degree and eigenvector centrality. The word 'breakfast' recorded a lower rank in frequency and degree centrality than in eigenvector centrality. The words 'spa', 'facility', 'quality', 'bar', 'amenity' recorded higher in degree and eigenvector centrality than in frequency. However, the word 'luxury' recorded higher in frequency than in degree and eigenvector centrality.

The CONCOR analysis is the connection of the relationship and discovering patterns between words, and the greater the similarity of the connection relationship patterns, the greater the degree of structural equivalence of the other words. It forms clusters that include keywords with similarities to each other [45]. In other words, the CONCOR analysis is a method of repeatedly analyzing correlations to search certain levels of similarity groups. This study identifies the blocks of nodes according to the correlation coefficient of the matrix of the concurrent keywords and forms clusters that include keywords with similarities [5]. The keywords extracted from the frequency histogram according to the frequency ranking were used and a matrix was constructed. To visualize the results, NetDraw in UCINET 6.0 program was applied. The nodes are presented as blue squares and their sizes indicate their frequency, and the network shows the connectivity between them.

The result of the CONCOR analysis is shown in Figure 5 with visibility. There are four groups that were intricately interwoven with each other. After looking at the words in the group, the group was named as "Intangible Service", "Physical Environment", "Location", and "Purpose".

To make it easier to see which words belong to each group, the words grouped in the cluster and the ones to be noted are listed in Table 4. As shown in Table 4, the group name was chosen as follows considering the characteristics of the words. The

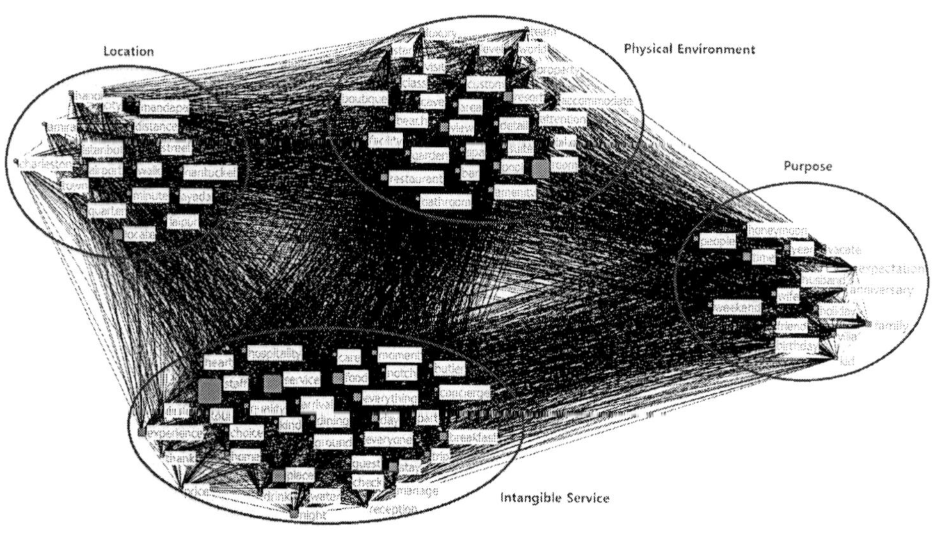

Figure 5. *Visualization of CONvergence of iterated CORrelation (CONCOR) analysis.*

"Intangible Service" group consists of 'staff', 'service', 'food', 'hospitality', 'concierge', 'dining', 'breakfast', 'drink', 'reception', 'moment', 'desk, 'quality' which are the significant terms for the hotel industry. "Physical Environment" comprises of 'room', view', 'resort', 'restaurant', 'spa', 'bar', 'beach', 'facility', 'cave', 'garden', 'pool', 'suite', 'bathroom', 'amenity' which contains various facilities. "Location" refers to several hotel brands such as 'Amira', 'Mandapa', 'Quarter', 'Ayada', 'Jai pur', and this group also contains words such as 'city', 'street', 'walk', 'locate', 'distance'. The last group, "Purpose" is composed of words relating with purpose such as 'honeymoon', 'vacate', 'anniversary', 'holiday', 'weekend', and also contains words relating to company such as 'people', 'wife', 'husband', 'kid', 'family', 'friend'. Accordingly, after the CONCOR analysis, 64 words that intimately associate with hotel experience and satisfaction were extracted for further research.

Table 4. *Result of CONCOR analysis.*

	Extracted Words	Significant Words
Intangible Service	staff/service/food/place/night/everything/experience/ day/breakfast/trip/stay/desk/heart/hospitalityquality/ tour/choice/home/thank/price/kind/arrival/dining/ ground/water/drink/guest/check/reception/manage/ care/moment/notch/butler/concierge/part	staff/service/food/experience/breakfast/ hospitality/quality/thank/dining/water/drink/ guest/care/notch/butler/concierge
Physical Environment	room/view/resort/pool/restaurant/property/world/ team/level/luxury/visit/star/class/cave/facility/boutique/ beach/garden/spa/bar/bathroom/amenity/detail/suite/ accommodate/attention/lake/custom/area	room/view/resort/pool/restaurant/luxury/ facility/garden/cave/boutique/beach/bathroom/ bar/spa/suite/amenity/suite/ accommodate/lake
Location	locate/minute/walk/airport/Quarter/Istanbul/distance/ street/Nantucket/Ayada/Jaipur/Mandapa/city/ Hanoi/Amira/Charleston/town	Locate/minute/walk/airport/Quarter/Istanbul/ distance/street/Nantucket/Ayada/Jaipur/ Mandapa/city/Hanoi/Amira/Charleston
Purpose	time/honeymoon/people/weekend/wife/husband/ year/vacate/expectation/anniversary/holiday/family/ villa/kid/friend/birthday	honeymoon/people/weekend/wife/husband/ vacate/expectation/anniversary/holiday/ family/kid/friend/birthday

Factor Analysis

The factor analysis can discover the commonalities among these keywords and show connection of variables through the variance of keywords within the same online hotel review. The purpose of the factor analysis is to reduce a large number of variables into smaller factors using an oblique rotation process. Common factorial criteria were used in extracting the factors, and the minimum factor loading was set to 0.400 in the final model. The factors also had to have Eigenvalues greater than 1.0 and had to explain a substantial percentage of total variance. Eight elements had low scores, which is less than 0.3. Ten elements loaded on two factors. Therefore, a total of 18 elements were excised from the 64 keywords. Finally, five factors with 22 keywords covering 22.099% of all variance to elicit the hotel experience were generated through the process of elimination of five times.

Table 5 shows the results of the factor analysis with 0.651 of KMO (Kaiser Meyer Olkin), which is higher than 0.6. Therefore, it was verified that the use of the factor analysis was suitable for this study. The Bartlett's test of sphericity value (X^2) was 113,025.397, with overall significance of the correlation matrix ($p < 0.001$). This result showed that the data did not produce an identity matrix, and it was multivariate normal and fit for using exploratory factor analysis. The five factors were named as "Access (Factor 1)", "F&B (Factor 2)", "Purpose (Factor 3)",

Table 5. *Result of the factor analysis.*

	Words	Factor Loading	Eigen Value	Variance (%)
Access	Locate	0.962	3.118	16.409
	Town	0.949		
	Amira	0.940		
	Walk	0.933		
Food and Beverage (F&B)	Food	0.928	2.818	14.832
	Breakfast	0.912		
	Drink	0.875		
	Dining	0.773		
Purpose	Weekend	0.817	2.306	12.135
	Birthday	0.815		
	Anniversary	0.685		
	Honeymoon	0.627		
Tangibles	Pool	0.747	2.004	10.547
	Spa	0.687		
	Beach	0.682		
	Restaurant	0.480		
	Bar	0.475		
	Room	0.437		
Empathy	Staff	0.844	1.858	9.778
	Care	0.738		
	Service	0.470		
	Friend	0.444		
Total variance (%) = 22.099				
KMO (Kaiser Meyer Olkin) = 0.657				
Bartlett chi-square(p) = 113,025.397 ($p < 0.001$)				

"Tangibles (Factor 4)", "Empathy (Factor 5)". Factor 1 contains 'locate', 'town', 'Amira', 'walk', which are related to the accessible location. Factor 2 has 'food', 'breakfast', 'drink', 'dining' which is related with F&B in the hotel. Factor 3 was about purpose containing 'weekend', 'birthday', 'anniversary', 'honeymoon'. In addition, Factor 4 consisted of aspects concerning intangibles, such as 'pool', 'spa', 'beach', 'restaurant', 'bar', 'room'. Factor 5 has 'staff', 'care', 'service' and 'friend', which is related with empathy.

Linear Regression Analysis

After the factor analysis, a customer experience and satisfaction was derived by using regression analysis as shown in Table 6. It has five independent variables: Access (A), F&B (FB), Purpose (P), Tangibles (T), Empathy (E), and one dependent variable: Customer Satisfaction (CS). The overall variance explained by the five predictors was 12% ($R^2 = 0.120$) and the standard error of the estimated value was calculated as 0.51021. The correlation between the independent and dependent variables was rather low because many factors affecting customer experience and satisfaction might not have been included among the five factors due to their low frequency in the online hotel reviews. In regression models related to opinion mining it is impossible to include all relevant variables to estimate output variables such as opinion from text mining data. Therefore, the R^2 value can be low [46,47,48]. There is a prior study saying that the R^2 value is 12.5%. This study also analyzed online review data for washing machines and used regression analysis and factor analysis [5].

Table 6. *Results of linear regression analysis.*

Model	Unstandardized Coef.		Standardized Coef.	*t*
	B	Std. error	Beta	
(Constant)	4.861	0.006		773.569
Access (A)	0.010	0.006	0.019	1.556
Food and beverage (FB)	0.019	0.006	0.036	2.947 **
Purpose (P)	0.015	0.006	0.029	2.377 *
Tangibles (T)	−0.002	0.006	−0.004	−0.359
Empathy (E)	0.045	0.006	0.087	7.114 ***

Notes: Dependent variable: Customer Satisfaction (CS); $R^2 = 0.120$; adjusted $R^2 = 0.100$; F = 13.894; * $p < 0.05$; ** $p < 0.005$; *** $p < 0.001$.

"F&B (FB, $\beta = 0.036$, $p = 0.003$)", "Purpose (P, $\beta = 0.029$, $p = 0.017$), and "Empathy (E, $\beta = 0.087$, $p = 0.000$)" are significant at the $p < 0.05$ level and positively related with customer satisfaction. In order to estimate the possible correlations among the predictors, a multicollinearity statistic was conducted. The tolerance level was less than 1.00, and the variance inflation factor (VIF) of the predictors was between 1.00 and 1.10, respectively, that is, the predictors were not significantly correlated to each other. Therefore, based on unstandardized β, the regression equation can be expressed as:

$$CS = 4.861 + 0.010A + 0.019FB^{**} + 0.015P^{*} - 0.002T + 0.045E^{***}$$

The "Empathy (E)" factor holds the highest standardized coefficients, which means this experience aspect of the hotel customer is the most important factor associated with customer satisfaction significantly. Reviews such as "Fantastic natural surroundings and friendly staff give you the best time" and "The thing that made this place so great for us was the staff service, especially our personal Concierge" are related to the hotel experience based upon "Empathy" attributes.

DISCUSSION

This study was conducted to enhance the customer's experience and satisfaction using online hotel reviews. For the online hotel review data analysis, the first process was extracting keywords by text mining and the second was calculating the frequency of words used by customers. Based on the frequency analysis, the degree and eigenvector centrality of top 99 frequent words were analyzed to search their connection and the most affected keywords among them. The CONCOR analysis was performed for grouping them. As a result, the top 99 keywords were divided into four groups, namely, "Intangible Service", "Physical Environment", "Purpose", and "Location". Moreover, they were visualized by drawing networks and nodes using NetDraw in UCINET 6.0. In addition, the study conducted factor analysis and linear regression analysis to understand the relationship between extracted factors and customer satisfaction. The factor analysis reduced the dimension of the original 64 keywords to 22 keywords and grouped them into five factors, which are "Access", "F&B", "Purpose", "Tangibles", and "Empathy". The clusters can be related between CONCOR analysis and factor analysis, such as "Intangible Service" with "Empathy", "Physical Environment" with "Tangibles", "Location" with "Access".

First of all, the group representing the highest beta coefficient was "Empathy" in the linear regression analysis, and the related words were 'staff', 'service', 'care', and 'friend' through the factor analysis. Especially, 'staff' and 'service' were most frequent words in the online hotel review, and through the CONCOR analysis, "Intangible Service" group was the biggest group compared with "Physical Environment", "Purpose", and "Location". According to Lee [49] the service from hotel staff is the most important attribute to making customers satisfied rather than the other luxurious or new facilities. In addition, Han and Chung [50] examined customers satisfied with excellent service by hotel staff rather than physical environment, such as room cleanness, comfort, and room condition. The results of this study show the same results as many prior studies show that intangible service has the greatest impact on customer experience and satisfaction. Therefore, Service by staff is an essential key attribute to create a good reputation in the service industry and can still be seen as a part of the hotel that must be managed at all times to keep up the image of the hotel. Therefore, it is important to improve the attitude of employees through systematic service training. In addition, providing an appropriate working environment to enhance employee satisfaction to produce better service to customers can be another way.

The second highest beta value was "F&B" in the linear regression analysis, and the related words were 'food', 'breakfast', 'drink', and 'dining' through the factor analysis and those keywords are recorded a very high position in the frequency analysis. In hotels with a high satisfaction index, F&B facilities should also be well equipped and restaurants providing high-quality food to customers are significant. Especially, as keywords for breakfast are derived, it will be helpful for hotel business to focus on breakfast rather than on other meals.

This study shows the academic implication that the study has extended its application area of the semantic network analysis. While given the significance of the hotel segment in the tourism industry, this study empirically explores hotel experience and satisfaction by big data analytics. Along the way, the hotel industry has the opportunity to gain an understanding of attributes on the online review, so as to infiltrate into this market and investigate corresponding marketing strategies for their significant advantages. Understanding online reviews as a manifestation of customers' experiences can help the hotel industry to identify the main attributes required to achieve positive post-purchase behaviors and to minimize negative intentions. Thus, the online reviews not only provide an efficient way for the hotel industry to collect feedback from hotel customers, but also provide an opportunity to discover how to generate positive intent after the experience. To create a high satisfaction score and a positive eWOM, the hotel industry should consider "F&B", "Purpose", and "Empathy". Among them, "Empathy" was the most influential attribute in the regression analysis. These key factors may be used to examine the customer satisfaction or to test theoretical models to have a better understanding of a hotel customer's behavior.

In practice, the analysis of online reviews can be used as a marketing tool by managers since customer review is an important source for a hotel to improve service and to create some promotion regarding profit. The analysis also provides the level of importance of these service attributes so the hotel industry can allocate their resources accordingly. The online review analyses can provide reliable satisfaction assessment. The hotel industry can also use this method to analyze their competitors' customer reviews so that they can benchmark themselves against competitors in terms of customer satisfaction. These reviews can be used for sustainable strategic marketing decisions against competitors.

However, this study shows limitations in data collection. Firstly, the data collected in this study is limited, because this study focuses on only the top 25 hotels in the world for the sample. That is why future research should collect online review data from more hotel industries to generalize the findings. Secondly, the collected text was analyzing based on the frequency of individual words, therefore, it is difficult to understand the additional meaning of words. In future studies, further analysis of positives and negatives and sentimental analysis is expected to be carried out to better understand the customer's experience and satisfaction. Therefore, it can provide stronger strategies to the hotel industry.

Author Contributions

H.-J.B. and H.-S.K. designed the research model, analyzed online review data and wrote the paper. H.C., E.-K.C., and S.L. were in charge of review and editing the paper.

REFERENCES

1. Siering, M.; Deokar, A.V.; Janze, C. Disentangling consumer recommendations: Explaining and predicting airline recommendations based on online reviews. *Decis. Support Syst.* **2018**, *107*, 52–63.
2. Kim, W.H. The impact of online reviews on customer satisfaction: An application of the American customer satisfaction index (ACSI). *Int. J. Tour. Hosp. Res.* **2017**, *32*, 65–78.
3. Rodríguez-Díaz, M.; Rodríguez-Voltes, C.I.; Rodríguez-Voltes, A.C. Gap analysis of the online reputation. *Sustainability* **2018**, *10*, 1603.
4. Gao, B.; Li, X.; Liu, S.; Fang, D. How power distance affects online hotel ratings: The positive moderating roles of hotel chain and reviewers' travel experience. *Tour. Manag.* **2018**, *65*, 176–186.
5. Kim, H.S.; Noh, Y. Elicitation of design factors through big data analysis of online customer reviews for washing machines. *J. Mech. Sci. Technol.* **2019**, *33*, 2785–2795.
6. Ban, H.J.; Kim, H.S. Understanding customer experience and satisfaction through airline passengers' online review. *Sustainability* **2019**, *11*, 4066.

7. Ban, H.J.; Kim, H.S. A study on the TripAdvisor review analysis of restaurant recognition in Busan 1: Especially concerning English reviews. *Culi. Sci. Hosp. Res.* **2019,** *25,* 1–11.

8. Ban, H.J.; Kim, H.S. Semantic network analysis of hotel package through the big data. *Culi. Sci. Hosp. Res.* **2019,** *25,* 110–119.

9. Cheng, B.L.; Gan, C.C.; Imrie, B.C.; Mansori, S. Service recovery, customer satisfaction and customer loyalty: Evidence from Malaysia's hotel industry. *Int. J. Qual. Serv. Sci.* **2019,** *11,* 187–203.

10. Nysveen, H.; Oklevik, O.; Pedersen, P.E. Brand satisfaction: Exploring the role of innovativeness, green image and experience in the hotel sector. *Int. J. Contemp. Hosp. Manag.* **2018,** *30,* 2908–2924.

11. Pizam, A.; Shapoval, V.; Ellis, T. Customer satisfaction and its measurement in hospitality enterprises: A revisit and update. *Int. J. Contemp. Hosp. Manag.* **2016,** *28,* 2–35.

12. Torres, E.N.; Kline, S. From customer satisfaction to customer delight: Creating a new standard of service for the hotel industry. *Int. J. Contemp. Hosp. Manag.* **2013,** *25,* 642–659.

13. Dominici, G.; Guzzo, R. Customer satisfaction in the hotel industry: A case study from Sicily. *Int. J. Mark. Stud.* **2010,** *2,* 3–12.

14. Olorunniwo, F.; Hsu, M.K.; Udo, G.J. Service quality, customer satisfaction, and behavioral intentions in the service factory. *J. Serv. Mark.* **2006,** *20,* 59–72.

15. Vijayadurai, J. Service quality, customer satisfaction and behavioural intention in hotel industry. *J. Mark. Comm.* **2008,** *3,* 14–26.

16. Gundersen, M.G.; Heide, M.; Olsson, U.H. Hotel guest satisfaction among business travelers: What are the important factors? *Cornell Hotel Restaur. Admin. Q.* **1996,** *37,* 72–81.

17. Hu, N.; Zhang, T.; Gao, B.; Bose, I. What do hotel customers complain about? Text analysis using structural topic model. *Tour. Manag.* **2019,** *72,* 417–426.

18. Saura, J.; Reyes-Menendez, A.; Alvarez-Alonso, C. Do online comments affect environmental management? Identifying factors related to environmental management and sustainability of hotels. *Sustainability* **2018,** *10,* 3016.

19. Belarmino, A.M.; Koh, Y. How E-WOM motivations vary by hotel review website. *Int. J. Contemp. Hosp. Manag.* **2018,** *30,* 2730–2751.

20. Kim, D.K.; Kim, I.S. An analysis of hotel selection attributes present in online reviews using text mining. *J. Tour. Sci.* **2017,** *41,* 109–127.

21. Saha, G.C.; Theingi. Service quality, satisfaction, and behavioural intentions: A study of low-cost airline carriers in Thailand. Managing Service Quality. *Int. J.* **2009,** *19,* 350–372.

22. Browning, V.; So, K.K.F.; Sparks, B. The influence of online reviews on consumers' attributions of service quality and control for service standards in hotels. *J. Travel Tour. Mark.* **2013,** *30,* 23–40.

23. Kotler, P.; Bowen, J.T.; Makens, J.; Baloglu, S. *Marketing for Hospitality and Tourism;* Pearson: London, UK, 2017.

24. Knutson, B.J. Frequent travelers: Making them happy and bringing them back. *Cornell Hot. Rest. Admin. Quart.* **1988,** *29,* 82–87.

25. Verma, V.K.; Chandra, B. Sustainability and customers' hotel choice behaviour: A choice-based conjoint analysis approach. *Environ. Dev. Sustain.* **2018**, *20*, 1347–1363.

26. Kim, S.; Kandampully, J.; Bilgihan, A. The influence of eWOM communications: An application of online social network framework. *Comput. Hum. Behav.* **2018**, *80*, 243–254.

27. Hunt, J.D. Image as a factor in tourism development. *J. Travel Res.* **1975**, *13*, 1–7

28. Bhandari, R.S.; Bansal, A. A study of characteristics of e-WoM affecting consumer's social media opinion behavior. *J. Indian Manag. Strateg.* **2019**, *24*, 33–43.

29. Klein, L.R. Evaluating the potential of interactive media through a new lens: Search versus experience goods. *J. Bus. Res.* **1998**, *41*, 195–203.

30. Gaikwad, S.V.; Chaugule, A.; Patil, P. Text mining methods and techniques. *Int. J. Comput. Appl.* **2014**, *85*, 42–45.

31. Hassani, H.; Huang, X.; Silva, E.S.; Ghodsi, M. A review of data mining applications in crime. *Stat. Anal. Data Min. ASA Data Sci. J.* **2016**, *9*, 139–154.

32. Sirsat, S.R.; Chavan, D.V.; Deshpande, D.S.P. Mining knowledge from text repositories using information extraction: A review. *Sadhana* **2014**, *39*, 53–62.

33. Joseph, G.; Varghese, V. Analyzing Airbnb customer experience feedback using text mining. In *Big Data and Innovation in Tourism, Travel, and Hospitality*; Springer: The Gateway, Singapore, 2019.

34. Kuhzady, S.; Ghasemi, V. Factors influencing g customers' satisfaction and dissatisfaction with hotels: A text-mining approach. *Tour. Anal.* **2019**, *24*, 69–79.

35. Berezina, K.; Bilgihan, A.; Cobanoglu, C.; Okumus, F. Understanding satisfied and dissatisfied hotel customers: Text mining of online hotel reviews. *J. Hosp. Mark. Manag.* **2016**, *25*, 1–24.

36. Philander, K.; Zhong, Y. Twitter sentiment analysis: Capturing sentiment from integrated resort tweets. *Int. J. Hosp. Manag.* **2016**, *55*, 16–24.

37. Kweon, S.H. A semantic network analysis of 4th industry revolution: News frame for on drone, AI, big data and IoT news. *Int. J. Adv. Sci. Tech.* **2018**, *110*, 115–128.

38. Shuting, T.; Kim, H.S. Cruising in Asia: What can we dig from online cruiser reviews to understand their experience and satisfaction. *Asia Pac. J. Tour. Res.* **2019**, *24*, 514–528.

39. Kim, Y.J.; Ban, H.J.; Kim, H.S. An exploratory study on the semantic network analysis of Busan tourism: Using Google web and news. *Culin. Sci. Hosp. Res.* **2019**, *25*, 126–134.

40. Lim, S.; Tucker, C.S.; Jablokow, K.; Pursel, B. A semantic network model for measuring engagement and performance in online learning platforms. *Comp. App. Eng. Edu.* **2018**, *26*, 1481–1492.

41. Zhang, L.; Yun, H.J. Tourism information contents and text networking (focused on formal website of Jeju and Chinese personal blogs). *J. Korea Cont. Asso.* **2018**, *18*, 19–30.

42. Shuting, T.; Kim, H.S. A study of comparison between cruise tours in China and USA through big data analytics. *Culin. Sci. Hosp. Res.* **2017**, *23*, 1–10.

43. Kim, H.S. A semantic network analysis of big data regarding food exhibition at convention center. *Culin. Sci. Hosp. Res.* **2017**, *23*, 257–270.

44. Bonacich, P. Some unique properties of eigenvector centrality. *Soc. Netw.* **2007**, *29*, 555–564.

45. Lee, Y.J.; Yoon, J.H. Exploring ways to utilize SNS big data in the tourism sector. *Int. J. Tour. Hosp. Res.* **2014,** *28,* 5–14.

46. Neter, J.; Wasserman, W.; Kutner, M.; Nachtsheim, C. *Applied Linear Statistical Models,* 4th ed.; McGraw-Hill: Chicago, IL, USA, 1996.

47. Freund, R.J.; Littell, R.C. *SAS System for Regression,* 3rd ed.; SAS: Cary, NC, USA, 2000.

48. Gennaioli, N.; Martin, A.; Rossi, S. Banks, government bonds, and default: What do the data say? *J. Monet. Econ.* **2018,** *98,* 98–113.

49. Lee, J.H. Understanding customer values by analyzing the contents of online hotel reviews. *J. Korea Cont. Assoc.* **2013,** *13,* 533–546.

50. Han, J.H.; Chung, N. Opportunities of big data applications to develop global marketing strategies: Analyzing hotel guest online reviews. *J. Tour. Lie Res.* **2017,** *7,* 233–251.

INDEX